Praise for *The Trump Paradox*

"Brings a plethora of fresh evidence to understand the US-Mexico relationship, particularly around immigration and trade debates that were central to Donald Trump's election victory in 2016, which will also remain pressing issues into the foreseeable future. Several of the chapters stand out as must-reads for scholars and students alike."

—David Scott FitzGerald, author of *Refuge beyond Reach: How Rich Democracies Repel Asylum Seekers*

"The volume is a timely analysis of the Trump administration's immigration and trade policies, and the public response—which the editors present as paradoxical on many different fronts. The chapters represent an impressive range of methodological and theoretical traditions, authored by a much-needed binational and interdisciplinary mix of leading migration scholars."

—Shannon Gleason, Cornell University

The Trump Paradox

The Trump Paradox

Migration, Trade, and Racial Politics in US-Mexico Integration

EDITED BY
Raúl Hinojosa-Ojeda and
Edward Telles

UNIVERSITY OF CALIFORNIA PRESS

University of California Press
Oakland, California

© 2021 by Raúl Hinojosa-Ojeda and Edward Telles

Library of Congress Cataloging-in-Publication Data

Names: Hinojosa-Ojeda, Raúl Andrés, 1956- editor. |
 Telles, Edward Eric, 1956- editor.
Title: The Trump paradox : migration, trade, and racial
 politics in US-Mexico integration / edited by Raúl
 Hinojosa-Ojeda and Edward Telles.
Description: Oakland, California : University of
 California Press, [2021] | Includes bibliographical
 references and index.
Identifiers: LCCN 2020023671 (print) |
 LCCN 2020023672 (ebook) | ISBN 9780520302563
 (cloth) | ISBN 9780520302570 (paperback) |
 ISBN 9780520972513 (ebook)
Subjects: LCSH: International trade—Political aspects—
 United States. | United States—Foreign relations—
 Mexico. | Mexico—Foreign relations—United States. |
 Mexico—Emigration and immigration. | United
 States—Emigration and immigration.
Classification: LCC E183.8.M6 T78 2021 (print) |
 LCC E183.8.M6 (ebook) | DDC 327.73072—dc23
LC record available at https://lccn.loc.gov/2020023671
LC ebook record available at https://lccn.loc
 .gov/2020023672

30 29 28 27 26 25 24 23 22 21
10 9 8 7 6 5 4 3 2 1

Dedicated to the millions of people currently suffering in the US, Mexico and Central America from our broken immigration system, inadequate trade agreements, and racialized politics, which require more equitable and inclusive policy approaches.

Dedicado a las millones de personas que viven en Estados Unidos, México, y Centroamérica, quienes ven su calidad de vida deteriorándose como consecuencia de un sistema migratorio fallido, políticas racistas, y acuerdos comerciales poco favorables. Esperamos que todas ellas puedan beneficiarse con los enfoques sobre políticas públicas novedosas, equitativas, e inclusivas.

Contents

List of Figures   *xi*
List of Tables   *xv*
Acknowledgments   *xvii*

Introduction   1
Raúl Hinojosa-Ojeda and Edward Telles

PART ONE. THE TRUMP PARADOX   13

1. How Do We Explain Trump's Paradoxical Yet Electorally Successful Use of a False US-Mexico Narrative?   15
   Raúl Hinojosa-Ojeda and Edward Telles

2. What Were the Paradoxical Consequences of Militarizing the Border with Mexico?   32
   Douglas S. Massey

PART TWO. MEXICO-US MIGRATION   47

3. How Did We Get to the Current Mexico-US Migration System, and How Might It Look in the Near Future?   49
   Silvia E. Giorguli, Claudia Masferrer, and Victor M. García-Guerrero

4. Recession versus Removals: Which Finished Mexican
   Unauthorized Migration?   63
   René Zenteno and Roberto Suro

5. How Is the Health of the Mexican-Origin Population on
   Both Sides of the Border Affected by Policies and Attitudes
   in the United States?   78
   *Fernando Riosmena, Hiram Beltrán-Sánchez, Megan Reynolds,
   and Justin Vinneau*

6. What Shall Be the Future for the Children of Migration?
   LASANTI and the Educational Imperative   88
   Patricia Gándara and Gary Orfield

7. What Are the Policy Implications of Declining Unauthorized
   Immigration from Mexico?   102
   Pia M. Orrenius and Madeline Zavodny

8. How Does Mexican Migration Affect the US Labor Market?   113
   Frank D. Bean, Susan K. Brown, and James D. Bachmeier

PART THREE. TRADE INTEGRATION   127

9. Before and after NAFTA: How Are Trade and Migration
   Policies Changing?   129
   Raúl Hinojosa-Ojeda, Sherman Robinson, and Karen Thierfelder

10. What Is the Relationship between US-Mexico Migration
    and Trade in Agriculture?   148
    *Antonio Yúnez-Naude, Jorge Mora-Rivera, and Yatziry
    Govea-Vargas*

11. Is Complementarity Sustainable in the US-Mexico
    Automotive Sector?   159
    Jorge Carrillo

12. What Policies Make Sense in a US-Mexico Trade Deal?   174
    Robert A. Blecker, Juan Carlos Moreno-Brid, and Isabel Salat

IV. RACIAL POLITICS — 189

13. What Is the Historical and Political Context for Trump's Nativist Appeal? — 191
    David Montejano

14. How Has the New Mexico-US Relationship Affected Mexican Nationalism? — 204
    Regina Martínez Casas and Rafael Elías López Arellano

15. What Are the Social Consequences of Immigrant Scapegoating by Political Elites? — 214
    René D. Flores

16. How Do Latinos Respond to Anti-Immigrant Politics? — 227
    Gary Segura, Matt Barreto, and Angela E. Gutierrez

17. Anti-Immigrant Backlash: Is There a Path Forward? — 244
    Zoltan L. Hajnal

List of Acronyms — 255
Notes — 259
Glossary of Key Terms — 271
References — 287
List of Contributors — 323
Index — 325

List of Figures

1.1 Map A, US Counties by Percent Voting for Trump (2016) – Percent Voting for Romney (2012); Map B, US Counties by Percent Mexican Immigrants; Map C, US Counties by Mexican Imports per Capita (in quantiles) / 22

2.1 Mexican Migration to the United States in Three Legal Status Groups / 34

2.2 Feedback Loop between Apprehensions and Border Enforcement, 1965–1995 / 37

2.3 Border Patrol Budget in Constant 2017 US Dollars, 1965–2010 / 38

2.4 Causal Effect of Border Enforcement on the Likelihood of Departing on and Returning from a First Undocumented Trip / 42

2.5 Estimated Size of the US Undocumented Population / 43

3.1 Mexican-Born Population Living in the United States, 1900–2017 / 51

3.2 (A) Total Fertility Rates; (B) Total Population Annual Growth Rates; (C) Annual Growth Rates of the Working Age (15–64) Population in North America and Selected Central American Countries / 60

4.1 Northbound Mexican Unauthorized Flows to the United States Measured on a Quarterly Basis, 2003–2017 / 68

4.2 Annual Percentage Change in the Flow of Unauthorized Migrants Measured on a Quarterly Basis, 2006–2017 / 68

4.3 Border Patrol Budget and Staff and Apprehensions of Mexican Migrants along the Southwest Border Sector, FY 2000–2017 / 73
4.4 Share of Repatriated Mexicans with More than One Year of US Residence Measured on a Quarterly Basis, 2004–2017 / 73
6.1 Income Inequality, 30 OECD Countries, Percent Above/Below Mean, 2014 / 90
6.2 Income by Educational Attainment as a Proportion of University Educated Income, Mexico, 1996–2014 / 92
6.3 Increasing Income Gap by Education Levels, Southern California Family Ratio of Income by Level of Education, 1980–2014 / 94
7.1 Estimated Number of Unauthorized Mexican Immigrant Workers / 105
7.2 Comparison of New Unauthorized Mexican Immigrant Workers and Border Apprehensions / 105
8.1 Annual Percent Change in GDP for the United States and California, 1990–2017, Two-Year Moving Average / 115
8.2 Legal Permanent Resident Migration from Mexico and the Countries of Next Largest Migration, 1981–2016 (in three-year moving averages) / 118
8.3 Nonimmigrant Admissions (1–94 only) from Mexico, Japan, the United Kingdom, and China/South Korea/Japan, 1993–2016 / 118
8.4 Number of Unauthorized Migrants in the United States and the Percentage of Mexican-Origin among Them, 1990–2016 / 119
9.1 Periods of Mexican Net Migration: Net Out-Migration, 1940–Mid-2000s; Net In-Migration, Mid-2000s–2015; Mexican and US Employment by Economic Sector as Share of Total Employment, 1890–2015: (A) Mexico; (B) United States / 133
9.2 (A) Relative US/Mexico GDP per Capita; (B) US Apprehensions and Deportations; and (C) US and Mexico Trade Shares of GDP / 135
9.3 Mexico Migration, Trade Contributions, and Remittances/FDI as a Share of US GDP / 140
9.4 Map A, Percent Change in County US Sectoral Output under NAFTA Trade War in Nonservice Sectors; Map B, Percent Change in County Output under Mass Deportation in All Sectors / 144
10.1 Corn: Volume of Imports under and over Tariff Rate Quota (metric tons) / 152

10.2 Migration of Mexican Farmworkers and Corn Production and Imports / *153*

10.3 Employment in Mexico/Mexican Farmworkers Crossing into the United States / *154*

10.4 Mexican Agricultural Workers Crossing US Border and Mexico Field Crops GDP / *156*

11.1 Evolution of Production and Automobile Sales in Mexico, 1966–2017 (units) / *162*

11.2 FDI by Country of Origin in the Automotive Sector (millions of dollars) / *163*

11.3 Main Automotive Clusters in Mexico / *167*

11.4 Mexico: FDI in the Automotive Industry by Mega Region / *168*

12.1 GDP per Capita and Labor Productivity in Mexico as Percentages of US Levels, 1991–2015 / *176*

12.2 Hourly Compensation of Mexican Production Workers, in Real Terms and as a Percentage of the US Level, 1994–2016 / *177*

15.1 Newspaper Coverage and Crime Rates in Hazleton, PA, 1999–2012 / *218*

16.1 Trump Favorability Interaction Models / *236*

16.2 Changes in Probability of Being Angry Often or All the Time during the 2016 Election / *238*

16.3 Predicted Probability of Being Angry Often or Always during the 2016 Election / *239*

16.4 Political Participation Models by State, National Origin, and Generation with Displays of the Marginal Effect of Going from the Lowest Value of Each Coefficient to the Highest Value while Holding All Other Variables at Their Mean / *240*

17.1 Effect of Latino Context on Corrections Spending / *251*

List of Tables

1.1 Statistical Models Predicting Republican Vote Share in 2016 Minus 2012 Republican Vote Share at Congressional District Level / 25
1.2 Statistical Models Predicting Trump Vote in 2016 / 27
1.3 Statistical Models Predicting Whether Flipped from Voting for Trump in 2016 Presidential Election to Voting for Democrats in 2018 House Election / 28
3.1 Total and Foreign-Born Population in North America and Selected Central American Countries, 2017 / 54
3.2 Migration Stocks in North America by Selected Countries of Origin, circa 2016 / 55
4.1 Mexican Immigrants in the United States and Annual Rate of Change, 1960–2017 / 65
4.2 Selected Characteristics of Repatriated Mexicans by Time of Stay in the United States / 75
7.1 Determinants of Mexico-US Unauthorized Worker Migration / 107
8.1 Average Annual Growth of US Working-Age Population (25–64), 1970–2015, by Nativity, Sex, and Education / 122
9.1 Postwar US-Mexico Trade and Migration Policy Initiatives / 136
9.2 US and Mexican Real GDP Aggregates by Scenario / 143

10.1 Percentage Weight of US Trade in Total Trade of Agricultural Commodities in Mexico, 2003–2015 / *150*
11.1 Milestones in the Mexican Automotive Industry / *161*
11.2 Mexico: Principal Exports and Imports / *166*
15.1 Ethnic and Racial Composition of Hazleton, PA, 2000–2010 / *217*
16.1 Summary of Response to the Racism Scale Items by National Origin Group / *233*
16.2 Racism Scale and Immigrant-Linked Threat / *234*
17.1 More Regressive Government Policy in Heavily Latino States / *248*

Acknowledgments

The Trump Paradox is the result of a multiyear transnational collaborative program of research, teaching, conferences, and policy action initiatives known as "Expanding Bridges and Overcoming Walls: University of California Collaborations with Mexican and North American Institutions." Starting with the 2016 election, we were alarmed at the destructive impact that the misinformed Trump discourse on trade and immigration would have on Mexico-US relations, reducing them to racialized politics and impeding progress towards an agenda for a more equitable, inclusive, and prosperous North American integration.

This collaboration was built across a number of UC campuses (primarily UCLA and UCSB but also UC units in Washington [UCDC] and Mexico [CASA California]) and Mexican institutions (primarily CIESAS [Center for Research and Advanced Studies in Social Anthropology] and El Colegio de Mexico but also El Colegio de Tlaxcala and Universidad Michoacan). As part of this collaborative, we held a series of forums in Mexico City, Washington DC and California with leading scholars and policymakers from the US, Mexico, and Central America. These forums focused on migration and trade in the context of US racial politics and international inequalities of employment income and development. We thank the participation of many people in these forums including congress people, union leaders, scholars, and others from both sides of the border. These included: Cuauhtémoc Lázaro Cárdenas, Amalia Garcia, Berta Lujan, Lydia Camarillo, Antonio Gonzalez,

Gabriela Lemus, Hector Sanchez Barba, Mexican Senador Armando Rios-Piter, and US Congressmen Jimmy Gomez, Luis Correa, Henry Cuellar, and Raul Grijalva.

We also entered into a data and modeling agreement with the Instituto Nacional de Estadística, Geografía e Informática (INEGI), the Peterson Institute for International Economics (PIIE), the Ministry of the Economy of El Salvador, Statistics Canada, International Food Policy Research Institute (IFPRI), and the North American Development Bank. In addition, we were able to use new video-conferencing technologies to teach a binational graduate seminar with students, professors, and policy experts across four universities: El Colegio de Mexico, CIESAS, UCLA, and UCSB. *Gracias a Regina Martinez Casas y Silvia Giorgiuli* for coordinating that in Mexico.

The series of meetings reached an apex with the milestone conference "Expanding Bridges and Overcoming Walls," held at UCSB on August 25–26, 2017, which would lead to the chapters produced in this book. We would like to thank, above all, Magali Sanchez-Hall of the UCLA NAID Center, who has been the main organizer of the conferences and forums, doing extensive legwork and always troubleshooting, from the very beginning to the present. We are also grateful to the leadership and excellent staff of the collaborating institutions on both sides of the border. For our UCSB conference, Lisa Blanco and Vera Reyes were the point staff and we also benefitted from the enthusiasm and hard work of many other UCSB staff. UCSB Chancellor Henry Yang made sure all the doors were open for a successful conference. The conference ran smoothly also thanks to the talented and pleasant assistance of Iliana Arroyo, Devin Cornell, Maria del Carmen García, Ruben Hoyos, Sania Mendez, Amanda Pinheiro, Liliana Rodriguez, and Omar Serrano.

We were fortunate to have Janet Napolitano (University of California systemwide President and former director of the Department of Homeland Security) and Xavier Becerra (California Attorney General) as keynote speakers. We also featured Ms. Napolitano in a Q&A session that was interrupted by the incredible and sad news that Trump had just pardoned Joe Arpaio! The conference was genuinely binational at all levels and we were honored with the presence and participation of Republic of Mexico Federal Senators José Narro and Alejandro Encinas Rodriguez, both of whom have been critical to Mexico's policies on immigration and trade. We were also graced with words by Salud Carbajal (US Congressman representing Santa Barbara) and Julie Chavez Rodriguez (State Director for US Senator Kamala Harris).

The many esteemed participants were critical to the conference's success and included innovative discussions between researchers and policymakers and between Mexico and the United States. Such binational encounters are, unfortunately, all too rare. In addition to the authors of this book's chapters, presenters and discussants at the conference included from the Mexican side: Agustin Escobar Latapi, Victor Lichtinger, Laura Carlsen, Alfredo Cuecuecha, Carlos Heredia, Isabel Hernandez, Mariana Carmona, Rafael Barrientos, and Gerardo Esquivel. From the US side, speakers and discussants also included Andrew Selee, David Hayes-Bautista, Erika Arenas, Graciela Teruel, Helen Shapiro, Howard Winant, Jeffrey Passel, Jonathon Fox, Narayani Lasala-Blanco, and Roger Waldinger. In addition, State Senator Hannah Beth Jackson, Alma Rios Nieto, Victor Rios, Leila Rupp, Helen Shapiro, Ray Telles, Marcos Vargas, and Astrid Viveros also participated in the conference activities.

The conference was made possible by generous funding by various institutions and the support of individuals. This included Leila Rupp and Charles Hale, incoming and outgoing Deans of Social Science at UCSB, Darnell Hunt, the Dean of Social Sciences at UCLA, the UCLA North American Integration and Development (NAID) Center, the Broom Center for Demography through Maria Charles, the UCSB Department of Economics, the Ford Foundation in Mexico City, the UC Irvine Center for Research on International Migration through Frank Bean, and former state senator Fabian Nuñez. A special shout-out goes to Abel Valenzuela of UCLA's Institute for Research on Labor and Economics (IRLE) for his ongoing support in various phases of our initiative.

Several individuals helped in other ways. At the University of California's Office of the President, Provost Michael Brown and Vice President for Research Art Ellis met with us and linked us to broader activities at the University of California. Thanks to Veronique Rorive and Cynthia Giorgio of the UC Mexico Initiative and Allert Gort-Brown of UC's Casa California for their ideas, networks, and participation. Gilberto Cardenas provided beautiful lithographs on immigration from leading Chicano and Mexican artists on immigration.

For the actual production of the book, we thank Naomi Schneider, Senior Editor of the University of California Press, whose support was unwavering since the beginning. We lucked out by having such knowledgeable and generous reviewers: David FitzGerald and Shannon Gleason. We greatly appreciate the assistance of Lisa Moore, our development editor, who shepherded the book project through, patiently communicating us and the authors. We are grateful also to UC Press's

Francisco Reinking, who supervised the production process, and to research assistance we received from Jiahui Zhang and Marcelo Pleitez. Special thanks to Sholeh Wolpé for her love and encouragement and for wonderfully designing the cover.

As editors of this volume and organizers of the initiative and collaborations, we have enjoyed the privilege of working with such talented and committed people, in Mexico and the United States. Unfortunately, such binational cooperation is all too rare but it is necessary to solve our shared fates. We hope our example is contagious. Finally, we also have learned much from each other, and together we have enjoyed every step of the process.

Just as we began with Trump's fearmongering of Mexican immigrants and trade with Mexico, we close-bracket the publication of this book with the end of the Trump presidency and, hopefully, the beginning of a new era in immigration, trade, and US-Mexico relations. We hope that we have fostered greater Mexico-United States cooperation in teaching, research, policymaking, and service. Our efforts are ongoing and we expect to be quite active in a new era of really "Expanding Bridges and Overcoming Walls."

Introduction

RAÚL A. HINOJOSA-OJEDA AND EDWARD TELLES

The Trump Paradox: Migration, Trade, and Racial Politics in US-Mexico Relations has been put together to explore one of the most complex and unequal cross-border relations anywhere in the world, especially in light of the rise of Donald Trump. The book examines current US-Mexico relations by looking at paradoxical immigration politics and policies and the current state of trade integration before and after the North American Free Trade Agreement (NAFTA). The current dynamics involve not only the changing migration demographics that have contributed to net zero Mexican migration to the United States but also the trillions of dollars contributed by Latino immigrants to the US economy. Trump's narrative blaming trade and migration for areas of the United States that are struggling economically must be understood instead in the context of the racialized historical roots of US-Mexico relations as well as their major implications for global trends in the twenty-first century.

Donald Trump's political rise utilized the narrative that America ceased being great because of "illegal" immigrants and trade agreements that produced deficits and took US jobs. The rise of Trump's electoral popularity has been conflated by many observers with measurable negative impacts from trade and migration on the lives of Trump supporters, as well as evidence of the need for more restrictive immigration and trade policy responses. An examination of the detailed geographic concentration of primary and general election voter support for Donald

Trump, however, indicates a negative correlation between Trump supporters and the presence of both Mexican immigrants and trade with Mexico. Thus, the Trump Paradox shows that those districts that voted for Trump are the least affected by Mexican trade and migration but still harbor anti-trade and anti-immigration views. The results of the 2018 elections show signs that the Trump Paradox is both deepening and unraveling. Forty congressional districts that voted for Trump in 2016 flipped in 2018, showing the unraveling of Trump's Mexico narrative. These formerly GOP districts are some of the districts that are most exposed to Mexican migration and trade. Recent research also shows that actually implementing highly restrictive trade and/or migration policies will significantly hurt Trump voting areas, despite their relatively low level of linkages with Mexico. While Trump voter regions are shown to be struggling economically, with high concentrations of white poverty, unemployment, and low income, neither the cause nor the solution is Mexico-related migration, and trade policies are neither the cause of nor the solution for these regions lagging behind economically.

This misguided Trump narrative is also paradoxical in the context of the recent historic shifts in US-Mexico trade and migratory labor integration. In the thirty-five years following World War II, deepening US-Mexico economic ties were characterized by relatively high trade protection and openness to migration, particularly in the Southwest where US agriculture depended on Mexican migrants for farm labor. But beginning in the 1980s and accelerating with NAFTA, US policy has shifted to increasingly liberal trade and investment policies. These policies have been accompanied by more restrictive immigration policies. Nearly a quarter century of a focus on trade liberalization has ignored areas of migration reform that are potentially much more beneficial, reforms that would recognize the positive impacts on the US GDP of the rising stock of migrants in the United States. Today, the United States and Mexico continue to share their long and unequal border, with intense trade, migration, and remittance interdependence involving billions of dollars per day and a Mexican-origin population in the United States that has contributed over $1 trillion to the US GDP, more than the size of the entire Mexican economy.[1]

Despite these regional complementarities and opportunities, the election of Donald Trump has led paradoxically to a highly conflictive period. The larger questions explored in this book are whether North America can shift to a new historic engagement that has the potential for beneficial migration and trade policy reforms. Such reforms could leverage a new historical complementarity for upward wage and productivity convergence, increased intra- and interregional trade, and reduced migration.

It is in this US-Mexico context that we must see the paradox and the history behind the rise of Donald Trump, the epicenter and model for the rise of neonationalist politics across the globe. Trump created momentum for his political movement by blaming trade with and migration from developing countries, particularly by demonizing Mexico and Mexicans, for the economic woes of the working class, especially those in manufacturing. In doing so, he played to the economic and social anxieties of his majority-white political base. For Trump and his supporters, US-Mexico relations are believed to be deeply rooted, once again, in the racialized clash of a white "America" with nonwhite contenders, particularly its neighbor to the south and the people coming from it. Trump, like others before him, turned what would normally be cast as an instance of international relations into a racialized relationship. That is why we situate racial politics as central to understanding Donald Trump's rise.

The Trump campaign and the Trump administration have stoked white anxieties, this time about losing their majority status and their privileged position, just as President James K. Polk did in the mid-nineteenth century in the Mexican-American War when the United States invaded Mexico and essentially seized its land. President Trump's rhetorical attacks on Mexico, which follow three decades of relatively serious and cordial relations, have inflicted damage on Mexico and US-Mexico relations and have marked Mexicans as a public enemy. In doing so, Donald Trump has also exposed anti-Mexican and anti-Mexico sentiments that have been brewing for more than 150 years, openly racializing not only Mexicans in the United States but also the country of Mexico and Mexico's relations with the United States. From this racialized US-Mexico narrative Trump provides a road map for how the "West" is to respond to a great new global convergence in which rich and poor countries come together (Spence 2011). Trump characterizes Latino immigrants, particularly those from Mexico, as an existential threat to the United States, reaffirming the "Hispanic Challenge" narrative advanced by the influential political scientist Samuel P. Huntington in his 1996 book, *The Clash of Civilizations and the Remaking of the World Order*. Huntington's argument is that "the persistent inflow of Hispanic immigrants" poses the biggest threat to the essentially Anglo-Saxon Protestant US national identity because their growing presence in the United States threatens "to divide the United States into two peoples, two cultures, and two languages[,] . . . rejecting the Anglo-Protestant values that built the American dream."[2]

The pivotal question is whether this monumental shift toward racialized nationalist anti-immigrant and anti-trade policy is a sustainable representation of a new world order or whether this fundamentally flawed narrative represents the last gasp of an old order—one that is soon to be replaced by a California-style transformation that embraces US-Mexico migration and trade integration. The chapters in this book have taken on this question from myriad perspectives, each bringing in empirical evidence and fresh research to illuminate both the conflicts and the complementarities of US-Mexico relations today.

ORGANIZATION OF THIS BOOK

This volume emerged from a binational conference that we convened at the University of California, Santa Barbara (UCSB), in late 2017. Its seventeen chapters present state-of-the-art analysis by scholars from both Mexico and the United States, sometimes working in binational teams. Most of the chapters were presented at the UCSB conference in an early version; others were later added to round out the volume. This has truly been a collective effort that we hope will contribute to greater cross-border understanding and cooperation. The views represented by the contributors to this volume are their own and not those of their respective institutions.

The seventeen chapters are organized in four parts, with the titles of each chapter bearing a central research question. Each chapter is also accompanied by suggested reading for those interested in further research on the subject. Key terms are boldfaced where they are first mentioned in the book, and a glossary (cross-referenced to that initial chapter) is included at the back of the book, along with a list of acronyms.

The Trump Paradox (Chapters 1 and 2)

The first two chapters frame the trade and migration paradoxes that inform the exploration of these issues in parts 2 and 3, on migration and trade, respectively, that follow. They also open the discussion of racialized politics as a driver of attitudes and policies in the current political climate, a subject that informs the whole book but is given particular context and focus in the book's final part. Of course, racialized politics have a long history in the United States, a history described in chapter 13, the foundational chapter for part 4, "Racialized Politics."

In chapter 1, *How Do We Explain Trump's Paradoxical Yet Electorally Successful Use of a False US-Mexico Narrative?*, we compare the Trump narrative about how Mexican migration and trade have hurt the United States to the economic and social exposure to Mexican trade and immigration in places that voted for Trump. Our research shows the existence of what we refer to as the Trump Paradox, whereby counties that voted for Trump are often struggling economically, with high concentrations of poverty and unemployment, but paradoxically with little exposure to immigration or trade with Mexico. We also analyze the 2018 midterm elections and the breaking down of the Trump Paradox. In both elections, we find that Trump was able to gain support by tapping into anti-immigrant and anti-trade attitudes—disproportionately and paradoxically in places where there was little actual exposure to Mexican immigration or trade.

In chapter 2, *What Were the Paradoxical Consequences of Militarizing the Border with Mexico?*, Douglas S. Massey further examines the Trump Paradox by describing and analyzing Trump's single-minded determination, fired up by millions of voters, to build a border wall and militarize the border. Massey illustrates the evolution of Mexican migration and US policy over the past several decades and exposes the "train wreck" that Trump created. Through ongoing data collection and analysis, Massey has long argued that militarizing the border would not solve the problem of undocumented migration. In fact, it would make it worse, actually increasing the size of the undocumented population as it disrupted patterns of circular migration and traditional migration routes. This has ironically led to more undocumented immigrants making the United States their home given the unlikely success and the financial and physical costs of crossing the border again. At the same time, border militarization has redistributed many of them away from traditional destinations and throughout the rest of the country.

Mexico-US Migration (Chapters 3–8)

The Swiss playwright and novelist Max Frisch famously said, "We wanted workers, but we got people instead." The chapters in part 2 continue to explore the transformation of Mexico-US migration, including issues of health, education, and work that affect an increasingly binational population. Several chapters pick up on the history of migration outlined in chapter 2 from relatively low-scale bracero recruitment of agricultural workers after World War II to large-scale migration tipped by the Immigration and Naturalization Act of 1965; these chapters go further to describe immigration as well as immigration enforcement over the past decade and illustrate the economic and demographic causes for the precipitous decline in immigration from Mexico since the Great Recession, one that has coincided with a fertility transition in Mexico. For the first time more Mexicans are leaving the United States than are arriving, though immigration from southern Mexico continues and that from Central America has exploded. Indeed, a dilemma for rich and aging societies like the United States is that for their economies to continue flourishing, they need immigrants. Several chapters describe the challenges that need to be addressed for future generations, including suggestions for sustainable policies.

Chapter 3, *How Did We Get to the Current Mexico-US Migration System, and How Might It Look in the Near Future?*, by Silvia E. Giorguli, Claudia Masferrer, and Victor M. García-Guerrero, explores the changing nature of migration between Mexico and the United States. Demographic projections that take into account Mexico's steep fertility decline and Mexico's relations with other neighbors—Canada, Guatemala, Honduras, and El Salvador—reveal a new migration system in the making, one that entails a slowing but persistent flow of Mexicans to the "North," a rapidly growing US-born population in Mexico, and the visible flow of Central Americans across Mexico to the United States, often for political reasons.

Given that, for now at least, mass Mexican immigration has ended, chapter 4, by René Zenteno and Roberto Suro, investigates the question, *Recession versus Removals: Which Finished Mexican Unauthorized Migration?* This chapter explores how the Great Recession suddenly stifled Mexican immigration and how the steep decline in Mexican fertility to near-US levels may keep it from returning to earlier levels. By its size, concentration, and duration, the authors note, Mexican immigration stood as a singular event in the annals of contemporary migrations worldwide and was unprecedented both in Mexico's experience as a sending country and in the long history of immigration to the United States. Zenteno and Suro point out that the circumstances of the migration finale are as important as its much-studied beginnings.

In chapter 5, *How Is the Health of the Mexican-Origin Population on Both Sides of the Border Affected by Policies and Attitudes in the United*

States?, Fernando Riosmena, Hiram Beltrán-Sánchez, Megan Reynolds, and Justin Vinneau explore the implications for health among the Mexican-origin population on both sides of the border. They note that because the United States and Mexico are deeply linked economically, environmentally, and socially, a shared, binational understanding of the well-being of these populations is required. The chapter concludes with policy suggestions for improving health care for these populations.

In chapter 6, *What Shall Be the Future for the Children of Migration? LASANTI and the Educational Imperative,* Patricia Gándara and Gary Orfield discuss the need for school integration in the deeply interdependent and contiguous region of Los Angeles–San Diego–Tijuana (LASANTI). This Baja California (a state in Mexico) and Southern California region is home to the most heavily transited international border in the world. In spite of the rhetoric about building walls and sealing borders, California and Mexico are highly interdependent, especially at this frontier, and their fortunes are inexorably tied. Yet this enormous resource is at risk unless both nations combine their efforts to raise the education level for the entire region, quickly, before the window of opportunity closes.

Pia M. Orrenius and Madeline Zavodny, in chapter 7, examine changes in the size and flows of undocumented immigration and discuss the policy implications of slowing undocumented immigration and growing labor demand. *What Are the Policy Implications of Declining Unauthorized Immigration from Mexico?* first estimates the size of inflows of unauthorized workers from Mexico and then examines the determinants of those inflows. As previous chapters have suggested, their estimates reveal that the current inflows of unauthorized Mexican workers are the lowest they have been in decades, and based on various indicators, they are unlikely to rebound. Nevertheless, US labor demand is growing. They point to the policy implications of creating a broad and sustainable temporary worker program that would allow for low-skilled, employment-based immigration as well as incorporate unauthorized workers who are already present.

Finally, in chapter 8, *How Does Mexican Migration Affect the US Labor Market?,* Frank D. Bean, Susan K. Brown, and James D. Bachmeier assess the extensive research on the impact of immigrants on US labor markets, explaining the complex interaction between them and the clearly positive economic and demographic gains from immigration in the long term. They note that numerous rigorous research studies demonstrate that allegations that immigrants take American jobs are false or grossly exaggerated. Since the end of World War II, economic and job growth in the United States has ranked among the highest in the world, especially in California. This alone, taken at face value, suggests that Mexican migrants and their descendants have not damaged the labor market of the United States.

Trade Integration (Chapters 9–12)

The chapters in part 3 review the long-term labor market and demographic transformations within and between the United States and Mexico over the post–World War II period. This part explores the positive impact immigration has had on the US economy, the effects of NAFTA on agriculture and the automobile sector, and the winners and losers under NAFTA, with an examination of some of the new provisions in the United States-Mexico-Canada Agreement (USMCA).

In chapter 9, *Before and after NAFTA: How Are Trade and Migration Policies Changing?*, Raúl Hinojosa-Ojeda, Sherman Robinson, and Karen Thierfelder take up the positive impact immigration has had on the GDP of the US economy and provide statistical models that show how immigration reform is a potentially much more significant economic factor than any trade deal could be. These models also estimate the cost and benefit of alternatives to immigration reforms, such as the collapse of NAFTA, trade wars among NAFTA countries, and the implementation of the new USMCA. These are then compared to (1) the effects of highly restrictive and mass removal migration policies or, alternatively, (2) the legalization and empowerment of 8 million undocumented workers in the United States. The results show the negative consequences of neonationalist policies and the trade policies that could potentially benefit both countries more than the relatively low impact of the USMCA—policies that could create complementary versus conflictual trade integration.

Chapter 10, *What Is the Relationship between US-Mexico Migration and Trade in Agriculture?*, by Antonio Yúnez-Naude, Jorge Mora-Rivera, and Yatziry Govea-Vargas, seeks to present an accurate diagnosis of the association of two events under NAFTA: the evolution of Mexico-US migration and the recent state of Mexican agriculture, particularly field crops and corn. Against common misconceptions of the relationship between NAFTA and migration, their data show that Mexican migration has decreased the most just as Mexican corn imports have increased the most in the past two decades. A better understanding of past and contemporary trends of these phenomena is needed in order to reflect about the future relationship between trade, migration, and agricultural development.

In chapter 11, *Is Complementarity Sustainable in the US-Mexico Automotive Sector?*, Jorge Carrillo analyzes the importance of the automotive sector to the Mexican economy and the impact of the trade relationship between Mexico and the United States. Trade in the automotive industry between both countries is not a zero-sum game in which one country gains and the other loses but rather a highly integrated and complex process that is complementary in various ways. While the asymmetrical dependence of Mexico on the United States increases, so too does the wage gap between the two countries. In the face of this paradoxical process of increased complementarity, there has been a growth in labor market disparities. In addition, a new Industry 4.0 of technological change, including robotics, is challenging traditional labor processes and will need to be confronted.

In chapter 12, Robert A. Blecker, Juan Carlos Moreno-Brid, and Isabel Salat consider the question, *What Policies Make Sense in a US-Mexico Trade Deal?* The renegotiation of NAFTA in 2017–18 at the behest of US president Donald Trump has focused public attention on trade "deals" as a key link between the Mexican and US economies. Like all trade agreements, NAFTA helped reshape the industrial structure of the three member economies (Mexico, the United States, and Canada) and created winners and losers along the way. NAFTA's trade and investment rules created incentives for industries to locate in one country or another and promoted the development of trinational "supply chains" among the three North American nations. Revising those rules in the new USMCA will affect the evolution of all three economies and will create new winners and losers in each one. USMCA includes a number of new provisions, such as a requirement to pay higher wages in a substantial part of automobile production, protections for the labor organizing rights of Mexican workers, and a mandate for future renegotiation, the consequences of which are difficult to foresee.

Racial Politics (Chapters 13–16)

Today, with globalization and growing diversification of the United States and particularly California, we would expect internationalist policies to be welcomed. But a nationalist reaction, led by the political impulses of President Trump, has led to increasing polarization between Mexico and the United States. Indeed, antiglobalization, anti-immigrant, and racist attitudes that we thought were going the way of the dinosaur are back with a vengeance. As a result, politics increasingly represents this clash of views on immigration and trade policies. These politics are increasingly tinged with racism and a long racialized history regarding Mexicans, as such viewpoints have become emboldened with the current administration. At the very least, the Trump administration has demonized Mexico and Mexicans, relying on the support of his base, many reclaiming inherent and historical anti-Mexican attitudes. In addition, immigration politics in the United States is racially divided, with Latinos reacting by tending to heavily support immigration reform. Chapters 13 through 16 reveal this turn to a racial politics in both American and Mexican nationalism.

In chapter 13, the social historian David Montejano describes how Donald Trump represents merely the latest in a long lineage of anti-Mexican and nativist leaders, critiquing the ideology of Manifest Destiny and the repercussions of the annexation of northern Mexico after the Mexican-American War. Montejano investigates the historical and contemporary conditions under which such racial politics and nativism arise, outlining the conditions under which nativist politics has surfaced once again. *What Is the Historical and Political Context for Trump's Nativist Appeal?* explores the rise of Trump and puts the roots of Trump's "Make America Great Again" slogan in the historical and political context of his nativist worldview.

In chapter 14, the anthropologists Regina Martínez Casas and Rafael Elías López Arellano observe how Donald Trump's "Twitter diplomacy" has stoked Mexican nationalist sentiments. In the context of Mexican nationalism—formed largely in response to US aggression and aggrievement throughout that country's history—the authors examine a series of tweets from then candidate and now president Trump. *How Has the New Mexico-US Relationship Affected Mexican Nationalism?* surveys Trump's attacks on Mexico and Mexicans and the way in which Mexico and Mexican nationalism have responded through a nationalist narrative of both estrangement and rapprochement.

Chapter 15, *What Are the Social Consequences of Immigrant Scapegoating by Political Elites?*, by the sociologist René D. Flores, looks at local anti-immigration initiatives and the rhetoric used by prominent leaders and explores the intended and unintended consequences that the targeting of immigrants has set in motion. Cases are presented of immigrant scapegoating in California, Florida, and Pennsylvania. The chapter concludes by providing some evidence of the short-term consequences of Trump's rhetoric and predicting some of its long-term consequences at the national level.

In chapter 16, the political scientists Gary Segura, Matt Barreto, and Angela E. Gutierrez explore the effects of "group threat" on racializing Latino identity and Latino responses to the anti-immigrant rhetoric of recent years. Their analysis of postelection survey data shows that Latino voters were indeed politically motivated by Trump's anti-Latino rhetoric. *How Do Latinos Respond to Anti-Immigrant Politics?* also presents evidence that Latino voters who were angry were more likely to engage in political activities during the 2016 election cycle. The findings hold for US-born Latinos as well as among non-Mexican Latinos who felt similarly targeted by Trump's rhetoric and proposals.

In the final chapter, chapter 17, the political scientist Zoltan L. Hajnal examines anti-immigrant backlash in state-level politics, most notably in California—a state that was in the 1990s at the forefront of the anti-immigrant backlash and may now be at the vanguard of pro-immigrant policy making. In particular, *Anti-Immigrant Backlash: Is There a Path Forward?* explores the lessons we might learn from California. The evidence leads Hajnal to conclude that growth in the Latino population initially provokes an anti-immigrant backlash. However, evidence also shows that once the Latino population crosses a demographic threshold, politics and policy begin to shift back toward inclusion and generosity.

BACKGROUND OF THIS BOOK

Even before Trump's election, a group of us at the University of California and leading Mexican institutions began discussions on how to understand this new context and its potential for long-term damage to US-Mexico relations. The U.S.-Mexico-California Collaborative, which we formed as a result, undertook a binational research agenda and organized a series of conferences on major policy arenas of trade, migration, integration, and racialized politics. We acted on the necessity of organizing a series of educational, research, and service activities that would bring together the best research on these issues to dismantle and replace Trump's misinformed and racially constructed policy narratives on immigration and international trade. Despite the scientific evidence and consensus that immigration and cross-border trade are generally beneficial to the US economy and US workers, he convinced his many voters of the opposite—that Mexican immigration and trade hurts them even though they tend to live in places with relatively little of either. Furthermore, the implementation of his anti-immigration and trade agenda will nevertheless have negative impacts in their relatively isolated communities. We believe that exposing this "Trump Paradox" is not only essential to clarify the nature of Trump's support but also opens up the potential for creating a counternarrative and a policy agenda based on real evidence, in contrast to Trump's divisive politics of fear and misinformation. It is also a way to communicate to the wider public policy community the large benefits of implementing policies leading to the legalization of immigration and sustainable trade integration.

The experience of California in the past three decades has been central to our thinking. In the 1990s, California elected an anti-immigrant governor and voted in anti-immigrant initiatives, including the notorious Proposition 187, banning government services and support for undocumented immigrants. Largely as a result of demographic change, with immigrants naturalizing and their children coming of age, as well as the growth of a college-educated population, California subsequently turned left and embraced immigration (Pastor 2018). We ask if California's rejection of the anti-immigration politics of Proposition 187 is a model for a demographic and political evolution that embraces a new phase of US-Mexico relations. California as a state can play a huge role in moving policy research and politics in this direction. For example, its economy strongly benefits from openness to technology, trade, migration, and integration with Mexico, and these factors provide widespread indirect benefits throughout the US economy. California's political leadership has demonstrated that it is committed to leading the way on sensible policies on immigration and trade (as well as progressive and sustainable environmental policies), based on evidence-based research and a concern for human rights rather than the current administration's nationalistic anti-immigrant and anti-trade policies that build on white anxieties about immigrants and minorities, as well as damaging environmental policies. We believe that California provides lessons for the nation today, and it has inspired us to produce this book.

PART ONE

The Trump Paradox

CHAPTER 1

How Do We Explain Trump's Paradoxical Yet Electorally Successful Use of a False US-Mexico Narrative?

RAÚL HINOJOSA-OJEDA AND EDWARD TELLES

Much has been made of early studies that tried to equate Donald Trump's victory in 2016 with voters who had been hard hit by free trade policies such as the North American Free Trade Agreement (NAFTA) and by job competition and social disintegration created by an increase in immigration—even though the actual economic and social impacts of Mexico-related trade and migration were not considered. In this chapter, we introduce (nonalternative) facts about Mexican migration and trade policies and compare the Trump narrative about how Mexican migration and trade have hurt the United States to actual economic and social exposure to Mexican trade and immigration. We focus on the following questions and hypotheses:

1. Was support for Trump based on the actual local presence of immigrants and trade, particularly from Mexico?
2. If we do not find that places with more trade and immigration predict Trump support, then is it attitudes about trade and immigration that predict Trump support instead? We thus open up the possibility that Trump may have tapped into attitudes about these rather than their actual impact.
3. Or perhaps both are operative: Trump support reflects negative attitudes about immigration and trade as well as a greater presence of immigration and trade, suggesting that negative attitudes would be a response to a greater local threat of immigration and trade.

4. Finally, does Trump support correlate with poorer socioeconomic conditions, and if so, how are these related to trade and immigration?

Our research shows the existence of a **Trump Paradox**. That is, while counties that voted for Trump are often struggling economically, with high concentrations of poverty and unemployment, and have negative attitudes about immigration and trade, these counties—paradoxically—have little exposure to immigration or trade with Mexico.

THE FALSE US-MEXICO NARRATIVE

From the launch of his campaign in June 2015, Donald Trump adeptly focused on US-Mexico relations to create a media narrative that America ceased being great because of border-raiding illegal immigrants ("murderers and rapists") and trade agreements like NAFTA that ship US jobs across the border (Green 2017). In this narrative, "real" American working people are hurt because America's border is being overrun by Mexico sending their worst people and because of "unfair" trade deals made by our "bad" leaders. This diagnosis leads to the magical solution that he can "Make America Great Again" by building a "big, beautiful wall," deporting millions, dismantling NAFTA, and imposing huge tariffs. "We have no choice," Trump says. "If we don't defend our borders, then we cease to be a nation." He has since continued to use this narrative with great success among his political base.

The dog whistle of this simply construed yet dangerously fictitious cross-border narrative—not to mention the full-throated denunciations of Mexicans and Central Americans—should not have been underestimated, especially given Trump's openly racist demonizing, unprecedented in modern presidential campaigns. His narrative of nostalgia, forged as it is by white ethnic identity politics, invokes a long historical legacy of privileged supremacy but with a twist. In this telling of the story it is an "embattled" white citizenry that must make a stand or be swallowed up by a demographic transformation to a nonwhite-dominant multiracial America. Trump's claim that "this is our last chance"—his presidential campaign's forthright appeal for a **white backlash**—should have made clear what was at stake for American democracy in the twenty-first century.

The collective failure by the media and political leaders to immediately counter not only the blatant bigotry of his initial position but also its manifest economic absurdity allowed Trump to elaborate a twenty-first century **nativism** based on anti-immigrant politics and similar to the nativist movements that emerged in the late nineteenth century, where "native-born" whites decried the upsurge in immigration from the "undesirables" of that day, painting the desperate immigrants from southern Italy, Ireland, Germany, and Eastern Europe with ugly ethnic stereotypes and slurs. Then as now, Trump's **nativist narrative** insults immigrants, particularly Mexicans, with calls for deporting all undocumented immigrants and their US-born children and making Mexico pay for the wall by seizing family remittances to Mexico. Today, the narrative is augmented by vilifying international trade, especially from Mexico, the same country that the despised immigrants come from. Trade policies promoted by Trump's narrative include voiding NAFTA and imposing tariffs as coercive threats around migration and trade.

Journalists, political leaders, and academics have sought to explain Trump's political rise, initially accepting at face value Trump's claim that immigration and the global economy threaten American workers. Journalists accepted preliminary scholarship suggesting that this was the basis for the popularity of his appeal and his electoral victory in key swing states (Davis and Hilsenrath 2016).[1] These journalists wrongly inferred that attitudes about immigration and trade were the result of actual immigration and trade, conflating these attitudes with the wrongheaded idea that Trump supporters had experienced negative impacts from both migration and US trade in a global economy.

Scholars have continued to debate the causes of Trump's or other nationalist candidates' unexpected electoral victory using a variety of techniques. Some economists use data on temporally specific regional impacts, looking for correlations between the "China shock" of increased imports in the early 2000s and voting that swung for Trump in 2016 (Autor, Dorn, and Hanson 2016; Autor et al. 2016). Chinese import penetration was also found to be a predictor of the rise of right-wing candidates and nationalism in Europe (Colantone and Stanig 2018). Other economists find a correlation between the decline in manufacturing employment and the counties that voted for Trump (Altik, Atkeson, and Hansen 2018). Prevailing theory in political science and journalistic readings of social science data expected that economic interests and support for Trump were positively correlated (Mutz 2018).

However, the political communication scholar Diana Mutz (2018), in a paper backed by the National Academy of Sciences, uses the leading election panel surveys and disputes the perceived economic interest explanation, instead finding that attitudes concerning **white status** were a better explanation for Trump's victory. In particular, candidate Trump was able to tap into white voter anxiety about globalization and diversity. Specifically, concerns and anxieties about immigration and job displacement predicted greater support for Trump (Mutz 2018). A careful reanalysis of those same data concludes that the **status threat** explanation was overstated; indeed, perceptions of economic interests were at least as important, and perceived economic interests are intertwined with status issues (Morgan 2018). The political scientists Marc Hooghe and Ruth Dassonneville (2018), who study electoral behavior, found that anti-immigrant attitudes and racial resentments explained much of the Trump vote, though neither they nor any of the other authors mentioned explored the actual impact of immigration or trade.

Economic Self-Interest, Anti-Immigrant Attitudes, and Racial Resentments

Our research demonstrates that using data on actual Mexican trade and migration impacts challenges both the economic and the attitudinal-based explanations for Trump support. It shows the existence of a Trump Paradox that exposes dual yet systematic contradictions between Trump voter behavior and actual county economic exposure to Mexican trade and immigration, as well as contradictions between the attitudinally perceived economic and social impacts compared to actual economic and social exposure to Mexican trade and immigration. We do, however, confirm that places that voted for Trump are more economically challenged by unemployment and poverty than others. Yet these challenging economic conditions are unrelated to exposure to Mexican trade and immigration.

Arguments for the importance of attitudes rather than real self-interest are based on sociological and political science research. Work in group position theory, for example, posits that increases in the size of a given racial minority group can be seen as a **group threat** to political and social resources by the majority, triggering the fear that immigrants pose a potential challenge to the dominance of the white majority and generating hostility and negative stereotyping of the minority group (Blalock 1967; Hood and Morris 1997; Quillian 1995). Because of the growing Latino population across the United States (Krogstad and Lopez 2015), Latinos, and Mexicans in particular, may be perceived as a major threat to the white majority, especially when those fears are activated by political candidates.

Similarly, growing trade may threaten whites by challenging their sense of not only racial but also global supremacy. In this way, white Americans situate themselves as the "real" Americans in a world where "America's" global leadership is at stake. On the other hand, white anxieties and negative attitudes about immigration and trade may be stirred up by political actors. These actors activate latent racial hostilities (Hopkins 2010; Valentino, Hutchings, and White 2002) as well as a preference for like-minded candidates (Mendelberg 2001), independent of actual immigration and trade.

Trump uses nationalist rhetoric to tie poor economic conditions to globalization and diversity (Monnat 2016; Rothwell and Diego-Rosell 2016), but this rhetoric obfuscates the deeper underlying dynamics of high unemployment and low income by falsely blaming trade and immigration for the economic challenges of unemployment and poverty. Our research shows that the challenging economic conditions in much of Trump country are real but are unrelated to local exposure to Mexican trade and immigration. We examine the actual volume of trade and immigration rather than simply attitudes about immigration and trade. As far as we know, no one has examined the effect of actual immigration and trade on the 2016 election, and the only paper that has examined **trade flows** (goods and services that are bought and sold between countries) is that by the labor economist David Autor and colleagues (2016) on Chinese imports. In particular, we focus on trade and immigration from Mexico, which has been particularly vilified by Trump's campaign and his presidency as a primary source of the nation's economic and social ills.

DATA AND METHODS: TRUMP SUPPORT, TRADE, AND IMMIGRATION

We analyze data at the county and congressional district (macro) and individual (micro) levels. We use county and congressional district data from the US Census and the American Community Survey, in addition to sources we indicate below. Our macro level data are composed of a mapping analysis of 1,925 counties, which account for 94.4 percent of the US population. Maps at the county level permit detailed geographic analysis. However, we were unable to get sufficient trade data for the smallest counties, which account for the remaining 5.6 percent, because their sales in **tradable sectors** (i.e., those goods and services large enough to trade internationally)[2] are too low to be included in the Economic Census at the county level.

For the macro analyses, we conducted a series of statistical models[3] that could quantify the relationship between Trump support and both trade and migration, as well as a host of other variables, at the congressional district level. We calculated the percent that voted for Trump in 2016 minus the percent voting for the Republican presidential candidate Mitt Romney in 2012. We examine the shift in Republican vote shares from 2012 to 2016 rather than Republican shares in 2016 since the percent of votes shares that go to one or another party in general elections largely depends on consistent partisan voting by a large percentage of Americans, which often is unaffected by candidate positions. By comparing 2012–16 vote shares we thus use a conservative or strict standard to assess the greater (or lesser) attraction of Trump over Romney, the previous Republican candidate. Alternatively, in a less strict test, we examined the percent voting for Trump, and the results are similar.

To quantify trade, we collected data on imports by sector (e.g., agricultural products, textiles) from the World Institute for Strategic Economic Research (WISER) trade database.[4] To distribute this trade data at the county level, we created a ratio based on county sales by sector and then distributed the higher-level data according to this ratio. This sector's sales data were collected from the US Census Bureau's 2012 Survey of Business Owners and Self-Employed (SBO). Our analysis sought to replicate core aspects of the methodology used by Autor, Dorn, and Hanson (2016) to measure regional trade exposures in US trade with China. Their analysis of US-China trade is based on the share of each industry in the region's (e.g., county's) total sales on the US market; it summarizes differences across US regions in industry specialization patterns (e.g., for the distribution of labor, goods, and services in particular industries). Thus their methodology captures variation in regional exposure to China's supply-driven export growth. For our analysis of US trade with Mexico, we also extended and, we believe, improved the specificity of this measurement by including imports from Mexico for counties. Finally, we divide this measure of variation in regional exposure by total population to get a per capita measure of trade with Mexico.

To quantify immigration, we use the percent foreign-born Mexican-origin population, which is based on the 2016 American Community Survey. We also control for demographic variables, particularly percent white, percent college educated, and percent over age sixty-five, which are commonly used in studies of voter behaviors (Altick, Atkeson, and Hansen 2018). We then control for the effect of economic conditions, including poverty levels, unemployment, median income, and whether employed in the manufacturing sector.

We first analyze macro level data for counties and congressional districts, using maps (for counties) and statistical models (for congressional districts) to illustrate the relation between places that voted for Trump and those where there is greater immigration and trade. Counties are used for the maps since they better illustrate geographical detail though we use congressional districts for the statistical analysis since voting and representation are done at that level. Since such ecological data cannot be used to deduce the voting behavior of individuals (King 2013), we complement our macro analysis with an analysis of a micro level data set from the Cooperative Congressional Election Survey (CCES) to see if actual immigration and trade are associated with the preferences of (non-Hispanic) white voters for Donald Trump, independent of individual social and economic characteristics and attitudes about immigration and trade. We are particularly interested in parsing the effects of actual trade and immigration versus attitudes about them, again independent of personal economic situations and social characteristics.

The micro analysis also allows us to examine non-Hispanic white voters in isolation.[5] The dependent variable is whether or not individuals voted for candidate Trump, with a control for whether the respondent voted for Romney in 2012 and for the political party he or she belongs to. The independent variables from the CCES data are (1) individual characteristics of voting history, partisanship, education, gender, age, income, and employment status; and (2) individual attitudes about immigration and trade, specifically those indicating agreement or disagreement on whether the US government should deport undocumented immigrants, and whether one supports the Trans-Pacific Partnership (TPP) Act.[6] Using statistical models, we analyze both individual and congressional district level variables (Raudenbush and Bryk 2002). We also include the independent variables Mexican immigration and per capita Mexican imports. To do this, we link the individuals in the CCES data to the information about immigration and trade in the congressional district in which they reside.

Finally, to analyze voters that flipped in 2018, we use statistical models with the 2018 CCES data to predict whether white voters who voted for Trump in 2016 then voted for the Democratic candidate in 2018. Among the independent variables, we changed only two variables from the 2016 to the 2018 analysis: we no longer control for whether they voted for Romney in 2012, and we use support for the border wall rather than support for deportations because the question itself changed in the CCES.

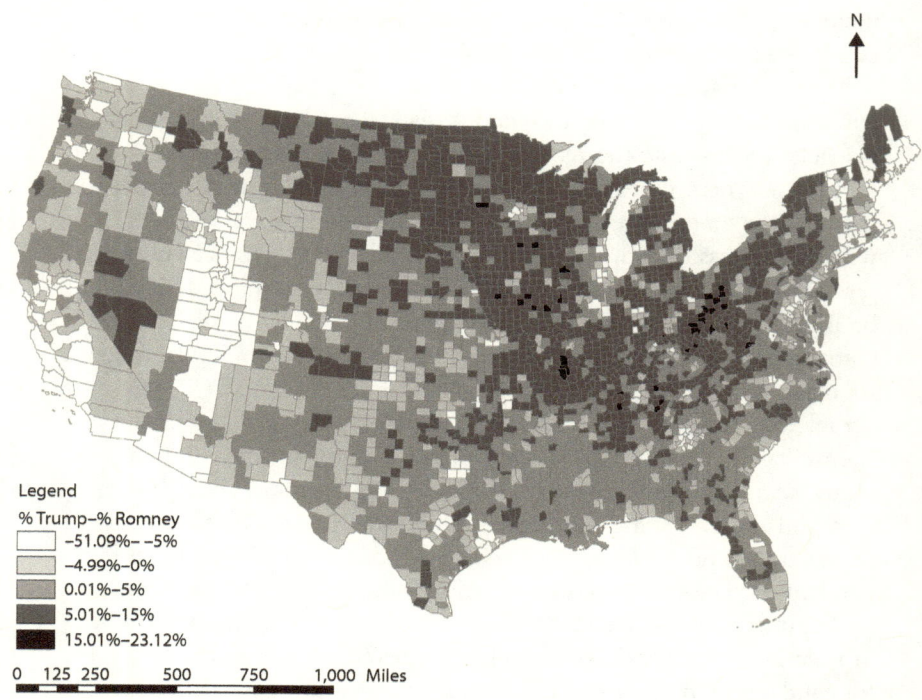

FIGURE 1.1A. US Counties by Percent Voting for Trump (2016) − Percent Voting for Romney (2012).

TRUMP SUPPORT GREATER WHERE THERE ARE FEWER MEXICAN IMMIGRANTS AND LESS TRADE

We illustrate how Trump voting, immigration, and trade were distributed across the country and then statistically examine the relation among these at the county level. At a descriptive level, **figure 1.1** shows several maps of US counties. As the white and light gray counties in Map A show, Trump lost support in much of California and Arizona, in some counties in the Northwest and New England, and in nearly all of Utah, but these were exceptions. Trump support expanded from the traditional Republican base throughout the rest of country but especially in the Midwest and surrounding areas. However, Map A shows that the county locations that shifted toward Trump are clearly distinct from the counties with Mexican immigrants (Map B), suggesting that the appeal of his narrative tended to be greater among voters who are

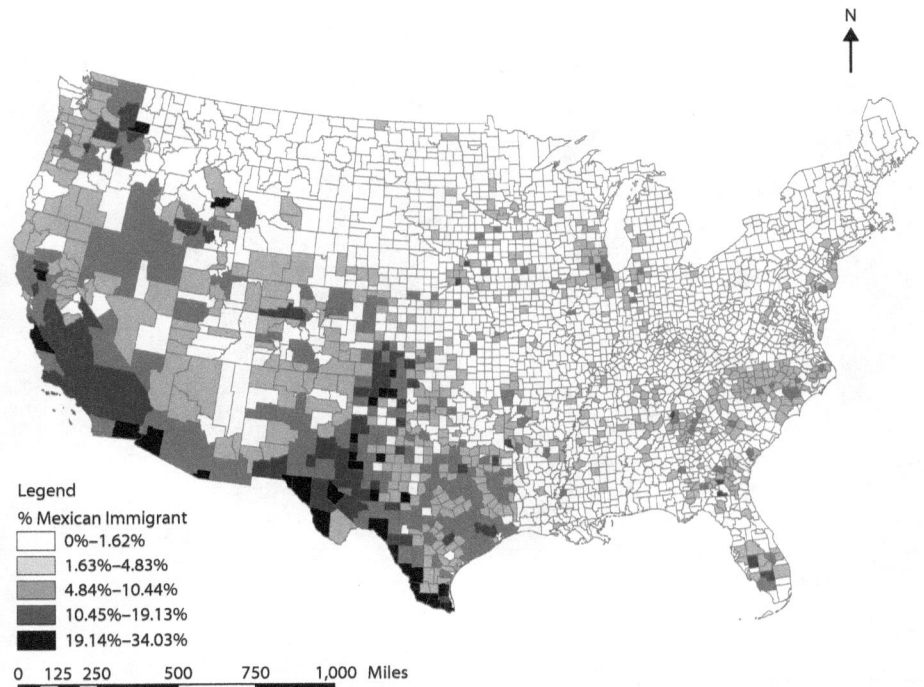

FIGURE 1.1B. US Counties by Percent Mexican Immigrants.

hardly affected by Mexican immigration. Most notably, the Midwest and northern states were regions with the lowest concentrations of Mexican immigrants, but support in those regions turned increasingly for the 2016 Republican candidate.

Map C shows that the relationship of Trump support to trade seems more mixed, at least descriptively. Map A and Map C together show that those counties that supported Trump often had little trade with Mexico, as evidenced by the fact that Mexican imports were concentrated on the Pacific Coast, along the Mexican border, in Utah, and in New England. These areas tended to vote for the Democratic candidate in 2016 and were often less likely to vote for Trump in 2016 compared to Romney in 2012. On the other hand, Map C shows that counties in the Great Lakes, the lower Midwest, and other regions also had very high levels of Mexican imports but widespread support for Trump, though the statistical analysis that follows shows these were exceptions.

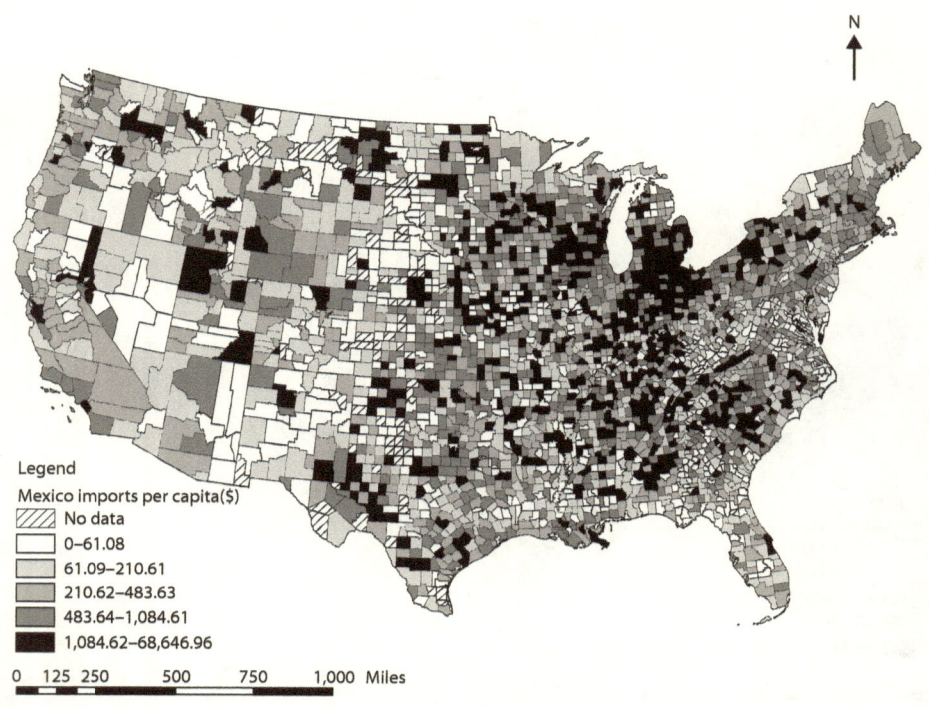

FIGURE 1.1C. US Counties by Mexican Imports per Capita (in quantiles).

Table 1.1 more precisely determines the relation among these and other variables.[7]

In table 1.1, we present our statistical models of 373 congressional districts predicting changes in Republican voting in 2016. As with figure 1.1, table 1.1 shows that Trump support was greater than Romney support in counties where there were fewer Mexican immigrants (% Mexican Immigrants). These results persist regardless of whether we use total Mexican immigration, total Mexican non-naturalized immigration, or total immigration instead of recent Mexican immigration or Mexican trade exports instead of imports (results not shown). Similarly, levels of Mexican imports, our indicator of trade, are negatively correlated with Trump voting (Mexico Import [$1,000]/Person); that is, no or very few Mexican imports occur in areas that supported Trump. These results held with other indicators of trade such as exports, net trade, and recent trade (data not shown). Last, results for the other variables show that congressional districts with higher proportions of

TABLE 1.1 STATISTICAL MODELS PREDICTING REPUBLICAN VOTE SHARE IN 2016 MINUS 2012 REPUBLICAN VOTE SHARE AT CONGRESSIONAL DISTRICT LEVEL

	Immigration and Trade (1)	+Demographic (2)	+Economic (3)	All Variables (4)
% Mexican Immigrants	−0.225***			−0.338***
	(0.044)			(0.055)
Mexico Import ($1,000) / Person	−0.005***			−0.003**
	(0.002)			(0.001)
% Non-Hispanic White		0.037***	0.023*	−0.045***
		(0.011)	(0.013)	(0.016)
% BA or More		−0.227***	−0.247***	−0.275***
		(0.019)	(0.034)	(0.033)
% 65+		0.373***	0.427***	0.434***
		(0.068)	(0.075)	(0.072)
% Female		1.361***	1.431***	0.644**
		(0.214)	(0.229)	(0.256)
Log Median HH Income			0.015	0.034
			(0.031)	(0.030)
% Unemployment			−0.040	−0.035
			(0.032)	(0.030)
% Manufacturing			0.100	0.334***
			(0.107)	(0.114)
Population Logged	−0.267***	−0.092**	−0.087**	−0.098**
	(0.050)	(0.039)	(0.040)	(0.040)
Constant	3.599	0.525	0.365	0.881
	(0.673)	(0.535)	(0.569)	(0.586)
Observations	373	376	376	373
R-squared	0.158	0.442	0.448	0.511

NOTE: All independent variables computed for 2016. HH = Household.
SIGNIFICANCE: ***p<0.01, **p<0.05, *p<0.1.

whites (% non-Hispanic White) tended to vote for Trump rather than Romney, while places with more college-educated persons (% BA or More) and more females (% Female) shifted away from Trump, as did those with more manufacturing (% Manufacturing).

Therefore, our macro analysis suggests that an economic interest explanation for the presumed negative effects of immigration and trade do not explain the Trump vote. The Trump narrative that seeks to stoke fear about Mexican immigration and trade had the opposite effect: it seems to work best where there is little actual immigration and trade. Our results are consistent with economic evidence that immigration and trade improve local economies, contrary to the Trump narrative that his base materially suffers because of immigration and trade with Mexico (Greenstone and Looney 2010; Furman 2018; National Academy of Sciences 2017).

ANTI-TRADE AND ANTI-IMMIGRANT ATTITUDES ACCOUNT FOR TRUMP SUPPORT, NOT ACTUAL IMMIGRATION OR TRADE

We further examine Trump voting and its relation to immigration and trade for individual voters, specifically white voters, rather than for counties. The county-level results in the previous analysis describe the geographic distributions and relations between Trump voting, immigration, and trade, but these are also subject to the effects of racial composition (e.g., Latino voters), as mentioned earlier, and the fact that in the previous analysis small counties carry as much weight as large urban counties. Thus, **table 1.2**[8] uses statistical models to examine whether non-Hispanic whites voted for Trump in 2016 while controlling for whether they voted for Romney and for their party affiliation. Moreover, data from the CCES also allow us to model voter attitudes about immigration and trade, with questions ascertaining the extent of agreement with the assertions that the United States should deport illegal immigrants or whether they are against the TPP Act. These models also allow us to gauge the extent to which voters were exposed to actual immigration and trade (% Mexican Immigrants; Mexico Import [$1,000]/Person).

Similar to table 1.1, table 1.2 shows that less educated (Completed College or More) and lower-income white voters (Family Income Logged) tended to vote for Trump, suggesting that Trump's candidacy appealed to less fortunate whites. Trump voters also tended to work in the manufacturing industries (Work in Manufacturing), suggesting that persons in that sector may have felt particularly vulnerable economically (Altick, Atkeson, and Hansen 2018). Models 2 and 4 show that percent Mexican immigrant (% Mexican Immigrants) and extent of Mexican trade (Mexico Import [$1000]/Person) were unrelated to voting for Trump among white voters, but they reveal that negative attitudes about immigration and trade were clearly related to support for Trump (Believes US Should Build a Border Wall; Against Trans-Pacific Partnership Act). Actual immigration was negatively related to voting for Trump. Trade and immigration were unrelated to Trump support, suggesting that anti-immigrant and anti-trade attitudes bore no relation

TABLE 1.2 STATISTICAL MODELS PREDICTING TRUMP VOTE IN 2016

	Model Numbers			
	(1)	(2)	(3)	(4)
Individual Level				
Voted Romney in 2012[a]	2.857***	3.003***	2.580***	2.721***
	(0.093)	(0.077)	(0.091)	(0.082)
Independent	0.909***	1.010***	0.783***	0.891***
	(0.083)	(0.090)	(0.085)	(0.091)
Republican	2.248***	2.392***	2.115***	2.255***
	(0.109)	(0.113)	(0.099)	(0.107)
Completed College or More	−0.857***	−0.855***	−0.728***	−0.743***
	(0.069)	(0.076)	(0.070)	(0.079)
Female	−0.210***	−0.229***	−0.085	−0.103
	(0.060)	(0.065)	(0.059)	(0.064)
Age 65 and Over	0.102	0.071	0.094	0.049
	(0.069)	(0.066)	(0.066)	(0.061)
Family Income Logged	−0.076**	−0.067**	−0.020	−0.017
	(0.037)	(0.033)	(0.038)	(0.036)
Temporarily Laid Off	−0.060	−0.131	0.003	−0.060
	(0.338)	(0.374)	(0.312)	(0.340)
Work in Manufacturing	0.411***	0.349***	0.246**	0.203*
	(0.109)	(0.121)	(0.112)	(0.120)
Believes US Should Deport Illegal Immigrants			1.612***	1.645***
			(0.064)	(0.061)
Against Trans-Pacific Partnership Act			0.655***	0.663***
			(0.070)	(0.064)
Congressional District (Groups) Level				
% Mexican Immigrants		0.565		1.383
		(2.085)		(2.274)
Mexico import ($1,000) / person		−0.013		−0.007
		(0.054)		(0.055)
Constant	−1.099	−1.324	−2.692	−2.879
	(0.409)	(0.408)	(0.423)	(0.440)
Observations	22,475	21,857	22,441	21,823
Number of groups		373		373

NOTE: Robust standard errors in parentheses.
SIGNIFICANCE: *** $p<0.01$, ** $p<0.05$, * $p<0.1$.
[a] Dummy variable for not voting in 2012 not shown.

TABLE 1.3 STATISTICAL MODELS PREDICTING WHETHER FLIPPED FROM VOTING FOR TRUMP IN 2016 PRESIDENTIAL ELECTION TO VOTING FOR DEMOCRATS IN 2018 HOUSE ELECTION

	Model Numbers			
	(1)	(2)	(3)	(4)
Individual Level				
Independent	−1.246***	−1.295***	−1.204***	−1.288***
	(0.208)	(0.214)	(0.207)	(0.220)
Republican	−2.350***	−2.450***	−2.312***	−2.462***
	(0.136)	(0.155)	(0.137)	(0.165)
Completed College or More	−0.137	−0.172	−0.222**	−0.292**
	(0.106)	(0.130)	(0.112)	(0.144)
Female	0.189*	0.238**	−0.021	−0.020
	(0.111)	(0.115)	(0.121)	(0.129)
Age 65 and Over	−0.559***	−0.609***	−0.316***	−0.337***
	(0.092)	(0.098)	(0.092)	(0.103)
Family Income Logged	−0.092	−0.140**	−0.024	−0.090
	(0.063)	(0.071)	(0.064)	(0.075)
Temporarily Laid Off	0.547	0.556	0.900	1.095
	(0.958)	(1.051)	(0.873)	(0.933)
Work in Manufacturing	0.275*	0.261	0.371**	0.353
	(0.153)	(0.188)	(0.177)	(0.216)
Believes US Should Build a Border Wall			−1.372***	−1.641***
			(0.138)	(0.199)
Against Trans-Pacific Partnership Act			−1.210***	−1.356***
			(0.142)	(0.143)
Congressional District (Groups) Level				
% Mexican Immigrants		3.378***		3.447***
		(1.285)		(1.279)
Mexico Import ($1,000)/ Person		0.036		0.037
		(0.037)		(0.037)
Constant	0.298	0.521	1.462	2.201
	(0.723)	(0.760)	(0.709)	(0.798)
Observations	8,855	8,585	8,807	8,538
Number of Groups		370		370

NOTE: Robust standard errors in parentheses.
SIGNIFICANCE: ***p<0.01, **p<0.05, *p<0.1.

to the levels of trade and immigration. Thus candidate Trump was able to mobilize anti-immigrant and anti-trade sentiments among white voters through his narratives, whether or not there was an actual presence or threat of immigration and trade. In our full model, which includes individual characteristics, attitudes about immigration and trade, and congressional district characteristics of immigration and trade (Model 4), all the aforementioned results held. (In another set of models, we also examined the change in immigration and trade between 2010 and 2016, and these revealed similar results.)

Finally, in **table 1.3** we analyze the midterm House elections in 2018 in which fully forty congressional seats flipped from Republican to Democrat, representing a voter backlash against the Trump presidency. Table 1.3 is set up to mirror the model in table 1.2. Positive coefficients in table 1.3 represent a tendency to flip to the Democratic candidate (whereas positive coefficients represented voting for Trump in table 1.2). For example, the coefficient for female in Model 1 shows that women who voted for Trump in 2016 were more likely than men to flip to Democratic candidates. Also, the less educated and those working in manufacturing, who were more likely to vote for Trump in 2016, flipped to voting for Democrats in the midterms. Negative attitudes about both immigration and trade continued to drive voters against Democrats. However, although the presence of Mexican immigrants was unrelated to Trump voting, congressional districts with more immigrants were more likely to flip to Democratic candidates in 2018. This suggests that perhaps proximity to immigrants may have led to turning away from the Republican Party, which had become increasingly anti-immigrant under the leadership of Donald Trump. Trade with Mexico, on the other hand, continued to be unrelated to voting.

CONCLUSION: THE TRUMP PARADOX

Our research, at both the macro (county) and micro (individual voter) levels, shows that *virtually no aspects of Trump's simple narrative to his voters has any factual basis in economic data*. Ironically, in analyzing counties or congressional districts across the United States, Trump's voters are less likely to live in places that have a significant number of Mexican immigrants and that have been affected by trade with Mexico. When examining white voters specifically, neither actual immigration nor trade context is related to where his supporters resided, but in the 2018 midterm elections, the immigration context became important as many Trump voters switched to vote for Democrats, especially in districts with more Mexican immigrants.

Our research shows the existence of a Trump Paradox that exposes dual yet systematic contradictions between Trump voter behavior and actual county economic exposure to Mexican trade and immigration, as well as contradictions between the attitudinally perceived economic and social impacts compared to actual county economic and social exposure to Mexican trade and immigration. While counties that voted for Trump are more economically challenged by unemployment and poverty than others, these challenging economic conditions are unrelated to exposure to Mexican trade and immigration.

Our research thus contradicts the core Trump narrative and demonstrates the need to develop a counternarrative. While many people in the United States are struggling financially in Trump voting counties, trade and migration are not to blame, even though many whites believe that to be the case. The difference between the two should not be understated. In fact, the evidence shows quite the opposite: places with more immigration and trade tend to do better economically, and there are only very small if any effects on native workers (National Academy of Sciences 2017). Trump's supporters may feel that trade and migration have damaged their economic prospects, but the empirical evidence says otherwise. Rather, candidate Trump successfully mobilized voters on the underlying sentiments that trade and immigration have hurt them. In the wake of Trump's political ascension, the worst thing that America's policy makers could do is treat Trump supporters' misdirected anger as a set of legitimate grievances in need of redress through anti-immigrant and anti-trade policies.

Trump's ability to successfully tap into anxieties about immigration and trade rather than the presence or threat of actual immigration and trade is consistent with social science research showing that economic self-interest generally has little effect on sociopolitical attitudes, especially those concerning issues of race and immigration (Sears and Funk 1991; Citrin et al. 1997; Green and McElwee 2018). Instead, attitudes about immigrants or racialized others may be based on factors such as media exposure (Héricourt and Spielvogel 2014), religious identity (Margolis 2018), racial anxieties (Sears and Funk 1991), or stereotypes about Latinos, all of which have been further stimulated during Trump's campaign and administration. Trump supporters may see nonwhites as altering their sense of American culture. They may see nonwhites growing in political power because of immigration and globalization, largely represented by international trade. They may feel that nonwhites, therefore, threaten American power (Mutz 2018). Our evidence suggests that Trump's support is based on such racialized beliefs, even though diversity and globalization tend to be beneficial to even these white working-class voters (National Academy of Sciences 2017).

The need to provide solid data and critical analysis is now more important than ever, particularly with respect to an understanding of the real forces driving the Trump phenomenon. Rarely does research examine actual trade and migration, and weakly informed questioning by the media and their misleading reports legitimizes Donald Trump's false claims about the real problems facing the economy. This has implicitly endorsed a dangerously wrong-headed set of solutions. Implementing the highly restrictive trade and/or migration policy that Trump proposes would disproportionately hurt those areas that voted for Trump.

Suggested Reading

Colantone, I., and P. Stanig. 2018. The trade origins of economic nationalism: Import competition and voting behavior in Western Europe. *American Journal of Political Science* (April 18). DOI.org/10.1111/ajps.12358.

Green, J. 2017. *Devil's Bargain: Steve Bannon, Donald Trump, and the Storming of the Presidency*. New York: Penguin.

Mendelberg, T. 2001. *The Race Card: Campaign Strategy, Implicit Messages, and the Norm of Equality*. Princeton, NJ: Princeton University Press.

Mutz, D. 2018. Status threat, not economic hardship, explains the 2016 presidential vote. *Proceedings of the National Academy of Sciences* 115(19): E4330–E4339. DOI.org/10.1073/pnas.1718155115.

National Academy of Sciences. 2017. *The Economic and Fiscal Consequences of Immigration*. Washington, DC: National Academies Press.

CHAPTER 2

What Were the Paradoxical Consequences of Militarizing the Border with Mexico?

DOUGLAS S. MASSEY

Watching a train wreck—that's what it has been like for me these past three decades, witnessing a disaster unfold in real time. I could see in my ongoing data collection and analysis that militarizing the border was not going to solve the problem of undocumented migration. In fact, it was going to make it worse, actually working to increase the size of the undocumented population rather than restraining it. At the same time, it would redistribute that larger population away from traditional destinations into the rest of the country, and in bringing a larger number of immigrants into wider contact with more Americans in states unused to foreigners a huge political conflict would ensue. I tried to warn people. I testified before Congress four times, trying to explain why militarizing the Mexico-US border was a bad idea and how it would backfire; but politicians in Washington live in a separate reality defined by alternative facts, and they paid little attention.

In the end, of course, the United States *did* militarize the border, quite drastically, and everything that I predicted came true. It pains me because it was so unnecessary. Once again, America shot itself in the foot and achieved a dysfunctional outcome that brought pain and hardship to millions of people. From 1988 to 2008, the number of Border Patrol officers increased by 471 percent and the Border Patrol's budget increased nearly fifteen times—yet the undocumented population grew from 2 million to 12 million. Obviously, something went wrong: all that money spent on border enforcement, only to have the undocumented population grow by a factor of six! My goal here is to explain how it all happened.

THE WATERSHED OF 1965

To understand how more border enforcement produced more **undocumented migrants,** we have to go back to 1965. At the stroke of midnight on January 1, 1965, Congress let the Bracero Agreement with Mexico expire. Over the previous twenty-two years, this binational treaty had offered temporary visas to many thousands of Mexicans for seasonal work in the United States, mostly in agriculture and food processing. Although begun in 1942 as a temporary wartime measure, the program grew after 1945 and eventually peaked at around 450,000 annual entries in the late 1950s. As the civil rights movement picked up momentum in the 1960s, however, the **Bracero Program** came to be seen as a discriminatory and exploitative labor system, on a par with black sharecropping in the Jim Crow South.

Having eliminated this source of injustice on January 1, Congress turned its attention to a reform of the Immigration and Nationality Act, which on racial grounds banned immigration from Asia, Africa, and the Middle East while favoring immigrants from northern and western Europe at the expense of those from southern and eastern Europe. In June 1965, Congress amended the act in the **Immigration and Naturalization Act of 1965** to create a new system that allocated residence visas uniformly on the basis of labor market needs and family reunification criteria. Annual worldwide immigration was capped at 290,000 visas, with 170,000 reserved for immigrants from the eastern hemisphere (Europe, Asian, Africa, and Oceania) and 120,000 set aside for those from the western hemisphere (the Americas). Beginning in 1968, immigration from nations in the eastern hemisphere was capped at 20,000 visas per year, and in 1976 this cap was applied to nations in the western hemisphere as well.

In the late 1950s, legal immigration from Mexico averaged around 50,000 per year, which when added to the 450,000 braceros produced an **annual inflow** of around half a million migrants. This was overwhelmingly a **circular migration.** Even migrants holding permanent resident visas often moved back and forth across the border rather than settling in the United States (Massey et al. 1987). Although the intent of Congress in 1965 was laudable—to eliminate racism and prejudice from the US immigration system—legislators gave little thought to what would happen to the annual circulation of half a million Mexican migrants

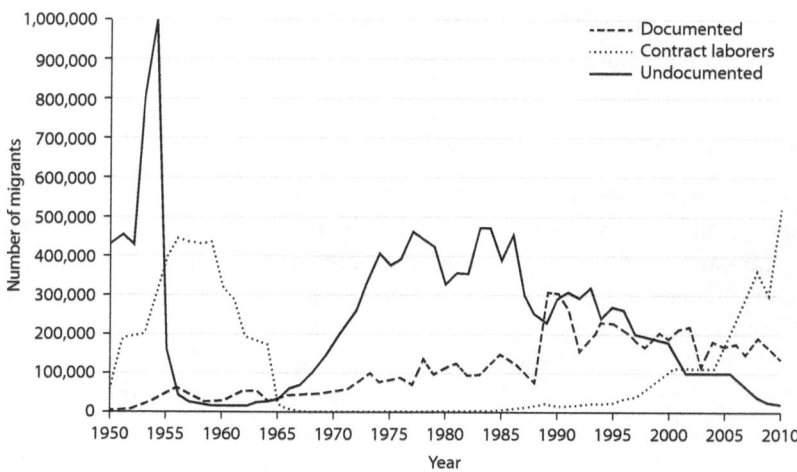

FIGURE 2.1. Mexican Migration to the United States in Three Legal Status Groups. Source: US Office of Immigration Statistics.

once opportunities for legal entry were curtailed by the cancelation of the Bracero Program and the imposition of country quotas.

The circumstances of labor supply and demand north and south of the border had not changed, of course, and by 1965 many millions of Mexican workers had established ties with US employers and were embedded in well-developed networks that connected them to jobs in the United States (Massey, Durand, and Malone 2002). As a result, when opportunities for legal entry suddenly evaporated, the flows quickly reestablished themselves under undocumented auspices. **Figure 2.1** illustrates this fact by showing trends in Mexico-US migration in three categories from 1950 to 2010. The dashed line shows entries by documented migrants holding permanent resident visas, the dotted line displays entries by migrants with temporary work visas, and the solid line shows the trend in undocumented entries, proxied by the number of border apprehensions per thousand Border Patrol agents. As can be seen, the years 1953–54 witnessed an intense but brief militarization of the border under the aegis of Operation Wetback, causing apprehensions per capita to surge to around one million and providing a highly visible display of the nation's resolve to control its borders. The operation drew in state and local law enforcement officials to assist in making arrests, which artificially inflated the apprehension count above what the Border Patrol could achieve on its own, so these years do not provide an accurate indication of the actual volume of migration.

Less visible was a massive expansion of the Bracero Program that coincided with the surge in apprehensions. From 200,000 temporary work visas in 1953, the program was expanded to some 450,000 visas in 1956. When combined with the 50,000 permanent resident visas annually going to Mexicans, the increase in bracero migrants was sufficient to accommodate labor demand north of the border and apprehensions fell to very low levels, causing **undocumented migration** to disappear as a political issue. The border remained quiescent until 1965, but after that date apprehensions per capita rose steadily to peak at 464,000 in the late 1970s, then leveled off and began to fluctuate cyclically through the mid-1980s. In essence, from 1965 to the late 1970s the bracero inflow of the late 1950s had been reestablished under undocumented auspices, with no sustained increase in **unauthorized migration** thereafter.

As before, Mexican migration during the undocumented era remained heavily circular, with the large majority of migrants moving back and forth across the border to undertake limited periods of labor abroad before returning to invest and spend their earnings at home. Most migrants repeated this back-and-forth process a few times over the course of their working lives and then retired to Mexico to enjoy the fruits of their labors. A small number developed a pattern of recurrent migration that involved regular annual trips back and forth across the border, but only a small share ended up settling permanently in the United States (Massey et al. 1987). From 1965 to 1985, 85 percent of undocumented entries were offset by departures, and the undocumented population grew very slowly (Massey and Singer 1995).

RISE OF THE LATINO THREAT NARRATIVE

The post-1965 migration system generally replicated the contours of the earlier bracero system, with migrants circulating back and forth to the same sorts of destinations to work for the same kinds of employers, only now they were doing so without authorization, leading to their framing in the media and public discourse as "illegal aliens." Although in practical terms, little had changed except the status of the migrants, in symbolic terms everything had changed, since the migrants were now "illegal" and thus easily portrayed in the media as "criminals" and "lawbreakers" and thus a clear menace to the nation, giving rise to what Chavez (2001, 2008) has called the *Latino threat narrative*.

This narrative drew on one of two metaphors to cast Mexican migrants in a threatening light. Initially marine metaphors portrayed undocumented migrants as a "rising tide" that would "flood the United States" to "drown" its society and "inundate" its culture. Over time, however, martial metaphors increasingly took hold in the media. In this narrative undocumented migrants became "alien invaders" who were "attacking" the United States, launching "banzai charges" against Border Patrol officers who desperately sought to "hold the line" to prevent the "conquest" of the United States and its "occupation" by "illegal hordes." Massey and Pren (2012a) traced the rise of these framings in the US media, using the Proquest Historical Newspaper Files to count instances in which the words *illegal, undocumented,* and *unauthorized* were paired with "Mexico" or "Mexican immigrants" and the words *crisis, flood,* and *invasion* in four leading newspapers: the *New York Times,* the *Washington Post,* the *Wall Street Journal,* and the *Los Angeles Times.*

Searching through these newspapers for the period from 1965 to 2010, they tabulated frequencies by year and took three-year moving averages to smooth the results. They found that these threat metaphors were hardly deployed at all in 1965. Thereafter, the frequency rose steadily, to peak around 1980, and then fluctuated thereafter with no consistent increase over time, much the same as we observed for apprehensions in figure 2.1. Indeed, the correlation over time between apprehensions and the frequency of threat metaphors is 0.96 (Massey and Pren 2012b). With each peak in the frequency threat metaphors, however, the United States implemented another piece of restrictive immigration legislation or border policy.

In a very real way, the rising number of apprehensions became the visible manifestation of the ongoing "invasion of illegal aliens," heralded by immigration officials, politicians, and pundits as evidence of the need for even more restrictive legislation and border enforcement, thereby creating a self-perpetuating cycle in which enforcement produced more apprehensions and more apprehensions justified more enforcement. **Figure 2.2** presents a path diagram developed by Massey and Pren (2012b) to summarize the resulting feedback loop. It uses data from the **Mexican Migration Project (MMP)** (which annually gathers detailed data on US migratory experiences), the US Department of Homeland Security, and the National Science Foundation's General Social Survey from 1965 to 1995 to estimate the strength of each causal pathway. At the far left of the figure we see that the number of illegal entries increased independently after 1965 owing to the curtailment of opportunities for legal entry. The rise in undocumented entries naturally produced more apprehensions, which were then used by politi-

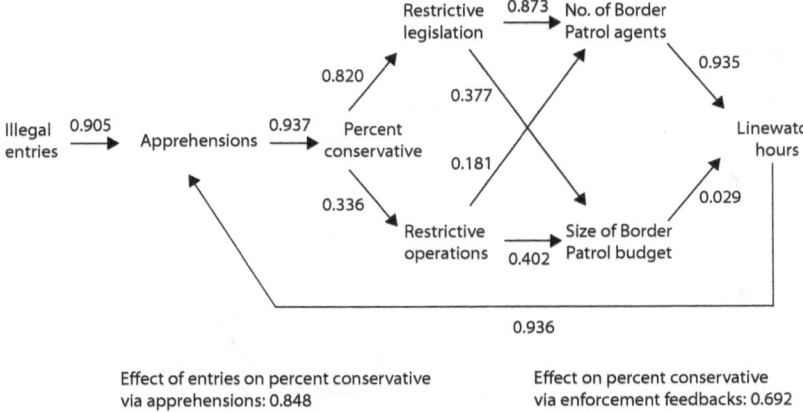

FIGURE 2.2. Feedback Loop between Apprehensions and Border Enforcement, 1965–1995. Source: Massey and Pren 2012.

cians and pundits to advance the Latino threat narrative, pushing public opinion in a more conservative direction to generate more restrictive legislation and more restrictive border operations, which in turn generated more Border Patrol agents and a larger Border Patrol budget.

More agents operating with a larger budget necessarily increased the number of linewatch hours (person-hours spent patrolling the border), which then fed back to drive up the number of apprehensions irrespective of the number of undocumented entries. After 1965 the number of apprehensions initially rose, owing to the growth in undocumented entries created by the elimination of the Bracero Program and the imposition of country quotas. Over time, however, the increase in apprehensions increasingly was generated by the feedback mechanism just described: more apprehensions pushed popular opinion in a more conservative direction, which increased public demands for restrictive legislation and stricter border operations, which generated more Border Patrol agents working with larger budgets, which yielded more hours spent looking for undocumented migrants, which ultimately produced more apprehensions, whereupon the cycle repeated itself.

The ultimate effect of the feedback loop is indicated in **figure 2.3**, which plots the Border Patrol budget from 1965 through 2010 in constant 2017 dollars. From 1965 through 1985 the budget was flat in real terms; then with the passage of the Immigration and Naturalization Act in 1965 it began to rise, accelerating with the launching of Operation Blockade in El Paso in 1993, the initiation of Operation Gatekeeper in San Diego in

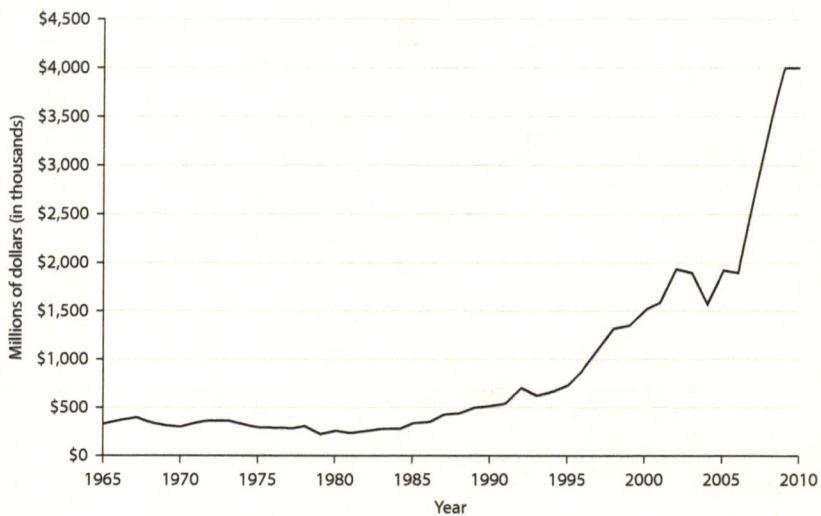

FIGURE 2.3. Border Patrol Budget in Constant 2017 US Dollars, 1965–2010. Source: US Department of Homeland Security.

1994, and the passage of the Illegal Immigration Reform and Immigrant Responsibility Act in 1996. The budget increase accelerated even further after the passage of the USA PATRIOT Act in 2001. Recall, however, that the exponential increase in the border enforcement budget after 1986 occurred despite the fact that the inflow of undocumented migrants had peaked in the late 1970s.

THE CONSEQUENCES OF MILITARIZATION

The militarization of the border was a massive policy intervention into what had been a stable migration system built up over four decades, and it was bound to have far-reaching consequences. The effects of the intervention have been well documented by Massey, Durand, and Pren (2016), who estimated a series of statistical models to assess how border enforcement affected patterns and processes of undocumented migration. Drawing on data from the MMP, they used retrospective life history data to follow household heads year by year from the point of entry into the labor force to the survey date. Using this event history, they estimated discrete time models to predict six migratory outcomes: the likelihood of crossing the border at a traditional location, the likelihood of crossing with a paid guide, the cost of the crossing guide, the likelihood of being apprehended while crossing, the likelihood of taking a first undocumented trip, and the likelihood of returning from a first trip within twelve months of entry.

The key predictor in their models was the size of the Border Patrol budget, which was measured in real terms and estimated as an instrumental variable using two-stage least squares to enable causal analysis. Their estimated models controlled for individual characteristics, household assets, community size, and region of origin, as well as national economic and demographic trends in Mexico and the United States. Predicted values for each outcome were generated by allowing the Border Patrol budget to follow its actual trend from 1970 to 2010 while holding all other variables constant at their mean values. The predicted values were then compared with observed values to assess the causal influence of border enforcement on each outcome.

The authors began by comparing the observed and predicted trends in likelihood of crossing at a traditional location (defined as Tijuana–San Diego or Juárez–El Paso). Looking first at the observed trend, they found that from 1970 through the late 1980s between 70 and 80 percent of all unauthorized border crossings occurred at traditional locations in the San Diego and El Paso sectors. Thereafter the share of traditional crossings fell sharply, from 77 percent in 1988 to around 30 percent in 2003. After a brief revival from 2005 to 2008, the decline resumed to reach an all-time low of 25 percent in 2010. Turning to the predicted trend, they found that it closely followed the observed decline, suggesting that the increase in border enforcement was the underlying cause of the shift away from traditional sites toward new locations elsewhere along the 2,000-mile border.

This outcome reflects the fact that enforcement efforts were initially targeted to the busiest border sectors, creating literal walls of enforcement resources that diverted migrants away from San Diego and El Paso into the Sonoran Desert and toward new crossing points along the border with Arizona. In doing so, the militarization of these two sectors pushed the **migration flows** away from relatively safe crossing locations in urbanized areas into much more dangerous desert terrain characterized by a scarcity of water, freezing temperatures at night, and excessive heat during the day. This geographic shift also left migrants many miles away from traditional destinations in California and Texas. In response to the more challenging circumstances of border crossing, migrants increasingly turned to paid guides known colloquially as coyotes to help them move across the border and onward to new job sites throughout the nation.

The use of coyotes has always been common, even before the border militarization. Even in 1970, when the vast majority of crossings were at traditional locations, around three quarters of all undocumented migrants were guided by a coyote. Over time, however, what was common became universal. The observed likelihood of crossing with a coyote rose from 0.75 to 1.0., a trend in the likelihood of crossing with a coyote that was entirely explained by the trend in likelihoods predicted by the rising enforcement effort. Moreover, as the difficulty of crossing rose, so did the cost of coyote services. From 1970 to around 1990 the observed cost of crossing with a coyote remained fairly flat at around $500 to $600 per trip in real terms. Thereafter it began rising rapidly, peaking at $2,700 in 2010—a trend that was again entirely predicted by the rising enforcement effort.

In addition to the rising cost of border crossing, the risks increased as the crossing routes shifted from urbanized areas into barren desert landscapes, dramatically increasing the odds of getting lost and dying from thirst, heat exhaustion, and hypothermia. Annual tallies of migrant deaths compiled from death certificates show the number of deaths actually declined from 1985 into the early 1990s, but after the 1993 launching of Operation Blockade in El Paso and the 1994 launching of Operation Gatekeeper in San Diego, the number of deaths climbed rapidly, from 72 in 1994 to 447 in 2012 (Massey, Durand, and Pren 2016), a trend that closely follows the trajectory predicted by the size of the Border Patrol budget.

The analysis of death rates makes clear that the militarization of the Mexico-US border had powerful effects on the locus, mode, cost, and risk of border crossing. Ironically, however, the border buildup had little effect on the likelihood of apprehension. The observed trend in the likelihood of being apprehended during an unauthorized crossing did *not* rise in a manner commensurate with the exponential increase in the enforcement effort. From values around 0.40 in the early 1970s the probability of apprehension fell to around 0.21 in 1990 before rising back to 0.40 in 2010. The predicted line, however, was relatively flat with values around 0.25 through the mid-1980s, slowly rising up to 0.43 in 2010.

Over the four decades from 1970 to 2010, the observed likelihood of apprehension averaged 0.33 while the predicted likelihood averaged 0.30; and no matter what the likelihood of apprehension was in any given year, the odds of ultimately gaining entry over a series of attempts were extremely high. Very few migrants turned back and went home after being caught on a first crossing attempt (Massey, Durand, and

Malone 2002). Calculations of the likelihood of ultimately gaining entry to the United States over a series of attempts averaged 0.97 over the four decades, and through 2008 the likelihood never fell below 0.95 (Massey, Durand, and Pren 2016). In short, the massive militarization of the border did very little to prevent aspiring undocumented migrants from achieving a successful border crossing.

THE NEW CONTEXT FOR MIGRANT DECISION MAKING

Despite its failure to increase the likelihood of apprehension or prevent unauthorized entry into the United States, the militarization of the border *did* have a profound effect on the context in which prospective migrants made their decisions about whether to depart and return. In 1970, Mexicans knew they could take an inexpensive bus to Tijuana or Juárez and easily connect with a coyote who would guide them across the border for around $500. Although surreptitious border crossing carried risks, migrants were moving from one urbanized area to another and thus did not face the prospect of death from dehydration, heat exhaustion, or hypothermia. Moreover, once across the border they could blend in with large Mexican-origin populations in San Diego and El Paso before moving on to labor markets located in nearby cities in California or Texas.

In 2010, however, migrants had to make their way to small, isolated staging areas in the Sonoran Desert that were not on major bus lines, and once there they would have to pay $2,500 or more to a coyote to guide them through open desert, with the possibility of losing one's way and dying of thirst, heat exposure, or hypothermia being very real. Moreover, once on the other side of the border there were no large population centers that the migrants could blend into before moving on to destinations in California and Texas, now hundreds of miles away. Despite these drawbacks, they nonetheless knew that the odds of apprehension remained low and that the odds of ultimately achieving a successful entry were very high. Moreover, although Los Angeles, Dallas, and Houston may have been far way, they also knew that other jobs were readily available at new destination areas throughout the nation, as unemployment rates fell to record low levels everywhere during the dot.com boom of the 1990s and the housing boom of the early 2000s.

In both 1970 and 2010, it therefore made economic sense to head to the United States in search of higher wages, but in the latter year it no longer made much sense to return after a period of work in the United States as part of a process of circular migration, for next year they would

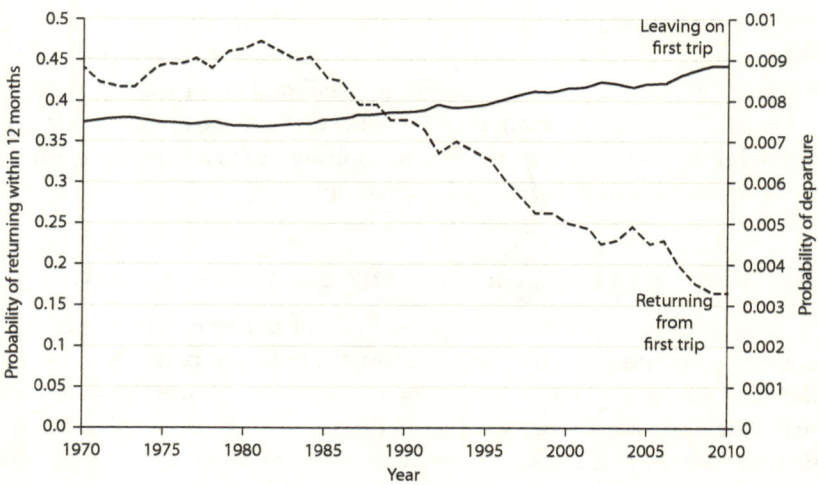

FIGURE 2.4. Causal Effect of Border Enforcement on the Likelihood of Departing on and Returning from a First Undocumented Trip.

have to face the high costs and risks of border crossing once again. The higher costs of border crossing also meant that migrants had to stay longer in the United States in order for a trip to become profitable. In 1970, if a migrant made $500 a month working in agriculture, for example, then after one month of labor the coyote fee would be paid off; but in 2010, with a fee of $2,500, it would take five months of labor for the trip to become profitable. Moreover, with fees steadily rising, the cost of crossing would probably be greater on the next trip. Thus it made sense to minimize border crossing, not by remaining in Mexico, but by staying longer in the United States to avoid facing the high costs and risks of unauthorized border crossing associated with circular migration.

Figure 2.4 draws on the estimates of Massey, Durand, and Pren (2016) to present the predicted causal effect of border enforcement (indexed by the size of the Border Patrol budget) on the likelihood of **in-migration** to the United States and **out-migration** back to Mexico (here assessed by the probability of leaving on and returning from a first undocumented trip to the United States). As shown by the solid line, the massive increase in border enforcement after 1986 had no significant effect in deterring Mexicans from initiating undocumented migration to the United States, with the rate of in-migration to the United States remaining fairly flat through the mid-1980s and then drifting up very slightly. In contrast, as indicated by the dashed line, it had a strong negative effect on the likelihood of

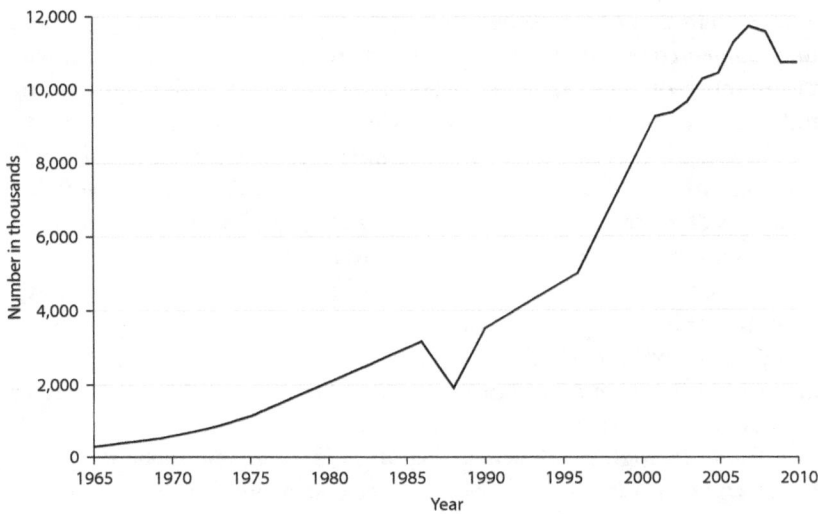

FIGURE 2.5. Estimated Size of the US Undocumented Population.

returning to Mexico beginning around 1985, suggesting a sustained drop in the rate of out-migration from the United States.

Since **net migration** equals in-migration minus out-migration, the end result of the border militarization paradoxically was to drive up the net volume of undocumented entries and thus sharply increase the rate of undocumented population growth. **Figure 2.5** confirms this fact by plotting annual estimates of the size of the undocumented population compiled by the immigration expert Ruth Ellen Wasem for the US Library of Congress's Congressional Research Service (2011). From 1965 to 1986, the undocumented population grew slowly, from 0.3 million to 3.2 million, before dropping back to 1.9 million in 1988 as a result of the legalization program authorized by the 1986 Immigration Reform and Control Act. After recovering to 3.5 million in 1990, slow growth resumed as the undocumented population increased to 5 million in 1996. Thereafter the curve turns sharply upward, reaching 9.3 million in 2001 before slowing down and ultimately achieving a maximum value of 11.8 million in 2007.

Whereas the undocumented population grew at a rate of 250,000 per year from 1990 to 1996, over the next five years it grew at a rate of 860,000 per year—not because more Mexican migrants were coming, but because fewer were going home. Although the growth rate slowed to 367,000 per year from 2001 to 2007, it never returned to the status quo ante, and, overall, the 1996–2007 growth rate was 65 percent greater than that observed between 1990 and 1996. Since 2007 the total undocumented population has fluctuated around 11 million persons, with the number of undocumented Mexicans actually trending downward, indicating net out-migration back to Mexico (Passel and Cohn 2016).

The reason for the decline and termination of undocumented Mexican migration was not the intensification of border enforcement but Mexico's demographic transition. In 1970 the total fertility rate in Mexico was 6.8 births per woman, whereas today it is 2.2 births per woman replacement level. As a result, Mexico has become an aging society, with the median age rising from around 17 in 1970 to 29 today. According to data from the MMP, the average age of household heads who are in the labor force but had not yet migrated to the United States was 22 in 1970 and had reached 46 by 2010 (Massey, Durand, and Pren 2016). Like most demographic events, migration is highly age dependent, rising sharply during the late teens to peak at around age 22 and then declining rapidly to low levels beyond age 30. If people do not begin migrating between the ages of 18 and 30 they are very unlikely ever to migrate at all; and as the average age has risen, the share of Mexicans in this age range has steadily dwindled, bringing the era of mass undocumented migration to a close.

ANATOMY OF A TRAIN WRECK

According to the *Urban Dictionary* (2018), the definition of a train wreck is a "total f***ing disaster[,] . . . the kind that makes you want to shake your head," and I think that US immigration and border policies implemented over the past several decades qualify under this definition. From 1986 to 2010 the United States spent $34.6 billion in border enforcement and in doing so transformed what had been a circular flow of mostly male workers going to three states into a settled population of families living in fifty states, thereby driving up the costs of immigration while creating long-term social, economic, and political difficulties for the nation. Massey, Durand, and Pren (2016) estimate that absent the border militarization, the undocumented population would have ended up being around a third lower than its eventual peak of around 12 million persons.

As we have seen, militarizing the border after 1986 reduced out-migration while leaving in-migration unchanged and thus *increased* rather than decreased net undocumented migration, thereby tripling the rate of undocumented population growth from 1996 to 2001 and raising it by 65 percent over the entire period from 1996 to 2008. At the same time, the selective hardening of the border in San Diego and El Paso transformed the geography of border crossing, pushing migratory flows away from these metropolitan areas into the Sonoran Desert and toward new crossing points in Arizona. The intense militarization of the San Diego sector, in particular, permanently redirected undocumented migrants away from California. Whereas 63 percent of all Mexican immigrants who entered the United States from 1985 to 1990 went to California, during the period 1995–2000 this share fell to 28 percent and from 2005 to 2010 it was only 33 percent (Massey and Capoferro 2008).

As male migrants spent longer durations north of the border, processes of family reunification took hold as married men were joined by their spouses and children and processes of family formation took hold among unmarried migrants as a result of union formation and childbearing. According to estimates prepared by the Migration Policy Institute (2018), today's undocumented population is 46 percent female, 60 percent have been in the United States for ten years or longer, 39 percent reside with a minor child, and of the latter 85 percent are parents of at least one US-born citizen child. Some 5.1 million children now reside with an undocumented parent, and nearly 80 percent are US citizens. Citizen children with an undocumented parent are more likely than other children of immigrants to live in poverty and are less likely to experience socioeconomic advancement over time (Capps, Fix, and Zong 2016). They also have less access to health care (Gelatt 2016) and poorer health both physically (Vargas and Ybarra 2017) and mentally (Delva et al. 2013).

Although the undocumented population stopped growing in 2008, it nonetheless stands at around 11 million persons and constitutes around a quarter of all immigrants and more than 60 percent of those from Latin America (Passel and Cohn 2016), making mass illegality a structural feature of today's Latino population, with around 17 percent being out of status. This is the largest number of US residents who lack many basic social, economic, or civil rights in the United States since the days of slavery, when slaves numbered just under 4 million. With 3.45 million deportations between 2008 and 2016, the undocumented population is under pressure as never before, inflicting great collateral damage on the families and communities from which they were taken, most notably their 4.1 million US citizen children.

Deportation brings about an agonizing choice for parents of US citizen children: either parents leave their children with friends or relatives to grow up in the United States without them or they bring their children home with them to grow up in a country they do not know and whose language most do not speak very fluently. In addition, they are forced into a school system vastly different from the one they knew in the United States and compelled somehow to integrate into an alien student population in which they are marked as outsiders. According to US Embassy and Consulates in Mexico (2018), around 600,000 US citizen children currently reside in Mexico with their deported parents, and an unknown number remain orphaned in the United States in the wake of their parents' removal, yielding a growing population of traumatized American citizens—future US workers whose well-being and productivity is therefore compromised.

The great irony is not simply that the United States spent $35 billion on border enforcement only to expand the size of the undocumented population and spread it more widely throughout the country, or that these counterproductive expenditures were made in a vain attempt to stop a migratory inflow that eventually would have stopped of its own accord as a result of Mexico's demographic transition. No, the greatest irony is that the current administration seeks to spend $25 billion on a border wall to stop a migratory inflow that ended ten years ago and has been zero or negative ever since. Since a border wall cannot have much of an effect on a net population movement that is already negative, its real purpose is symbolic: to signal to white nationalists that Donald Trump shares their rejection of persons originating to the south of the wall as potential Americans and underscoring his resolve to block any increase in the number of such persons moving forward. Of course, $25 billion is a lot to spend for a symbol, especially one that expresses racism and hatred toward our closest neighbors.

Suggested Reading

Chavez, L. R. 2008. *The Latino Threat: Constructing Immigrants, Citizens, and the Nation*. Stanford, CA: Stanford University Press.

Golash-Boza, T. 2015. *Deported: Immigrant Policing, Disposable Labor, and Global Capitalism*. New York: New York University Press.

Massey, D. S., J. Durand, and N. Malone. 2002. *Beyond Smoke and Mirrors: Mexican Immigration in an Age of Economic Integration*. New York: Russell Sage Foundation.

Massey, D. S., J. Durand, and K. Pren. 2014. Explaining undocumented migration to the U.S. *International Migration Review* 48(4): 1028–61.

———. 2016. Why border enforcement backfired. *American Journal of Sociology* 121(5): 1557–1600.

Nevins, J. 2010. *Operation Gatekeeper and Beyond: The War on "Illegals" and the Remaking of the U.S.-Mexico Boundary*. 2nd ed. New York: Routledge.

PART TWO

Mexico-US Migration

CHAPTER 3

How Did We Get to the Current Mexico-US Migration System, and How Might It Look in the Near Future?

SILVIA E. GIORGULI, CLAUDIA MASFERRER, AND
VICTOR M. GARCÍA-GUERRERO

Perceptions of international migration are based on the specific political and economic context at both the sending and receiving communities. Therefore, it often occurs that the images we see in the media as well as the particular information we receive regarding trends or recent events tip the balance toward a more positive or negative perception of migration. It is also true that migration is often used in political discourse, mainly in receiving countries, as a scapegoat to enhance anti-immigrant sentiments that most of the time do not correspond to empirical facts. This has been the case in the United States, where an increase in anti-immigrant political discourse has motivated anti-Mexican sentiments.

This chapter has two goals. First, we provide a long-term reading of the international mobility between Mexico and the United States. The long-standing interaction between the countries dates back more than a hundred years, changing in its nature and profile but building a strong connection at the community and national levels (Selee 2018). Second, the nature of migration flows between Mexico and the United States has changed gradually over the past decade, since the years of the **Great Recession**. The current trends and the clear involvement of new actors in the shared flows, mainly from Central America, have built a new narrative incorporating the changes in the persistent flow of Mexicans toward the "North," the increasing arrival of a US-born population in Mexico, and the visible flow of Central Americans across both countries. These connections are not limited to Mexico and the United States.

Demographic projections and relations with their neighbors—Canada, Guatemala, Honduras, and El Salvador—can anticipate to a certain extent the future profile of the migration flows in what can be read as a migration system in the making (Giorguli, García-Guerrero, and Masferrer 2016). In our view, a long-term perspective on migration flows within North America and Central America and the broad analysis of the current trends are crucial to building a fact-based, efficient, human rights–centered approach to the governance of migration.

MORE THAN A HUNDRED YEARS OF HUMAN MOBILITY BETWEEN MEXICO AND THE UNITED STATES: THE CONSTRUCTION OF STRONG LINKAGES

After more than 130 years of migration between Mexico and the United States, in both directions, the construction of strong linkages between both countries is not a surprise. The continuous back-and-forth movements of a large population, the growing number of **dual citizens** (a population we share), and the strong connections that technology and communications facilitate contribute to maintaining these bonds. For the first eight decades of the past century, the demand of the US labor market was the main driver of migration flows (the number of people entering or leaving the United States with or without legal authorization) from Mexico, and the nature of migration policies in the United States resulted in a large unauthorized population. Even if labor is still a strong factor, the flow today is more heterogeneous. Family reunification is also very important, but increasingly other social and political factors like violence and insecurity have motivated emigration from Mexico (Chort and de la Rupelle 2016). Changes in the demand for labor and the impact of migration policies on the characteristics of the flow have defined six stages in the history of Mexico-US migration, as suggested by Jorge Durand (2016) (**figure 3.1**).

Although migration started as a circular pattern made up primarily of males in the regular flows, it eventually led to the incorporation of other family members, including children, into the flows. Not only the sex composition of the flows have changed, but the origin and profile of the flows have changed as well (Garip 2016). Over time, Mexico became more urban and more educated, and flows originated not only from rural areas but also from all cities and metropolitan areas (Riosmena and Massey 2012). Family migration and the loss of circularity have been one response to the more restrictive migration policies enacted

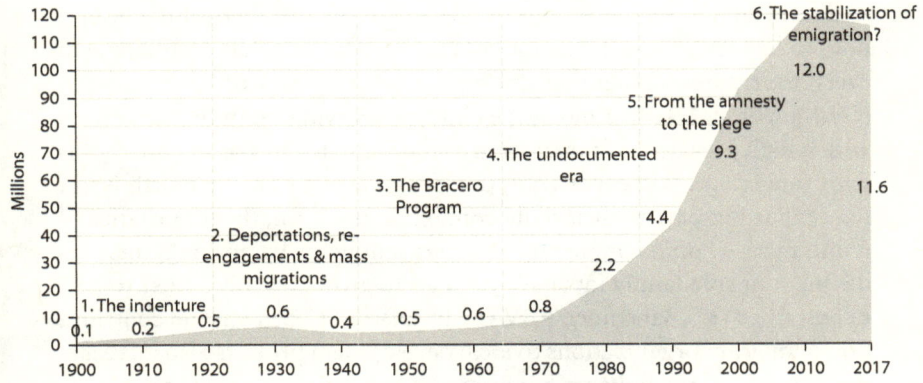

FIGURE 3.1. Mexican-Born Population Living in the United States, 1900–2017. Source: Authors' estimates based on information from the US Census Bureau: 5% Census samples from 1900, 1% Census Samples from 1910 to 1970, 5% Census Samples from 1980 to 2000, American Community Survey, 2010 and 2017. This is an updated version of a similar figure in Giorguli and Angoa 2019.

since the **Immigration Reform and Control Act (IRCA)** was implemented in 1986. While IRCA legalized the status of unauthorized immigrants who had come to the United States prior to 1986, it also made it illegal to hire unauthorized immigrants (i.e., those who arrived after 1986). Other changes in migration included year-round work and settlement in urban areas. Such changes help explain to a large extent the rapid growth of the Mexican-born population living in the United States since the mid-1980s (Riosmena 2004). However, emigration from Mexico to the United States declined dramatically after 2008 (Villarreal 2014), and policies have had a strong effect on increasing **return migration**—those leaving the United States to return to Mexico—in recent years (Massey, Durand, and Pren 2015).

From the Mexican perspective, the number of Mexicans living in the United States, almost 12 million, represents close to 10 percent of the total population living in Mexico and 17 percent of the working-age population. International migration has spread all over the country, and it is not limited to the traditional or historical sending communities located in western Mexico, just as returnees arrive increasingly in non-traditional sites of out-migration (Masferrer and Roberts 2012). According to the more recent estimates available, almost all the municipalities (2,446 of 2,457) report households receiving remittances, return migrants, or some out-migration (CONAPO 2010).

At the family level, it is not rare for one of the members of the household to have migrated. Different data sources suggest that around one in every four parents migrated during the school years of their children (Giorguli et al. 2018). Among the children growing up in municipalities with a high prevalence of migration to the United States or in households with some migration experience, the idea of leaving for the North is not unfamiliar but part of their daily context. In addition, the importance of **remittances**—familial monetary transfers sent home by out-migrants—as the main or sole family income continues to grow (reaching close to $28 billion in 2016) (Bancomer, BBVA, and CONAPO 2018). The contribution of migrant organizations to local development projects also increases the visibility of the linkages between Mexico and the United States.

Mexico-US migration has changed in recent years. The current situation regarding mobility across the border in both directions reflects prior contradictions and unresolved issues regarding the management of the flows but includes new elements that will define the nature of the population exchanges between the two countries in the future. Five features describe this new stage in the history of Mexico-US migration, as follows:[1]

1. A decline in emigration since 2008, the stabilization of annual arrivals from Mexico to the United States (less than 160,000 a year), and the persistence of a strong predominance of the United States as the preferred country of destination (Pew Research Center 2018; Giorguli and Angoa 2019).
2. The steady increase in involuntary return migration after 2008, motivated by economic hardship due to the Great Recession, which lasted from 2007 through 2010 and included severe increases in poverty and unemployment. In addition, there was an increase in criminalization, deportations, and other forms of immigration enforcement (Masferrer and Roberts 2012).
3. The continuous flow of a US-born population to Mexico, most of them minors under the age of eighteen. These children of Mexican parents are potentially dual citizens; however, they face challenges in integrating into the educational system and Mexican society in general (Medina and Menjívar 2015; Zúñiga and Hamann 2015; Zúñiga and Giorguli 2019).
4. The diversification of the profile of Mexicans in the United States, which includes an even proportion of documented and undocumented migrants, along with a steady increase in the number of **temporary work visas** issued since 2008 (Giorguli, García-

Guerrero, and Masferrer 2016); such visas for noncitizen workers include those with highly specialized expertise (**H1B visas**), seasonal agricultural workers (**H2A visas**), and nonagricultural domestic workers (**H2B visas**), among others.

5. The consolidation of a large community of Mexicans living in the United States who have spent long periods in the country, with and without authorized status. Among the Mexican unauthorized population, four of every five arrived to the United States more than ten years ago, and half have lived in the United States for fifteen years (Pew Research Center 2018).

Finally, two additional aspects characterize the current context. The first has to do with the importance of migration in the bilateral relationship between Mexico and the United States. Although it has changed over time, international migration has gained relevance in the discussion of broader bilateral issues and in the negotiations over a renewed trade agreement migration was used as an exchange card. Second, our understanding of the migration flows between both countries and the options to manage them have been traditionally seen only in relation to Mexico-US flows. The increase in **in-transit flows** through Mexico and their visibility (in **migrant caravans**), the current crises in the asylum-seeking system in the United States, and the challenges for the Mexican government of managing the flows suggest that when talking about a shared responsibility in the governance of migration we need to add **Central American flows** to the discussion.

Is There a Migration System Comprising North America and Central America?

Geographic proximity, historical linkages, sustained social ties, and the building of large foreign-born communities at the main destination countries—United States and Canada—support the idea of an emerging **migration system** that includes the six countries of North and Central America. Within this system, Honduras, El Salvador, and Guatemala are mainly places of origin, whereas Mexico is a country of origin, transit, return, and, increasingly, destination. The migration flows among the six countries constitute one of the most dynamic systems in the world. Although stable in its persistence, it responds to the socioeconomic changes, political events, and demographic dynamics in each of the countries and to the migration policies at the three main destinations.

TABLE 3.1 TOTAL AND FOREIGN-BORN POPULATION IN NORTH AMERICA AND SELECTED CENTRAL AMERICAN COUNTRIES, 2017

Country	Total Population (thousands)	Total Foreign-Born Population (thousands)	Percentage of Total Population
Canada	36,624	7,861	21.5
United States	324,459	49,777	15.3
Mexico	129,163	1,224	0.9
Gautemala	16,914	82	0.5
El Salvador	6,378	42	0.7
Honduras	9,265	39	0.4

SOURCES: United Nations, Department of Economic and Social Affairs, Population Division (2017); World Population Prospects: 2017 Revision.

One of the characteristics of the migration system is the differential in the size of their populations and the volume of the stocks of the foreign born (**table 3.1**). The United States dominates in terms of size (324 million inhabitants), but Canada has a larger proportion of population born outside of the country (one in five). Mexico, although increasingly a destination, still shows a very low proportion of immigrants (less than 1 percent). There is one additional aspect to highlight regarding the size of each of the countries. The population of Honduras, El Salvador, and Guatemala amounts to almost 33 million, which represents less than the total population of Canada (36.6 million). Even in the case of a larger exodus from any of the three Central American countries, the number of potential migrants will be small compared to the total amount of immigrants already living in the United States (50 million).

In terms of the size of the stocks from each of the countries of this migration system (**table 3.2**), one in three immigrants living in the United States was born in Canada, Mexico, or the three Central American countries. Mexico remains the major point of origin: nearly one in four immigrants in the United States were born in Mexico. This is different in Canada, since other origin countries, like the United Kingdom, China, India, and the Philippines, have larger stocks living there. Of the total 7.8 million immigrants, those from the other five countries in the system represent less than 8 percent (see table 3.2). The largest stock from these countries was born in the United States (close to 350,000), followed by Mexico (more than 95,000) and El Salvador (close to 50,000).

TABLE 3.2 MIGRATION STOCKS IN NORTH AMERICA BY SELECTED COUNTRIES OF ORIGIN, CIRCA 2016

	Canada	US	Mexico	Guatemala	El Salvador	Honduras
Canada (2106)		338,630	95,410	18,725	49,260	8,570
United States (2017)	957,203		11,597,633	979,851	1,414,285	660,101
Mexico (2015)	9,816	739,168		42,874	10,594	14,544

SOURCES: For Canada, Statistics Canada, 2016 Census of Population, Statistics Canada Catalogue no. 98–400-X2016184; for United States, American Community Survey, 2017; for Mexico, National Intercensal Survey, 2015.

Finally, in Mexico more than 75 percent of the foreign born come from the United States. In 2015, more than half a million US-born minors lived in Mexico, most of them with at least one Mexican parent, because these movements are closely related to the return of their parents (Masferrer, Hamilton, and Denier 2019). Note also in table 3.2 the small number of immigrants from Guatemala, El Salvador, and Honduras compared to the size of the stock from the United States. Nonetheless, the recent increase in the number of immigrants from Central America in Mexico has raised concerns about the size of the flows and its manageability. Although there is no clear answer to those concerns, Mexican history shows prior experience of successful reception of **political migrants**. In the early 1940s Mexico received in a short period close to 20,000 exiles from the Civil War in Spain (Lida 2006), at a time when the country had 19.7 million inhabitants (INEGI 2014).

Immigration policies are key to defining migration trends and patterns and how the foreign-born population is integrated into the receiving communities. The proportion of undocumented migrants in the main countries of destination captures well how migration policies lead to different results. While in the United States undocumented migrants represent 22 percent of the total immigrant population (i.e., 11.3 million; Gelatt and Zong 2018), in Canada they are practically nonexistent. Canada receives immigrants that arrive as permanent residents based on economic considerations linked to the labor market and regional needs, as well as family reunification or humanitarian concerns, while also receiving temporary migrants under work or study permits or applying for asylum. In addition, the country has implemented an integration policy that includes a specific budget for actions such as language acquisition, coupled with a multicultural approach to diversity.

Another characteristic of mobility within the system is the diversification of the drivers of migration and the legal options to migrate. Along with **labor-driven migrants,** we can trace migration linked to political turmoil—mainly in Guatemala and El Salvador—and to natural disasters, such as Hurricane Mitch in 1998 and Hurricane Stan in 2005. As a result, the documented stock includes migrants who have naturalized as Canadian or US citizens, dual citizens, **legal permanent residents** (**LPRs**; noncitizens who are lawfully authorized to live permanently in the United States), those with temporary work visas, refugees, and those granted **temporary visas,** distinct from temporary work visas. Temporary visas are granted to noncitizens who will not work while in the United States, such as students, tourists, and those recovering from the occurrence of catastrophic natural events.

Mexico is a receiving country, both of Mexican returnees and of US-born immigrants, as well as Central Americans. Although Mexico installed refugee camps in the early 1980s to receive Guatemalans and Salvadorans, these were concentrated close to the southern border and only a limited number of applications for refugee status were approved. Two-thirds of Guatemalan migrants returned to their country fifteen years later, once they considered the situation in their communities of origin improved (Castillo and Rojas 2019). Is Mexico increasingly becoming a receiving destination, in need of a clear integration policy? The close to 1.5 million returned migrants within the last ten years, the almost 750,000 US born living in Mexico, and the 60,000 coming from the three Central American countries suggest that there is a need to think about how to integrate them into Mexican society.

In summary, the migration system comprising North America and El Salvador, Guatemala, and Honduras is dynamic, persistent in time, and complex given the diverse nature of the flows and the diverse situation of migrants upon arrival. Since 2016, more Central Americans have been apprehended at the Mexico-US border than Mexicans. The context of social violence in the three Central American countries and in Mexico poses an additional challenge as it is increasingly a reason for migrating. The current anti-immigrant sentiment and sociopolitical context have added risks to the journey from the countries of origin through Mexico and all the way to the US border. Along with direct threats, economic reasons motivate people to migrate from violent communities. This challenges the traditional concepts of refugees and asylum seeking, but **refugee systems** often respond to other political needs. For example, even if Canada has had an open and assertive approach to the provision of protection to refugees from all over the world and received thirty thousand Syrian refugees in 2015, there has been no response to those from Mexico and Central America who are in need of protection.

The context in the United States is less favorable. The **asylum crisis** along with the restrictive measures inhibiting humanitarian protection in the United States that were implemented by the Trump administration have created an adverse scenario in regional migration management (Meissner et al. 2018). The major backlog of cases (close to 320,000 direct claims and 750,000 claims through immigration courts in 2018) and the waiting periods of years leave asylum seekers and other claimants in an uncertain situation (Meissner, Hipsman, and Aleiikoff 2018). Moreover, recent changes such as eliminating gang and domestic violence as valid reasons for requesting asylum have narrowed access to this path for many Central American migrants (Meissner, Hipsman, and Aleiikoff 2018).

Mexico is also facing diverse challenges that make it difficult to build a coherent, effective, and human rights–centered approach in its asylum system. It faces the bureaucratic inertia of the past, the lack of human and financial resources for timely response to claims, US pressure to stop the flows, and an unsolved scenario of internal violence that overlaps with migration routes. While the management of the violence-related flows, mainly from Central America but also from Mexico, requires a coordinated approach with a shared responsibility perspective that integrates the six countries into the system, the political conditions for such an approach are not present today.

PLAYING GUESS: PROBABLE FUTURE SCENARIOS IN THE NORTH AMERICA–CENTRAL AMERICA MIGRATION SYSTEM

Of the three main demographic variables, fertility, mortality, and migration, the latter is the most uncertain and the most difficult to predict even in contexts of low and controlled migration. The other two have been highly unpredictable in different temporal and geographic contexts; fertility was highly uncertain during the first stages of **fertility transition** in Mexico, and mortality at present is highly unpredictable due to the high rates of homicides caused by the thirteen years of war in Mexico and Central America. Regarding migration flows specifically, after reaching a peak of almost 700,000 Mexicans arriving in the United States in 2005, there was an unanticipated large drop during the years of the Great Recession and stable low numbers (below 160,000 persons) thereafter. It was not until specialists obtained information from the 2010 Mexican and US Censuses that new estimates pointed out the dramatic change in the flows. In spite of the potential volatility in migration estimates, when analyzed in the longer term there are some hints that can anticipate the scenarios within the North America–Central America migration system. Overall, projections suggest that migration from Mexico and Central America to the North will decline in the future, whereas emigration from other areas, like Asia and Africa, will increase (Hanson and McIntosh 2016).

Demographic dynamics are an important determinant of migration flows, especially when they are labor driven. High fertility and population rates exert additional pressure on labor markets, favor the scarcity of jobs, and become an incentive to move to another region or country. Changes in fertility, in the population growth rates, and, especially, in the working-age population growth rates will have an impact on the size of migration flows. In addition, an aging society may require migrant work as **dependency ratios** increase and therefore the need for jobs in the service sector rises, in particular, for care work. A stable or declining native working-age population may not suffice to cover the requirements of an increasing elderly population.

In the case of the migration system suggested in this chapter, there are clearly differences in the size of the six countries, as shown in table 3.1. Interestingly but not unexpectedly, there is a clear converging trend in the main demographic indicators (Giorguli, García-Guerrero, and Masferrer 2016; García-Guerrero, Masferrer, and Giorguli 2019). In fact, except for Guatemala, today all the countries show a total fertility rate (TFR) close to or below replacement (i.e., below 2.2). According to **figure 3.2A**, all six countries, including Guatemala, will have converged in terms of fertility levels by 2050.

The reduction in fertility anticipates also a continuous **fertility decline** in the total population and working-age population growth rates in the six countries (**figures 3.2B, 3.2C**) but at different paces. Today El Salvador has the lowest total population growth rate, even lower than that of Canada and the United States. Even by 2050, the last observation in figures 3.2A–C, El Salvador will remain the country with the lowest growth rates. According to UN projections, Mexico will be converging with Canada and the United States around 2040. Guatemala will remain the fastest growing, although the rate of change will decrease rapidly.

There is a lagged effect of reduction in fertility and population growth on the size and rhythm of change in the working-age groups. Guatemala, Honduras, Mexico, and El Salvador show, in all cases, a declining trend that will continue beyond 2050 (see figure 3.2C). By that year, UN projections estimate even lower rates for El Salvador and Mexico than for Canada and the United States. Especially significant to illustrate the potential scenarios is the most rapid decline in the rates for the population ages 15 to 64 in Honduras and Guatemala.

With regard to demographic pressure on the labor market, in Guatemala, Honduras, El Salvador, and Mexico, the future scenario suggests less pressure and thus fewer incentives to migrate. In terms of the size of the population, Honduras, Mexico, and El Salvador have reached their largest cohort of young population (15 and younger), and before 2050 they will have passed the most numerous cohort of young working adults ages 15–30 (Giorguli, García-Guerrero, and Masferrer 2016). For these four countries, first-time migrants tend to concentrate in this age group. A decrease in the size of the cohort of young adults may result in lower migration flows.

Parallel to the fall in fertility and the slow pace of growth, all the countries in the system are experiencing rapid growth of the population 65 and older. It is the fastest-growing group, and it will remain at this pace of change beyond 2050. We have paradoxical scenarios. On the one hand, as the number of young people entering the labor market dwindles, the incentive to migrate will also decrease in the main four countries of origin. On the other hand, there will be a rising demand for labor because of the aging process. Canada and the United States will have the fastest change in the dependency ratios and may consequently increase the demand for migrant work. However, the other four countries in the system will also be experiencing a rapid aging process that will create an internal need for care work. In demographic terms, in the future it is hard to imagine that migration from Central America and Mexico will reach the historical peaks of the past (for Mexico) and today (for Honduras, El Salvador, and Guatemala). To a certain extent, this trend builds a more positive scenario for the discussion on the regional management of migration.

CONCLUDING REMARKS: TOWARD THE MANAGEMENT OF INCREASINGLY HETEROGENEOUS FLOWS WITHIN A HIGHLY MOBILE REGION

The extended migratory system that comprises Canada, the United States, Mexico, Guatemala, Honduras, and El Salvador has proved to be one of the largest in the world. It can be characterized by the heterogeneity of the flows, which include diverse documented statuses and, at least

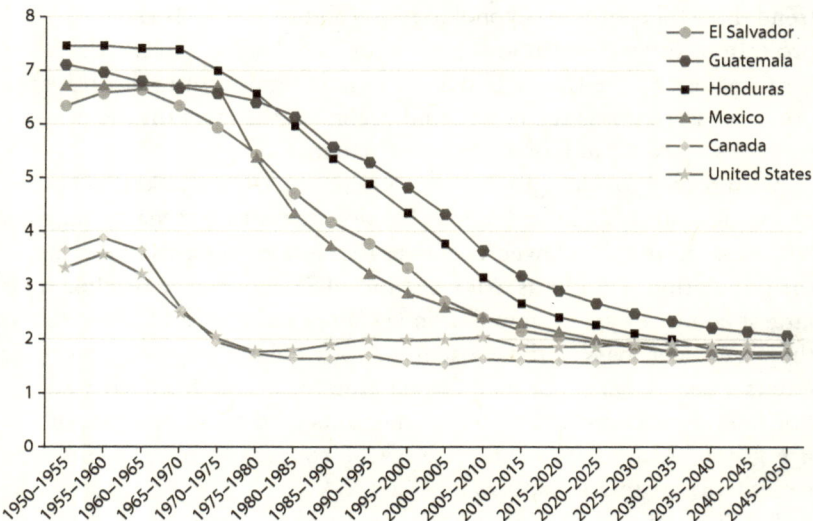

FIGURE 3.2 (A). Total Fertility Rates. Sources: United Nations, Department of Economic and Social Affairs, Population Division (2018); World Population Prospects: The 2017 Revision.

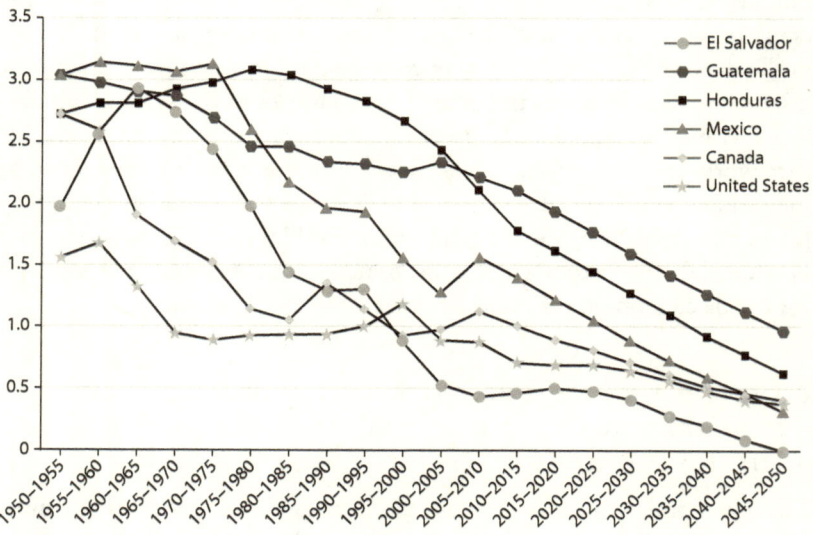

FIGURE 3.2 (B). Total Population Annual Growth Rates. Source: United Nations, Department of Economic and Social Affairs.

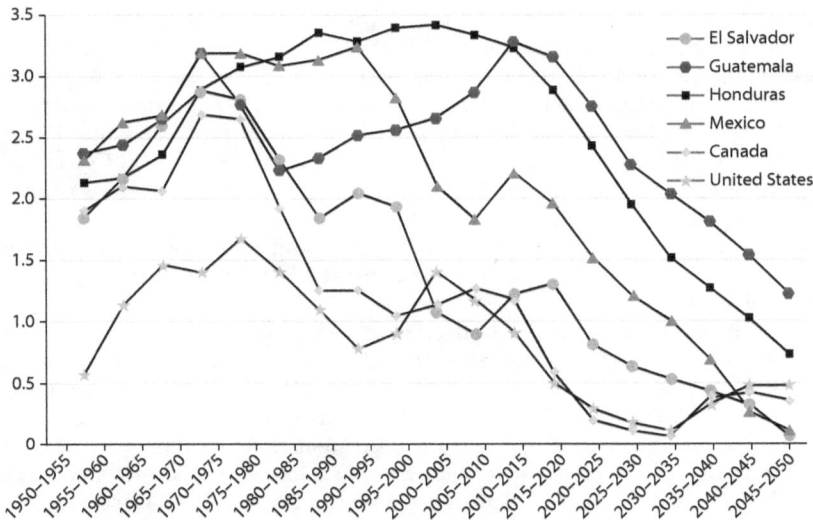

FIGURE 3.2 (C). Annual Growth Rates of the Working Age (15–64) Population in North America and Selected Central American Countries. Sources: United Nations, Department of Economic and Social Affairs, Population Division (2018); World Population Prospects: The 2017 Revision.

for the United States as a receiving country, a large undocumented migrant population. The social and economic ties built through the international moves among countries allow us to anticipate that migration will continue for the next decades, under a different path and with the potential presence of flows from the North to the South. A large population of dual citizens and the concentration in young age groups also support the possibility of persistent large linkages through migration.

Demographic dynamics in the six countries anticipate that the size of the flows may stabilize and may even decline as fertility rates tend to converge. In addition, the profile of potential migrants will change as education expands in the main countries of destination. Nonetheless, there is an increasing mismatch between the demographic dynamics and the migration policies, especially in the United States. When analyzed in the medium or long term, the population change in the migration system offers a unique opportunity to define a strategy to manage migration efficiently.

Suggested Reading

Durand, J. 2016. *Historia mínima de la migración México–Estados Unidos* [Brief History of Mexico-US Migration]. Mexico City: El Colegio de México.

Garip, F. 2016. *On the Move: Changing Mechanisms of Mexico-U.S. Migration*. Princeton, NJ: Princeton University Press.

Giorguli, S.E., V.M. García-Guerrero, and C. Masferrer. 2016. A migration system in the making: Demographic dynamics and migration policies in North America and the Northern Triangle of Central America. Policy Paper. Center for Demographic, Urban, and Environmental Studies, El Colegio de México. Available at http://cedua.colmex.mx/images/_micrositios/amsitm/Giorguli_Garcia_Masferrer_2016.pdf.

Massey, D.S., J. Durand, and K.A. Pren. 2015. Border enforcement and return migration by documented and undocumented Mexicans. *Journal of Ethnic and Migration Studies* 41(7): 1015–40.

Pederzini, C., F. Riosmena, C. Masferrer, and N. Molina. 2015. Three decades of migration from the Northern Triangle of Central America: A historical and demographic outlook. CIESAS, CANAMID Policy Brief Series. Guadalajara, Mexico. Available at www.canamid.org/en/publication.

Pew Research Center. 2018. U.S. unauthorized immigrant total dips to lowest level in a decade. Report, November 27. Available at www.pewresearch.org/hispanic/wp-content/uploads/sites/5/2019/03/Pew-Research-Center_2018-11-27_U-S-Unauthorized-Immigrants-Total-Dips_Updated-2019-06-25.pdf.

Zúñiga, V., and S. Giorguli. 2019. *Niñas y niños migrantes internacionales en México: La generación 0.5* [What children know about international migration: The 0.5 generation]. Mexico City: El Colegio de México.

CHAPTER 4

Recession versus Removals: Which Finished Mexican Unauthorized Migration?

René Zenteno and Roberto Suro

From 1965 to 2015, more than 16 million persons left Mexico for the United States.[1] By its size, concentration, and duration, this stands as a singular event in the annals of contemporary migrations worldwide and unprecedented both in Mexico's experience as a sending country and the long history of immigration to the United States. Scholars have identified numerous drivers that explain the origins and vitality of this migration. The available evidence offered nary a hint that this big, robust migration phenomenon could end suddenly. The circumstances of that finale are as important as its much-studied beginnings. Simple lines of causality are difficult to draw. Nonetheless, valuable scholarship is already under way to explain how and why the era of large-scale, Mexico-US migration came to a halt in the 2000s and what replaced it in the 2010s.[2] Advancing that work will require an ever more detailed understanding of the time line that marks the evolution of these migration trends, and that is our focus.

The chapter begins with a composite picture of developments in Mexican migration to the United States since the onset of the Great Recession. Carrying the time line forward to 2017, we use multiple sources of publicly available information in combination with our original analysis of recent data from the Border Survey of Mexican Migrants. Second, we

The authors gratefully acknowledge the support of Marie Laure Coubes and Mauricio Rodríguez-Abreu with the Border Survey of Mexican Migrants.

summarize some of the analyses put forward to explain this evolution. Third, we examine the role of border enforcement in greater detail, particularly its deterrence effect among recent Mexican deportees.

THE STEADY RISE AND SUDDEN FALL OF MEXICAN EMIGRATION TO THE UNITED STATES

The fifty years prior to the Great Recession saw a migration from Mexico to the United States that was driven by structural differences in the two economies, public policies on both sides of the border, and family reunification. Annual emigration from Mexico to the United States rose gradually after the end of the Bracero Programs (1964) and the enactment of the Immigration and Naturalization Act (1965). **Table 4.1** shows that the gross influx of migrants from Mexico to the United States grew progressively from 1970 to 2010. In 1970, the 759,700 Mexicans residing in the United States represented only 1.6 percent of the native population of Mexico. This population tripled between 1970 and 1980 and doubled in each of the following two decades to reach 9.2 million in 2000. By then, 9.5 percent of the Mexican-born population was already living in the United States.

The upsurge of **northbound flows** took place in a context of growing disparities between Mexico and the United States, as well as escalating regional polarization in Mexico in terms of economic and social opportunities. The peak of the Mexican exodus occurred in the 1990s as conditions in both countries created a "perfect storm": (1) demographic pressures in Mexico; (2) the Mexican peso crisis of 1994; (3) economic prosperity in the United States (the "roaring nineties"); (4) the consolidation of migrant networks; and (5) the 1986 Immigration Reform and Control Act's (IRCA's) massive legalization of undocumented immigrants (in exchange for stronger immigration enforcement). By that time the Mexican diaspora north of the border was well established. The millions of Mexicans residing in the United States, including the many who achieved legal status through IRCA, provided material support for migrants, knowledge of the transit corridors north, and, in many cases, the added attraction of family reunification. In the period between 1990 and 2000, the Mexican migrant stock grew at an annual rate of change of 7.6 percent and 500,000 Mexican migrants were added annually to the population of the United States.

This persistent growth continued until 2007, the last year in which there is a record of an increase in the United States of both the total

TABLE 4.1 MEXICAN IMMIGRANTS IN THE UNITED STATES AND ANNUAL RATE OF CHANGE, 1960–2017

Mexican Immigrants		Growth Rate	
1960	575,900	1960–70	2.8
1970	759,700	1970–80	10.6
1980	2,199,200	1980–90	6.7
1990	4,298,000	1990–2000	7.6
2000	9,177,500	2000–2010	2.4
2010	11,711,100	2010–17	−0.6
2017	11,269,900		

SOURCES: Migration Policy Institute (MPI) Data Hub, www.migrationpolicy.org/programs/data-hub/charts/mexican-born-population-over-time?width=1000&height=850&iframe=true; and authors' calculations.

number of low-skilled immigrants and the Mexican-born population (Zenteno 2012; Hanson, Liu, and McIntosh 2017). Mexico-US migration entered a new era in 2007 when the number of migrants coming north started to decline, coinciding with a slowdown in the construction industry that presaged the Great Recession (Pew Hispanic Center 2007). Soon after, as the US economy hit bottom, net migration appeared to hit the zero point.

The 2008 US financial crisis exposed a fundamental reality about Mexico-US migration: its strong ties to labor demand in the US economy (Villarreal 2014; Massey, Durand, and Pren 2014). Mexican emigration to the United States declined radically as a result of the Great Recession. The total number of Mexican immigrants added to the US population during the period 2000–2010 was 2.5 million, which was about half the number for the previous decade and the lowest annual growth rate (2.4 percent) since the 1960s. According to data from the Pew Research Center, only 265,000 Mexicans were counted as new immigrants in the United States by 2008, a figure much lower than the 615,000 registered just four years earlier (Cohn, Passel, and Gonzalez-Barrera 2017).

Table 4.1 also shows that the number of immigrants in the United States from Mexico seems to have stabilized or even declined slightly in the current decade. As of 2017, the Mexican-born population in the United States was 11.3 million. The most recent estimates of the annual inflow of Mexican migrants show 165,000 new arrivals for 2015 (Cohn, Passel, and Gonzalez-Barrera 2017). As we can infer from the Mexican migrant stock, new immigrant arrivals from Mexico have been offset by equally significant **outflows** of residents of the United States moving in the opposite direction. The near-zero net migration rate between Mexico and the United States has been described in detail elsewhere (Passel, Cohn, and Gonzalez-Barrera 2012).

BORDER SURVEY OF MEXICAN MIGRATION

The core findings of this chapter are formulated on the basis of data from the **Border Survey of Mexican Migration** (Encuesta sobre Migración en la Frontera Norte de México [EMIF]). Operating since 1993, the border survey is the oldest continuous research program tracking original data on the number of people crossing the US-Mexico border legally or illegally. It is conducted at select border-crossing points and at airports in the interior of Mexico by El Colegio de la Frontera Norte (COLEF), a government-funded research institution. The border survey offers a unique glimpse at the size and characteristics of migration in both directions across the border, with data systematically assembled on a quarterly basis.

In this chapter we are primarily concerned with changes in the size of migration flows over time, and the border survey is particularly valuable in this regard because the methodology has been repeated consistently over many years. Moreover, EMIF's sampling design allows flows to be tracked by calendar quarters. Annual comparisons for the same quarter allow analyses that account for seasonal variations in the flow. Conducted in Mexico by Mexican interviewers, the survey asks northbound respondents whether they are crossing into the United States legally or not.

This chapter also draws on survey data based on interviews conducted with a random sample of Mexicans who have been delivered to the Mexican side of the border by US authorities. In the survey, these Mexicans are categorized as having been "repatriated," and the term has been selected to distinguish the survey findings from the terminology used to describe enforcement actions by US authorities. Repatriated Mexicans in the EMIF have been forcibly returned to Mexico for a variety of reasons. They may have been caught by the Border Patrol hours earlier, or they might have been apprehended in the interior of the United States, detained, and then deported. In addition to collecting demographic data and information on their stay in the United States, the survey asks respondents where they were taken into custody.

THE COLLAPSE OF UNDOCUMENTED BORDER CROSSING

In understanding the evolution of the Mexico-US stream during the post-1965 period, we must ponder the role played by undocumented immigrants. Undocumented immigrants account for a large share of the Mexican-born population in the United States. In 2006, Mexicans accounted for 57 percent of the 12.2 million unauthorized immigrant population in the United States. Ten years later, the proportion of Mexicans had decreased to almost 50 percent. Thus, the number of unauthorized Mexican immigrants in the United States dropped from 7.0 million in 2007 to 5.5 million in 2016 (Passel and Cohn 2018).

The shift in the undocumented population in the United States stems in part from the fact that the number of Mexicans crossing the border without proper documentation have been substantially declining in recent years. Unauthorized migrants almost uniformly travel in search of work, and the contraction of the US labor market coincided with a major decline in that flow. The upsurge of Mexican unauthorized northbound flows before the Great Recession can be seen in figure 4.1, and figures 4.1 and 4.2 illustrate its most recent collapse.[3]

Several observations can be made from these figures based on EMIF data. The flows of unauthorized migrants present important seasonal variations during the years of heightened demand in the US labor market (see dotted line in figure 4.1). This seasonal pattern tied to labor market demand disappeared after absorbing the effects of the economic recession. Overall Mexican unauthorized migration flows skyrocketed from 330,000 in 2002, surged in the mid-2000s, and peaked in the first quarter of 2006. What happened after 2007 needs to be understood as a comedown from a peak. And it was a temporary and somewhat artificial peak to the extent that migration was pumped up by the home construction bubble and other economic activities in the United States that proved subject to collapse and slow to recover. Finally, the Great Recession had a sharp impact on the northbound flow, unfolding a new chapter in the history of contemporary Mexico-US migration.

The survey data show that the number of undocumented migrants heading into the United States declined steadily for sixteen straight quarters starting at the beginning of 2008 (see figure 4.2) but that the pace slowed in 2011 and then reversed. In the first two quarters of 2012, the border survey registered annual gains in the undocumented flow for the first time since the onset of the Great Recession. In the first

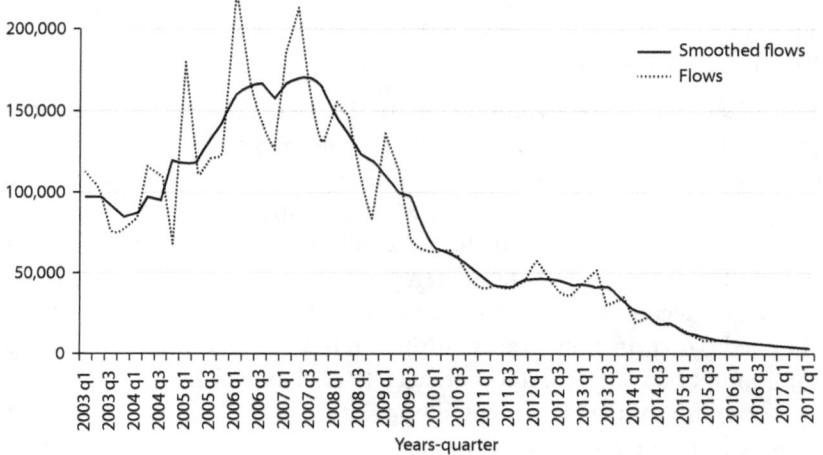

FIGURE 4.1. Northbound Mexican Unauthorized Flows to the United States Measured on a Quarterly Basis, 2003–2017 (smoothed data to show secular trend*). Source: Border Survey of Mexican Migration (EMIF). Note: Smoothing function applied using Stata was $(1/4)*[x(t-2) + x(t-1) + 1*x(t) + x(t+1)]$; $x(t)$ = flow.

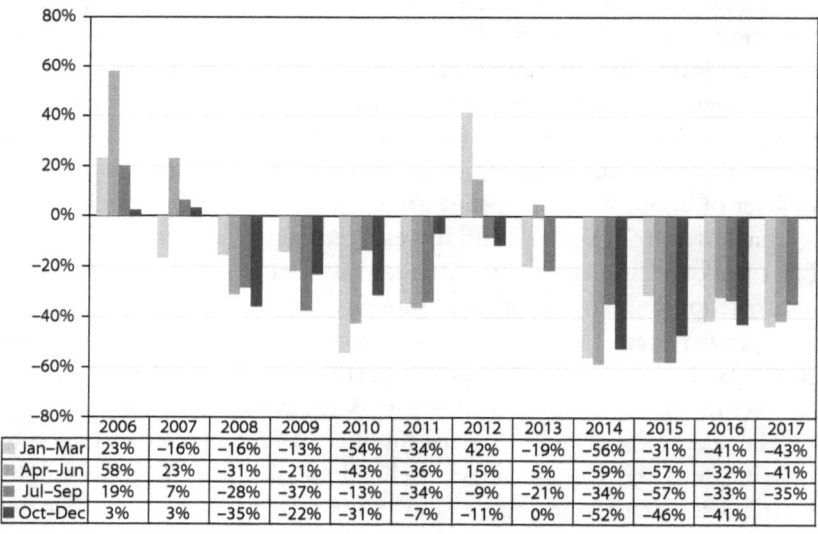

	2006	2007	2008	2009	2010	2011	2012	2013	2014	2015	2016	2017
Jan–Mar	23%	−16%	−16%	−13%	−54%	−34%	42%	−19%	−56%	−31%	−41%	−43%
Apr–Jun	58%	23%	−31%	−21%	−43%	−36%	15%	5%	−59%	−57%	−32%	−41%
Jul–Sep	19%	7%	−28%	−37%	−13%	−34%	−9%	−21%	−34%	−57%	−33%	−35%
Oct–Dec	3%	3%	−35%	−22%	−31%	−7%	−11%	0%	−52%	−46%	−41%	

FIGURE 4.2. Annual Percentage Change in the Flow of Unauthorized Migrants Measured on a Quarterly Basis, 2006–2017. Source: Border Survey of Mexican Migration (EMIF).

quarter of 2012, the survey registered an unauthorized flow 42 percent higher than that in the same quarter of 2011. The second quarter marked a year-over-year increase of 15 percent.

After some signs of a renewed northbound flow and relatively steady numbers in 2012 and 2013, the decline of undocumented migration from Mexico appears to have initiated a new gradual decline. Starting in the first quarter of 2014, flows of unauthorized migrants continued their downward trend and dipped sharply for fifteen consecutive quarters. The EMIF data show the sharpest slide over the course of 2014 and 2015 (annual declines of more than 50 percent in five quarters). The number of northbound migrants continued declining steadily in 2016 and the first three quarters of 2017. During the last seven quarters recorded by the EMIF, illegal border crossings attempted by Mexicans were only 17 percent of the crossings recorded just in the first quarter of 2006.

UNDERSTANDING THE COLLAPSE OF UNDOCUMENTED MEXICAN IMMIGRATION: ECONOMIC DOWNTURN

Today's unauthorized northbound flows are at an all-time low. The decline in the number of Mexicans leaving for the United States is the result of many factors. Striking evidence of the impact of the Great Recession on the decline of Mexican emigration to the United States comes from a 2014 research paper by the sociologist Andrés Villarreal. Villarreal uses panel data from Mexico over the period 2005–13 to demonstrate that the contraction of employment in key US economic sectors hiring Mexican-born workers played a significant role in lowering the migration of Mexican men. That, in turn, resulted in more positive selection among young migrants in terms of education. Other economic factors contributing to the low volume of migration from Mexico are decreasing volatility of Mexico's economic performance relative to the United States in the postrecession period and improvements in the Mexican economy (Hanson, Liu, and McIntosh 2017).

UNDERSTANDING THE COLLAPSE OF UNDOCUMENTED MEXICAN IMMIGRATION: DEMOGRAPHIC TRANSITION

The new era of Mexico-US migration should also be understood in the context of Mexico's demographic transition. The magnitude of the Mexican exodus had a strong demographic component: the greater growth of Mexico's labor supply in comparison to the neighboring country.

Mexico's demographic "subsidy" to the US economy has been eroded as a result of low birthrates and the reduction of family size in Mexico. In 1970, before the introduction of family planning in Mexico, Mexican women had on average 4.3 more children than women in the United States. This difference dropped to 0.2 by the end of the century.[4] Gordon Hanson and Craig McIntosh were the first scholars to examine the connection between the size of Mexican cohorts (labor supply) and the great Mexican migration to the United States in two seminal papers (Hanson and McIntosh 2009, 2010). More recently, Hanson and colleagues have extended their research to examine Mexican migration between 2000 and 2010. They find strong support for the hypothesis that labor supply shocks and, to a lesser extent, changes in the US business cycle played an important role in driving the decline of out-migration of Mexican individuals ages fifteen to forty (Hanson, Liu, and McIntosh 2017), a result consistent with the reduction of the stream of Mexican emigration at the turn of the century which was only reversed by the home construction bubble.

UNDERSTANDING THE COLLAPSE OF UNDOCUMENTED MEXICAN IMMIGRATION: BORDER ENFORCEMENT

In addition to elements related to economic and demographic factors in Mexico and the United States, other factors have had an impact on the dynamics of Mexican emigration, with tougher border and interior enforcement topping the list. The past thirty years have seen a rapid acceleration of **immigration enforcement** in the United States (Massey, Durand, and Pren 2016), with enhanced border security at historical levels during the Great Recession and the postrecession period (Argueta 2016). The most notorious transformation in border enforcement does not come from the Trump administration but from the previous more sustained escalation from 2008 to 2013.

Establishing the nature of the relationship between border enforcement and unauthorized migration has proved challenging. One hurdle is its endogeneity; that is, these two phenomena influence each other. For example, migration is shaped by border and interior controls, yet it also influences the size and strategy of enforcement. Also, it is difficult to quantify how prospective migrants perceive their risk of apprehension at the border and to measure the consequences of detention and deportation among current migrants.

Overall, studies have found the deployment of massive resources on border security had little effect on the inflow of undocumented migrants from Mexico from 1977 to 1988 (Espenshade 1994), on attempted undocumented migration from 1983 to 1997 (Dávila, Pagan, and Soydemir 2002), on migration propensities of unauthorized migration from 1972 to 2003 (Gathmann 2008; Angelucci 2012), on the initiation of Mexican undocumented migration from 1970 to 2010 (Massey, Durand, and Pren 2016), or, more recently, on the intention of Mexican deportees to remigrate between 2005 and 2012 (Amuedo-Dorantes and Pozo 2014).

Examining the enforcement-migration relationship before the Great Recession, the picture that has emerged is threefold. First, the border buildup was incapable of preventing migrants from entering the United States without proper documentation. Second, it resulted in increased health risks for undocumented migrants. And third, the costs of migration (smuggler prices, harsher sentences for recurring illegal crossing) were large enough to create a "caging effect" and encourage millions of undocumented migrants to settle permanently in the United States (Massey, Durand, and Pren 2016).

Although most studies find that the deterrent effect of enhanced border security is small, there are reasons to believe that we underestimate its real impact for three reasons. First, border buildup has a deterrent effect among potential migrants at an unknown rate. Second, past evidence suggests that there are increasing returns to scale on tighter enforcement efforts (Hanson and Spilimbergo 1999; Angelucci 2012). Third and finally, in the past the escalation of border buildup might have not approached a threshold level sufficiently high to distress the volume of unauthorized migration.[5]

After 2007, push-pull economic factors driving Mexico-US migration went through a substantial transformation, but the process of border militarization and interior enforcement changed dramatically as well. The labor economist Catalina Amuedo-Dorantes and colleagues were the first to illustrate the effects of federal and local enforcement policies on rising fear of deportation and curbing intentions to remigrate among unauthorized Mexican returned migrants interviewed in 2009–10 (Amuedo-Dorantes, Puttitanun, and Martinez-Donate 2013). Other recent works on the relationship between immigration enforcement and migration patterns have found that interior enforcement has contributed to a reduction of the share of Hispanic noncitizen population in places like Arizona (Amuedo-Dorantes and Lozano 2015) and that border enforcement is an important determinant of the areas where Mexican immigrants settle in the United States (Bohn and Pugatch 2015).

EXAMINING THE IMPACT OF IMMIGRATION ENFORCEMENT

Starting in 1993, successive US administrations have invested heavily in Border Patrol personnel, electronic sensors, and physical barriers, all aimed at impeding the movement of undocumented migrants across the US-Mexico border. In the years since the Great Recession, enforcement activity on the border, as measured by apprehensions, has dropped off along with the northbound flow. Meanwhile, new federal enforcement efforts have gotten under way along the border and within the interior of the country.

Figure 4.3 illustrates the consistent decline in the number of Mexicans apprehended at the US-Mexico border since 2000, as captured in data from the US Department of Homeland Security (DHS). In 2017, US authorities made only 128,000 apprehensions of undocumented Mexicans along the Southwest border sector (the lowest total since 2000), down from the peak of roughly 1.0 million annual apprehensions just before the Great Recession. However, as illustrated in figure 4.3, US investments in border enforcement accelerated even after the northbound flow declined. Both the budget and staffing levels of the Border Patrol rose more steeply after Mexican migration began to decline than at any time since the initial effort to ramp up the agency from a skeleton force of less than 4,000 officers. Between 2006 and 2013, the personnel numbers increased from 11,032 to 18,611, a jump of 68 percent. This reflected both long-term spending authorized by Congress and year-to-year budgetary decisions.

This hefty increase in control efforts during a decline in the phenomenon meant to be controlled raises obvious public policy questions about the federal government's ability to adapt to changing circumstances. Then again, nimbleness is not a trait commonly associated with Washington. But another issue, more relevant to this discussion, arises from the contrast between enforcement efforts and northbound flow: What is the relationship between the two? If the largest increases in enforcement occurred after the flow had begun to decline, how much causality can be ascribed to enforcement in explaining that decline? We will return to that question later in this chapter.

Data from the EMIF in **figure 4.4** show that ramped up enforcement coincided with a distinct change in one key characteristic of the Mexicans being removed from the United States: their longevity as migrants. Before the Great Recession, 2004–7, less than 12 percent of repatriated Mexicans had lived in the United States for more than a year. Thus, the

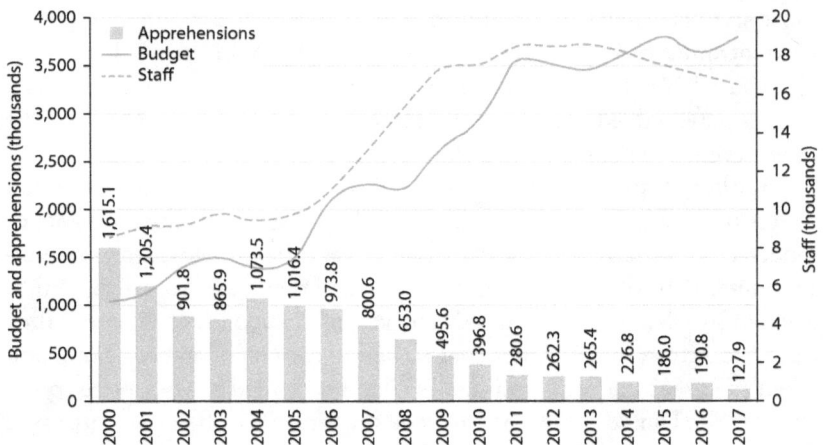

FIGURE 4.3. Border Patrol Budget and Staff and Apprehensions of Mexican Migrants along the Southwest Border Sector, FY 2000–2017. Source: US Department of Homeland Security (DHS).

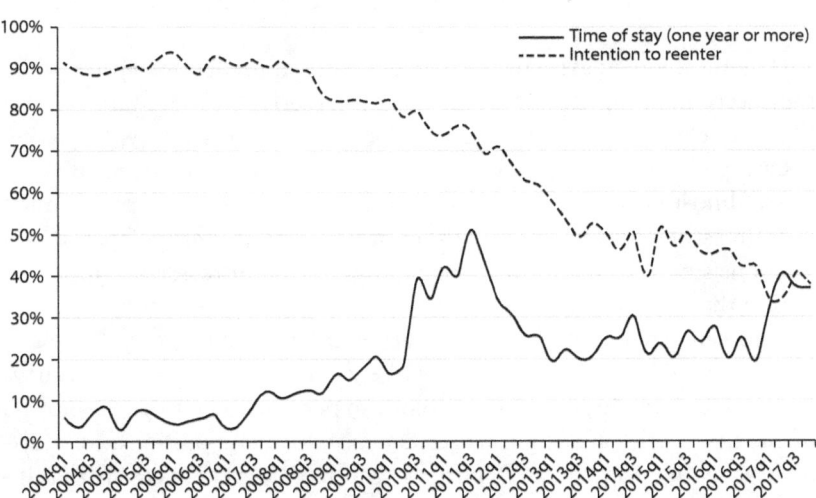

FIGURE 4.4. Share of Repatriated Mexicans with More than One Year of Residence in the US and Stating an Intent to Return to the US Measured on a Quarterly Basis, 2004–2017. Source: Border Survey of Mexican Migration (EMIF).

most serious impact of US enforcement efforts fell overwhelmingly on new entrants who were caught at the border. By 2011, nearly half of the repatriated Mexicans had lived in the United States for at least a year. The data available for 2017 show that between 32 and 41 percent of the most recently repatriated were longer-term migrants.

Another strand of data from the EMIF suggests that the potential effects of removal on future migration plans are greater for migrants of longer tenure than the recently arrived. Repatriated Mexicans are typically interviewed for the EMIF the same day they have been returned to Mexico by US authorities, and the survey asks respondents whether they intend to return to the United States. Before the recession took hold, and when the great majority had just been apprehended as they were trying to enter the United States, as many as 90 percent of the repatriates said they planned to head back north (see figure 4.4). That share began to drop in 2009 and has continued to slide since the last two quarters of 2016. The intent to return is at about 41 percent or less now.

Not surprisingly, the EMIF data reveal some important differences in the profiles of new entrants to the migrant stream compared to those who have already set up residence in the United States. **Table 4.2** compiles data on selected characteristics of repatriated Mexicans from surveys conducted from 2012 to 2017.

Among the new arrivals, 68 percent were apprehended either while they were crossing the border or in the desert and mountain regions immediately to the north of the border. That is consistent with having been repatriated as a result of a Border Patrol apprehension. In contrast, almost two-thirds of the longer-term migrants were apprehended in traffic stops and 23 percent either at home or at work. Those shares are consistent with the effects of immigration enforcement conducted within the interior of the country.

The centerpiece of the new interior enforcement efforts has been longer-term migrants who are more likely to be older (45 percent, thirty-five or older) and heads of households (69 percent). The forced removals of Mexicans who are longtime residents of US communities have a distinct psychological effect. Deportees who have experienced the disruption of being removed from a home, job, and community are less interested in returning to the United States. This could reflect other factors, such as a weak US job market and heightened border and interior enforcement. However, it is important to note that a clear majority of Mexican migrants who are interviewed just after they have been forcibly removed from the United States do not declare their intent to return.

TABLE 4.2 SELECTED CHARACTERISTICS OF REPATRIATED MEXICANS BY TIME OF STAY IN THE UNITED STATES (PERCENTAGES)

	2012–2017	
	Less than One Year[a]	One Year or More[b]
Sex		
Male	85	91
Female	15	9
Age Group		
15–24	34	13
25–34	38	41
35+	27	45
Marital Status		
Single	40	34
In union	54	57
Once in union	7	9
Household Position		
Head	55	69
Spouse	5	5
Son/daughter	25	13
Other[c]	15	14
Place Arrested		
Work	1	10
Home	1	13
Street or highway	28	62
Crossing the border	41	4
Desert or mountain	27	3
Other	2	7

SOURCE: Border Survey of Mexican Migration, 2012–17.
NOTES:
[a] Migrants who reported staying in the United States less than a year.
[b] Migrants who reported staying in the United States one year of more.
[c] Siblings, parents, or other relation.

This applies in equal measure to those who have just been caught trying to cross the border for the first time and those who have been removed from a home, job, and community.

As the northbound flow declined, the data make clear the enforcement effort shifted from migrants in transit to those with an established presence in the United States. This development raises a number of normative and political issues beyond the scope of this chapter, which is focused on the relative effectiveness of these enforcement strategies. However, the data on intentions to return suggest that the removal of long-term migrants might have a greater impact on future flows than did the heightened border enforcement that followed the Great Recession.

CONCLUSION

By 2017, a full decade had passed since the flow of undocumented Mexicans had declined precipitously. Indeed, the period between 2014 and 2017 saw a stark acceleration of that trend, suggesting that this phenomenon has not spent itself but rather has gained momentum. If anything, the available data indicate that unauthorized migration from Mexico will not again add to the US population any time soon. Extensive research points to multiple causal factors, including demographic and economic trends in both Mexico and the United States. Increased US enforcement efforts also undoubtedly played a part. The difficult remaining question is how to ascribe relative weights to these causal factors.

Claims that border enforcement was a dispositive factor, however, must be treated with skepticism. Evidence from the EMIF, when examined in the context of other measures of migration phenomena as well as data on US immigration enforcement efforts, suggests that enforcement, especially border enforcement, may have reinforced the decline but did not initiate it. Rather, the chronology alone points to the centrality of the Great Recession. The northbound flow showed a sharp, unquestionable decline as the home construction industry collapsed at the onset of the economic downturn and was well in place by the time the economy as a whole was crippled. The most substantial enforcement efforts came into effect afterward. And it is only with the passage of time and a shift of enforcement from the border to the interior that we have seen deep discouragement set in among returning migrants.

Much of the research points to structural trends, such as lower fertility rates in Mexico, as causes of the reversal in Mexican unauthorized migration. Our research seeks to refine the time line of the change in the migration flow and the drivers behind it. One very clear finding is that structural trends do not explain why the decline in the northbound flow began so sharply at a precise point in time, the last two quarters of 2006, and then was rapidly entrenched within a year. Demographic trends that gain momentum across decades seem unlikely suspects for producing a phenomenon that takes shape over the course of months. The data suggest focusing on short-term developments instead. The most sudden of the developments associated with the change in migration patterns is the onset of the Great Recession, and the specific timing correlates closely with the drop in migration. Meanwhile, the heightened enforcement that took place under the Obama administration actually followed the onset of the decline in migration.

Our study of the chronology of the changes in migration patterns points to something like a one-two punch. The Great Recession hammered the brakes down on the flow of unauthorized Mexican migration and then enforcement reinforced the trend, prolonging it and allowing the decline to develop what now appears to be a hard permanence. Given the importance of these migration trends to both Mexico and the United States, we believe that still further study is required of the events between 2007 and 2017 when an era of mass migration came to an end. Only by better understanding that extraordinary turn of events can we attempt to understand the new era now emerging.

Suggested Reading

Border crossings have been declining for years, despite claims of a "crisis of illegal immigration." 2018. *New York Times,* June 20. Available at www.nytimes.com/2018/06/20/us/politics/fact-check-trump-border-crossings-declining-.html.

Donato, K., and A. Armenta. 2011. What we know about unauthorized migration. *Annual Review of Sociology* 37: 529–53.

Gonzales, R., B. Ellis, S. A. Rendón-García, and K. Brant. 2018. (Un)authorized transitions: Illegality, DACA, and the life course. *Research in Human Development* 15(3–4): 345–59.

Hanson, G., C. Liu, and C. McIntosh. 2017. Along the watchtower: The rise and fall of U.S. low-skilled immigration. Brooking Papers on Economic Activity. Available at www.brookings.edu/bpea-articles/along-the-watchtower-the-rise-and-fall-of-u-s-low-skilled-immigration/.

Massey, D., J. Durand, and N. Malone. 2002. *Beyond Smoke and Mirrors: Mexican Immigration in an Era of Economic Integration.* New York: Russell Sage Foundation.

Villarreal, A. 2014. Explaining the decline in Mexico-U.S. migration: The effect of the Great Recession. *Demography* 51(6): 2203–28.

CHAPTER 5

How Is the Health of the Mexican-Origin Population on Both Sides of the Border Affected by Policies and Attitudes in the United States?

FERNANDO RIOSMENA, HIRAM BELTRÁN-SÁNCHEZ, MEGAN REYNOLDS, AND JUSTIN VINNEAU

The United States and Mexico are intimately linked economically, environmentally, and socially. Because the deep demographic linkages bridging the two nations require a shared, binational understanding of the well-being of their populations, this chapter provides an overview of the health of the Mexican-origin population on both sides of the border. First, major changes in contemporary migrations between both countries are examined. Next, these changing conditions are linked to the health of Mexican migrants and US-born Mexican Americans in the United States. Finally, given sizable movements South by Mexican-origin individuals in recent years, the chapter explores the health of return migrants and of the increasing number of US-born (Mexican) Americans living in Mexico. The chapter concludes with policy suggestions for improving health care for these populations.

THE POPULATIONS BOTH COUNTRIES SHARE: MAJOR TRENDS IN CONTEMPORARY MOBILITY

For well over a century, a large and storied stream of migrations has forged durable demographic linkages between Mexico and the United States. Two very important contemporary shifts in these movements have further deepened these links.

First, in the 1990s, the Mexican immigrant population in the United States increased more rapidly than in prior decades as Mexico-US migration shifted away from the solo male sojourner typical of the 1940s through 1980s (Massey, Durand, and Malone 2002). At that point, a larger share of undocumented migrants began settling in the United States for longer periods, often accompanied or eventually joined by their families. This change occurred at least partly in response to enforcement shifts that lowered the incentives for circulation between the two countries (Massey, Durand, and Pren 2015).

Second, the hardening of US immigration enforcement continues to alter these population flows, contributing to reduced immigration from Mexico (Villarreal 2014) and, especially, to the increasing number of Mexican-origin individuals moving from the United States to Mexico, including via mass deportation (Masferrer and Roberts 2012).

These seismic changes in the dynamics of Mexican migration have likely had important implications for **migrant well-being,** including their mental and physical health. The challenges to the welfare of Mexican-origin migrants to the United States and of those suddenly uprooted from the United States and returning to Mexico are taken up separately in the rest of this chapter.

THE HEALTH OF THE MEXICAN-ORIGIN POPULATION IN THE UNITED STATES

Over the past four decades, scholars have uncovered a consistently bipolar picture of the health of Mexican-origin populations in the United States. On the one hand, Mexican Americans—particularly immigrants—exhibit several health-related advantages relative to non-Hispanic whites. This **immigrant health advantage** is seen in health outcomes as important as adult mortality, which is in turn a result of better Mexican American chronic health in some types of cancers and, especially, many measures of cardiovascular function (Cunningham, Ruben, and Narayan 2008).

In contrast to this outlook, and perhaps more expectedly given the lower socioeconomic position of Mexican Americans, the health of this population is poor in many dimensions. Most notably, **Mexican American health disadvantages** compared to non-Hispanic whites include worse and worsening health in a variety of cardiometabolic conditions, particularly in diabetes (Beard et al. 2009), as well as on levels of the so-called good cholesterol and triglycerides (Beltrán-Sánchez and Riosmena 2017).

Likewise, the Mexican-origin population experiences many challenges in mental health. Even if they are less likely to report being *diagnosed* with depression and anxiety, Mexican Americans and undocumented immigrants in particular are more likely to report a few important *symptoms* of these mental health problems as well as some forms of stress (e.g., McGuire and Miranda 2008), suggesting underdiagnosis.

In addition to these outright disadvantages, over time Mexican immigrants experience a deterioration of many of the conditions in which they exhibited some advantage (Lara et al. 2005), often leading to a total loss of the prior immigrant health advantage. As a result of the accumulation of disadvantage and the erosion of advantage, Mexican Americans may live longer than non-Hispanic white individuals but spend a larger proportion of their life spans suffering from often underdiagnosed or mistreated chronic diseases, with some form of cognitive impairment, or with depression (e.g., Garcia et al. 2018; Garcia et al. 2017).

Because of the existence of the immigrant health advantage, it is assumed that Mexican migrants are—upon departure—in better health than the people they leave behind, a phenomenon known as **selectivity**. The act of migrating for those crossing without documents and the work that undocumented and legal immigrant laborers perform require a fair degree of physical endurance (Holmes 2013; Horton 2016). As such, those with a stronger constitution may be better able to both make the trek and stick with the grueling work.

Although migrants tend to exhibit *some* favorable "risk factors" that, in turn, often lead to better health than nonmigrants (Riosmena, Kuhn, and Jochem 2017), selectivity is unlikely to explain the full immigrant health advantage as it is much less clear when examining more direct measures of chronic health (e.g., Diaz, Zeng, and Martinez-Donate 2018).

Because the health status of people is deeply affected by their prevailing environment and as the Mexican immigrant population today has, on average, spent more than a decade in the United States, it follows that the **context of reception**—the way in which immigrants are perceived and received—is increasingly relevant in influencing people's well-being over the life course. Before arrival in the United States—if they make it at all—people trying to cross without documents suffer considerable grief or, at a minimum, the threat of grief.

Over the past half century, temporary guest worker programs and other legal avenues for labor migration have been arguably outpaced by labor demand. At the same time, over the past quarter century, the US government has dedicated substantial resources to making crossing more dangerous while failing to address with commensurate seriousness the economic and social forces that stimulate undocumented labor migration (Massey, Durand, and Malone 2002). For example, US labor recruitment has traditionally played a large role in these migrations, even though conditions at home and (deeply constrained) individual choices are factors as well (Massey and Riosmena 2010; Ryo 2013). Because the focus on border enforcement does not address these economic and social forces and focuses far too narrowly on apprehension, it has been an ineffective and inefficient policy tool to manage labor migration.

Crossing the border without documents has become an increasingly dangerous and expensive proposition filled with all sorts of pitfalls. The riverine and, especially, the remote, hilly desert and isolated environments along the **migrant trail** of the Mexican and US borderlands present many hazards, leading to the annual death of roughly four hundred migrants on the US side of the region (Ortega 2018)—even in recent years, despite much lower undocumented crossings from Mexico—where people most commonly die by drowning, suffocation, heat exhaustion, or heat stroke. On the Mexican side of the trail, migrants also face the risk of extortion and kidnapping by criminal organizations and of robbery and sexual violence (Martínez 2013), the trauma of which often lingers, especially if left untreated.

In recent years, immigration management has become even harsher with the enactment of **zero tolerance policies** aimed at criminally prosecuting anyone and everyone caught trying to cross the border in an irregular way, as opposed to the previous practice of detaining and deporting people without bringing criminal charges.[1] Longer detention times as a result of these and other practices have led to the warehousing of people (including young children) in subpar detention facilities housing thousands of asylum seekers and undocumented migrants caught in the borderlands and the interior. In addition to the general harm caused by detention—a punishment that many observers argue does not fit the crime of crossing without documents, let alone seeking asylum—detainee abuse is unfortunately not uncommon in these facilities (Jorgensen 2017). These practices are very likely to produce considerable, long-lasting trauma to detainees, particularly children (Isacson, Meyer, and Hite 2018).[2]

Other aspects of the context of reception are also increasingly relevant to migrant well-being. Migrant health is particularly sensitive to conditions in destinations, especially as immigrating often involves radical changes in the social environment. These experiences are likely to affect migrants' health in ways that would not have occurred had they stayed in Mexico—sometimes for the better but more often, in the long run, for the worse. The negative context of reception that migrants experience is also likely to further complicate the **modes of incorporation** (within a wide assimilation spectrum) of those who make it to the US interior—irregularly or legally—as well as the well-being (or assimilation) of their US-born children (Waters and Pineau 2016).

A large majority of Mexican migrants in the United States today have spent more than a decade in the country (e.g., Gonzalez-Barrera and Krogstad 2017), including at least one million people brought by their parents during childhood. Given the existence of an immigrant health advantage in some outcomes, factors operating in the United States could be "protecting" people from the types of factors that lead to poor health. In particular, Mexican American and/or immigrant communities could be acting as a "buffer" against stresses of daily life such as poverty, discrimination, or lack of legal documents (e.g., Eschbach et al. 2004). However, these protective effects are either an artifact of healthy (unhealthy) people moving in (out) of neighborhoods or otherwise short-lived in the sense that they may be eventually overrun by the accumulation of disadvantage leading to the aforementioned health erosion.

This deterioration has often been thought of as being part of the process by which immigrants "acculturate," or adopt the attitudes, sentiments, values, and, especially, behaviors typical of "mainstream" US society, including the adoption of health-deleterious practices such as increased smoking, binge drinking, drug use, and poorer eating habits (Lara et al. 2005). However, scholars have increasingly pointed to flaws in the acculturation explanation, instead advancing the idea that disadvantage—in terms of ethnic, racial, or immigration status–related discrimination and the related and resulting class position and labor conditions—accumulates and eventually somatizes into negative health outcomes (e.g., Holmes 2013).

Anti-immigrant sentiment and associated policies and practices in particular stand out in the current political climate as an important conduit by which the context of reception affects the health of immigrants (and, as we discuss in the next section, their descendants). This is particularly the case in perinatal and mental health outcomes, including post-traumatic stress, depression, anxiety, and other forms of psychological distress. Social isolation, separation from one's traditional sources of emotional and social support, internalized guilt resulting from stigma, and fear of deportation—all affected by anti-immigrant sentiment to some extent—take a toll on migrants' mental health (Sullivan and Rehm 2005).

Comparatively little research exists on how anti-immigrant sentiment and other forms of disadvantage "get under the skin," increasing physical morbidity or mortality. However, we know that forms of disadvantage related to legal and socioeconomic status eventually affect chronic health. For instance, many Mexican Americans—both foreign and US born—continue to engage in dangerous and otherwise repetitive labor, leading to more accidents and injuries (Horton 2016). This may help explain higher disability rates in the Mexican-origin population (Hummer and Gutin 2018).

Likewise, cumulative disadvantage processes may affect Mexican American—especially immigrant—health with continued poor systematic access to quality health care. The Affordable Care Act (ACA) increased access to insurance mechanisms for 13 million people, including 1.1 million Latinos (Collins et al. 2016). However, largely because the ACA provisions further blocked the 11 million undocumented migrants in the country from accessing less expensive private health insurance plans, and as these people are also ineligible for most kinds of public insurance (most notably, Medicaid and Medicare), Hispanics today represent an even more disproportionate share of the uninsured than in the past (40 percent in 2016 vs. 29 percent in 2013) (Collins et al. 2016). Late detection due to this lack of health care can cause pain and a higher bill for patients, and—on many occasions—all taxpayers, who foot the bill via the patchwork of care that helps the uninsured.

While health insurance and care are extremely important, Mexican Americans and other people of color experience differential treatment and discrimination in doctors' offices, hospitals, clinics, and emergency rooms (Hausmann et al. 2011), leading to poorer health. This applies to undocumented Mexican migrants in particular, who are even more likely to report negative health care experiences than US-born Mexicans, partly explaining the former's lower rates of health care utilization (Ortega et al. 2007).

Despite the challenges immigrants may disproportionately face, US-born Mexican American health is less favorable than that of their foreign-born coethnics almost invariably (e.g., Cunningham, Ruben, and Narayan 2008). Likewise, within the US-born group, the children of immigrants (the second generation) have better health than the third-plus generations (e.g., Afable-Munsuz et al. 2014). This suggests that the assimilation of Mexican Americans (and other immigrants) to US society comes with worse health, a paradox given that people migrate to the United States to improve their children's well-being in particular.

Mexican Americans of all generations are experiencing some progress relative to their parents in terms of schooling attainment and other measures of socioeconomic status (Telles and Ortiz 2008). Yet the social, economic, and policy conditions immigrant and other parents face do have repercussions on their descendants. Most clearly, lack of parental legal status negatively affects the well-being and functioning of US-born children (Landale et al. 2015), in part perhaps by virtue of the fact that rising anti-immigrant sentiment is associated with lower parental claims and utilization of different types of public support these children are otherwise entitled to (Pedraza and Zhu 2015), like Medicaid. This chilling effect is bound to become more relevant once the Trump administration fully implements its proposed changes to the so-called public charge rule (Perreira, Yoshikawa, and Oberlander 2018), which would deny permanent residence to applicants living in the United States if they or their dependents—including their US-born children—use most public health services.

THE HEALTH OF MEXICAN MIGRANTS RETURNING TO MEXICO

As with out-migration, to understand the health of return migrants one first needs to consider the selectivity of this group. Studies had traditionally focused on older return migrant adults because of interest in the well-being of this more vulnerable population and on assessing whether the immigrant health advantage—which is particularly pronounced in old age—is an artifact of the return of less healthy individuals to the sending country. Indeed, people going back to Mexico in older adulthood have worse chronic health, higher rates of physical limitations, and higher mortality rates than fellow Mexican migrants remaining in the United States (Riosmena, Palloni, and Wong 2013; Turra and Elo 2008), contributing to but not fully explaining the immigrant health advantage.

More recent research has begun to examine the health of younger adults returning to Mexico, a particularly relevant population given the recent trends discussed above. While younger adult returnees are *not* in worse (or better) chronic physical health than migrants remaining in the United States, they do have worse perceptions of their own health, have worse mental health, or exhibit more negative health behaviors (Arenas, Goldman, et al. 2015; Diaz, Zeng, and Martinez-Donate 2018). This status is perhaps the result of the more chronic cumulative disadvantage processes discussed above and, certainly with regard to mental health, the deportation process itself. Either way, the relatively poor health status of those returning presents clear challenges for the Mexican health care system, which we discuss while assessing how health may further change as returnees and ethnic return migrants (re)adapt in Mexico.

Although the manner in which return migrants and, especially, US-born Mexican Americans are readapting or adapting on their return or move to Mexico is the issue in need of most research of those discussed in this chapter, there is some indication that this adaptation has been unfavorable in ways that may ultimately affect returnee and ethnic returnee health, perhaps mental health in particular. Recent returnees are having worse labor market outcomes than prior waves of migrants (Parrado and Gutierrez 2016). Return migrants also have worse health insurance and health care coverage than nonmigrants, both because return migrants are less likely to currently or previously hold public and formal private sector jobs that provide access to insurance and because migrants are less likely to be part of Seguro Popular (Riosmena, González, and Wong 2012; Ross, Pagán, and Polsky 2006), a public health insurance program established in 2004 that has dramatically increased coverage and utilization and reduced out-of-pocket expenditures for Mexicans (Arenas, Parker, et al. 2015). Even after reforms of the Seguro Popular program (now called Instituto de Salud para el Bienestar [INSABI]; Institute of Health for Wellness), return migrants are still less likely to have access to it due to, for example, lack of access to identity and other documents.

More recent return migrants have experienced a marked improvement in health insurance coverage in more recent years thanks to Seguro Popular. However, these improvements have not closed their coverage gap relative to other Mexicans (Wassink 2016), a situation that has not improved with recent reforms, including the elimination of premiums. Most likely, this expansion has been slower among return migrants, in part because the program requires that applicants present specific documents that are often difficult to obtain for migrants. Indeed, because some of the required documents to apply are only available for Mexican-*born* individuals,[3] the US-born population of Mexican descent (to the best of our knowledge, even those with dual nationality) remains ineligible for this insurance program. Indeed, Mexico requires a more flexible health care system so that the large number of return migrants and their US-born children can have better access to Seguro Popular and other health systems in the country.

CONCLUSION: FUTURE OUTLOOK, POLICY RECOMMENDATIONS

The picture of the health of Mexican-origin populations on both sides of the border provided here is generally negative (with a few notable but fleeting exceptions), and the outlook is likely to worsen further in the future. Scholars have already forecasted that some aspects of the immigrant health advantage would continue to erode given trends in chronic health in both countries (Hummer and Hayward 2015). The situation, however, is particularly concerning; since the inauguration of Donald Trump the political and social climate, including but not limited to social policy affecting immigration and immigrant well-being, has deteriorated considerably (see note 2). This includes the debilitation of public and subsidized health programs.

Given the mobility trends briefly discussed at the beginning of this chapter and the economic and social integration of both countries in other domains, addressing the health challenges for these populations should include efforts—in both the United States and Mexico—to improve their legal standing, living and working conditions, and access to health care. The latter should include specific binational health care solutions, like portable Medicare for all US retirees (including the large population of pensioners without prior ancestral connections to Mexico living in the country) (Schafran and Monkkonen 2017), as well as a portable binational health insurance program for Mexican citizens.

We recognize that these recommendations are unrealistic in the current political climate since it is this climate that has produced many of the conditions challenging the health of the Mexican-origin population on both sides of the border. Yet that does not make them inadequate approaches. More important, regardless of the political climate, there are no other realistic solutions to the challenges faced by the populations the countries share, and the United States and Mexico will continue to be deeply intertwined by these and other linkages. Evidence-based rational and humane policy making will eventually become realistic again.

Suggested Reading

Holmes, S. 2013. *Fresh Fruit, Broken Bodies: Migrant Farmworkers in the United States*. Berkeley: University of California Press.

Riosmena, F., E. Root, J. Humphrey, E. Steiner, and R. Stubb. 2015. The waning Hispanic paradox. *Pathways* (Spring). Available at https://inequality.stanford.edu/sites/default/files/Pathways_Spring_2015_Riosmena_et-al.pdf.

Viruell-Fuentes, E. A., P. Y. Miranda, and S. Abdulrahim. 2012. More than culture: Structural racism, intersectionality theory, and immigrant health. *Social Science & Medicine* 75(12): 2099–2106.

Waters, M. C., and M. Gerstein Pineau. 2015. *The Integration of Americans into American Society*. Washington, DC: National Academies Press.

CHAPTER 6

What Shall Be the Future for the Children of Migration?

LASANTI and the Educational Imperative

PATRICIA GÁNDARA AND GARY ORFIELD

The region that extends from Los Angeles through Tijuana, a region we call **LASANTI** (Los Angeles–San Diego–Tijuana), was the eleventh largest economy in the world in 2016. It is larger than the economies of Spain and Russia, and it is critically important for the economic well-being of the state of California, for the United States, and for Mexico. In spite of the rhetoric about building walls and sealing borders, California and Mexico are highly interdependent, especially at this frontier, and their fortunes are inexorably tied. This is also the site of the world's most active border and home to hundreds of thousands of *students we share*—those young people who are the product of both the United States and Mexico and on whom the fortunes of both countries are highly dependent. Yet this enormous resource is at risk unless these nations combine efforts to raise the educational level for the entire region and do so quickly, before the window of opportunity closes.

THE CONTEXT

The creation of this Pacific megalopolis we call LASANTI is a triumph of promotion and creativity over reality. As the population soared and money poured into Southern California at the beginning of the twentieth century, civic leaders managed to transform what was barren desert—taking water from the north—into a stunning garden filled with midwestern trees. The lack of a natural harbor was overcome by building a huge man-made one.

Los Angeles alone, in urban terms, is perhaps the world's greatest self-fulfilling prophecy. The city has always had a talent for creating and marketing powerful images, manifest now as the world center of film, television, and popular music. And so it has created its own image, wrought from a desert with few natural assets. In 2016 Brookings Institution scholars, using a wide array of data to classify metropolitan areas according to measures of technological innovation, creation of new industries, capital and knowledge resources, and investment, identified the world's six most powerful, defining them as "global giants" (Leal and Parilla 2016). These extremely large, wealthy metropolitan areas are hubs for financial markets or major corporations and great universities and serve as key nodes in the global flow of capital, innovation, and talent. One of the six is Los Angeles. Another part of LASANTI, Metro San Diego, is identified as one of nineteen **knowledge capitals** of the world by the same Brookings study. These nineteen areas are midsized, highly productive innovation centers, with talented workforces and elite research universities.

On the other side of the border is Tijuana, one of Mexico's largest cities (much larger than San Francisco and twice the size of Seattle or Portland). It is located in Baja California, one of Mexico's wealthiest states. American firms and multinationals have built and operate modern factories producing goods for the world and plentiful jobs for local residents. Lively universities add intellectual capital to the region and great numbers of US citizens cross every day to visit and take advantage of less expensive services, while many Mexicans cross every morning to work or go to school in the United States. In fact, it is the most traversed border in the world.

A major asset that this area holds, which too often is overlooked, is the cadre of young bilingual, bicultural workers who can be a bridge between the economies and the societies of the two nations. In a recent survey we conducted in San Diego and Tijuana middle and high schools, most of the young people in Tijuana reported having connections to the United States through family, friends, or other interactions, and many on both sides of the border have dual language skills that are highly sought after by employers.

ENORMOUS INEQUALITY IN BOTH MEXICO AND THE UNITED STATES

Yet as prosperous and dynamic as the region is, it is also a site of profound **economic inequality**. California, as well as the border area of Baja

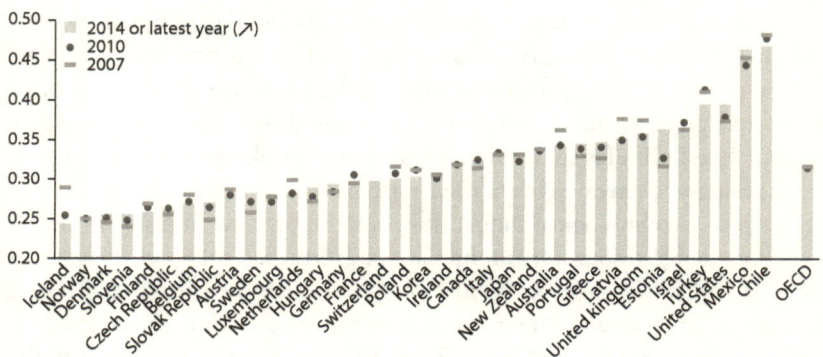

FIGURE 6.1. Income Inequality, 30 OECD Countries, Percent Above/Below Mean, 2014. Source: OECD 2017, www.oecd-ilibrary.org/development/development-co-operation-report-2017_dcr-2017-en.

California, has produced millions of good jobs, but large segments of the population have almost no chance for mobility. This is increasingly the case in all of LASANTI. Economic inequality is very severe in both countries. Southern California is one of the most unequal regions in the United States, and the United States ranks third and Mexico second worst among the thirty member countries of the **Organization for Economic Cooperation and Development (OECD)** with respect to income inequality. (See figure 6.1.)

The California Department of Education reports that 80 percent of Latino students in the state qualify for free or reduced-price lunches (California Department of Education 2016). Most Latino parents cannot afford to pay for their children's lunches, and LASANTI has a majority of Latino students. Conditions for children and youth are exacerbated by the high percentage of immigrant families in California. Half of all children in California have at least one immigrant parent, and a quarter of all immigrants are undocumented (Johnson and Sanchez 2018), meaning that many immigrant children live in very unstable circumstances given current immigration enforcement policies. Moreover, because federal policy does not allow even legal immigrants to access many federally supported social services for a period of five years, these families too are often reluctant to seek basic health care and nutritional services for which their US citizen children are eligible.

Income inequality in Mexico is only exceeded by Chile among the thirty OECD countries, as shown in figure 6.1, and is extremely high compared to the average for all countries listed. Mexico also suffers from extremely high poverty rates. While international definitions of poverty vary greatly, researchers at the Universidad de Iberoamerica calculate the poverty figure at slightly above 50 percent of the Mexican population (Teruel, Reyes, and López 2017). A very low minimum wage, currently at 88.3 pesos per day, or about US$5.00, contributes to this problem. Workers who earn minimum wage fall below the poverty line in Mexico. It is clear that for Mexico to prosper it must attack the problems of poverty and deep inequalities, which are exemplified in the extremely low minimum wage. The new government of Andrés Manuel López Obrador ordered a 16 percent increase in the minimum wage, to about $5.40 per day, and a doubling of the minimum wage along the northern border, to over $9.00 per day effective in 2019 (Harrup 2018). More increases may be on the way to meet the terms of the United States-Mexico-Canada Agreement (USMCA). However, low levels of **educational attainment** go hand in hand with the minimum wage.

EDUCATIONAL CHALLENGES ON THE MEXICAN SIDE

While many jobs have been created in Baja, inflation has outpaced wage increases, resulting in declining real incomes. Although the jobs are mostly entry level with little or no mobility, they have been attractive enough to lure many young workers from other parts of Mexico. While attractive to an 18-year-old without major responsibilities, such jobs do not pay enough to raise a family out of poverty. Dramatic progress in raising educational levels in Baja has been seen at the high school level for 15- to 17-year-olds. The graduation rate was 39.5 percent in 2004 but increased to 58.9 percent a decade later, in 2014 (Instituto Nacional de Estadística y Geografía [INEGI] and Gobierno de Baja California 2016). Nonetheless, very low levels of higher education attainment and still very high numbers of young people who fail to finish high school are features of the Baja region that seriously limit its development. Unfortunately, the income gap of individuals with middle school or less education and those with a college degree or more has *decreased* in recent years (Mordechay 2014). Nonetheless, although college completion affects only a small proportion of the society so far, it appears to yield a much more substantial premium. **Figure 6.2,** taken from research for the Inter-American Development Bank (IDB) by Santiago Levy and Luis Feipe López-Calva (2016), illustrates the limited financial advantages to simply finishing high school. Lack of opportunity also results in more than 20 percent of Mexican 18- to 24-year-olds who are neither

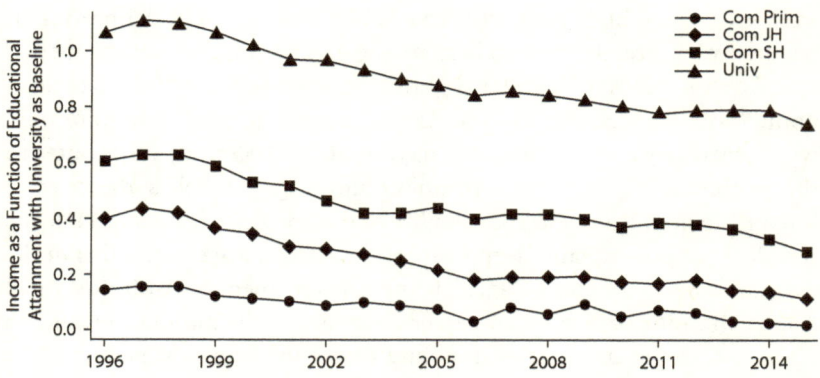

FIGURE 6.2. Income by Educational Attainment as a Proportion of University Educated Income, Mexico, 1996–2014. Sources: Levy and López-Calva 2016; figure created to include percentage of income, completed (Com) schooling (Primary [Prim], Junior High [JH], Senior High [SH]) and at least some university [Univ]). Source: Labor earnings, misallocation, and the returns to education in Mexico, IDB Working Paper Series No. IDB-WP-671, IDB, https://publications.iadb.org/publications/english/document/Labor-Earnings-Misallocation-and-the-Returns-to-Education-in-Mexico.pdf; figure reformatted for "Will More Education Increase Growth in Mexica," Report for Brookings Global/Ceres Economic and Social Policy in Latin America Initiative, www.brookings.edu/research/will-more-education-increase-growth-in-mexico/.

in the labor market nor in school, double the average for comparison OECD countries (Guthrie et al. 2018).

The region has a severe shortage of high school spaces, and the pathway to college is opaque for most students and their parents whose education ended long before college. For example, in Baja California in 2017, twelve thousand students found themselves without the possibility of attending a public high school because there were no spaces left when they applied (Reyes 2017b). Students not familiar with the school system and the application and testing processes are the most likely to be left out. The Mexican government provides scholarships to private high schools, but many of these are inferior "pop-ups" that offer few hours of instruction and a weak curriculum (Reyes 2017b). Given the lack of viable options, many students simply end their educations before completing high school.

With respect to higher education, 35 percent of 18- to 22-year-olds in Baja California who seek admission to college are unable to find a space in the public system (Reyes 2017a). Thus, while it is important to stimulate students' interest in furthering their education, very real barriers exist for even the convinced. Only 17 percent of Mexicans between the ages of

25 and 64 had attained a college degree (*licenciatura*) by 2016 (Barshay 2018). Moreover, at the master's and doctorate levels by far the highest completion rates occur in the social sciences and education.[1] Local universities are producing very few workers trained at the graduate level in science, math, or business. But there are excellent schools in other parts of Mexico that do such training at a very high level. If the Mexican side of LASANTI is to be much more richly integrated into the region's economy, the US institutions could help greatly with the development of serious training programs for promising young workers. Even modest steps in expanding top-level higher education could produce large changes in cross-border relations and joint possibilities for the future.

At the primary and middle school levels, recent reforms have been passed in the congress to streamline the matriculation of students coming from outside the country, principally "returnees." Mexican primary and secondary (middle) schools are now required to accept students as they present themselves with or without paperwork. However, reports continue that this is not always respected or perhaps even known in some parts of the country (Jacobo and Jensen 2018). Many problems continue to exist with respect to integrating the students we share into the Mexican school system. Teachers often fail to notice that these students are "behind" because they have not yet learned to read and write in Spanish or they have been in a different school system with different expectations and different curricula. The US-educated students, who generally appear to be Mexican, may be evaluated by teachers as being learning disabled or delayed when in fact their problem is one of language acquisition. Mexican teachers are not trained to address these students' needs and often even feel resentment at having to deal with them at all. Mexico does not provide Spanish as a second language classes for immigrants or orientation programs such as newcomer programs, as the large number of new immigrants without strong Spanish skills is a relatively new phenomenon. Thus it is extremely challenging to new arrivals to adapt to a new curriculum and a new set of expectations while simultaneously acquiring reading and writing skills in Spanish and trying to keep up with their Mexican-educated classmates.

EDUCATIONAL CHALLENGES ON THE CALIFORNIA SIDE

While there are clear differences in remuneration in Southern California according to level of education completed, wages have actually been

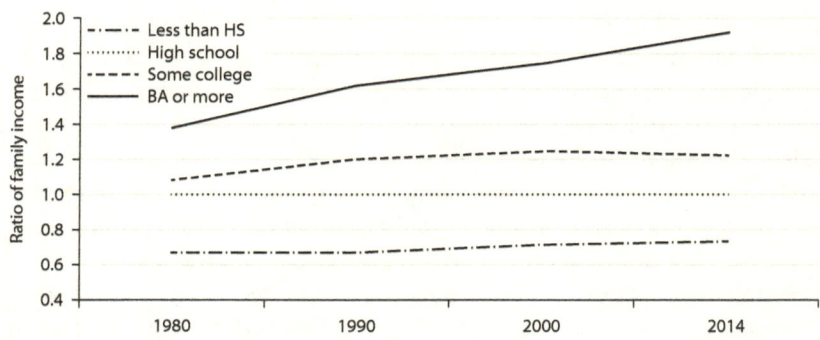

FIGURE 6.3. Increasing Income Gap by Education Levels, Southern California Family Ratio of Income by Level of Education, 1980–2014. Source: Authors' computations based on US Census, American Community Survey (ACS), 2016.

pretty flat for several decades, which means that real buying power has gone down. Social mobility is accessed only through the completion of higher education. **Figure 6.3** shows the relationship of average family income to level of education completed over the past two and a half decades. Income has grown very little over the entire period for all levels of schooling completed except college degrees. This is consistent with the growing inequalities in US society, with economic advantages accruing almost exclusively to better-educated individuals.

California assesses its students annually on both English Language Arts and Mathematics in grades 3–8 and 11. For example, in 2017, 57 percent of Euro-American fourth-graders were able to meet or exceed the state's standard for mathematics achievement at that grade level, 74 percent of Asian students met or exceeded the standard, but only 29 percent of Latino students were able to perform at this level. In the eighth grade, just before entering high school, almost 52 percent of white students met or exceeded the standard, compared to 73 percent of Asians and only 23 percent of Latinos (California Department of Education 2017). Thus Latino students in California enter high school with vastly different preparation from their white and Asian counterparts. This results in substantial differences in persistence to graduation, with 87 percent of white students, 94 percent of Asians, and 80 percent of Latinos graduating four years later. In other words, 1 in 5 Latino students do not graduate with their class, and of these only 42 percent graduate with the required courses to enter a four-year college or university. Almost 55 percent of white students complete these courses, as do 76 percent of Asians. All along the pipeline from high school to college, fewer and fewer Latino students are prepared to enter and succeed in college. In 2016, while 64 percent of Asians and 47 percent of whites had completed at least a BA degree in the California LASANTI region, only 15 percent of Latinos had done so by age 29.[2] Given the predominance of the Latino population in this region, these statistics are reason for alarm. California economists now project that the state is going to be well over a million college graduates short of what the future labor market is projected to need within the next decade (Bohn and Cuellar Mejia 2017), and since Latinos are the majority of the state's and the region's students, this creates a major misalignment of human resource supply and economic demand.

California's economic strength was built on huge educational gains for earlier groups of white baby boomers that reaped the benefits of a strong postwar economy invested in building a world-class education system. But the state's investments in education have dwindled since that time, and there has been a poor record for Latinos, mostly of Mexican origin, who are inheriting the region. In this rich and successful region, California has, by some accounts, an extremely high level of poverty and dangerous polarization due in good part to the undereducation of the Mexican-origin population (Shellenberger 2018).

UNIVERSITY OF CALIFORNIA–MEXICO INITIATIVE

Janet Napolitano, president of the University of California (UC) System, launched the **University of California–Mexico Initiative** in 2014 in response to her surprise that in a state with such a huge percentage of students of Mexican origin there was no systemwide initiative to coordinate research and researchers in California and Mexico and to push for a broader policy agenda with Mexico. At that time there was not even a master list of persons within the UC System who were engaged in research in or with Mexico. Napolitano asked Kim Wilcox, chancellor of the Riverside campus, to oversee the initiative. The initiative launched with five working groups, which could later be modified but which appeared to have the greatest head start on moving Napolitano's agenda to heighten the visibility and importance of broad alliances between Mexico, Mexican universities, and the UC System. Over time the focus shifted to energy, health, and education, as these areas were the most active. Included in the mission statement of the University of California–Mexico Initiative (2014) is the mandate to "inform public policy [and] address issues of common interest," in addition to academic collaborations. That is, the mission is broad and the vision is to connect not just at an academic level but with civil society as well.

The Education group immediately identified the issue of students we share as our focus because of work that the Civil Rights Project at UCLA had been immersed in.[3] We were aware of the urgent need to foster greater cooperation between Mexico and California regarding US-born, Mexican-origin students who were falling through the cracks on both sides of the border and putting both nations' economies at risk. We identified academic and governmental colleagues who were anxious to partner with us on these issues, and we also identified the natural partnership with the U.S.-Mexican Studies Center at UC, San Diego (UCSD). The UCSD Center connected the Education group to its many colleagues at the Universidad Autónoma de Baja California (UABC) and El Colegio de la Frontera Norte (COLEF), and both readily pledged resources to begin work on Students We Share. The first goals were (1) to establish relationships with academics from both countries who were doing scholarly work in the area of binational education and students we share, as well as with policy makers from both sides and media representatives who could promote the work; (2) to collect data about the students at the California-Baja border that could inform our broader research agenda (which would also require establishing strong relationships with the public schools on both sides of the border); (3) to create a conference that would bring all of these entities together in the same place to hear from one another; and (4) once having identified key areas of opportunity, begin doing the applied research that would allow us to launch pilot projects in the border region. Given our limited resources and to sharpen our focus, it made most sense to work in our California-Mexico border area. Between 2014 and 2018, the Education group undertook to accomplish each of these goals.

ESTABLISHING RELATIONSHIPS: STUDENTS WE SHARE

A primary means of developing deep relationships between UC and sister institutions in Mexico was a conference on the students we share in Mexico City in 2016. The proposal was met with enthusiasm and support from the Colegio de Mexico, the Centro de Estudios Superiores en Antropología Social (CIESAS), the Centro de Investigación y Docencia Económicas (CIDE), and the Universidad Nacional Autónoma de México (UNAM), as well as the US embassy and the Secretaría de Relaciones Exteriores (SRE), the Instituto de Mexicanos en el Extranjero (IME), and the Secretaría de Educación Pública (SEP). Key legislators from both California and Mexico also agreed to take part. The year long planning formed the basis for ongoing collaborations among the academics and with policy makers and laid the groundwork for a summit between key researchers and the Secretariat of Education and the Superintendent of Public Instruction and their teams in Mexico City in June 2017. These meetings then culminated in hearings in both the Mexican and California legislatures and the signing of the historic Memorandum of Understanding (MoU) to continue collaborative work among the University of California, the Mexican Secretariat of Education and the California Superintendent of Public Instruction on May 8, 2018.

DATA COLLECTION ON THE STUDENTS WE SHARE

During 2015, the Education group built relationships with school districts in the border area of California to allow us to conduct surveys of high school students. Our goal was to know more about what these students understood about opportunity and its connection to education. The San Diego Unified School District and the Sweetwater High School District both agreed to cooperate with data collection, as did the public and private schools of Tijuana. In all, data were collected on approximately 6,500 high school students on both sides of the border. In Tijuana, the 2016 survey consisted of a representative sample of about 3,000 ninth- and tenth-grade students in the public and private schools in the city.[4] The survey showed that 87 percent of students thought that schooling was "necessary for success in the future" and 93 percent recognized that schoolwork "matters for success in the workforce." Only 3 percent thought that they would not finish high school, but this was clearly overly optimistic given that almost half do not.

As is true in many such surveys in the United States, the Tijuana students reported much higher expectations for their level of educational attainment than were being achieved in their society: only 10 percent said a college degree was enough, and most wanted a graduate or professional degree, including 17 percent who expected to be lawyers. Only 40 percent expressed strong confidence about "finding a good job when I finish my studies," but the vast majority of the remainder was hopeful. Eighty-four percent said that their parents wanted them to study for a technical career, and 94 percent said that their parents wanted them to go to a university. Almost a quarter (23 percent) said that they would try to go to a university in the United States, and another 32 percent said they were interested but did not know how to apply.

A total of 91 percent of students agreed that it was "important to finish university to get a good job," but almost two-thirds of students (64 percent) saw cost as the most serious barrier to their hopes. Among the latter, 23 percent cited transportation, 26 percent cited academic qualifications, and 18 percent cited the lack of information about higher education. Interestingly, only 13 percent said that they knew how to apply to college and 66 percent said "more or less," which any teacher knows actually means very little. Students often do not know what they do not know. More than half the students said that their "parents have to make big sacrifices so that I can study." These representative data basically show extremely high levels of aspiration, wide recognition that higher education is a critical asset for future prospects, and great optimism but serious life obstacles and lack of critical information.

Similar numbers of high school students (approximately 3,500) were surveyed on the US side of the border, and many of the findings were the same, with students' aspirations outpacing likely reality and a lack of understanding of exactly how to get from high school to college and how to create a career path for themselves. The primary difference we saw between the two groups was the greater poverty and fewer resources of the students on the Tijuana side. Among both groups, although aspirations are high, they lack the tools to realize their dreams.

DEMONSTRATION PROJECTS

Again, unlike most academic research, the Education group took very seriously the initiative's mission to use research to "address issues of common interest." That meant linking the findings of the student surveys and other research being done by colleagues as well as ourselves to see if we could introduce research-based pilot projects. To date there are six.

(1) Project SOL (Secondary Online Learning). This pilot project attempts to respond to the problem that students we share have gaining access to key college prep courses in a language that for them is not strong. It is a project to test the viability of developing

and then providing, free of charge, bilingual, binationally accredited, online math and science courses that incorporate content required for college prep in both Mexico and California.

(2) The "Formadores" Project. This pilot project addresses the problem that students on both sides of the border are unlikely to have bilingual teachers who can support them linguistically and that teachers do not understand the challenges of students who find themselves on the other side of the border. The project brings together teacher trainers from Baja California with teacher preparation faculty at San Diego universities to jointly create and pilot a binational, bilingual curriculum to prepare teachers for the students we share.

(3) The Seal of Biliteracy. This is an idea that has captured the imagination of educators across the United States. Currently thirty-three states and the District of Columbia offer the seal to their graduating seniors who can demonstrate competency (reading, writing, speaking, and understanding) in two or more languages, including English (SealofBiliteracy.org). The Seal of Biliteracy will be implemented in Tijuana for a group of 1,250 students in *secundaria* (secondary schools), along with support for teachers to increase their English competency, in part using bilingual *retornados* (returnees). The objective is to strengthen and reward the English skills of the students we share

(4) The Near-Peer Mentoring Project. One of the things uncovered in the surveys that were conducted with high school (*secundaria* and *preparatoria*) students was that there is almost no college counseling available to students in Baja, which has a system of higher education that can be even more complicated than in the United States. The Center for U.S.-Mexican Studies (USMEX) is launching a near-peer mentoring pilot training and sending twenty undergraduate students from UABC who need to meet their service requirements to seven *preparatorias* in the Baja schools to help explain higher education to the students and to support them in preparing for college and university matriculation.

(5) Cross-Border Business Pathway—San Diego High School. USMEX is supporting San Diego High School in the launch of the Cross-Border Business Pathway. The pathway began in fall 2018 with a group of sixty students. It leverages the University of California

Curriculum Integration (UCCI) curriculum (see http://ucci.ucop.edu/) and will include collaboration with San Diego community colleges for students to earn a translation certificate. UCSD's Center for U.S.-Mexican Studies will help facilitate work-based learning opportunities and curriculum development.

CONCLUSION

LASANTI has a reservoir of human capital in the form of skills, understandings, and institutions to make cross-border contacts work. It has produced thousands of jobs and fostered intense development, but the social and economic mobility it has produced has been extremely limited, and inequalities are becoming increasingly acute. The region has yet to reach the next stage of development. The primary weakness that distinguishes it from other world metropolises and the primary impediment to its further development is its failure to create the capacity for higher educational attainment. This is especially the case with respect to completion of high school and college education, particularly in STEM (Science, Technology, Engineering & Math) areas in Tijuana. In Southern California, high school completion is at an all-time high, but college completion is extraordinarily low, especially for the Latino population that forms the majority of the youth of the region. Protecting the region's DACA students would be one important step as we now have clear evidence that offering DACA protections does foster greater college matriculation among undocumented students (Wong et al. 2017). Currently, the region is squandering its most critical resource and lacking a clear vision for its future. The priority in the immediate future must be to get more Baja students through high school and college and many more California Latinos into and graduated from college. We can do this, but it will require a shared vision for the region and a strong collaboration across the California-Baja border. Nowhere is it more critical to tear down walls and build bridges.

Suggested Reading

Edsource. 2017. Understanding DACA and education in California: A quick guide. Available at https://edsource.org/2017/understanding-daca-and-education-in-california-a-quick-guide/586829.

Floca, M., A. B. Mungary, and M. Matus. 2020. Educational challenges and opportunities facing binational youth in San Diego and Tijuana. *Journal of Borderlands Studies*, June 4. DOI:10.1080/08865655.2020.1768883.

Gándara, P. 2016. Policy report: The students we share. *Mexican Studies / Estudios Mexicanos* 32: 357–78. DOI:10.1525/mex.2016.32.2.357.

Hamann, E.T., and V. Zúñiga. 2011. Schooling and the everyday ruptures transnational children encounter in the United States and Mexico. In C. Coe, R. Reynolds, D. Boehm, J. Meredith Hess, and H. Rae-Espinoza, eds., *Everyday Ruptures: Children, Youth, and Migration in Global Perspective*, 141–60. Nashville, TN: Vanderbilt University Press.

White, G. 2017. U.S. ranks 23rd out of 30 developed nations for inequality. *The Atlantic*, January 16. Available at www.theatlantic.com/business/archive/2017/01/wef-davos-inequality/513185/.

CHAPTER 7

What Are the Policy Implications of Declining Unauthorized Immigration from Mexico?

PIA M. ORRENIUS AND MADELINE ZAVODNY

Policy makers and the public are again focusing considerable attention on unauthorized immigration, perhaps because some believe that the large presence of unauthorized immigrants in the United States creates adverse economic and fiscal effects. Most unauthorized immigrants are from poorer countries where they earn much less than they can earn working illegally in the United States. The number of unauthorized immigrants from Mexico present in the United States is more than ten times larger than the number from any other country (National Research Council 2013), which is not surprising given that a worker can earn $10 a day at home or cross the border into the United States and earn that much per hour.[1] Nonetheless, the number of unauthorized Mexican immigrants working in the United States has, if anything, been on a downward trajectory since about 2006. This chapter investigates the causes and policy implications of that decline.

We first estimate the size of the inflows of unauthorized workers from Mexico and then examine the determinants of those inflows. About 11 million unauthorized immigrants were present in the United

This chapter is a revised and shortened version of Center for Global Development Working Paper 436. We thank Unal Unsal and Alex Abraham for research assistance and Michael Clemens for helpful comments on an earlier version. Zavodny thanks the Center for Global Development for financial support. The views expressed here are those of the authors and do not reflect those of the Federal Reserve Bank of Dallas or the Federal Reserve System.

States in 2016, about half of them—some 5.6 million—from Mexico, a share that has fallen in recent years.[2] Our estimates suggest that annual inflows of unauthorized Mexican workers are the lowest they have been in decades and are unlikely to rebound. Nevertheless, US labor demand is growing. The policy implications point to creating a broad temporary worker program that would allow for low-skilled employment-based immigration as well as incorporate unauthorized workers already present in the country.

ESTIMATING THE NUMBER OF UNAUTHORIZED IMMIGRANT WORKERS

It is challenging to measure the stock and flow of unauthorized workers from Mexico. Unauthorized immigrants are a difficult population to count since they either successfully evade detection when they enter the United States or, if they enter legally, fail to leave when their visa expires.

This chapter presents new estimates of the gross inflow of unauthorized workers from Mexico. Widely cited estimates of the stock of unauthorized immigrants from Mexico are available from the Pew Research Center and the Department of Homeland Security, but we are not aware of other estimates of the gross inflow of unauthorized workers from Mexico. Knowing the gross inflow of unauthorized workers is important for analyzing US employers' unmet demand for domestic labor as well as for crafting immigration enforcement policy.

We use three methods to estimate the inflow of unauthorized immigrant workers from Mexico. The first method involves predicting the legal status of new Mexican immigrant workers in two large-scale US Census Bureau surveys, the Current Population Survey (CPS) and the American Community Survey (ACS), that include questions about migration and labor market behavior but not about legal status.[3] We predict Mexican-born workers' legal status based on another survey that does ask about legal status: the 2008 Survey of Income and Program Participation (SIPP). The second method counts the number of new immigrant workers from Mexico in the CPS and ACS and subtracts an estimate of the number of such workers coming legally. The third method involves creating simple rules of thumb that help screen out legal migrants from Mexico based on factors like education, occupation, veteran status, and government benefit receipt.[4] While the last two methods are fairly widely used, for example, by the Pew Research

Center and the economist George Borjas (2017), the first method is an innovative approach that merits wider use.[5]

RECENT TRENDS IN UNAUTHORIZED IMMIGRATION FROM MEXICO

Before introducing our estimates of new unauthorized workers, which are flow measures, we present baseline estimates of the total number of unauthorized workers from Mexico, a stock measure (**figure 7.1**).[6] There are about 3.2 million unauthorized workers from Mexico in 2014, according to our estimates. This number is down from its peak of 4 million in 2007. As shown in figure 7.1, the number generally rose during the late 1990s and early 2000s and then fell after 2007. The number failed to rebound even as the US economic recovery accelerated after 2010. The pattern in the figure is consistent with other estimates of unauthorized migration from Mexico.[7]

The decline in the number of unauthorized workers from Mexico since 2007 is due to several factors. The first is changes in economic conditions. The Great Recession of 2007–9 and subsequent slow economic recovery in the United States weakened the jobs magnet. The recession began with a widespread collapse of the US residential construction sector, which hit Mexican migrant workers particularly hard (Orrenius and Zavodny 2009). Meanwhile, the downturn was sharp but short-lived in Mexico, and the recovery there was stronger because there was no housing bust like that in the United States. In addition, the dramatic drop in the birthrate in Mexico a generation ago has led to a smaller cohort of potential immigrants (Hanson and McIntosh 2009).

Changes in US immigration enforcement contributed to the drop. Increases in border enforcement during the 1980s and early 1990s largely shifted *where* immigrants crossed the border, not *whether* they crossed. But by the mid-2000s, the border became difficult and expensive to cross, reducing the number of entries (Orrenius 2014). In addition, deportations increased and some states adopted laws that made it more difficult for unauthorized immigrants to live and work there (e.g., Bohn, Lofstrom, and Raphael 2014; Orrenius and Zavodny 2016).

Figure 7.2 presents our estimates of new unauthorized Mexican workers.[8] These estimates are gross, not net, inflows and therefore are not the change in the stock of unauthorized workers shown in figure 7.1. Nonetheless, a pattern similar to the changes in figure 7.1 emerges in figure 7.2: the number of new unauthorized Mexican workers was high

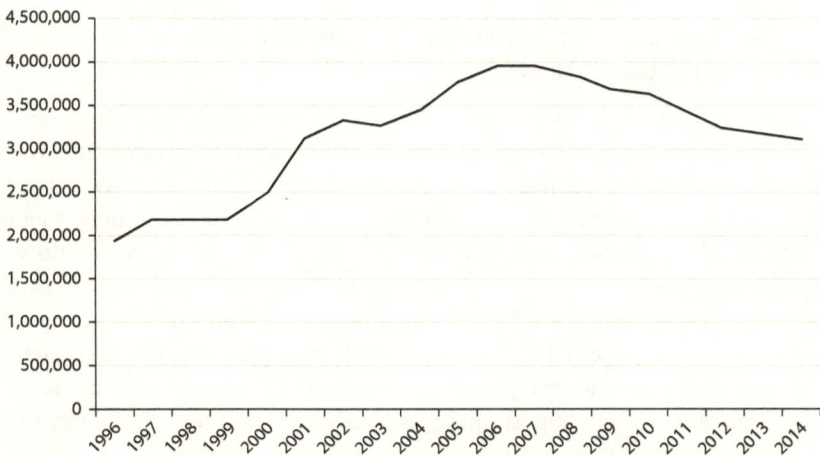

FIGURE 7.1. Estimated Number of Unauthorized Mexican Immigrant Workers. Sources: Current Population Survey (CPS); American Community Survey (ACS); authors' calculations.

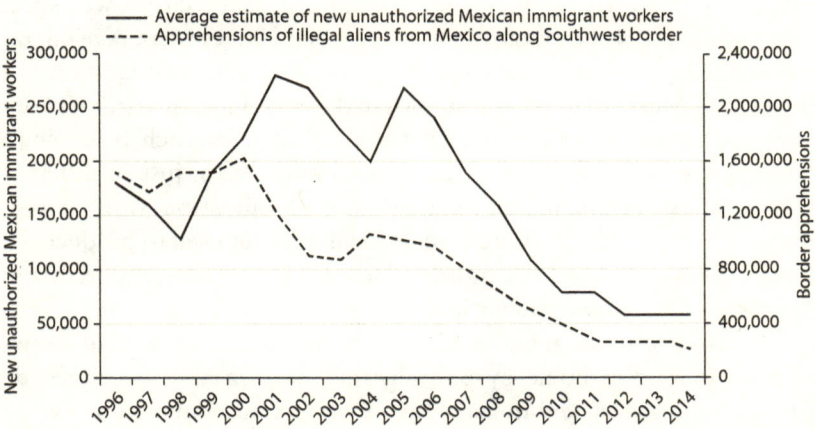

FIGURE 7.2. Comparison of New Unauthorized Mexican Immigrant Workers and Border Apprehensions. Sources: Current Population Survey (CPS); American Community Survey (ACS); US Border Patrol; authors' calculations.

and often rising during the late 1990s and early 2000s, and it began falling after 2006. To gauge how well our estimates capture inflows, we compare them in the figure with apprehensions of illicit border crossers from Mexico.[9] The two measures show similar trends, particularly after 2000.

DETERMINANTS OF UNAUTHORIZED WORKER INFLOWS FROM MEXICO

Figures 7.1 and 7.2 indicate that inflows are cyclical, but which economic variables should experts turn to if they want to predict inflows? Do Mexican or US economic conditions matter more? To answer these questions, we estimate time series regressions in which the dependent variable is the average of our three methods of estimating gross inflows (as plotted above in figure 7.2). **Regressions** are statistical models that allow us to estimate the effect of explanatory variables on the outcome of interest, migration in this case. **Table 7.1** presents the estimated effects (coefficients); we report three different specifications because of concerns about the short time series and some collinearity among the measures of economic conditions.

We measure US economic conditions using the real average wage, construction permits, and total employment; we measure Mexican economic conditions using the real average wage and total employment.[10] We include construction permits for the United States because of the large number of unauthorized immigrants working in that sector.[11] We expect that higher wages and employment in the United States encourage migration while higher wages and employment in Mexico deter migration.

We add Mexican exports to the United States and Canada.[12] Theory suggests migration and trade can be substitutes for each other since labor flows to the destination country in both cases, just in different forms (Borjas, Freeman, and Katz 1997). With migration, workers represent the labor transfer. With trade, the labor input used to produce the traded good represents the transfer. Hence, more trade—exports from Mexico—should lower migration.

We also add remittances to Mexico. Remittances are familial monetary transfers sent home by out-migrants, as measured by Banco de México, and are in real dollars. Remittances could have a positive or negative effect on migration, although when controlling for wages in both countries remittances should probably have a negative effect on migration since this additional income reduces the incentive to migrate for work. Moreover, remittances raise spending in origin communities, which boosts economic activity. If remittances are sizable enough, they will result in job creation and possibly higher wages.

All economic variables are logged. The measures of economic conditions are lagged one year in order to use information that migrants should have in hand.[13]

TABLE 7.1 DETERMINANTS OF MEXICO-US UNAUTHORIZED WORKER MIGRATION

Independent Variable	(1)	(2)	(3)
US labor demand			
Wages	13.9***	—	8.1*
Employment	—	13.7*	12.8*
Mexican labor demand			
Wages	-3.1*	—	-4.5**
Employment	—	-4.0	-6.0*
Trade			
Mex exports to US & Canada	0.0	-0.6	-0.7
Remittances			
Familial transfers to Mexico	0.0	-0.4*	0.0
Labor supply			
US births 15–19 yrs prior	-16.7	27.3	-15.3*
Mexican births 15–19 yrs prior	20.9***	-0.2	16.5**
Border enforcement			
Number of Border Patrol agents	-1.1**	-1.5**	-2.9**

SOURCE: Authors' calculations; see text for details.

NOTE: Results shown are based on estimated coefficients from AR(1) regressions of unauthorized immigration of workers on labor market conditions, trade, remittances, border enforcement, and birth cohorts. All specifications include a time trend and its square; the third specification also includes construction permits (not shown). All variables are in natural logs, and economic variables are lagged one year. Asterisks denote statistical significance at the *0.1, **0.05, and ***0.01 levels. The time period spans 1996–2014 (18 observations).

The regressions also include US Border Patrol staffing along the Southwest border to control for the difficulty or cost of crossing the border and birth cohort size to control for labor supply shocks.[14] Cohort size is measured as the number of births fifteen to nineteen years ago in each country. The regressions also include a linear time trend and its square. Caution is warranted in interpreting the regression results given the short time series available. A time-series regression rule of thumb suggests that a minimum of thirty observations is required for standard distributional assumptions to hold.

REGRESSION RESULTS

The results in table 7.1 indicate that economic conditions in both the United States and Mexico significantly affect unauthorized worker inflows. Higher wages in the United States attract more unauthorized immigrant workers, with a 1 percent increase in the average real wage boosting average inflows by 8 to 14 percent, depending on the specification used. This is a very large sensitivity, presumably because average wages were flat or falling in the United States during much of the period that we examine. An increase in the average wage in Mexico reduces migration, with a 1 percent increase reducing outflows by 3 to 4 percent.

An increase in total employment in the United States also boosts inflows. A 1 percent increase in employment (about 1.4 million jobs on average during this time period) increases migration by 13 to 14 percent. Increases in total employment in Mexico reduce emigration. A 1 percent increase in employment there (about 460,000 jobs) leads to a 6 percent decline in migration.

We find that pull factors have a very large effect on migration. Pull factors may be more important than push factors during the period we examine since wage volatility has lessened considerably in Mexico over time. The economists Gordon Hanson and Antonio Spilimbergo (1999) note that economic conditions in Mexico as a push factor appear to have dominated US economic conditions as a pull factor during the period 1968–96, which is unusual in studies of migration behavior.

The results in table 7.1 show that increased border enforcement reduces the number of new unauthorized workers, as expected. Recent studies have linked tighter enforcement to higher smuggler fees, which act as a deterrent to illegal migration by making it less affordable (and more dangerous). A 1 percent increase in Border Patrol staffing, about 150 additional agents, leads to a 1 to 3 percent decline in gross worker inflows in our results.

A larger cohort of US teenagers reduces the number of new unauthorized workers from Mexico in the third specification. This negative relationship makes sense if US teens fill jobs that otherwise might be filled by unauthorized immigrants. Meanwhile, a larger cohort of Mexican teenagers boosts out-migration from there; their entry into the labor force may push down their relative wage, which raises the incentive to migrate.

The results in table 7.1 also show that the trade variable appears unrelated to migrant inflows, except in the third column, where the coefficient is negative and more precisely estimated than in columns 1 and 2. The coefficient on remittances, meanwhile, is small and not statistically significant, except in the second specification, which excludes wages.

We do not examine several other demographic variables that are likely to affect migration patterns, namely, average age and educational attainment. Rising average age and educational attainment in the United States have boosted the demand for low-skilled foreign-born workers.

Meanwhile, falling birthrates, rising average age, and increasing educational attainment in Mexico have reduced the supply of low-skilled workers from there. Our data, which cover only a nineteen-year period, are not ideal for examining demographic factors like age and education, which typically change slowly and smoothly.

POLICY CONSIDERATIONS

Unauthorized immigrants play a nontrivial role in the US economy, accounting for nearly 5 percent of the labor force. They play a particularly important role in agriculture, where they account for 16 percent of workers; in construction, where they account for 12 percent; and in the leisure and hospitality sector, where they account for 9 percent (Passel and Cohn 2015).[15] In many cases, unauthorized workers may not account for a large share of workers in a given industry or occupation, but a dynamic analysis will show that they account for a disproportionate share of job growth. Hence, curtailing unauthorized immigration without creating a legal means for employers to hire foreign workers creates economic strain on these sectors. Difficulty hiring in these cases can actually stall growth by either preventing normal operations or choking off investment. Prices go up and small, labor-intensive businesses such as roofing companies or fruit and vegetable farms can go out of business.

The good news is that we now know that enforcement can reduce illegal migration. The bad news is that this means policy makers have to come up with legal ways for workers to enter if they want to ensure adequate labor supply as the economy expands. Among the legal avenues that already exist, we have seen large increases in usage, such as a threefold increase in H2A farmworker visas just over the past decade (from 52,000 in 2007 to 162,000 in 2017).

Trade policy can also have repercussions for immigration. Restricting trade through tariffs and tougher trade agreements can backfire by creating greater impetus for unauthorized migration. Preliminary evidence here suggests that trade with Mexico reduces emigration to the United States, which is consistent with theory. With higher exports come greater production; the thriving auto and vehicle parts manufacturing industry in Mexico, for example, has attracted billions in **foreign direct investment (FDI)** (whereby a significant share of ownership in an enterprise is located in a foreign country) and employs over 800,000 workers. This economic development slows emigration by increasing economic opportunity at home.

Other policy proposals, such as taxing the remittances that unauthorized immigrants send home, would also have unintended consequences for potential migrants left behind. If they receive fewer transfers and are made worse off, they have greater incentives to migrate themselves.

WHAT WOULD A TEMPORARY WORKER PROGRAM LOOK LIKE?

Employment-based visa programs grant work permits to foreign workers and could be instrumental in channeling unauthorized immigration into legal streams and boosting the economic gains from immigration. However, they will work best if they adopt the features of unauthorized immigration that result in economic benefits. These would include automatically adjusting to changes in economic conditions in the United States and Mexico (or other source countries) that affect labor demand and supply. It would also mean allowing employers, not government bureaucracies, to choose the workers they want and allowing workers to easily move between jobs in the destination. Unauthorized immigrants are readily hired, which is attractive to many employers. A visa program that replicates this timeliness aspect will entice employers to use it instead of hiring unauthorized workers, particularly if coupled with work site enforcement, such as E-Verify. E-Verify enables employers to digitally check eligibility documents provided by workers against federal records.

Before bringing in new low-skilled workers legally, it makes sense to create ways for unauthorized immigrants already here to receive permission to work, either temporarily or permanently. Giving unauthorized immigrants legal status would likely boost their employment, particularly among women.

Concerns about the current H2 programs and the Bracero Program, which brought in over 200,000 Mexican farmworkers per year from 1942 to 1964, offer a number of additional lessons for a **temporary foreign worker program** to succeed. Under a temporary foreign worker program, employers typically sponsor foreign workers for stints in seasonal industries. However, workers are particularly vulnerable to abuse, and downward pressure on wages and working conditions is greater when workers are trapped with one employer, as is the case under current temporary foreign worker programs. Relatedly, it should not be cheaper for firms to bring in foreign workers than to hire similar American workers. Employers must pay market wages and payroll taxes, plus a visa fee. Temporary foreign workers need to be covered by employer-provided health insurance requirements and other labor standards on the same terms as other workers. Finally, a program should not withhold a portion of pay until workers return home or retire unless policy makers are confident that workers will be able to receive it when eligible. The US government should hold any such funds (often called "bonds" by economists), not employers or foreign governments.

A binational program with Mexico would be a logical pilot, but it would make sense to expand the program to other countries that are major sources of low-skilled immigrant workers. Ongoing instability in Central America combined with higher birthrates there than in Mexico mean that the region is likely to continue to comprise a sizable and growing share of unauthorized migrants in the United States.

CONCLUSION

The number of Mexican immigrants entering the United States has declined sharply in recent years. While it is too early to know if this marks a long-term secular trend or a temporary shift, several structural changes point to it being a permanent change. That said, there has been little convergence between US and Mexican wages in recent decades, so one of the fundamental drivers of migration remains in place (Gandolfi, Halliday, and Robertson 2015). On the other hand, Mexico's exports have grown rapidly while its population growth has slowed and its cohort of young workers ages fifteen to twenty-four is currently peaking and will soon begin to shrink. Partly as a result, other areas, particularly Central America, are growing sources of unauthorized immigrants (Massey, Durand, and Pren 2014). An employment-based visa program with only Mexico would reduce the number of unauthorized workers in the United States but would be unlikely to entirely eliminate unauthorized migration.

The end of the Bracero Program marked the beginning of large-scale unauthorized immigration from Mexico (Hanson 2006). For decades, US employers of less-skilled workers turned to unauthorized workers instead of relying on costly and complex visa programs. The difficulty of entering or staying *legally* in the United States became an important, if little understood, contributor to unauthorized immigration. However, when unauthorized immigration failed to bounce back after the Great Recession and employers were faced with difficulty hiring, use of the H2A agricultural and H2B nonagricultural visa programs rose. There is considerable scope for those programs to be made more attractive to employers and workers and a viable alternative to large-scale unauthorized immigration. Reducing unauthorized immigration without major dislocations to the US economy will require expanding existing visa programs or creating new ones. Doing so would bring several benefits, not least of all to immigrants, who would no longer risk their lives trying to cross the border and then be limited to living in the shadows in the United States. It would also benefit American consumers and producers. Even US workers could benefit since legally present foreign workers will ensure a level playing field. It is time for a new approach to immigration policy, beginning with a broad, inclusive employment-based visa program for Mexican workers.

Suggested Reading

Clemens, M., and N. Hashmi. 2016. Modernizing U.S. migration policy for domestic and development gains. Center for Global Development. Available at www.cgdev.org/sites/default/files/whw-migration.pdf.

Krogstad, J. M., J. S. Passel, and D. Cohn. 2017. 5 facts about illegal immigration in the U.S. Pew Research Center. Available at www.pewresearch.org/fact-tank/2017/04/27/5-facts-about-illegal-immigration-in-the-u-s/.

Massey, D. S., J. Durand, and K. A. Pren. 2014. Explaining undocumented migration to the U.S. *International Migration Review* 48: 1028–61.

Zavodny, M., and T. Jacoby. 2013. Filling the gap: Less-skilled immigration in a changing economy. Immigration Works and American Enterprise Institute. Available at www.aei.org/wp-content/uploads/2013/06/-zavodny-filling-the-gap-immigration-report_140631709214.pdf.

CHAPTER 8

How Does Mexican Migration Affect the US Labor Market?

FRANK D. BEAN, SUSAN K. BROWN, AND
JAMES D. BACHMEIER

Over the past several years, President Trump has repeatedly asked Congress to support building a wall along the US-Mexico border, claiming that Mexican migrants to the United States disproportionately commit crimes and harm native workers. Numerous rigorous research studies, however, demonstrate that such allegations are false or grossly exaggerated (National Academy of Sciences 2015, 2016). Since the end of World War II, economic and job growth in the United States has ranked among the highest in the world, especially in California (Bean, Brown, and Pullés 2018). This alone, taken at face value, implies that Mexican migrants and their descendants have not damaged the labor market of the United States. This chapter seeks to assess in more detail the extent to which this is true.

Our assessment begins with an introduction to common notions about labor market competition and an examination of less-skilled labor in particular. Many observers seem to assume that jobs are filled under conditions of fixed resources, with employers being unable to hire immigrant workers without discharging others. But hiring often takes place under dynamic versus static external conditions. Taking note of shifting trends in the various kinds of Mexican entrants, we assess changes in the numbers of Mexican migrants over the past several decades. Finally, this chapter explores the implications of some of the nation's broad demographic trends (e.g., educational upgrading, baby boom changes in the workforce population, and fertility decline) for increases in Mexican migration. In conclusion, we speculate about policy implications for the country.

JOB GROWTH COMPARED TO POPULATION GROWTH

For at least the past forty years, US economic and job growth has outstripped population growth to such a degree that it suggests that not much labor market competition between immigrants and natives has occurred. Since 1980, US population growth has almost always fallen below 1 percent per year, even when both newly arrived unauthorized and legal immigrants are included as constituent parts of such growth. And since 1990, population growth has even more notably fallen *below* this level, especially since 2000. Also, economic growth over the period was quite high. Until the Great Recession in 2008, the annual percentage change in gross domestic product (GDP) averaged more than 3 percent annually in the country overall (**figure 8.1**). Even including periods of recession, the past five decades have enjoyed average job growth substantially above the level needed to absorb population growth. For example, during the 1970s, economic growth generated more than 1.9 million new jobs per year, or about 50 percent *more* than the number that would be required just to absorb both the baby boomers (persons born in 1946–64) then coming of workforce age and the new immigrants that were increasingly arriving (Bean and Stevens 2003).

During the 1980s, job growth was almost as high, about 1.8 million new jobs per year, and during the 1990s, considerably higher still, averaging more than 2.1 million jobs per year (US Bureau of Labor Statistics 2018). In the 2000s, at least until 2008 and the onset of the Great Recession, the economy still only needed to add 1.3 million new jobs each year just to keep up with population expansion from both natural increase (any excess of births over deaths) and immigration. In fact, job growth surpassed that threshold by more than half a million new jobs per year (Bean et al. 2012). And since the end of the recession in 2010, a similar pattern has emerged, with rates of job growth again exceeding rates of population growth. Hence, it seems abundantly clear that during periods of normal economic growth, which comprise the vast majority of years since 1990 (Peri 2013), job growth has easily been enough to accommodate immigration growth. In sum, immigration did not come at the expense of native jobs and wages and substantial job competition would not have been likely in normal periods of economic growth.

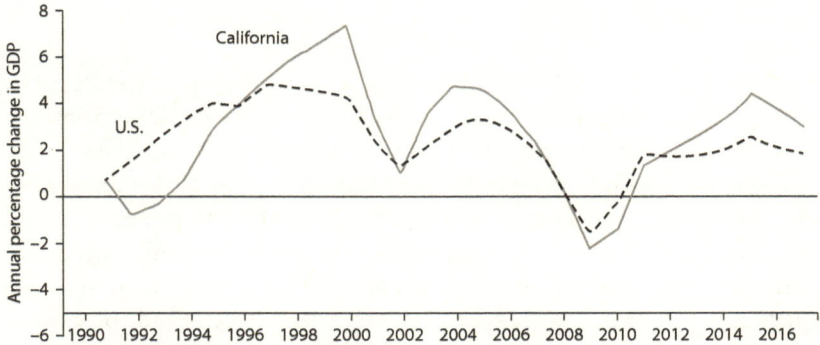

FIGURE 8.1. Annual Percent Change in GDP for the United States and California, 1990–2017, Two-Year Moving Average. Source: US Bureau of Labor Statistics 2018.

LABOR COMPETITION AND LESS-SKILLED WORKERS

Is this conclusion possibly different for natives with only high school degrees or less—**less-skilled workers**—or in periods of economic downturn? After all, the Great Recession hit such workers especially hard. By the end of 2009, the Great Recession had stripped the nation of more than 8.7 million jobs (US Bureau of Labor Statistics 2018), ravaging the labor market to a degree not seen since the Great Depression of the 1930s, particularly in the case of less-skilled workers. In April 2010, for example, the unemployment rate for the workforce *with only* a high school diploma or less was 14.6 percent, a rate more than triple that for college-educated workers (4.5 percent). For blacks, it was even higher—16.1 percent—and among Hispanics, a majority of whom were foreign born and Mexican, it was an unusually high 11.8 percent. Clearly, the brunt of the recession fell on blue-collar workers, while the jobs of higher-skilled workers were barely touched.

Although the United States may face a surplus of less-skilled immigrant labor during steep recessionary times, the idea that a relatively constant number of less-skilled jobs exists in the country in general reflects a **lump of labor fallacy.** This notion entails a zero-sum depiction of the labor market (Krugman 2003) that ignores additional jobs that immigrants inevitably generate (National Academy of Sciences 2016). Any new immigrant worker, through their own consumption, if nothing else, increases aggregate demand by at least a small amount. Moreover, the mere availability of new workers creates demand for some kinds of work. This is true especially for "luxury" services, such as providing manicures or landscaping or lawn maintenance services (Bean et al. 2012).

More broadly, immigration-induced job growth also results from immigrant labor reducing the cost of many goods and services to natives, boosting demand and production in the process and thus subsequent additional job growth (Cortes 2008). Moreover, to the extent that immigrant labor complements that of natives (i.e., that its presence makes some native workers more productive—through, for example, child care and elder care), less-skilled newcomers raise economic growth, fostering further job increases in this way as well (Peri 2013). And, of course, some work done by immigrants involves tasks that could probably be carried out with either presently available or new technology, especially in manufacturing and agriculture (Martin 2009)—jobs that might be eliminated without immigration.

This is not to deny that *some* less-skilled natives may lose their jobs owing to competition with newly arrived unauthorized immigrants. But it implies that these losses are offset by positive labor market effects, at least for natives. However, research does show that less-skilled immigrants exert some downward pressure on the employment and wage prospects of two categories of less-skilled workers in particular: (1) less-skilled immigrants and to a small degree (2) native high school dropouts (National Academy of Sciences 2016). Unauthorized migrants appear especially to make it more difficult for other unauthorized migrants to find jobs.

These broad trends suggest little job competition between immigrants and natives overall. Researchers generally agree that higher-skilled immigration benefits the economy (Fix, Papademetriou, and Sumption 2013) and that only negligible negative consequences occur for less-skilled workers (National Academy of Sciences 2016). The research that has explicitly focused on the labor market impacts of unauthorized Mexican migration, the flows of which have been both the most sizable and the least skilled among less-skilled labor migrants, found that such workers complement both native and legal immigrant workers (Bean, Lowell, and Taylor 1988). These results align with the research literature finding that less-skilled unauthorized workers seem *not* to compete much with other less-skilled workers (Hanson 2013).

Why, then, is there such confusion about the generally positive effects of immigration, and why does the debate over immigration's labor market impacts persist with such fervor? The United States does in fact need and benefit from less-skilled immigrant Mexican workers, but in difficult economic times not as many unauthorized immigrants may be needed as have arrived (with most of the negative effects falling on similar earlier arriving migrants). Because immigration's benefits are diffuse and not readily experienced, it is not easy for people to see how immigrant workers benefit native workers. As a result, some natives fall back on what they can see, which is often that more less-skilled immigrants, especially unauthorized migrants, may be coming to their communities than their communities need. They also worry about the local-level fiscal repercussions of such workers and their families. What is positive at the national level can sometimes be negative at the state and local governmental levels (National Academy of Sciences 2016), particularly during dire economic times when state and local tax revenues decline and the costs associated with schooling and health care continue.

TRENDS IN MEXICAN MIGRATION

What were the actual Mexican migration patterns that coincided with economic growth and the beginnings of declines in the less-skilled working-age population of the United States? Since 1990, the numbers of Mexican migrants arriving each year in the United States has increased. The yearly numbers of Mexicans becoming legal permanent residents (LPRs) steadily rose (**figure 8.2**), exceeding considerably those of the second-largest sending country (which varied over the period from the Philippines to India to China). In 2016, the flow of Mexican LPRs decreased, but it still was almost twice as high as that year's second-leading country (China). Today's levels of Mexican LPRs thus continue to dominate those from any other single national-origin country. A similar general trend has occurred involving the overall numbers of **temporary visitors,** which have risen over threefold, from about 6 million in 2007 to about 20 million in 2016 (**figure 8.3**). Most of these are *not* immigrants but rather students, tourists, businesspeople, exchange visitors, and temporary workers. Significantly, persons from Mexico have dominated the immigrant and temporary worker flows.

In the case of unauthorized migrants, the total number of such persons in the country seems to have slowed somewhat in recent years. Entries have apparently dropped and return migration to Mexico has actually increased, resulting in declining levels of annual net migration (consisting of comparable annual numbers of Mexican entrants and departures), with the result that the total number of unauthorized Mexicans in the country stabilized at around 6 million during the past

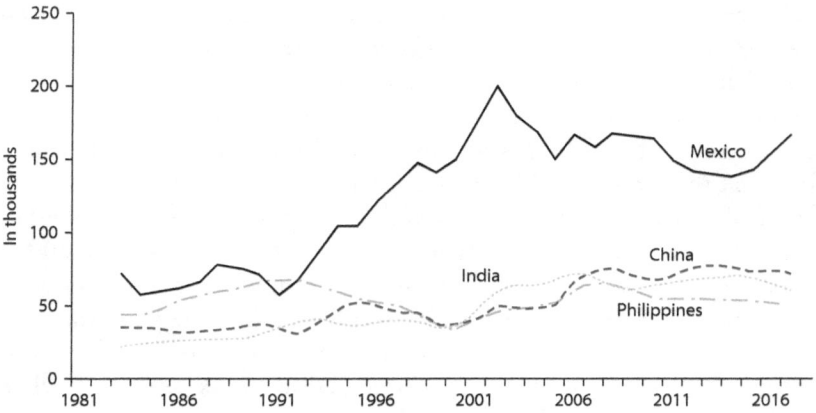

FIGURE 8.2. Legal Permanent Resident Migration from Mexico and the Countries of Next Largest Migration, 1981–2016 (in three-year moving averages). Source: US Department of Homeland Security, Office of Immigration Statistics.

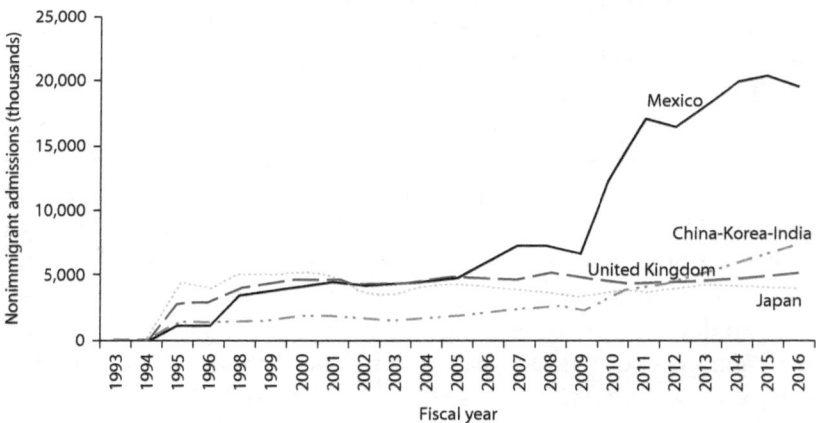

FIGURE 8.3. Nonimmigrant Admissions (I-94 only) from Mexico, Japan, the United Kingdom, and China/South Korea/Japan, 1993–2016. Source: US Department of Homeland Security, Office of Immigration Statistics.

few years (**figure 8.4**). In sum, nearly three in every five unauthorized immigrants here today are from Mexico, a fraction roughly similar to that of earlier decades (Passel and Cohn 2017). But it should be noted that increasing flows of Mexican *nonimmigrants* (temporary visitors and unauthorized migrants) raise the likelihood that the numbers of Mexican visa overstays may have risen both absolutely and relatively.

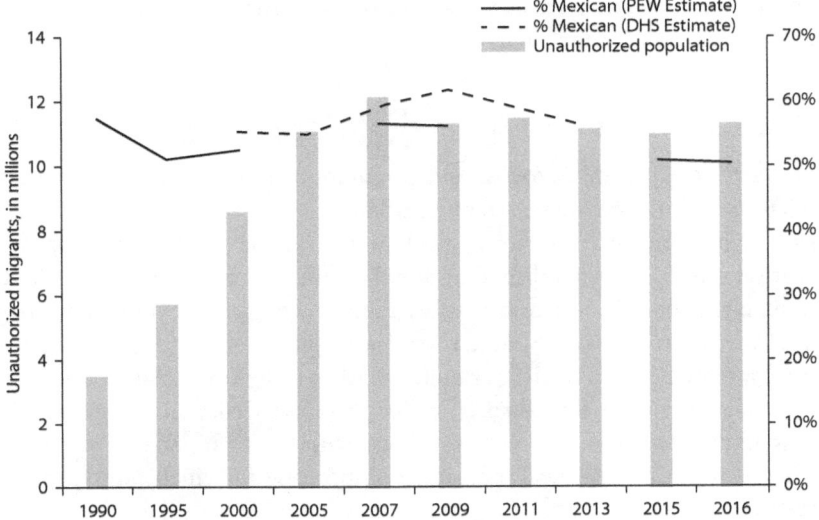

FIGURE 8.4. Number of Unauthorized Migrants in the United States and the Percentage of Mexican-Origin among Them, 1990–2016.

At the same time, the number of *temporary* legal Mexican workers has also climbed substantially. These workers are not included in statistics on total legal nonimmigrant admissions, which consist overwhelmingly of students and tourists. When we looked at the history of nonimmigrant admissions more closely, we noted that Mexican nonimmigrant admissions began to increase noticeably in the 1990s, coinciding with the high-tech economic boom. Tens of thousands of high-skilled temporary technology workers—H1B visas, for those workers with highly specialized expertise—began to arrive from India and China, as did larger numbers of less-skilled Mexican seasonal agricultural workers (H2A visas) and nonagricultural domestic workers (H2B visas). These latter categories of temporary Mexican workers reached levels in 2015 that were about ten times their 1970 levels. In sum, recent marginal migrant flows to the United States (those involving either unauthorized or temporary entrants and temporary workers) are sharply distinctive in two ways: their consistent rise and their overwhelming Mexican character. No other country has provided the US blue-collar workforce with so many laborers, especially labor migrants with unauthorized status. Because of this status, Mexican unauthorized migrants have disproportionately filled difficult, dirty, and sometimes dangerous jobs (Hall and Greenman 2015), a fact that underscores their exceptional contributions to the US economy.

IMMIGRATION REFORM

Other than economic growth and population decline discussed earlier, what explains these increases in Mexican migration? The steady rise in such migration since the late 1970s had its origins in the 1965 US immigration reforms that abolished national origins quotas, a policy that had limited effect on Eastern and Southern European, Asian, Middle Eastern, and African immigrants but did not impose quotas on Mexican immigration, largely because of the agricultural lobby. The Immigration Reform and Naturalization Act of 1965, called the Hart-Celler Act, changed all that and passed both houses of Congress with strong bipartisan support. This legislation involved a political compromise in which **immigration restrictionists** acceded to front-door policy modifications (i.e., changes in the criteria for legal immigration) in exchange for what was hoped would be less backdoor migration by putting a ceiling on western hemisphere entrants (Zolberg 2006). Combined with the end of the long-standing Bracero Program—the temporary worker program instituted in 1942 to combat labor shortages, particularly in agriculture, during World War II—the legislation spurred unauthorized Mexican migration.

After 1965, the cap of 120,000 Western Hemisphere—mostly Mexican—entrants, as well as a per-country limit of 20,000 visas, could not accommodate the demand for legal entrants, thus tending to generate unauthorized migration. For many Mexicans, especially circulatory labor migrants (those migrants who returned to Mexico at the end of the work season), the only option was to enter the country illegally since they could no longer do so as braceros. The Bracero Program, by providing employers with legal temporary agricultural workers, also raised demand among employers for such workers. This demand increased substantially as California agriculture expanded in the 1960s because of the completion of major irrigation projects. Not surprisingly, during the 1970s, the vast bulk of Mexican unauthorized migration to the United States took place in California.

Although the 1965 reforms and the end of the Bracero Program both created an impetus for Mexican unauthorized migration to increase, they do not fully explain why the numbers of unauthorized entrants as well as other nonimmigrant entrants rose. Nor do they account for an increasing rate of increase in the 1990s and up to 2007. Nor do they explain the persistence of nonimmigrant and temporary migrant increases after the Great Recession of 2008. Although the stock of unauthorized migrants stopped growing after 2007, undoubtedly in part because US housing construction did not recover appreciably until several years later, other kinds of less-skilled employment recovered quickly and other kinds of Mexican migration continued to increase. What explains this? Changes in the country's demography were leading to shrinkages in the native-born working-age population, especially among lesser-skilled natives, and this created new needs for Mexican migrant workers. These demographic factors are taken up next.

DEMOGRAPHIC FACTORS IN INCREASED MEXICAN MIGRATION

Increases in education—**educational upgrading**—began early in the twentieth century with the "high school completion" movement and continued after World War II with the expansion of public higher education, a benefit provided for veterans under the GI Bill. Although college attendance slowed in the 1990s and 2000s—only to rise again recently—the population with exposure to postsecondary schooling has steeply risen for most of the past six decades. Adults age 25 and over with *more* than a high school education now make up nearly 60 percent of the population, up from 5.3 percent in 1950 (Current Population Survey 2010; Minnesota Population Center 2011). The number of native-born Americans with a high school diploma or less has thus fallen in both relative and absolute terms. In 1950, more than 87 percent of US adults (25.7 million) never finished high school. By 2010, only 12.9 percent (80 million) did not finish high school. In short, by 2010, there were 68 percent *fewer* persons in the country without a high school diploma or its equivalent than in 1950 (Minnesota Population Center 2011; Current Population Survey 2010). Strikingly, this figure is for the *entire* adult population, which includes the substantial number of poorly educated immigrants who have come here over the past three decades.

From 1970 to 2015, the adult prime working-age segment (ages 25–64) of the US population grew on average by 1.77 million persons per year—an increase of 1.75 million persons per year (see **table 8.1**). This occurred in part because of the size of the **baby boom cohort** that moved into this age range and in part because of the arrival of new immigrants. Despite educational upgrading, the baby boom cohort was so big that the numbers of younger natives (ages 25–44) with only a high

TABLE 8.1 AVERAGE ANNUAL GROWTH OF US WORKING-AGE
POPULATION (25–64), 1970–2015, BY NATIVITY, SEX, AND EDUCATION

	Average Growth
Total	1.77
Native born	1.12
Foreign born	0.65
Males	0.90
Females	0.87
Native-born males	0.57
Native-born females	0.55
Foreign-born males	0.33
Foreign-born females	0.32
Native-born males, no college	0.00
Native-born males, college	0.57
Native-born females, no college	−0.18
Native-born females, college	0.73

school diploma or less also grew appreciably from 1970 until 1990. This growth was almost evenly divided between males and females (900,000 and 870,000, respectively, per year), and about two-thirds of the annual growth (1.12 million persons per year) took place in the native-born population. About one-third (650,000 per year) were in the foreign-born population. The strong expansion of the economy at that time more than absorbed the growth of the workforce. In broad outline, it is extremely unlikely that immigrants were taking jobs away from natives during the past four and a half decades. If anything, by 2015, the labor market had been needing immigrant workers for some time.

By 1980, when the earliest baby boomers started to move beyond age 45, the numbers of younger-age boomers (25–44) started to shrink. This tendency accelerated through the 1990s and 2000s as the numbers of older boomers leaving the workforce increased. In addition, once the baby boom ended in 1964, the fertility decline in the United States was sharp. By the mid-1970s, the total fertility rate had dropped by about half, reaching levels below 2.1, the point at which population nonreplacement starts to set in. The levels hovered for years in the 2.0 to 2.1 range (US Department of Health and Human Services 2010) before falling again during the 2008 recession. Thus, over time, there have been ever fewer natives to do the less-skilled work the expanding economy was generating.

Thus, demographic changes (educational upgrading, cohort change from the the aging of baby boomers, and lower fertility in the native-born population) have led to large declines in the pool of natives with only high school diplomas or less, the native-born group most likely to fill less-skilled jobs. From 1970 through 2015, the size of the native-born, less-skilled male working-age population did not increase. Its change was *zero*. That is, the number of non-college-educated native-born males ages 25 to 64 living in the United States in 2015 was the *same* as the number in 1970. This decline was more pronounced for less-skilled working-age women. There were fewer non-college-educated women in 2015 than there were in 1970. The less-skilled native workforce most likely to experience labor market competition from Mexican migrants (Bean, Brown, and Bachmeier 2015) actually *lost* about 5.5 million workers from 1990 to 2015. Thus, the native male workforce of this age range and skill level *shrank considerably more* than the immigrant workforce expanded.

In an economy that was rapidly expanding, especially during the 1990s and especially in agriculture in California, this left a void in the workforce. Immigrants, mostly from Mexico, filled that void. In 1970, there were few Mexican-born males in the workforce. But by 2015, the number of foreign-born, less-skilled persons had increased by 2.5 million, about two-thirds since 1990. This helps explain both the persistence of unauthorized Mexican migration and its growth since 1990. Mexican immigrant workers have increasingly filled the jobs that there were no longer enough native-born workers in the country to do. More and more of these immigrant workers were temporary or unauthorized because there were not enough alternative ways to enter the country legally.

CONCLUSION: FUTURE GROWTH AND INTEGRATION

A combination of immigration reform, which redefined the legal status of temporary workers in the United States, and demographic change led to increased Mexican migration generally and unauthorized migration in particular. The demographic factors with the most impact were (1) gains in education that resulted in smaller numbers of less-skilled natives; (2) declining native fertility rates that lowered the relative number of younger natives; and (3) baby boomers starting in 1990 to "age out" of the younger groups of lesser-skilled native workers, who were most likely to do manual labor and compete with immigrants. These changes led to large declines in the pool of younger US-born persons with only high school diplomas or less, the group of natives most likely to fill arduous, less-skilled jobs. These same dynamics seem likely to continue to contribute to a less-skilled workforce void through 2030. To fill this gap, a need for less-skilled migration will remain, especially if the economy and the job market continue to be robust across the next decade.

What is the likelihood that Mexican migrants will continue to fulfill this need? The annual flows of legal immigrants, unauthorized migrants, and nonimmigrants on temporary visas have all increased for quite some time. Unauthorized Mexican migration, which appeared to stabilize after 2008, upticked in the past couple of years (Passel and Cohn 2017) as strong job growth continued in the United States, reflecting now-recent gains in construction that had previously remained weak. The extent to which Mexican migrants will fill much of the future US workforce void remains an open question, but there are many reasons to think they will, not the least of which is the ever-strengthening US job market. In the past this factor has been the strongest magnet for such migration. Also, the increasingly insecure and often dangerous political situation in Mexico, which breeds ever more uncertainty, has also become a greater force for departure.

If Mexican migration were thus to continue, what would be the prospects for successful integration of the migrants and their descendants in the United States? Recent research results on this question have been somewhat mixed (National Academy of Sciences 2015). This results in part because of a sharp divide between those migrants and their offspring who have been able to legalize compared to those who have not. Studies of just the immigrant generation itself indicate that those who do not come legally or attain legalization fare badly. Given the enormous contributions that Mexican migrants have made to fill the less-skilled workforce needs of the United States since 1990 especially, it would make considerable sense for US immigrant integration policies to include pathways to legalization and citizenship for workers fulfilling this role. Both the immigrants and the United States would be better off for doing so.

Suggested Reading

Bean, F.D., S.K. Brown, and J.D. Bachmeier. 2015. *Parents without Papers: The Progress and Pitfalls of Mexican-American Integration.* New York: Russell Sage Foundation.

Castles, S., and M. Miller. 2009. *The Age of Migration: International Population Movements in the Modern World.* 4th ed. New York: Guilford Press.

Fix, M., D. G. Papademetriou, and M. Sumption, eds. 2013. *Immigrants in a Changing Labor Market: Responding to Economic Needs*. Washington, DC: Migration Policy Institute.

Martin, S. F. 2011. *A Nation of Immigrants*. New York: Cambridge University Press.

National Academy of Sciences. 2015. *The Integration of Immigrants into American Society*. Washington, DC: National Academies Press. DOI:10.17226/21746.

PART THREE

Trade Integration

CHAPTER 9

Before and after NAFTA

How Are Trade and Migration Policy Options Changing?

RAÚL HINOJOSA-OJEDA, SHERMAN ROBINSON, AND KAREN THIERFELDER

The North American integration of trade, migration, and remittance markets has undergone significant and intertwined transformations during the post–World War II era. The unequal juxtaposition of a high-income United States and a low-income Mexico has always contained the possibility for policies to leverage the potential for complementary regional economic integration and development. Achieving optimal migration and trade policy coordination for more productive and equitable development across North America, however, has proved to be an elusive goal. This chapter focuses on the impact that major changes in US immigration policy will have in the economic context of alternative post–North American Free Trade Agreement (NAFTA) reform or trade war scenarios.

We first review the long-term labor market and demographic transformations within and between the United States and Mexico over the post–World War II period. Second, we review the evolution of trade and migration policies during this period, focusing on the expansion of restrictive immigration enforcement policies since NAFTA and their acceleration in the Trump era. Third, using economy-wide simulation models, we measure the costs and benefits to the United States and Mexico arising from alternative NAFTA collapse and trade war scenarios or the implementation of the new United States-Mexico-Canada

The views expressed in this chapter are not those of the authors' respective institutions.

Agreement (USMCA). And finally, we compare these trade scenarios to the effects of highly restrictive and removal migration policy or the legalization and empowerment of 8 million undocumented workers in the US labor force and their remittance flows.

AN EMPIRICAL FRAMEWORK FOR US-MEXICO MIGRATION POLICIES

Over seventy-five years of deepening economic ties after World War II, US policies have shifted from an early period of relatively high trade protection and openness to migration to a period, beginning in the late 1980s and accelerating with NAFTA, characterized by increasingly liberal cross-border trade policies accompanied by more restrictive immigration policies and border barriers.[1] The renegotiation of NAFTA into the USMCA and the continued threats of tariff wars by the Trump administration have reversed the past thirty years of increasing North American **trade liberalization**,[2] which sought to remove or reduce barriers (e.g., tariffs or duties or licensing rules). In addition, the Trump administration has initiated aggressive changes in immigration policy, tightening restrictions on new immigrants, increasing border security, and threatening the use of mass deportation and seizing of remittances. This anti-integration mix of policies has the potential to severely disrupt the US and Mexican economies. At the same time, however, the potential legalization and empowerment of migration and remittances (money sent home to family by out-migrants) with sustainable regional **trade integration** has the potential for significantly enhancing economic growth and well-being in both countries.

To explore the economic impacts of alternative policy options in US-Mexico trade and migration, we developed economy-wide simulation models of the United States and Mexico. These simulation models incorporate the direct and indirect linked impacts of trade and migration policies on gross domestic product (GDP). They also incorporate the effects of trade, migration, and remittance flows on the various US and Mexico national household categories. The analysis utilizes a multicountry, multisector computable general equilibrium (CGE) model, called the **GLOBE model**.[3] This type of model is used widely for analysis of the implications of changes in trade policy. For the US CGE model, we add undocumented labor in ten different occupation categories and provide an empirical framework for analysis of further restricting or legalizing regional labor migration. We specify the effects of alternative policy scenarios for restricting or liberalizing trade and migration flows, comparing the direct and indirect effects on GDP, income, and cross-border exchange. The analysis reaffirms what some researchers predicted during the original NAFTA negotiations, namely, that the impacts of significant changes in the labor force arising from changes in immigration policy are potentially much larger than impacts arising from alternative scenarios in trade policy (Robinson et al. 1991; Bustamante, Reynolds, and Hinojosa-Ojeda 1992).

Current draconian immigration policy scenarios combined with possible anti-integration trade confrontations compound negative impacts, potentially creating a worst-case scenario that will significantly hurt economic development across the North American region.

The current turn to restrictive trade and immigration policies is occurring as the long arc of Mexican net out-migration has passed it peak.[4] The irony is that the process of regional integration and structural change in the Mexican economy coupled with demographic changes have reduced the potential supply of migrants to the United States just as we see a reduction of major employment dislocations due to earlier phases of regional trade integration. The major result for North America in the current era is that trade and supply chain integration has significantly matured just as net out-migration from Mexico has rapidly dropped in the past ten years and is currently negative just as US labor demand is rapidly growing (Gonzalez-Barrera 2015). The potential gains from complementary prodevelopment trade and migration legalization policies are stronger than ever. Such a coordinated policy program is possible and well worth pursuing, while the costs of the current anti-integration trade and immigration policies are now being realized as extremely destructive.

Our previous economic modeling was among the first to hypothesize, in 1991, that during Mexico's "demographic hump"[5] an immediate rapid liberalization of Mexican agriculture could have the consequence of accelerating out-migration in the absence of a major development effort directed to Mexican rural areas. This research was used to create the North American Development Bank (NADBank) and to support a fifteen-year tariff-elimination schedule for Mexican corn and agriculture negotiated under NAFTA. This is particularly important because corn is Mexico's main agricultural crop and a staple in the Mexican diet. The gradual tariff elimination was designed to allow time for this rural-to-urban structural and demographic transition to work itself out.[6] Our earlier modeling also supported the idea that comprehensive immigration reform that would legalize the flow of mutually beneficial circular migration and generate remittance income for Mexico would raise GDP and wages on both sides of the border (Hinojosa-Ojeda, Lewis, and Robinson 1995; Hinojosa-Ojeda 2010, 2011).

ECONOMIC DEVELOPMENT AND INTEGRATION: TRADE AND LABOR MIGRATION

The North American integration of commodity and labor markets has undergone two major and interrelated transformations during the post–World War II era. The first was the shift from nationally oriented commodity production and consumption within both countries to a much more liberalized cross-border production and market sharing pattern of regional interdependence in North America that began to emerge in the 1980s and continued with NAFTA. The integration of commodity production and consumption across borders has accelerated since NAFTA began in 1994, particularly through the expansion of **value chains** (also called **supply chains**), where various stages of the production process (e.g., design, parts and components production, assembly, packaging, sales, distribution) are dispersed among different countries, depending on where each stage can be performed at the lowest cost or under optimal conditions. As one example, value chains in the automotive industry start with raw materials sent to parts makers to make auto parts; these parts are then sent to manufacturers (companies like Ford or Toyota) to put together to manufacture vehicles; these vehicles are then sold to consumers through a dealership. The increased trade in intermediate inputs (e.g., automobiles and parts) supports associated productivity growth. The United States, Canada, and Mexico have since the 1970s been operating more and more as an integrated and competitive **trade and production bloc**—that is, a group of countries that have agreements that reduce barriers to trade among those countries.[7]

The second major transformation occurred as North America created a highly interdependent regional labor market, driven by a growing supply of migrant labor as Mexico transitioned from an agricultural to an industrializing urban society (**figure 9.1A**), accompanied by demographic change that increased the share of the working-age population. Mexico experienced a classic model of structural transformation that increased the supply of nonagricultural labor and a slowdown of population growth with urbanization. This is the Lewis model of economic growth with an "unlimited" supply of labor.[8] This process ends with a "Lewis model turning point," whereby the structural transformation comes to a natural end, with a lower share of the labor force in agriculture and a

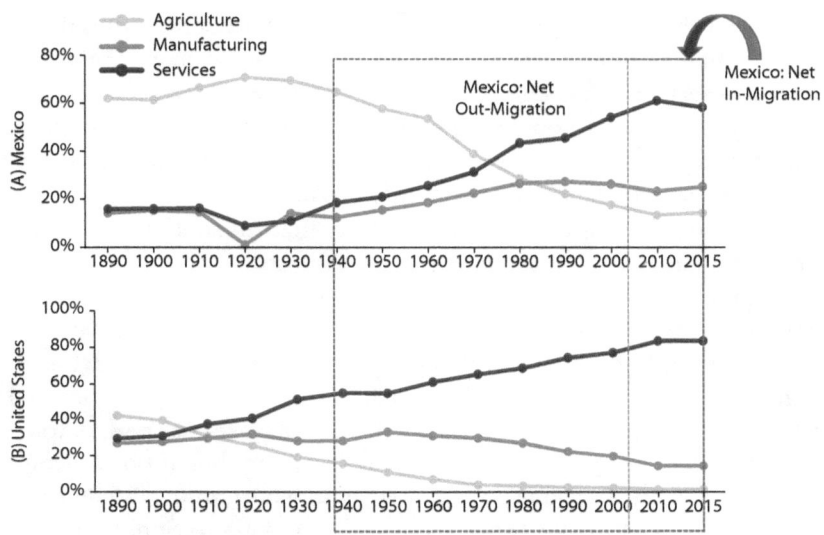

FIGURE 9.1. Periods of Mexican Net Migration: Net Out-Migration, 1940–Mid-2000s; Net In-Migration, Mid-2000s–2015; Mexican and US Employment by Economic Sector as Share of Total Employment, 1890–2015: (A) Mexico; (B) United States. Sources for Mexico: from 1895 to 1910: Estadísticas económicas del Porfiriato: Fuerza de trabajo y actividad económica por sectores [Porfiriato period economic statistics: Workforce and economic activity by sectors], El Colegio de México; from 1921 to 1990: Instituto Nacional de Estadistica y Geografica [INEGI; National Institute of Statistics, Geography, and Informatics]; from 1996 to 2016: *Encuesta Nacional de Ocupación y Empleo* [National survey of occupation and employment], INEGI and ILOSTAT [International Labor Organization Statistics]; "El Empleo en México en los Ochenta: Tendencias y Cambios" [Employment in Mexico in the eighties: Trends and changes], Banco Nacional de Comercio Exterior, México, revistas.bancomext.gob.mx/rce/magazines/250/3/RCE3; El empleo en México en los ochenta: Tendencias y cambios. Sources for US: Lippolis 2013, based on Berthold Herrendorf, Richard Rogerson and Akos Valentinyi, Growth and structural transformation, in *Handbook of Economic Growth*, vol. 2B, https://ourworldindata.org/grapher/employment-by-economic-sector?stackMode=relative&tab=data; http://www.public.asu.edu/~ bherrend/Published%20 Papers/Handbook%2013.pdf.

rising share of urban sectors (see figure 9.1A). The result is a dramatic slowdown in both internal Mexican migration and Mexico to US migration, documented as well as undocumented.[9]

The original high postwar growth in Mexican migration was complemented and encouraged by a growing US demand for agricultural labor and services, as the United States matured into a highly urban, postindustrializing, and increasingly service-oriented economy (**figure 9.1B**). Mexican migration became even more complementary and crucial to the United States as the postwar baby boom matured and began aging to retirement, generating even greater demand for labor-intensive services. This current phase of complementary US aging and slowing of Mexican population growth can potentially lead to rising wages and productivity across borders, as well as large-scale remittances. Much will depend on the ability of North America to produce a mutually supporting and development-oriented mix of trade, migration, labor, and remittance policies going forward.

The post–World War II period of US-Mexico migration and trade integration was built on fortuitous complementary endowments and proved to be beneficial to both countries. **Figure 9.2A** shows that Mexico achieved significant convergence in GDP per capita from 1942 to 1980, followed by divergence since the 1980s. During this seventy-five-year period, trade and migration policies were at times complementary but at times incompatible and working against efficient economic integration. While trade policy has been pro-integration, moving from a protectionist to open regime since the mid-1980s (**figure 9.2C**), migration policies, barriers, and enforcement have grown ever more restrictive, significantly distorting labor markets on both sides of the border. Rather than move toward increased orderly labor mobility, migration has been increasingly restricted due to US politics with no meaningful coordination with Mexico.

While Mexican migration has contributed significantly to US GDP growth throughout the postwar period, the lack of a well-functioning legal framework for managing migration flows and ensuring workers' rights has led to many problems. Immigrant wages have been kept artificially low and unproductive in the US labor market through increased undocumented migration in the 1990s through 2010 from both Mexico and Central America. This burst of undocumented migration (**figure 9.2B**) resulted from both supply and demand effects and was encouraged in the United States because the migrants were needed and had been made relatively cheaper due to their undocumented status (Brown, Hotchkiss, and Quispe-Agnoli 2012). The increasing stock of undocumented migrants after the Immigration Reform and Control Act (IRCA) of 1986 broke the postwar pattern of circular migration, legalizing most unauthorized immigrants who arrived in the United States prior to January 1, 1982, and thus ironically "fencing in" and increasing the permanent undocumented settlement in the United States (Massey, Durand, and Malone 2003). While much of the international policy negotiations has been focused on trade liberalization in NAFTA and the USMCA, the lack of regional or even national US immigration reform

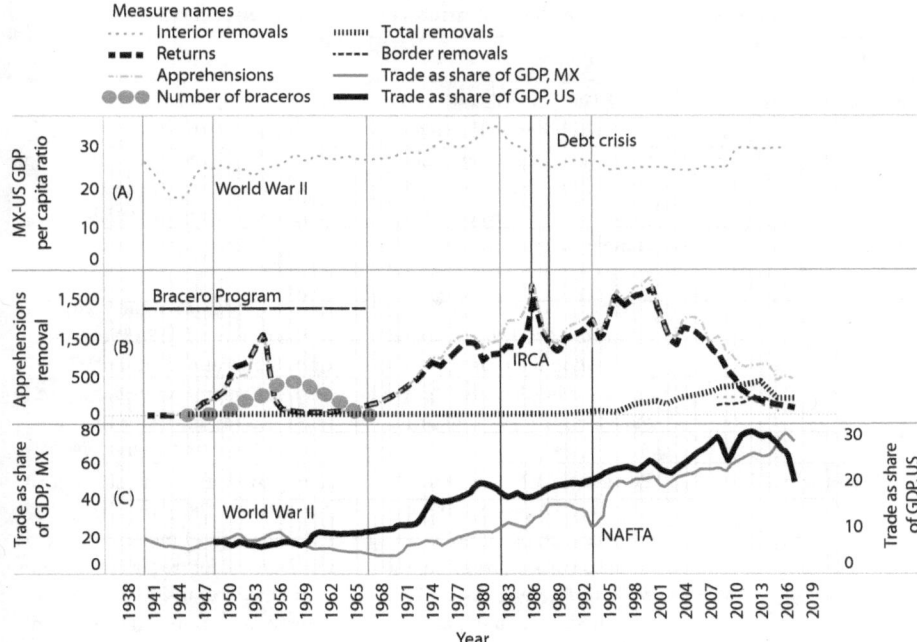

FIGURE 9.2 (A) Relative US/Mexico GDP per Capita (MX-US GDP Per Capita Ratio); (B) US Apprehensions and Deportations (Apprehensions, Removals); (C) US and Mexico Trade Shares of GDP (Trade as Share of GDP, MX; Trade as Share of GDP, US). Sources: Maddison Project Database, version 2018, Bolt et al. 2018; ICE Immigration Return and Removals Reports for Each Fiscal Year, www.dhs.gov/immigration-statistics/enforcement-actions; Trade as Share of GDP, for US: WTO, Time series on international trade; US Census Bureau, Historical series: US international trade in goods and services; and for Mexico: World Bank, Imports and exports of goods and services; INEGI, Estadísticas históricas de México [Historical statistics of Mexico].

and legalization in this period encouraged exploitation of undocumented labor in the low-wage labor market. Ironically, this growth in undocumented migration has produced much greater economic benefits to the United States than trade liberalization, as we show below, a fact lost in discussions on relatively minor distributional implications that were hotly debated in academic circles.[10]

POSTWAR US MIGRATION AND TRADE POLICY INITIATIVES

To understand the degree to which various US trade and immigration policies have succeeded or failed, it is important to review the major

TABLE 9.1   POSTWAR US-MEXICO TRADE AND MIGRATION POLICY INITIATIVES

Period	Trade Policy	Immigration Policy
1940s and 1950s	1942 (WW II): US and Mexico negotiate a comprehensive trade, investment, and debt agreement. Chapultepec Conference (1946) continued complementary pro-integration trade (ISI) policies.	Migration agreement: Bracero Program (1942–64) Post-WW II, US became less hospitable to Mexican migrants: Operation Wetback (1952–53)
1960s and 1970s	Border Industrialization Program (BIP, 1965) fostered Mexican industrialization along the border (also known as the Maquiladora Program).	Bracero Program terminated. Immigration bill (1965) expanded overall migration but limited Mexican migration beginning in 1976. Result: gradual expansion of undocumented migration.
1980s and 1990s	The idea of a North American Free Trade Agreement first received significant policy attention arising from the work of the congressional commission on immigration and development that accompanied the legislative reform process that created IRCA in 1986. NAFTA in force in 1994.	Immigration Reform and Control Act (IRCA, 1986). Legalized existing stock of migrants but did not increase future legal migration. Continued expansion of undocumented migration and disruption of circular migrations after 1996 legal restrictions and border enforcements.
2000s	Expanded trade under NAFTA, including major increase in value chain trade in intermediates, with associated productivity increases. Continuing pro-integration trade policies and acceleration of agricultural trade liberalization.	2001 was the peak year of undocumented crossings and apprehensions, while total removals via deportation increased as did enforcement expenditures under Bush and stabilized under Obama. CIR failed Congress in 2007 and 2013, as Obama issued DACA and DAPA as executive orders.
2017	Trump adopts a protectionist anti-integration approach with potential for tariff war and trade collapse. Trump threatens to cancel NAFTA and raise tariffs, forcing renegotiation into a very similar USMCA.	Trump embraces restrictive immigration policies, including rescinding DACA, building walls, increasing immigrant incarceration rates even as deportations and border crossings continue to fall, restricting access to legal immigration and refugees.

NOTE: DAPA = Deferred Action for Parents of Americans and Lawful Permanent Residents.

periods of migration and trade policy implementation in the post–World War II era. **Table 9.1** summarizes four periods. First, in the early 1940s, the United States launched the Bracero Program and a series of trade, investment, and debt agreements (Hinojosa-Ojeda 1999). The mid-1960s saw the end of the Bracero Program, a reorganization of legal immigration quotas in the Immigration and Naturalization Act of 1965, and the launch of the **1965 Border Industrialization Program,** which allowed for industrial production on the Mexican side of the border to enter the United States without paying tariffs.

In the mid-1980s to early 1990s, the United States enacted IRCA and NAFTA. In the 2000s, the United States enacted new laws and increased appropriations to the Department of Homeland Security (DHS) that were designed to restrict migration and penalize undocumented migrants in the United States. While trade across borders grew and attempts at comprehensive immigration reform were made, Congress was unable to agree on any major reforms, including legalization of the large stock of undocumented migrants. In the Trump era, the administration pursued anti-trade and extreme anti-immigration measures, with heavy-handed use of tariffs and enhanced restrictions on undocumented and legal migration, all of which could have serious negative impacts on the US labor force and the economy.

IRCA AND NAFTA: 1986–1994

The Immigration Reform and Control Act of 1986 represented a major change in post–World War II immigration policy. Its major achievement was to legalize the status of the large stock of undocumented migrants then in the United States. Congress and President Ronald Reagan's administration of the 1980s recognized that earlier policies, including tolerance of weak border and employer enforcement, had created a massive stock of undocumented migrants and that the solution was, correctly, large-scale legalization rather than large-scale deportation.

The major failing of IRCA, however, was reproducing the error of the 1965 Immigration and Naturalization Act by not expanding avenues for legal immigration from Mexico. There clearly was a continuing US demand for Mexican labor and an increasing supply of surplus labor in Mexico arising from continuing structural change. Migrant communities in the United States had strong linkages to Mexican communities, providing channels to respond to the demand and supply pressure for increased migration. IRCA did succeed in reducing undocumented migration for five years because it legalized many of the people engaged in circular migratory patterns. However, because it did not significantly expand legal migration avenues, it provided no mechanism for dealing with the next wave of workers coming of age in rural Mexico and entering Mexican labor markets and an already aging US workforce. In an acknowledgment of the larger regional challenge, however, Congress did establish the US Commission for the Study of International Migration and Cooperative Economic Development, which, in its 1990 report, prominently mentioned the need for freer trade between the United States and Mexico. Echoing the 1965 Border Industrialization Program, which allowed industrial production on the Mexican side of the border to enter the United States without paying tariffs, the commission envisioned that a North American free trade project could encourage increased trade and employment, but it did not anticipate the still-massive, and demographically driven, out-migration from the countryside to meet the growing US demand over the next twenty-five years.

When NAFTA was finally negotiated in 1992, the United States argued that immigration issues were too controversial to be included in NAFTA, and Mexico agreed on the condition that the United States accept its condition that oil would be excluded. The original NAFTA negotiations also ignored labor market issues as they focused on liberalizing trade and investment relations. Only after the signing of NAFTA in 1992 did the new administration of President Bill Clinton negotiate "side agreements" on environment, labor, and creation of the NADBank, which despite showing embryonic promise was not provided with the sufficient resources or power to meet the scale of the US-Mexico development challenge.[11] These early side agreements were thought to be the basis of what Robert Pastor (2001) would later see as a potential movement "toward a North American Community."

While ignoring calls for a more comprehensive migration, trade, and development compact, NAFTA negotiators did, however, take into consideration the potential impact of rapid liberalization of agricultural trade on the Mexican labor market. Research at the time indicated that trade liberalization that was too rapid could result in accelerated outmigration in Mexican agriculture, due to pressure for increased migration to the United States (Robinson et al. 1993; Levy and van Wijnbergen 1992, 1994). US and Mexican negotiators later agreed that agricultural trade liberalization would have the longest adjustment period (fifteen years) so that NAFTA would not constrain Mexican management of structural change. As previously mentioned, the scheduled elimination of corn tariffs was part of this adjustment. International financial institutions such as the World Bank also worked with the Mexican government to establish adjustment programs for rural families, with assistance from such programs as **Oportunidades (Opportunities)** that provided cash for school attendance and nutrition, among other supports, and is credited for decreasing poverty, particularly in rural Mexico. Other programs include **PROCAMPO (Programa de Apoyos Directos al Campo [Program for Direct Support to Rural Areas])**,[12] which subsidized small farmers.

NAFTA AND IMMIGRATION: 1994–2016

Despite the fact that NAFTA-related trade and financial liberalization flows were subject to much public debate, binational negotiations, and legislative action in both countries, immigration policy has seen no such binational or national action or urgency. On the contrary, the United States has seen a series of unilateral actions to restrict migration accompanied by massive growth of border enforcement expenditures. The result is that the cost per apprehension of an undocumented migrant has grown from $1,000 in 1991 to $45,000 in 2013 (Hinojosa 2013).

This is particularly illogical since a review of the **post-NAFTA era** shows that Mexican migration has had a much larger positive impact on the US labor market and has contributed much more to US GDP than have US-Mexico trade or financial flows. **Figure 9.3** shows that Mexican-origin and Mexican immigrant labor contributions to the US GDP have grown dramatically in the post-NAFTA era from 1994 to 2016. During this period, the GDP contribution of the **Mexican diaspora** (i.e., the total Mexican-origin population in the United States, including immigrants and the native born) totals $13.4 trillion, with Mexican foreign-born immigrants contributing $4.8 trillion, compared to a total GDP contribution of exports to Mexico of $3.3 trillion. The direct and indirect employment impacts of Mexican immigration is also significantly higher than employment supported by exports to Mexico.

Compared to the labor market impacts of post-IRCA migration, the post-NAFTA labor market effects were relatively small. Different academic and policy estimates from a range of political perspectives are actually in close agreement concerning the US employment impacts of post-NAFTA economic integration (around one million jobs), including the Economic Policy Institute (EPI); Public Citizen; and the University of California, Los Angeles, North American Integration and Development

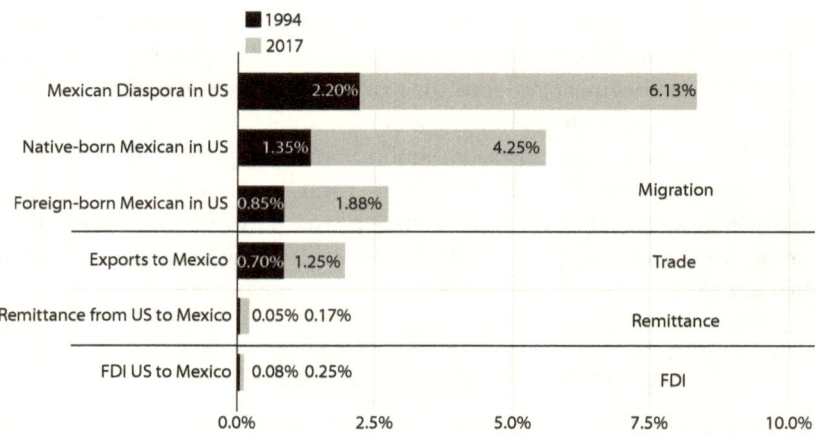

FIGURE 9.3. Mexico Migration, Trade Contributions, and Remittances/FDI as a Share of US GDP. Sources: US Census data was used to calculate Native- and Foreign-Born Mexican in US, as well as US Exports to Mexico. World Bank data were used to calculate remittance and trade shares of GDP.

(UCLA NAID) Center.[13] These estimates closely converge with the actual number of beneficiaries of various trade adjustment policies related to NAFTA, including the Small Business Association (SBA), Rural Development Advance (RDA); and the NADBank Community Adjustment and Investment Program (NADB CAIP), from 1994 to 2017. The NAD-Bank CAIP Federal Agency Program, which subsidized fees through SBA and RDA loans, likely generated approximately 10 to 21 percent of the reemployment of workers in CAIP's Designated Eligible Areas (DEAs) (Hinojosa 2019).

The post-IRCA and post-NAFTA era first saw a decline and then a rapid rise in undocumented migration based largely on the US business and unemployment cycle in the 1990s that determined US demand for labor. By the beginning of the 2000s, the continued demographic and structural change in Mexico had reached a tipping point and Mexico entered a new phase, moving toward the "end of labor abundance" (Taylor, Charlton, and Yúnez-Naude 2012). Starting in 2001, undocumented immigration not only peaked, but began a rapid decline that has continued to the present, with net migration turning negative in 2007. While total undocumented migration recovered slightly with the US business cycle, Mexican undocumented migration has continued its net negative slide, reducing the stock of Mexican undocumented labor for the first time in the post–World War II era. Migration from Central America has continued to grow. This trend is also reflected in the sharp decline in apprehensions by US enforcement agents during this period (figure 9.2B).

NAFTA itself had little direct effect on migration, contrary to some popular perceptions. The fifteen-year adjustment period for NAFTA agricultural trade liberalization ended just as the trends in demographic and economic structural change had largely worked through the Mexican economy. The Mexican government did, however, decide to implement a series of agricultural policy reforms outside of NAFTA, including the PROCAMPO and Oportunidades programs, constitutional changes to communal land rights, and accelerated corn imports that were faster than allowed by NAFTA. The combined effects of these policy changes do not appear to have influenced the rate of Mexico undocumented out-migration, which peaked in 2000, nor are they responsible for the continuous decline and net return migrations in recent years.[14] In further contradictions to popular perceptions, Mexican migration began declining after 2001, just as US corn exports to Mexico saw their most expansive rise.[15]

Mexico is in a new development phase, with less surplus labor and declining supply pressure for migration, which means that Mexico and the US policy makers are now in a different economic and demographic environment. Mexico benefited from the presence of the US labor market that provided an outlet for Mexican surplus labor during its period of dramatic demographic and structural change, but this has now slowed considerably (Hanson, Liu, and McIntosh 2017). The United States has benefited greatly from past migration, which supplied needed labor and improved the age structure of the US population, and will continue to so into the future. Going forward, the two countries need to consider policies that manage continued integration of their labor markets in an environment of much less migration pressure, as well as continue the long process of trade integration that has benefited both countries.

TRUMP ERA

With the election of Donald Trump in 2016, the United States is threatening to reverse the process of North American integration that has greatly benefited the three NAFTA countries. The Trump administration called for a renegotiation of NAFTA but resulted in a USMCA that had few changes but increased risks (Pulaski, Capaldo, and Gallagher 2019; Burfisher, Lambert, and Matheson 2019). Trump, meanwhile, has continued to use protectionist rhetoric and threats that may well poison all negotiations on trade and migration.

On immigration policy, the Trump administration is moving toward a highly restrictive policy on new immigration and draconian treatment of currently undocumented immigrants. Instead of a policy to legalize the large existing stock of 11 million undocumented immigrants, as was done in earlier immigration reform policies, the administration is moving rapidly to a hugely expensive policy of mass incarceration, deportation, and increased security (the "Wall") along the border.

The irony of the Trump administration policies to increase border security is that they address a problem that is already largely being resolved through demographic change, economic growth, and development trends in both Mexico and the United States.[16] The trade, immigration, and mass deportation policies that the administration proposed would likely set back the process of economic integration in North America and would lead to new pressure for undocumented immigration if, as is likely, they damage the economies of Mexico and Central America.

ECONOMIC IMPACTS OF SCENARIO RESULTS OF ALTERNATIVE IMMIGRATION AND TRADE POLICIES

To explore the economic impacts of alternative policy options in US-Mexico trade and migration, we utilize a GLOBE model, discussed earlier—the multicountry, multisector CGE model of global trade. We also use a US model specified for immigrant labor markets. There are thirty-five industries in the models, 10 labor occupation categories, capital, and five household groups (defined by quintiles of the overall income distribution), which differ by sources of income and expenditure patterns, providing an empirical framework for analysis of further restricting or liberalizing regional trade and labor migration.

We use these models to estimate the effects of alternative policy scenarios for restricting or liberalizing trade and migration flows, comparing the direct and indirect effects on GDP, income, and cross-border exchange. Alternative trade policy scenarios include (1) NAFTA disintegration, (2) trade war among NAFTA countries, and (3) the USMCA. We also specified two sets of migration scenarios: (1) comprehensive immigration reform (CIR), including the legalization of undocumented workers as well as future worker flows; and (2) migration collapse, specified by increasing reductions in the immigrant labor force by category.

In **table 9.2** we present the results of our CGE modeling scenarios, comparing the impact on the United States and Mexico of our alternative migration and trade policy scenarios on GDP, exports, imports,

TABLE 9.2 US AND MEXICAN REAL GDP AGGREGATES BY SCENARIO

	GDP	Exports	Imports	Employment Loss (1000s, ILO 2017)
US Scenarios				
NAFTA collapse short run US	−0.23	−0.78	−0.41	−372
NAFTA collapse medium run US	−0.05	−0.5	−0.41	−151
NAFTA trade war short run US	−1.9	−8.81	−4.25	−2,931
NAFTA trade war medium run US	−0.5	−6.98	−4.25	−1,284
Migration collapse ⅙ US	−0.97	−1.15	−0.92	−1,466
Migration collapse 100% US	−5.93	−7.04	−5.65	−8,793
USMCA	0.1	0.1	0.1	
CIR	2.38	1.21	2.01	
Mexico Scenarios				
NAFTA collapse short run Mexico	−4.62	−6.9	−3.14	−2,444
NAFTA collapse medium run Mexico	−0.51	−3.1	−3.14	−751
NAFTA trade war short run Mexico	−16.27	−21.92	−15.46	−8,877
NAFTA trade war medium run Mexico	−2.03	−9.24	−15.46	−3,140
Remittance Losses	−0.06	4.35	−3.31	
USMCA	−0.1	0.1	0.1	

SOURCES: Authors' calculation; Hinojosa-Ojeda 2010; Robinson and Thierfelder 2018; Burfisher, Lambert, and Matheson 2019.

and employment losses. The results indicate that for the United States, comprehensive immigration reform would increase GDP by $1.5 trillion over ten years while deportation of 5 percent of the labor force would result in a fall in GDP of up to almost 6 percent, depending on how labor and capital markets adjust. Tax revenue would rise and fall with GDP, and the government deficit would decrease and increase accordingly. The mass deportation scenario amounts to a policy-induced severe recession for the United States, with negative GDP impacts in Mexico (and Central America) as a result of the collapse of remittances due to migrant employment losses. Legalization and CIR generate growth of income and productivity as undocumented immigrants are allowed to move to more productive employment. CIR also has very positive impacts on trade with Mexico, further reducing out-migration pressures. Most interestingly, imports and exports in the United States fall more due to a **migration collapse scenario** than the worst effect of a **trade war scenario.** As previously calculated by the UCLA NAID Center in 2009 and corroborated by the Congressional Budget Office in 2013, projections of future immigration indicate continued decline. In addition, it is estimated that legalization, if implemented, would significantly reduce the

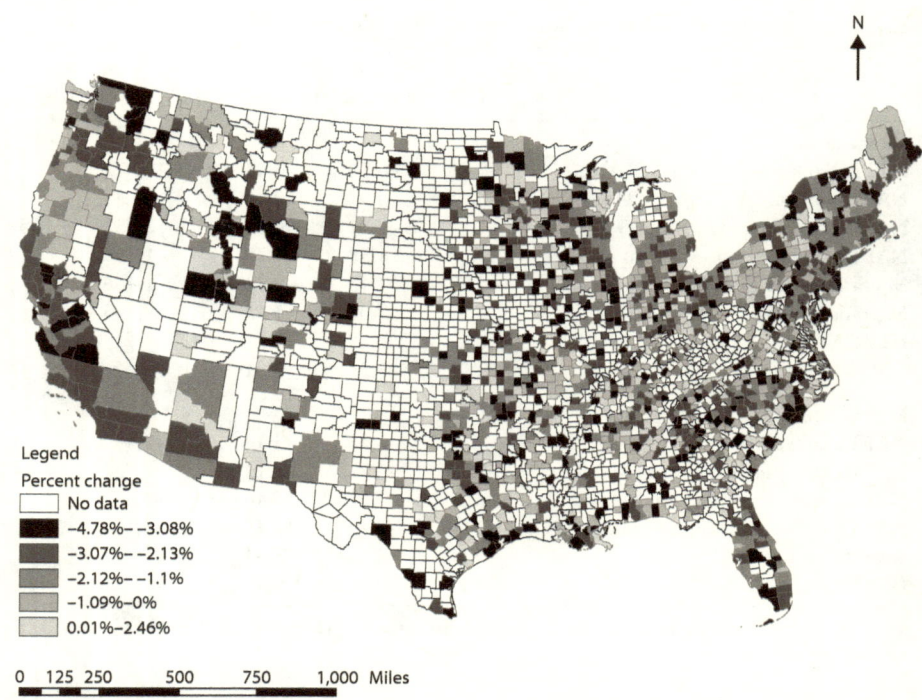

FIGURE 9.4A. Percent Change in County US Sectoral Output under NAFTA Trade War in Nonservice Sectors.

number of undocumented crossings, as occurred after the 1986 reform that legalized the then stock of undocumented immigrants.

With respect to trade scenarios, we find that the impact of the USMCA is minimal and was not worth the risk of more serious confrontations. In a NAFTA collapse scenario in the short run, when there is unemployment and producers cannot change capital-labor ratios, real GDP declines for all NAFTA countries but with relatively small declines for the United States. Mexico is hit especially hard (GDP falls by 4.6 percent), given that it has a much higher share of unskilled labor that is subject to unemployment. The NAFTA trade war scenario is more serious, however, damaging all three countries, and it is especially damaging to Mexico and Canada. The long-run scenario of disintegration of the North American trade bloc, which starts from the NAFTA trade war scenario and also assumes that Mexico and Canada will pursue free trade agreements with the European Union (EU) and East and South-

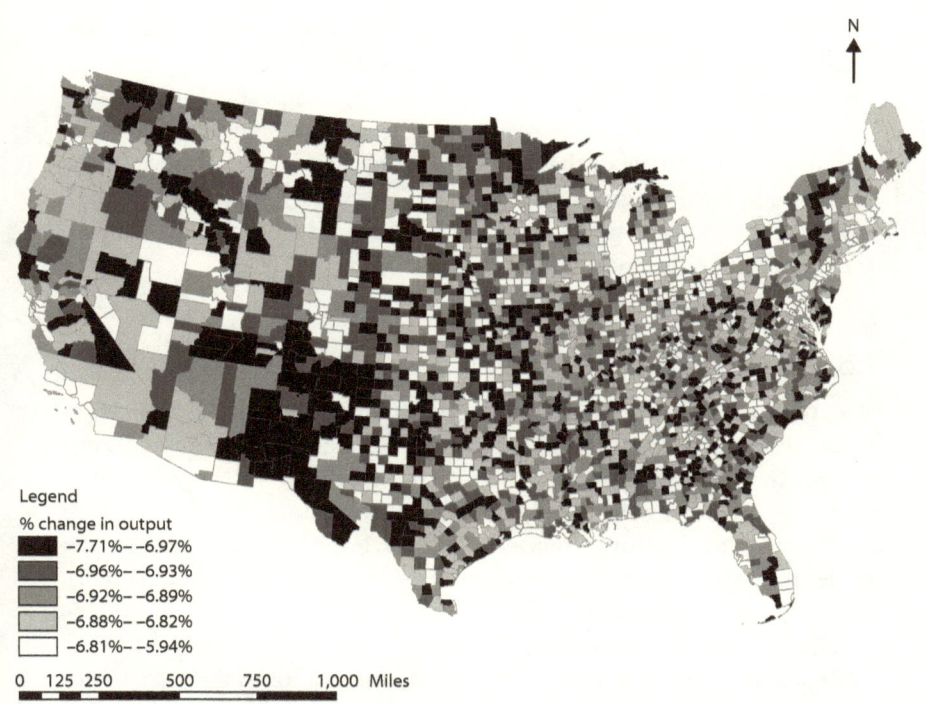

FIGURE 9.4B. Percent Change in County Output under Mass Deportation in All Sectors.

east (E&SE) Asia, also yields large impacts on all three countries. Trade diverts away from the United States so that it becomes more isolated in the global economy. US real exports decline overall, and exports to both NAFTA and non-NAFTA countries decline. Real exports from Mexico and Canada decline overall, but those countries increase their exports to non-NAFTA countries after severe adjustments.

The geographic dispersion of the impacts of these alternative policy scenarios are very interesting, particularly with respect to the paradox that those who support Trump's policies the most are the most likely to be hurt by them. The declines in production and income would not be restricted to industries and regions that directly compete with imports or where undocumented laborers work. The reductions in employment and sectoral output would be spread across industries, and the recession-induced reductions in GDP and household incomes would be spread across states and counties, many of which voted for Trump (**figures 9.4A and 9.4B**).

While some of these scenarios are speculative, they do yield a robust result: a trade war and migration collapse in North America is the worst option for all of the participants. In contrast, the impact of a USMCA is minimal, despite the intense hype and resource use. These new modeling results also reaffirm that the impacts of significant changes in the labor force via immigration policy are potentially much larger than from changes in trade policy (Hinojosa-Ojeda and Robinson 1991; Bustamante, Reynolds, and Hinojosa-Ojeda 1992).

CONCLUSION

We are now at a critical juncture in North America, with a largely completed trade liberalization and supply chain integration occurring simultaneously at the end of the period of surplus labor in Mexico that is naturally decreasing the supply of potential migrants. We now have an opportunity to develop a mutually supporting mix of pro-integration trade, migration, and labor policies that will result in rising incomes across North America.

The Trump administration, however, is moving to a protectionist trade policy and a draconian, restrictive immigration policy. This mix threatens to become the worst-case scenario, with a negative labor supply shock in the United States due to mass deportations threatening to overwhelm any positive gains from trade liberalization, past or future. The new policy is in sharp contrast to past bipartisan immigration reform that acknowledged that the large stock of undocumented migrants was due to policy choices by the US government and that legalization made sense in terms of both economic and humanitarian concerns. The potential gains from complementary prodevelopment trade and migration legalization policies are stronger than ever. Such a coordinated policy program is possible and well worth pursuing, while the costs of the current anti-integration trade and immigration policies are now being realized as extremely destructive.

Suggested Reading

Clausing, K. A. 2019. *Open: The Progressive Case for Free Trade, Immigration, and Global Capital*. Cambridge, MA: Harvard University Press.

Goldin, I., G. Cameron, and M. Balarajan. 2011. *Exceptional People: How Migration Shaped Our World and Will Define Our Future*. Princeton, NJ: Princeton University Press.

Hing, B. O. 2010. *Ethical Borders: NAFTA, Globalization, and Mexican Migration*. Philadelphia, PA: Temple University Press.
Massey, D. S., J. Durand, and N. J. Malone 2003. *Beyond Smoke and Mirrors: Mexican Immigration in an Era of Economic Integration*. New York: Russell Sage Foundation.
Sachs, J. D. 2015. *The Age of Sustainable Development*. New York: Columbia University Press.

CHAPTER 10

What Is the Relationship between US-Mexico Migration and Trade in Agriculture?

ANTONIO YÚNEZ-NAUDE, JORGE MORA-RIVERA, AND YATZIRY GOVEA-VARGAS

This chapter presents the state of knowledge—and an accurate diagnosis—of the association of two events under the North American Free Trade Agreement (NAFTA): (i) the evolution of Mexico-US migration and (ii) the recent state of Mexican agriculture, particularly field crops and corn. With this we hope to contribute to a better understanding of past and contemporary trends of these phenomena, which is necessary to reflect about the future.

The chapter is divided into five sections. The first section describes the trends in Mexico's agriculture and rural migration during NAFTA. In the next section special attention is given to corn because of its importance in the domestic supply and demand of foodstuffs in Mexico and because corn and trade liberalization under NAFTA have been singled out by some academics and in liberal political circles and the press as a main factor in the increase in rural migration to the United States. This discussion is followed by a series of hypotheses presented to explain these trends and by an exploration of recent changes in agricultural trade and migration whose causes are not yet fully understood. The chapter ends with a reflection on what these trends and changes mean for Mexican rural development, trade, and migration.

We thank George A. Dyer for his comments, but all errors remain ours.

AGRICULTURAL PRODUCTION, TRADE, AND RURAL MIGRATION TRENDS

The result of the renegotiation of NAFTA and the election of Andrés Manuel López Obrador (AMLO) as president of Mexico will have implications for the economies of both Mexico and the United States. In early 2019, Mexico and the US Congress had yet to approve what was agreed to in NAFTA renegotiations by their respective executive branches (called by President Trump the United States-Mexico-Canada Agreement, or USMCA). At that time, the prospects for US migration policy reform remained uncertain, and only a few details of López Obrador's rural **development policies** had yet to be announced. Furthermore, the discussion of the effects of NAFTA on Mexico-US **rural migration** and bilateral agricultural trade remained plagued by ideological arguments on both sides of the border. In addition to the above policy uncertainties, there is a lack of scholarly explanations concerning the relationship between recent changes in Mexico-US migration and agricultural **trade balances,** as well as agricultural production in Mexico.

Based on the observed trends in rural migration and the agricultural sector of Mexico during the past twenty-five years and on recent changes in these trends, however, what is clear is that the rates of migration and agricultural, particularly corn, production during this period cannot be solely attributed to NAFTA. First, evidence suggests a long-term relationship—dating at least from the beginning of the 1980s—between the Chicago Board of Trade and Mexico's prices for major grain imports (see, e.g., Jaramillo, Yúnez-Naude, and Serrano 2015; Fiess and Lederman 2004).

Second, despite negative projections of the expected bilateral trade impact of NAFTA (Robinson et al. 1993; Levy and van Wijnbergen 1994), domestic output (production) of major grains—corn, barley, sorghum, and wheat—has *not* declined sharply. The unexpected high levels of production of these crops is explained by several factors, from the structural characteristics of Mexican agriculture—**rural households** producing staples for subsistence alongside **commercial farmers**—to government supports to grain farmers (Yúnez-Naude 2010). Corn remains particularly resilient as it is produced by all types of farmers, small and large, using a wide range of technologies and facing different transaction costs. And it is still the main field crop produced in Mexico. The volume of corn production has actually increased during NAFTA.[1]

TABLE 10.1 PERCENTAGE WEIGHT OF US TRADE IN TOTAL TRADE OF AGRICULTURAL COMMODITIES IN MEXICO, 2003–2015

Weight of US Exports by Volume (and Value)		Weight of US Imports by Volume (and Value)	
Staple Field Crops		*Vegetables*	
Rice	96 (95)	Tomatoes	98 (97)
Barley	73 (71)	Broccoli/cauliflower	97 (98)
Corn	97 (95)	Peppers	99 (97)
Sorghum	97 (97)	Carrots	80 (83)
Wheat	71 (71)	Onions	75 (80)
Beans	92 (92)	Cucumbers	99 (91)
Soybeans	94 (93)		
Meats and Dairy		*Fruits*	
Bovine	81 (82)	Avocados	65 (67)
Poultry	95 (90)	Citrus	93 (85)
Goats and mutton	11 (13)	Melons	95 (88)
Pork	89 (89)	Papaya	100 (99)
Milk	81 (79)	Pineapple	99 (97)

SOURCES: Authors' estimates based on http://www.siap.gob.mx/comercio-exterior/. Imports: FAOSTAT (Fao.org 2017). Quotas: Tariff cuts and reduction periods from SECOFI 1994.

(The unique characteristics of Mexico's agricultural sector are discussed further in "Understanding Trends," below.)

By contrast and as was expected, overall agricultural trade has grown substantially during NAFTA. Imports of major grains and oilseeds and meat, as well as exports of fruits and vegetables, have increased continuously. Mexico's agricultural trade balance was negative until 2014 (except in 1995, when a macroeconomic crisis hit harder) and turned positive since 2015. With respect to grains and oilseeds—considered basic **noncompetitive** crops by the Mexican government during NAFTA negotiations—imports of corn, rice, and wheat stand out. From 1999 to 2015, calculated in constant pesos, the annual average growth rate (AGR) for imports of these three crops was 8.8, 5.3, and 28.5 percent, respectively. Increases in oilseed imports include an AGR of 3.3 percent for soybeans. From 1999 to 2015, the AGR of exported avocados, citrus products, and melons was 32.9, 21.5, and 8.5 percent, respectively. The AGR for tomato, broccoli/cauliflower, and cucumber exports was 20.4, 20.6, and 10.4 percent, respectively.[2] The AGR for meat imports was the highest for pork, at 15.5 percent, followed by poultry, at 9.9 percent.[3]

Both production and exports of fruits and vegetables have grown under NAFTA. The ratio of agricultural exports to **agricultural output** has increased, in real terms, for avocados, citrus, and tomatoes.[4] Imports of noncompetitive, major staples have increased as well, yet domestic output of these crops has not collapsed as expected. The ratio of imports to output increased for corn, rice, and wheat. The ratio decreased for sorghum and soybeans, whereas it remained relatively low and unchanged for barley.[5] In fact, the overall growth of Mexican agriculture has been slow during NAFTA and appears even slower when comparing the sector to the Mexican economy as a whole: their respective simple AGR during the period 1995–2015 was 1.68 and 2.62 percent, respectively (Yúnez-Naude and Hernández-Solano 2018). Whether or not NAFTA has caused **trade diversion**—that is, Mexico's imports and exports to the United States have grown at the expense of trade with other countries—is an open question that has to be studied empirically.[6] It is clear, however, that the weight of US-Mexican agricultural trade is overwhelming (**table 10.1**).

CORN AND TRADE LIBERALIZATION UNDER NAFTA

Corn deserves special attention here because it remains a staple in rural diets and the main production and consumption crop in Mexico. Its weight in agricultural trade also is considerable. It has been said repeatedly that American-corn imports made net losers out of corn farmers in Mexico, pushing them and their workers out of rural areas.

What is the NAFTA corn argument? The economist Jorge Calderón (2004) points out that the agricultural crisis began before NAFTA, yet was exacerbated by it, with corn and bean farmers—representative of net losers in the agricultural sector—leaving rural Mexico for US destinations. García Zamora and Gaspar (2017), experts in sociodemographic change, emphasize that the corn trade liberalization that reduced trading barriers allowed cheap American corn (cheap because American corn subsidies keep prices low) to flood Mexico, devastating prices and forcing many Mexican farmers to leave their land. This argument proposes that migration thus became an escape valve for victims of NAFTA. The law and development scholar Chantal Thomas (2010) concludes, therefore, that corn imports were responsible for displacing agricultural workers and causing flows of surplus labor into Mexican cities, and the cultural anthropologist Elizabeth Fitting (2006), who has studied food and rural displacement, also argues that the "**neoliberal** corn regime" has exacerbated the long-standing problems faced by maize producers

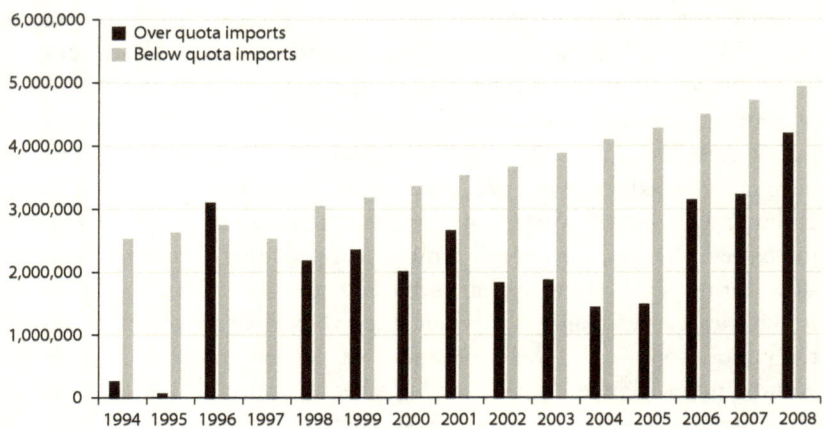

FIGURE 10.1. Corn: Volume of Mexican Imports under and over Tariff Rate Quota (metric tons). Sources: Imports, FAOSTAT (Fao.org, 2017); quotas: Tariff cuts and reduction periods from SECOFI 1994.

by favoring market liberalization over domestic corn production. Fitting points out that farmers have adapted by combining seasonal corn work in Mexico with periods of US-bound rural migration.

Despite this argument, however, there is in fact little evidence to date that the Mexican corn sector in general has diminished under NAFTA. The sector has held out even though the Mexican government did not use the over-quota tariffs that were part of the NAFTA transition period to protect Mexico from an unlimited supply of US corn. From 1994 to 2008, quotas free from tariffs averaged just 30.56 percent of total corn imports, all of which entered Mexico practically free (**figure 10.1**). Increasing corn imports notwithstanding, domestic corn production has increased in both value and volume almost continuously under NAFTA (Dyer et al. 2018).[7]

The number of Mexican farmworkers crossing the border into the United States decreased under NAFTA in the years leading up to 2001. It then climbed sharply, reaching its highest rate in 2007. But it has experienced a profound drop since then (**figure 10.2**). By 2016, the annual flow had decreased by some 22 percent since the start of NAFTA, while both domestic corn production and imports have increased gradually. Employment in Mexico's corn and bean sector has increased since 2004 (**figure 10.3**). (In fact, employment in the entire primary sector—agriculture, forestry, and fisheries—has increased in the past decade.) This indicates that during NAFTA there has not been a simple associa-

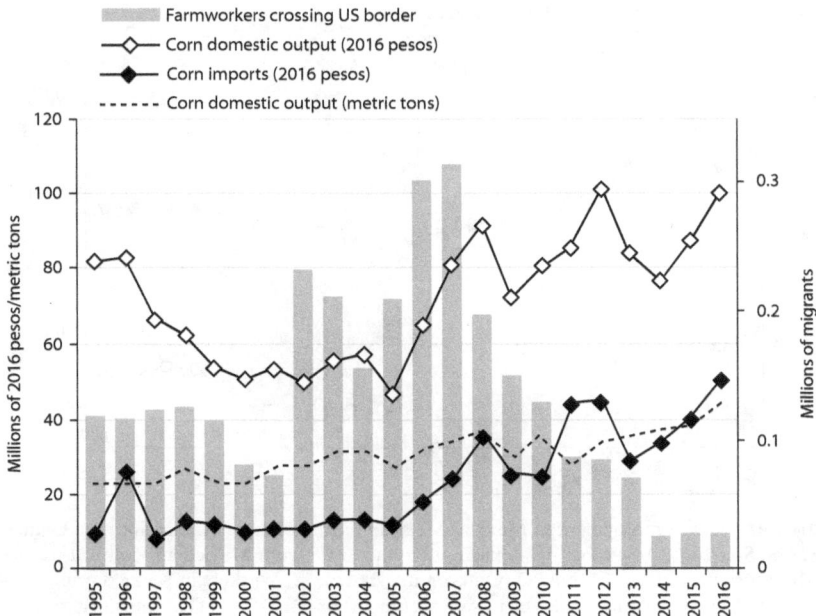

FIGURE 10.2. Migration of Mexican Farmworkers and Corn Production and Imports. Sources: (1) Number of Mexican migrants to US from Mexico agricultural sector: Migratory Series from the National Population Council (CONAPO) (Omi.org.mx, 2017); (2) Corn imports: Authors' elaboration with data from INEGI (Inegi.org.mx, 2017) and Bank of Mexico price index (Banxico.gob.mx,2017); (3) Value and volume of production: Agrifood Information Consulting System (SIACON 2017) and Agriculture and Fisheries Information System (SIAP 2017a).

tion between domestic corn production and corn imports or between these two variables and rural migration to the United States.

UNDERSTANDING TRENDS

To the extent that most of Mexico's agricultural trade is with the United States, it can be argued that, overall, NAFTA has contributed to output growth (i.e., domestic production) in Mexican agriculture. The argument is supported by the positive and statistically significant correlations we found between the gross value of output and trade of field crops: 0.68 for imports, 0.65 for exports. Whereas the sustained growth of corn imports can be attributed to NAFTA,[8] the maintenance of corn as Mexico's major cultivated staple cannot. Since the beginning of

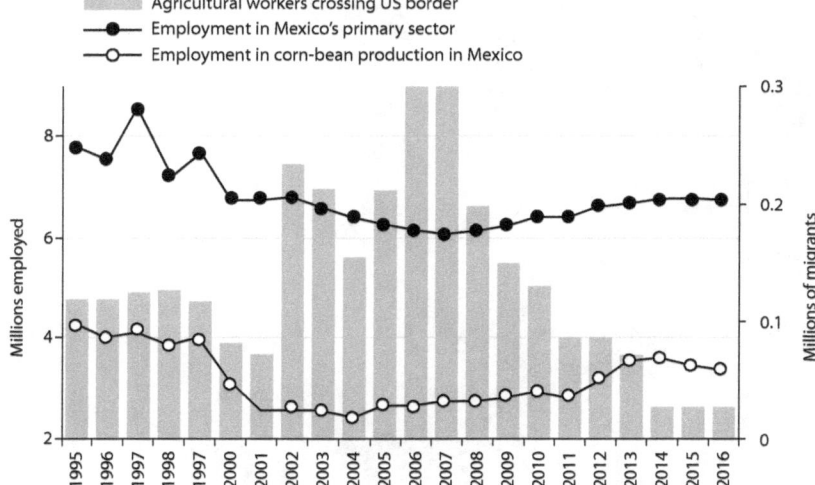

FIGURE 10.3. Employment in Mexico/Mexican Farmworkers Crossing into the United States. Sources: (1) Number of Mexican migrants to US from Mexico agricultural sector: Migratory series from CONAPO (Omi.org.mx, 2017); (2) Workers in Mexico primary sector: Occupation and employment series from Labor Ministry (STPS) (Stps.org.mx, 2017); (3) Workers in Mexico corn and bean sector: Authors' elaboration with data from National Survey of Employment (ENE) and National Survey of Occupation and Employment (ENOE) (Beta.inegi.org.mx, 2017).

NAFTA, Mexico followed more closely international and US corn prices, and these prices decreased until 2005 (Jaramillo, Yúnez-Naude, and Serrano 2015). Thus phenomena other than price reduction is needed to explain the persistence of corn production—as well as other basic crops—in Mexico.

One reason for continued corn production is related to government agricultural policies. In 1991, the Mexican government created **ASERCA (Agencia de Servicios a la Comercialización y Desarrollo de Mercados Agropecuarios [Agency for Support and Services to Agricultural Marketing])** to support farmers producing noncompetitive staple crops while transitioning from state regulation to a market orientation. ASERCA had two main programs: PROCAMPO (Programa de Apoyos Directos al Campo [Program for Direct Support to Rural Areas]) and agricultural marketing supports. Beginning in winter 1994, PROCAMPO made payments not linked to production decisions—that is, **decoupled payments**—to farmers who cultivated noncompetitive crops between 1991 and 1993. The program continued up to 2014. In addition to PROCAMPO,

ASERCA established combined income and price **marketing supports** to commercial farmers in specific regions as well as to their buyers, mainly multinational corporations. Marketing supports allow buyers to become "price indifferent" regarding imports and domestically produced staples (COFECE 2015). Among others, ASERCA supports have been meant to reduce the effects on Mexican farmers of US government subsidies to American farmers. These two programs help explain the persistence of Mexican corn production (Sumner and Balagtas 2007; Dyer 2007; Yúnez-Naude, Martínez, and Orrantia 2007).

Preference among groups of Mexican consumers for white corn rather than imported yellow varieties, which are used mostly for animal feed and other industrial uses, also helps explain the persistence of the domestic corn sector (Yúnez-Naude, Martínez, and Orrantia 2007; Yúnez-Naude 2014). Also important has been the perverse response of subsistence corn farmers to price shocks (Dyer, Taylor, and Boucher 2006). While the corn-price elasticity among commercial farmers is negative, it can be positive among **subsistence farmers** benefiting from lower land rents and wages (Taylor, Dyer, and Yúnez-Naude 2005; Dyer, Taylor, and Boucher 2006). Although lower corn prices also promote rural migration, this estimated effect is small: for example, a 10 percent reduction in the price of corn provokes just a 0.2 percent increase in rural migration to the United States.

RECENT CHANGES IN AGRICULTURAL TRADE AND MIGRATION

Beginning around the second half of 2000, Mexico experienced perceptible changes in trends in rural migration, agricultural production, employment, and trade. Estimates show a decrease in the total Mexican-born population living in the United States and perhaps even a zero rate of net migration (Massey 2012; Passel, Cohn, and Gonzalez-Barrera 2012). This change is consistent with the observed decrease in rural migration from Mexico to the United States (Taylor, Charlton, and Yúnez-Naude 2012; Charlton and Taylor 2016). Since 2005, Mexico's agricultural gross domestic production (GDP) has grown after years of stagnation or decline (**figure 10.4**),[9] and the agricultural trade balance turned positive in 2015 and 2016 (Yúnez-Naude 2018). Whereas Mexican corn output and employment within this sector has increased, the number of Mexican farmworkers crossing into the United States has decreased.

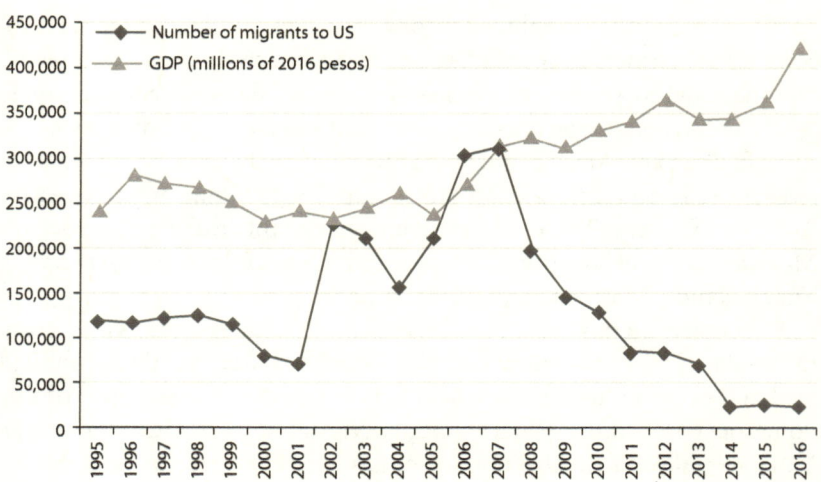

FIGURE 10.4. Mexican Agricultural Workers Crossing US Border and Mexico Field Crops GDP. Sources: (1) Number of Mexican migrants to US from Mexico agricultural sector: Migratory series from the CONAPO (Omi.org.mx, 2017); 2) Corn value of production: Agrifood Information Consulting System (SIACON 2017) and Agriculture and Fisheries Information System (SIAP 2017a); (3) Agricultural GDP (BIE, Banco de Información Económica; Inegi.org.mx, 2017).

Recent changes in rural migration to the United States deserve an explanation. The decrease in migration of rural and agricultural workers to the United States coincides with an overall declining trend in Mexicans migrating to the United States. Indeed, estimates show that the Mexican-born population in the United States has diminished since 2010, reaching around 12 million people today, meaning that the total number of net Mexican immigrants has remained relatively unchanged (Bancomer Foundation, BBVA Research, and CONAPO 2017; Passel, Cohn, and Gonzalez-Barrera 2012). This represents a pronounced change in a trend observed over the past four decades, prompting debate in both academic and political circles. The most frequently cited explanations include tighter border enforcement at the border, increasing deportations beginning in 2008, and rising costs of crossing the border, as well as greater difficulties finding jobs since the US recession of 2008–9.

Data from three rounds of Mexico rural household surveys (2003, 2008, and 2011) and data on changes in employment by sector of destination in Mexico and the United States show that the impact of the US financial crisis on Mexico-US migration was temporary. The data also show that the effects of border controls and deportations were secondary to other phenomena, such as changes in the elasticity of the Mexican rural labor supply with respect to US demand for farm laborers and changes in Mexico's rural demography. In addition, in recent years Mexican rural laborers tended to get jobs in Mexico rather than migrate for jobs to the United States (Taylor, Charlton, and Yúnez-Naude 2012; Charlton and Taylor 2016; see figure 10.3).

CONCLUSION

There is no evidence of a simple association between Mexican corn output or agricultural gross product and the flow of **farm labor** across the border when considering the whole period of NAFTA. If we add to this the fact that during the same period Mexico's agricultural GDP is positively and significantly correlated to Mexico's agricultural imports and exports, it is possible to argue that from 1995 to 2016 rural migration to the United States was not directly linked to agricultural, particularly corn, production in Mexico. Instead agricultural trade did not negatively affect this sector's growth in Mexico. In addition, data for the past ten years show that corn imports from Mexico continued to be high, whereas the number of workers migrating to the United States declined.

Notwithstanding the prevailing uncertainties about further US-Mexico border restrictions and the results of USMCA approval, recent trends in Mexico (e.g., increasing agricultural production and employment and exports of fruits and vegetables) could have important implications across various economic sectors in both countries. One of them is that a higher demand for farm labor on both sides of the border, coupled with a decreasing supply of Mexican farmworkers in the United States, could promote the employment in US agriculture of migrants from other countries, such as El Salvador, Guatemala, and Honduras (Taylor, Charlton, and Yúnez-Naude 2012; Peri 2016).

Under the USMCA, binational **market access** of agricultural products will basically prevail, just as it had under NAFTA. However, the current restriction in Mexico on imports of **genetically modified seeds** (**GMS**) could conflict with the USMCA's chapter 3, "Agriculture," "Section A, Agricultural Biotechnology" (USMCA 2018). With the USMCA, imports of GMS could further reduce the genetic **corn biodiversity** that has characterized corn cultivation by small farmers in several regions of Mexico (Dyer et al. 2014).

To know more than this, it is necessary to wait: USMCA began to be implemented a short time ago and the COVID-19 pandemic has disrupted the economies and societies globally and in North America. So at this time we have no clues about how rural migration, farm labor, and Mexican agriculture will be affected by the USMCA and by the pandemic. But to deliberate about the future, an accurate assessment of past and present trends regarding NAFTA's impact on migration and Mexican agriculture is necessary.

Suggested Reading

Fox, J., and L. Haight, eds. 2010. Subsidizing inequality: Mexican corn policy since NAFTA. Woodrow Wilson International Center for Scholars, Centro de Investigación y Docencia Económicas (CIDE; Center for Research and Teaching in Economics), University of California, Santa Cruz. Available at www.wilsoncenter.org/sites/default/files/Subsidizing%20Inequality_0.pdf.

Organization for Economic Development (OECD). 2006. Agricultural and fisheries policies in Mexico: Recent achievements, continuing the reform agenda. OECD, Paris, France. Available at www.oecd.org/tad/39098498.pdf.

World Bank. 2009. Mexico: Agriculture and rural development: Public expenditure review (PER). World Bank, Washington, DC. Available at http://documents.worldbank.org/curated/en/500971468299092123/Mexico-Agriculture-and-rural-development-public-expenditure-review.

Yúnez-Naude, A. 2010. Las transformaciones del campo y el papel de las políticas públicas: 1929–2008 [The transformations of the rural sector and the role of public policies: 1929–2008]. In Sandra Kuntz Flicker, ed., *Historia económica general de México: De la colonia a nuestros días* [General economic history of Mexico: From the colony to our day], 729–55. Mexico City: El Colegio de México and Secretaría de Economía. DOI: 10.2307/j.ctv47wf39.

Yúnez-Naude, A., F. Rivera Ramírez, A. Chávez Alvarado, J. Mora Rivera, and J.E. Taylor. (2015). *La economía del campo mexicano: Tendencias y retos para su desarrollo* [The economy of the Mexican countryside: Trends and challenges for its development]. Mexico City: El Colegio de México.

CHAPTER 11

Is Complementarity Sustainable in the US-Mexico Automotive Sector?

JORGE CARRILLO

This chapter analyzes the importance of the automotive sector to the economy in Mexico and the impact of the trade relationship between Mexico and the United States. Trade in the automotive industry between both countries is not a zero-sum game in which one country gains and the other loses but rather a highly integrated and complex process that is complementary in various ways. While the asymmetrical dependence of Mexico on the United States increases, as well as its importance, so too does the labor gap between the two countries. In the face of this paradoxical process of increased complementarity, for example, there has been growth in disparity. In addition, new technological challenges arise and need to be confronted.

THE ECONOMIC IMPORTANCE OF THE AUTOMOTIVE INDUSTRY IN MEXICO

The **Mexican automotive industry** (**MAI**) was not born with the North American Free Trade Agreement (NAFTA); it dates back more than ninety years. State intervention in the automotive sector, through public policies, has been present in Mexico for several decades. Historically, there have been specific policies aimed at this sector (sectoral policy), but there have also been *horizontal policies* that have indirectly affected their performance. Four phases can be established: (1) Completely Knocked Down (CKD) (1920–61), which began with the establishment of the first American assemblers in the country, in and around Mexico City (Buick, Ford, GM, Automex, and Vehículos Automotrices Mexicanos [VAM]) and was based on the assembly of imported vehicle components; (2) Industrialization for Substitution of Imports (1962–89), which had the objective of protecting and strengthening the national automotive industry; (3) Industrialization for Export (1990–2009), which has been delineated by four key initiatives, industrial modernization, the signing of NAFTA, the strengthening of competitiveness, and the promotion of Manufacturing, Maquiladora, and Export Services (IMMEX); and (4) Technology Development (2010–present), aimed at transforming the automotive sector into a highly technological one, boosting research, development, and innovation in order to raise its international competitiveness. Changes in Mexico's growth model have occurred approximately every thirty years (**table 11.1**).

Sustained growth in the MAI can be observed dating back to the 1980s and was boosted further during the financial crisis of 2007–8 with the bankruptcy of many US companies, the collapse of the US real estate market, and the drastic reduction in the US economy (**figure 11.1**). This provoked a change in expansion and localization strategies for dozens of companies and gave rise to a spike in investments in automotive plants in Mexico. The MAI is structured in a kind of pyramid with levels or tiers: above are the assemblies (OEMs, or original equipment manufacturers, such as GM, Nissan, etc.); below are auto parts suppliers, mainly Tier One—those companies that supply parts directly to OEMs—followed by Tier Two companies that specialize in particular parts but do not sell directly to OEMs, then Tier Three companies that basically supply the raw materials; and finally Tier Four, small and medium-sized enterprises basically in the informal self-employed sector.

The enormous dynamism of the MAI has afforded it global recognition. In 2016, it was the seventh largest producer of automobiles, the sixth largest producer of auto parts, the fourth largest exporter of automobiles, and the fifth largest exporter of auto parts. In Latin America, it has been the number one producer since 2014. In 2017, vehicle production reached a record of 4,068,415 units (OICA 2018) and employed close to a million workers. Eighty percent of production is for the export market (AMIA 2017), with finished products sent to approximately one hundred countries.

The industry's insertion in the external market, as well as its integration into global production chains, sometimes called **global value chains**

TABLE 11.1 MILESTONES IN THE MEXICAN AUTOMOTIVE INDUSTRY

Mexican Growth Model	Period	Milestones
CKD	1930s–1950s	Start of the Industry
ISI (Industrialization by Import Substitution)	1960s–1980s	**Consolidation of the Industry** Industrialization Decrees Development of Industrial Complexes in large Urban Zones Company Unions Beginning of Trade Openness at the end of the period
EXP (Exportations)	1990s–2010s	Sustained Growth NAFTA Development of Maquiladoras/IMMEX in new zones Limited Automation Broad Dissemination of the Lean Manufacturing & Management Industrial Escalation/Centers of R&D Development of Clusters Union Contracts for Protection Global Financial Crisis
Industry 4.0 (Exponential and Disruptive Technologies); ISI	2020s–2040s (?)	**Rupture: New Energies, Interconectivity, Autonomy** Technological Convergence (nanotechnology, biotechnology, new materials) New Environmental Standards Broad Digitalization Dissemination/Internet of Things Reduction of Cost of Robots Development of New Alternative Energies Changes in Mobility with new uses New Actors from other Industries/Changes in Governance of the CVG

or **global supply chains,** has allowed it to expand its production levels and maintain its great dynamism: between 1993 and 2016, the MAI grew at an annual average rate of 5.9 percent, while the national gross domestic product (GDP) and the manufacturing rates grew by 2.5 and 2.4 percent, respectively (CEFP 2017). While one year before NAFTA came into effect, in 1993, the automobile GDP represented 8.3 percent of the total Mexican GDP, by 2017, it reached 18.4 percent. In the same

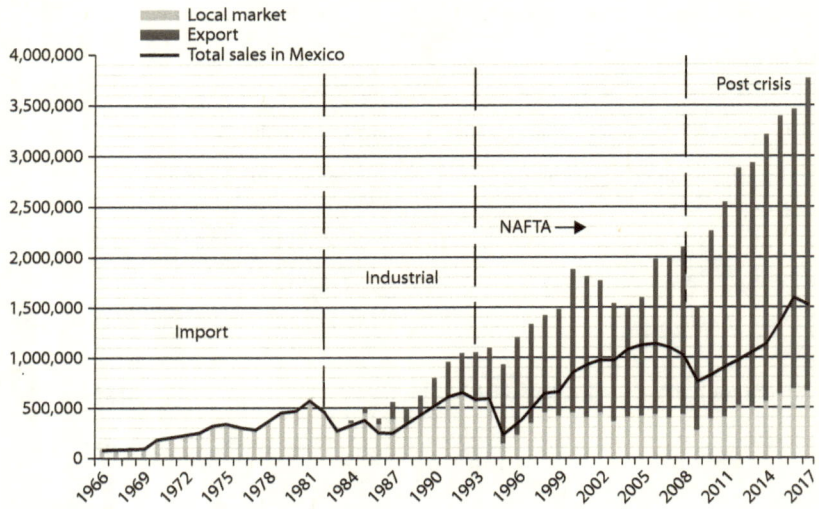

FIGURE 11.1. Evolution of Production and Automobile Sales in Mexico, 1966–2017 (units). Source: Author's elaboration based on data from AMIA and INEGI 2018. Note: Total sales include vehicle imports.

period, auto parts went from representing 4.2 percent of the total GDP to 8.1 percent (Albin 2017).

The MAI is by far the largest generator of foreign exchange in the country. In 2017, it generated double that of remittances ($56.9 billion vs. $28.3 billion, respectively) and almost five times that of tourism ($11.8 billion). In addition, it represents 11 percent of Mexican foreign direct investment (FDI). During the period 1999–2017, the FDI reached $59.7 billion. A large part of these investments came from the United States and represented 53 percent of FDI accumulated during these eighteen years. Historically, this growth in investment has not been linear but rather has come in waves (**figure 11.2**), with an increasingly greater American presence, particularly since the financial crisis of 2007–8.[1] The result, however, has been a gradual decrease in production in the United States (from 12.19 million vehicles in 2016 to 11.8 in 2017) (Albin 2017; OICA 2018). Furthermore, according to *IHS Market* and *Automotive News,* in 2017, for the first time, the trend regarding production according to country of origin changed, with American companies ceasing to be the main producers in the NAFTA market. In 1995, Detroit's "Big Three" represented 79 percent, while in 2016 this dropped to 50.4 percent, and it is predicted that it will fall further to

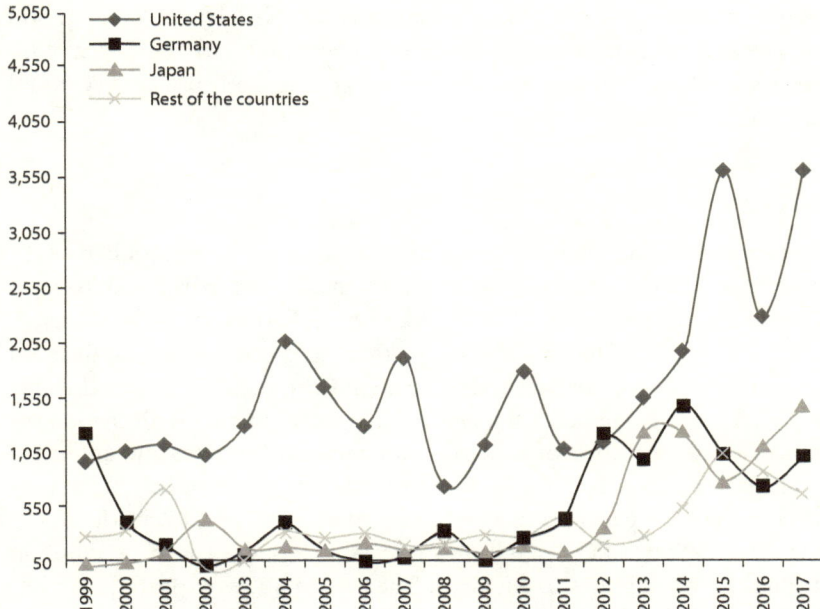

FIGURE 11.2. FDI by Country of Origin in the Automotive Sector (millions of dollars). Source: Author's elaborated data from the Secretariat of Economy, Direct Foreign Investment (conjuntodedato.gob) 2018.

20.9 percent by 2022. In contrast, non-American companies increased their participation from 20.8 to 49.6 percent, and it is expected that this will rise further to 52.4 percent (Albin 2017).

Within the MAI, the auto parts industry has a singular economic and social relevance. In 2017, Mexico was the sixth largest producer worldwide, with $85 billion, and it is expected that by 2021 this will reach $91 billion (Albin 2017). According to the Instituto Nacional de Estadística y Geografía (INEGI), the value of the production of auto parts in 2017 reached 39.6 percent of the total value of the MAI, in contrast to 47.6 percent in the light vehicles assembly industry and 12.8 percent in heavy vehicles.

Thus, and in summary, it can be said that (a) the presence of the automotive industry in Mexico is associated with different internationalization strategies by foreign assembly and auto parts companies and (b) that US FDI has had an important presence and will continue to grow in the country. While the productive participation of the United

States decreased slightly in the context of NAFTA in comparison to Mexico, it will continue to be complementary to the latter, with the two countries increasingly more integrated, both productively and commercially.

INTEGRATION OF AUTOMOTIVE CHAINS

Automotive value chains begin with the sale of raw materials to auto suppliers, which use these materials to make auto parts and systems that in turn are used by OEMS—like Ford, Toyota, or Volkswagen—to manufacture vehicles, which are then sold to consumers through dealerships. These automotive value chains are highly integrated in the NAFTA region (Mexico-US-Canada). They deal mainly with the importation and exportation of parts, components, and systems and are based on intra- and inter-firm trade. By 2016, the levels of production integration in the auto parts trade were by far mainly flowing from Mexico to the United States ($52.7 billion in 2016 as opposed to $28.4 billion from the United States to Mexico). The United States exports $25.5 billion to Canada and receives $16.0 billion from it. Trade between Mexico and Canada is less and also favors Mexico.

Due to the high trade deficit of the United States with Mexico, the Trump administration has been extremely critical of NAFTA. NAFTA renegotiations aim to counteract the trade deficit and generate employment in the United States by proposing an increase in the value of regional content for vehicles and auto parts from the current rate of 62.5 percent, with 50 percent "made in the USA" for automobiles made in Mexico and Canada and exported to the United States.[2] By August 16, 2018, the United States and Mexico had agreed ("in principle") on 75 percent regional content (25 percent from the rest of the world). From this 75 percent, 40 percent of the value of the vehicle is to be made in regions that pay $16 per hour. The imported vehicles from Mexico that fail to meet these requirements must pay a 2 to 3 percent tariff. Around 70 percent of the vehicles exported to the United States from Mexico meet these requirements.

Regardless of the uncertainty caused by the NAFTA renegotiations, in 2017 the automotive industry in Mexico achieved the highest FDI in its history, amounting to $6,850 million, or 23 percent of the total FDI. A review of the data on the accumulated FDI from 1999 to 2017 shows that the auto parts sector surpassed the manufacture of automobiles and trucks by 61 percent auto parts to 35 percent manufacture, almost double (Secretaría de Economía 2018).[3] The dominance of auto parts over assembly (on various economic indicators) is a characteristic particular to the Mexican case. In 2000, auto parts from Mexico made up 16 percent of American imports, and by 2017, this had increased to 35 percent, making Mexico the main supplier of the US auto parts market—overtaking Canada and Japan (Gortari 2018). The fact is that 2.8 times more auto parts are exported from Mexico to the United States than are imported to Mexico from the United States.

Nine main auto parts exported from Mexico in 2017 represented 47.6 percent of total exports (**table 11.2**). The main component is wire harness cables with a value of $7,505 million, followed by seats at a value of $5,551 million and internal combustion engines at $4,237 million. Wire harnesses, seats, and engines alone contributed 23.7 percent (Albin 2017). Imports of vehicle parts to the United States depend 63 percent on low-cost countries, of which more than half come from Mexico. In other words, $1,890 billion in auto parts are imported from Mexico, $1,589 million comes from other low-cost countries, and $2,078 million comes from countries that are not low cost (Albin 2017).

By successfully concluding the NAFTA renegotiation with the passage of the US-Mexico-Canada Agreement (USMCA), auto parts companies avoided the **World Trade Organization (WTO)** tariffs that could have been imposed if the renegotiation had failed and the contract had been canceled. The WTO sets and governs international trade regulations if no other agreement supersedes the WTO regulations. Production in Mexico would no longer have been competitive under WTO tariffs, since the maximum average auto parts depreciation is 5 percent (Albin 2017) and the WTO tariff goes above 5 percent. In the case of auto parts, the tariffs falling under the rules of the WTO would increase from 1 to 6 percent.

In summary, it is worth mentioning that (a) the existing intense trade in the North American region is based on the integration of global value (production/supply) chains; (b) trade is not only based on the exchange of vehicles, but more especially on intermediate goods; and (c) crucial components exist in this exchange such as wire harnesses, seats, and engines from Mexico and airbags, stamped parts, and gearbox components that go to Mexico.

TABLE 11.2 MEXICO: PRINCIPAL EXPORTS AND IMPORTS

Main Auto Parts Exported by Mexico *(millions of dollars)*

Auto Parts	2016	2017	Variation (%)
Harnesses, threads, and cables	7,953	7,505	−5.6
Seats and parts	5,552	5,551	0.0
Internal combustion engines	4,909	4,237	−13.7
Differential axles and parts	3,693	3,685	−0.2
Gearbox and parts	3,204	3,444	7.5
Stamped parts and accessories for car bodies	3,476	3,346	−3.7
Airbags and parts	2,570	2,536	−1.3
Braking mechanisms	2,015	2,204	9.4
Apparatus for air-conditioning	1,857	2,150	15.8
Total Selected Auto Parts	35,229	34,659	−1.6
Total Auto Parts	70,822	72,751	2.7

Main Auto-Parts Imported by Mexico *(millions of dollars)*

Auto Parts	2016	2017*	Variation (%)
Stamped parts and accessories for car bodies	2,440	2,570	5.4%
Components for gear boxes	1,991	2,271	14.1%
Components for harnesses	2,527	2,104	−16.7%
Internal combustion engines	1,554	2,024	30.2%
Components for playback devices (audio/vídeo)	2,025	1,920	−5.2%
Components for brakes	1,364	1,489	9.1%
Components for differential axles	1,157	1,466	26.7%
Components for seats	1,441	1,448	0.5%
Components for airbags	1,410	1,427	1.2%
Total Selected Auto Parts	15,909	16,719	5.1%
Total Auto Parts	44,096	47,797	8.4%

SOURCE: Author elaborated with data from INA 2017.

TECHNOLOGY LEVEL AND PRODUCTIVITY

Automotive companies, both OEMs and Tier One and Two suppliers, have dozens of plants throughout the North American region where most of the production, employment, and technology is concentrated. From the moment they are established in Mexico, many companies introduce the most advanced technology, the best organizational practices available, and the certification of their processes—within the framework of broad labor flexibility and a young and qualified labor

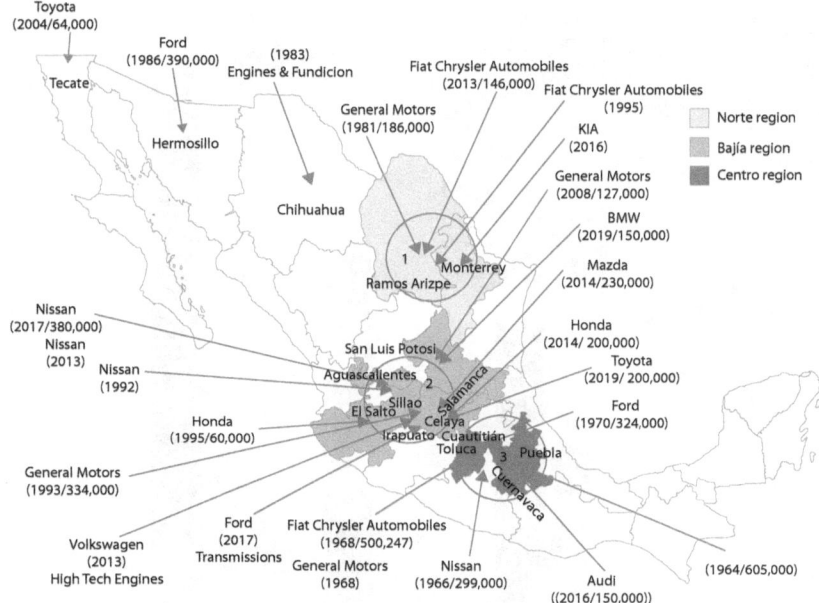

FIGURE 11.3. Main Automotive Clusters in Mexico. Sources: Author's elaboration. Graphic with data from the Secretaría de Economía, Direct Foreign Investment, Flows by Federal Entity, 2017. Map with data from AMIA and INEGI.

force. This process, which perhaps started with the Ford plant in Hermosillo in 1986, was followed by companies such as Delphi (a spin-off of General Motors), which coordinated with the Monterrey Technology Center (MTC) to open its first technology center outside the United States in Juárez in 1995, and many others. The recently created Audi plant in the state of Puebla similarly has the highest levels of automotive technology, and BMW in San Luis Potosí has announced its new computer-based paint system product. In addition, Continental and Bosch recently established new technical centers with strong expertise in software in order to meet the new trends in connectivity.

Regarding the manufacture of light vehicles and engines, these are distributed in eleven states in Mexico. Eighteen foreign production complexes have created three mega clusters: the Norte (northeast), the Bajío (west central), and the Centro (**figures 11.3 and 11.4**). Auto parts companies, both foreign and Mexican, are located in twenty-six states. The majority of plants and employment is concentrated in the Norte (45.9 percent), the Bajío (29.9 percent), and the Centro (13.4 percent)

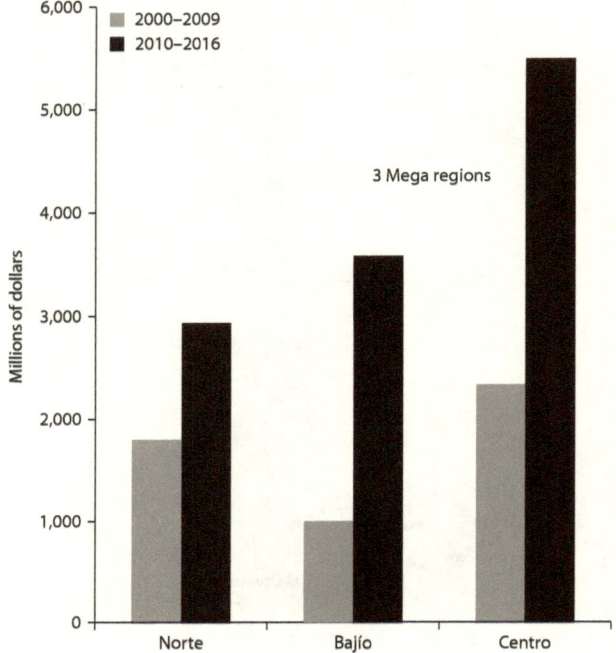

FIGURE 11.4. Mexico: FDI in the Automotive Industry by Mega Region. Source: Author elaboration based on Secretaria de Economia, 2018.

(Albin 2017). It is important to highlight that of the total auto parts plants, around a quarter are Tier One suppliers. Of the hundred main global players in this sector, 91 percent are in Mexico (Albin 2017). Some of these companies serve eighteen of the assembly plants located in Mexico that produced more than 4 million vehicles in 2017.

Despite this concentration of global firms (producers and suppliers), the supply chain is inverted in comparison to the structure in developed countries and other emerging economies such as China and India. That is, Mexico does not have any national OEMs and has only 1 percent of Tier One companies, with the majority of the few Mexican companies concentrated at the Tier Three and Tier Four levels, although no specific information exists in this regard.

So what is it that has changed since the establishment of NAFTA in 1994? First, the supply base is currently wider. Second, all levels of the chain have grown. Third, the segments that have grown the most are Tier One and Tier Two, resulting in the chain being inverted. And fourth, there are more Mexican companies, although they tend to be found at the lower levels of the chain.

THE NAFTA PARADOX

Although the passage of the USMCA begins to address some of the issues of wage disparity between Mexican and US workers, the **NAFTA paradox** remains: as Mexican workers increase their production, their incomes decrease (Shaiken 2016). In the case of the **maquiladora** industry (i.e., factories in Mexico owned by foreign companies that import products to assemble strictly for export), this paradox is understood as the enrichment of work with the impoverishment of employment. That is, workers are increasingly more qualified and better trained and able to deal with new technologies and have better organizational practices and international certifications but are experiencing a process of increasing labor precarity—irregular employment, job insecurity, low wages, and few benefits.

Precarious employment began with the restructuring of the automotive industry at the beginning of the 1980s (Carrillo 1993) and continues to this day. In the 1980s, American car makers responded to the new dominance of Japan by creating leaner operations and pursuing cost-saving strategies—particularly automation—while also expanding their offerings to include minivans and sport utility vehicles. In Mexico, where the automotive sector employed close to 1 million people in 2016 (108,143 in OEMs and 757,000 in auto parts),[4] wage variation is consistent with such strategies for saving production costs. Labor segmentation—with unskilled workers at the bottom of the wage scale and executives at the top—is not the only factor evident. Other factors are (a) substantive differences in salaries paid by OEMs, where top companies can pay up to double that of those that pay the least (Covarrubias 2014); (b) salary differences between regular and subcontracted workers within the OEMs and Tier Ones; and (c) variation in wages between companies, plants, and regions and also within the same company (García and Carrillo 2017).

In addition, the enormous salary differences between a newly hired automotive worker in the United States and Canada and a newly hired worker in Mexico are abysmal: 7.8 times greater, or $17.80 per hour in the United States, compared to $2.30 in Mexico in 2017. This is viewed by Canadian and American unions as *social dumping*. According to INEGI and AMIA (2016), in 2014 wages paid to employees in the MAI reached $7.82 per hour, more than double the average registered in all the manufacturing industry and contrasting with the $3.40 an hour in the auto parts industry.[5] In addition, salary differences are evident between long-established companies and those recently created, including producers of luxury cars (Heim 2016). Finally, salaries in various OEMs, in terms of their purchasing power (living wage), are below the urban poverty line (García and Carrillo 2017).

This behavior contrasts with the growth in productivity of the automotive sector. According to the Comisión Económica para América Latina y el Caribe (CEPAL) (2017), between 1990 and 2012, automotive production was greater than the average productivity within the manufacturing sector. Not only does Mexico place last regarding salaries paid in comparison to other Latin American countries, but it is also a paradigmatic case with high productivity and low wages (Moreno-Brid and Garry 2015). In general terms, it is possible to state that during the period 1999–2015, while productivity in the MAI grew by 45 percent, wages stagnated, to say the least, with a reduction of −10 percent. This relationship was more evident in the OEMs than in auto parts. Thus, a dichotomous process is evident: economic upgrading with social downgrading.

The recent trade agreement between the United States and Mexico established a chapter on labor issues. So, instead of a parallel agreement (which is more best intentions than reality), this new chapter brings International Labour Organization (ILO) standards. Although Mexico requires "secondary legislation" in order to have a law on these issues, the new phase looks better for working people, with the real possibility of upgraded wages.

In summary, (a) automotive companies in Mexico are labor-intensive, both final assembly plants and first- and second-level suppliers; and (b) growth in productivity in the sector is not associated with a corresponding increase in wages but rather the contrary.

CHALLENGES IN THE FACE OF EXPONENTIAL NEW TECHNOLOGIES

The automotive industry finds itself at a crossroads in the face of exponential new technologies. The "fourth technological revolution," known as **Industry 4.0**, is changing the ecosystem of the automotive sector. Some of the tendencies influencing Industry 4.0 are new concepts of mobility (e.g., autonomous driving, car sharing, car pooling), patterns of consumption more concerned about the environment, and energy efficiency. Although changes in production and consumption are still quite limited, the central question is not if these new technologies will arrive (summarized in Industry 4.0) but rather how quickly they will be introduced and where they will take place. For example, the average automobile currently has sixty microprocesses, four times more than ten years ago (CEPAL 2017).

Three technological tendencies are currently evident worldwide in the automotive industry and will, no doubt, impact Mexico:

1) Electrification. Power trains will move toward hybrid-electric, electric, and fuel cell technology, as electrification matures and becomes cheaper.
2) Diverse mobility. As the sharing economy expands and consumer preferences change, the standard model will move from individual buys to rentals or car sharing (car sharing, car pooling, autonomous vehicles, cellular vehicle-to-everything, car-to-x connectivity).
3) Connectivity. The possibilities of *infotainment innovations,* new traffic services, and new business and service models will increase as cars become connected to each other, to broad infrastructure, and to people. The development of 5G technology will facilitate technological convergence (intersectoral coevolution and cooperation/automotive and information and communication technologies [ICTs]). As technologies mature (including the 5G network), the operation of autonomous cars will move from drivers' assistance systems to totally autonomous driving systems.

In the case of the automotive sector, automation has always been at the heart of the debate. The automated assembly line, an essential characteristic of Fordism, has been present since the 1920s (Coriat 1992) and gave rise to the configuration of a production model based on mass production, with repercussions on all economic sectors (Boyer and Freyssenet 2002). The wave of automation in the 1980s substituted, for example, all work in welding and painting departments of the automotive assemblies, not only with robots, but also with numerical control machines. Currently, various predictions indicate that an important volume of work in the automotive sector could be automated: up to 69 percent, depending on whether it is predictable manual labor, information processing, or information gathering (US Bureau of Statistics, cited in McKinsey Global Institute 2017).

The discussion focuses on (a) whether this impact is directed principally at routine manual activities or also at other activities; (b) whether the reduction in the cost of robots (generic and specialized) will stimulate a massive substitution of labor; or (c) whether the impact will be equitable between regions with different levels of development. What is certain is that parallel to the great dynamism in innovation is great uncertainty.

Firms have great incentives to substitute labor with automated processes (Autor 2015). Robots, for example, can work more reliably, cheaper, and quicker, in addition to the fact that they neither complain nor go on strike. Furthermore, labor continues to be relatively expensive in highly industrialized countries, including some recently industrialized (or emerging) countries. Despite this, in cases such as Mexico, predictions are even more difficult to make given the relatively low salaries (sometimes below the urban poverty line) (García and Carrillo 2017) as well as the prevailing system of labor relations that has become a factor in attracting foreign investment (Bensusán, Carrillo, and Ahumada 2011). In addition, the existence of flexible, productive labor with a long tradition in the export sector and longer workdays than most other countries may be sufficient to delay the massive wave of automation. However, the foreseeable future remains uncertain.

CONCLUSION

The automotive industry in the Mexico-US-Canada region is highly integrated. It involves the same global players confronting crucial challenges to reduce costs, elevate productivity, and strengthen capacity in the so-called Industry 4.0. **Intraregional trade**—trade between regional neighbors, such as the countries in North America—is intense and comprises complex value chains. Firms not only compete internationally but also in the regions where they are located and even among their own subsidiaries. Within this process, grading of work, exportation vocation in the regions, and innovation ecosystems play a central role in incentivizing new investments and quickly appropriating new digital technologies. Thus, while national borders are less clear with exponential new technologies, and certainly exacerbate the process of complementarity between the United States and Mexico, they are likely to simultaneously increase social inequalities in these countries, unless the Mexican government seriously considers the necessary socio-labor upgrading. The new trade agreement between the United States and Mexico will affect some investment due to new rules of origin, but it will also bring the possibility for social upgrading from rising wages and the reduction of "protection agreements."

Suggested Reading

Center for Automotive Research (CAR). 2017. NAFTA briefing: Trade benefits to the automotive industry and potential consequences of withdrawal from the agreement. Center for Automotive Research, Detroit, MI.

Comisión Económica para América Latina y el Caribe (CEPAL). 2018. La inversión extranjera directa en América Latina y el Caribe [Foreign direct investment in Latin America and the Caribbean]. CEPAL–Naciones Unidas, Santiago de Chile.

de Gortari, Alonso. 2018. *How much of your car is made in Mexico?* EconoFact Network, Edward R. Murrow Center for a Digital World, Tufts University.

Holmes, J. 2017. NAFTA and the automotive industry: A Canadian perspective. Paper presented at the Ontario Auto Mayors Meeting, August, Queen's University, Oakville, ON.

Moreno-Brid, J., and E. Garry. 2015. El salario mínimo en México: En falta con la Constitución mexicana y una aberración en América Latina [The minimum wage in Mexico: Missing the Mexican constitution and an aberration in Latin America]. In M. Á. Mancera, ed., *Del salario mínimo al salario digno* [From the minimum wage to the living wage], 105–21. Mexico City: Consejo Económico y Social de la Ciudad de México.

ProMéxico. 2016. *La industria automotriz mexicana: Situación actual, retos y oportunidades* [The automotive industry in Mexico: Current situation, challenges, and opportunities]. Mexico City: Secretaría de Economía.

Secretaria de Economia. 2018. Registro Nacional de Inversiones Extranjeras (RNIE). Secretaría de Economía, Mexico.

CHAPTER 12

What Policies Make Sense in a US-Mexico Trade Deal?

ROBERT A. BLECKER, JUAN CARLOS
MORENO-BRID, AND ISABEL SALAT

The renegotiation of the North American Free Trade Agreement (NAFTA) in 2017–18 at the behest of US president Donald Trump focused public attention on trade "deals" as a key link between the Mexican and US economies. Like all trade agreements, NAFTA helped to reshape the industrial structure of the three member economies (Mexico, the United States, and Canada) and created winners and losers in all three countries along the way. NAFTA's trade and investment rules created incentives for industries to locate in one country or another and promoted the development of trinational "supply chains" among the three North American nations. Revising those rules in the newly renamed United States-Mexico-Canada Agreement (USMCA)—which went into effect on July 1, 2020—will affect the future evolution of all three economies and will create new winners and losers in each, in rather unpredictable ways.

On the one hand, USMCA was launched while the Covid-19 pandemic was dramatically reducing economic activity and international trade, breaking global value chains, interrupting international travel, and undermining investment prospects—not to mention killing hundreds of thousands of people—in North America and elsewhere. All these elements introduce enormous uncertainty, which depresses the business climate for the short and medium term. On the other hand, as occurred with NAFTA, USMCA will facilitate overall trade in the region. But its ultimate impact on employment and economic growth will depend on whether or not other key policies, especially industrial, innovation and labor policies, are implemented.

Indeed, policy makers and civil society should be very careful to prevent the renegotiation of NAFTA and its transformation into USMCA from becoming merely a distraction from the need to apply other policies that could truly improve living conditions for the vast majority of workers in all three member countries. Such policies would be pretty much the opposite of what the Trump administration has promulgated in the United States. Nothing in the rebaptized USMCA will do much if anything to address the two greatest economic problems in the region: the huge disparity in wages and per capita income between Mexico and its richer northern neighbors and the high degree of inequality within all three countries. Nor will the new trade agreement help Mexico escape from its trap of slow long-term growth unless a new agenda for development is put in place.

WHAT NAFTA DID AND DIDN'T ACCOMPLISH

When NAFTA went into effect in 1994, it was widely hailed as the first modern **preferential trade agreement**—an agreement that reduces trade barriers, particularly tariffs, but only among the member nations—between a developing nation, Mexico, and two advanced economies, Canada and the United States. The hope or expectation was that the enactment of this agreement would lead to a renewed process of upward **economic convergence** between Mexico and its northern neighbors, in which average Mexican wages, productivity, and per capita income would rise toward US and Canadian levels while the latter would continue to increase—as occurred between 1950 and 1980 but was reversed thereafter (see Blecker and Esquivel 2013).

Some of the expectations for Mexican-US integration did come to pass.[1] Intraregional trade has mushroomed: between 1993 and 2016, Mexican exports to the United States increased sevenfold in value, while Mexican imports from the United States grew about four times.[2] Mexico's transformation from a country that mostly exported oil and other primary commodities into one of the world's largest exporters of manufactures began with its initial trade liberalization and opening to foreign investment in the late 1980s but accelerated greatly under NAFTA. Foreign direct investment (FDI) inflows into Mexico increased from an average of about 1 percent of the country's gross domestic product (GDP) before NAFTA to nearly 3 percent after.[3]

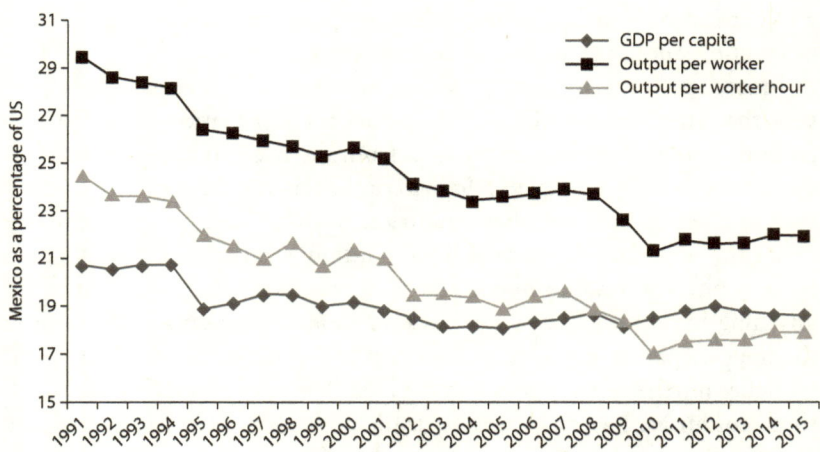

FIGURE 12.1. GDP per Capita and Labor Productivity in Mexico as Percentages of US Levels, 1991–2015. Source: World Bank, *World Development Indicators*; OECD statistics, accessed October 15, 2017; and authors' calculations.

In spite of these increases in trade and FDI, however, the larger goals that the Mexican government proclaimed for NAFTA when it was adopted in 1994 have not been achieved. As shown in **figure 12.1**, Mexico has actually diverged from the United States in GDP per capita, and even more in **labor productivity** (output per hour or per worker), since that time. Although productivity has grown rapidly in the largest firms and in export sectors, average productivity growth for the entire Mexican economy has been held down by stagnant or even falling productivity in other sectors, especially services and the informal sector—where workers are either self-employed or work in small enterprises without social insurance or protections (Moreno-Brid and Ros 2009; Bolio et al. 2014)—and real (inflation-adjusted) wages have lagged behind productivity in export-oriented manufacturing industries and in the economy in general (Blecker 2016).

Thus, the hoped-for convergence of Mexico with the United States never occurred. Mexico's real GDP per capita, measured in **purchasing power parity (PPP)** terms (i.e., corrected for differences in the cost of living in each country), grew at a paltry 1.2 percent average annual rate from 1994 to 2017, far below the 6.2 percent rate achieved in the Asian developing and emerging economies over that same period and even below the 1.5 percent rate in the United States during those years.[4] Furthermore, the expected convergence between the wages of Mexican

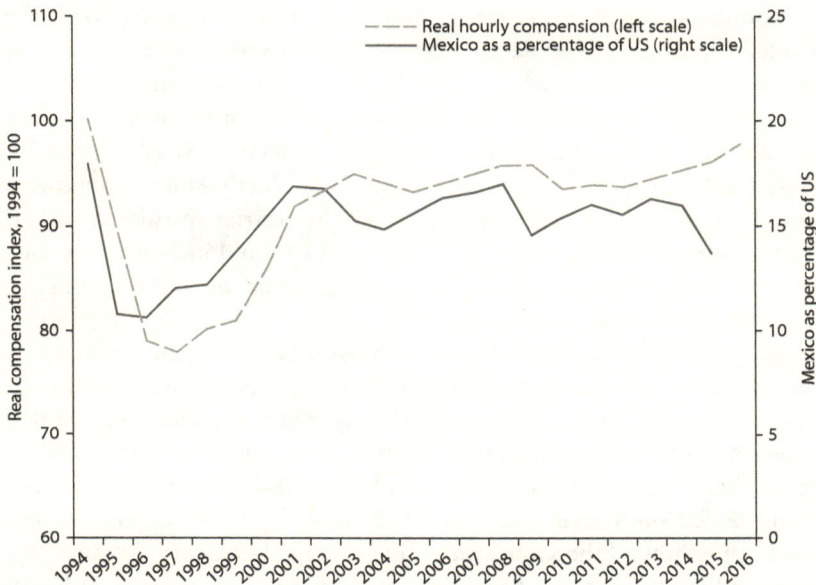

FIGURE 12.2. Hourly Compensation of Mexican Production Workers, in Real Terms and as a Percentage of the US level, 1994–2016. Source: Authors' calculations based on data from Banco de México (www.banxico.org.mx), INEGI, EMIM, www.inegi.org.mx; and BLS, International Labor Comparisons, retrieved from www.bls.gov.

and US workers never occurred. As figure 12.2 shows, as of 2016, real hourly compensation in Mexican manufacturing was still below its absolute level from 1994, while as of 2015 (the last year for which comparable data are available), Mexican hourly compensation in manufacturing was also a lower percentage of the US level than in 1994. As the Harvard economist Dani Rodrik writes, "Probably no other country in the world presents a starker contrast between external success and domestic failure" than Mexico (Rodrik 2014).

INDUSTRIES, JOBS, AND INEQUALITY

Although Mexico exports many types of manufactures, including electronic products, electrical equipment, televisions, and other consumer appliances, by far its largest export industry and the most successful example of regional integration in North America is the automotive sector (Dussel Peters and Gallagher 2013; Moreno-Brid et al. 2018). In recent years, Mexico has specialized in labor-intensive parts and components (e.g., brakes and brake pads) and smaller cars, while the United States and Canada have specialized in more capital-intensive, technologically advanced inputs and larger vehicles, such as SUVs, minivans, and light trucks. Ironically, one reason for the strength of the automotive sector is not the free trade provisions of NAFTA—although NAFTA did provide for zero tariffs for intra–North American trade in automobiles and auto parts—but rather the restrictive **rules of origin** that required 62.5 percent of the value of a car sold in North America to consist of North American (Canadian, Mexican, or US) inputs in order to receive that tariff exemption.

Aside from automobiles, however, most other Mexican manufacturing export sectors have continued to focus mainly on the assembly of imported parts and components, the so-called maquiladora model, where manufacturing plants transform imported materials into finished or semifinished goods for export—with limited domestically generated value added—a system that predated NAFTA. These export sectors have not exhibited the same kind of increases in **backward linkages** and **value added** that have been observed in the automotive industry (Moreno-Brid, Santamaría, and Valdivia 2005; Moreno-Brid et al. 2018). That is, the assembly operations carried out in many Mexican export industries create little demand for domestically produced inputs and add relatively little value to the imported inputs used in the assembly process. Thus, the good news is that Mexican export industries across the board have become highly integrated into global value chains (sometimes referred to as supply chains or production chains), in which the different stages of the production process are located across different countries; the bad news is that outside of the automotive sector Mexican production is mostly located on the segments of those chains that generate the least domestic value added. This lack of value added in Mexican exports largely accounts for why the domestic economy has grown so slowly in the post-NAFTA period, in spite of the rapid increase in the total value of Mexican exports (which is exaggerated by the inclusion of the value of imported inputs).

On the US side, the "success" of the regionally integrated automotive sector presents a less favorable view for labor. US employment in motor vehicles (including parts and components) fell by about a half million between the late 1990s and 2018, while Mexican employment in the same industries rose by a comparable amount.[5] Although this coincidence does not prove that those jobs "moved" to Mexico, on the whole automotive employment in North America shows a net gain in Mexico in the past two decades relative to its neighbors. In the process, many US auto workers and their communities in rust belt states like Michigan lost out, which may help to explain the political swings in auto-producing regions of the United States. Nevertheless, one could argue (even though it's a hard sell to US workers) that what remains of the US motor vehicle sector is more competitive as a result of the regional rationalization of production across North America and the reliance on lower-cost parts and components sourced from Mexico.

In spite of the losses in US manufacturing jobs (and the accompanying US trade deficit with Mexico, which consists mostly of automotive products), it is not true that Mexico "won" from NAFTA and the United States "lost" as Trump has claimed. On the one hand, US corporate interests (such as the automobile companies) have profited handsomely from their ability to rationalize production and establish supply chains throughout North America, with the more labor-intensive operations carried out in lower-wage Mexico. Middle-class US consumers of cars and other manufactured imports benefited from lower prices for such goods, while less-educated US workers in affected industries and regions were surely the main losers (Hakobyan and McLaren 2016). On the other hand, although Mexico did gain some manufacturing jobs, the numbers involved pale in comparison with the country's employment needs,[6] and, as noted earlier, Mexico never achieved the convergence in wages and incomes with the United States that it originally sought with NAFTA. Moreover, Mexico's trade deficit with other countries exceeds its bilateral surplus with the United States, so that it has a small deficit overall, even in manufactures. As a result, Mexico is neither a surplus country nor a truly dynamic economy (Moreno-Brid 2013; Blecker 2019).

Moreover, since the late 1990s, both Mexico and the United States have experienced significant increases in inequality, as measured by rising top income shares and falling labor shares in national income (Piketty 2014; Esquivel 2015; Ibarra and Ros 2019). At the core of this rising inequality in both countries is the fact that workers' real wages have stagnated even in the manufacturing sector, where productivity has increased most rapidly, contributing (along with increasing market power of large corporations) to higher profit margins of firms and stagnation of economic growth (Bivens 2017b; Autor et al. 2020; De Loecker, Eeckhout, and Unger 2020).

Trade and **offshoring** of jobs are only some of the forces causing these trends in inequality, but they are likely important ones, and a trade agreement like NAFTA that privileged property rights of corporations over labor rights of workers is certainly a suspect—along with many other trade agreements and policies—in having contributed to some degree (see Bivens 2017a). Nevertheless, other policies and events surely also played a role, including privatization of state enterprises (often transforming them into private monopolies) in Mexico; the merger-and-acquisition boom (which has enhanced the monopoly power of corporations) in the United States; the transformation of corporate governance to a shareholder value orientation; and the weakening of labor unions and deregulation of markets in both countries. Dwindling public expenditures on infrastructure (as percentages of GDP) have also contributed to weak growth in industrial employment on both sides of the border (where most job growth has been in services).

THE USMCA DEAL ON AUTOMOBILES

After President Trump pushed to have NAFTA renegotiated—after being persuaded by his advisers in April 2017 not to simply withdraw—US Trade Representative (USTR) Robert Lighthizer designed the US strategy in the renegotiation process. The US objectives for the NAFTA renegotiation (USTR 2017) stemmed from Lighthizer's focus on key manufacturing sectors like automobiles and his concern to weaken what he saw as incentives in NAFTA for US producers to outsource production to Mexico.

Not surprisingly, given the importance of the automotive sector, much of the NAFTA renegotiation focused on this industry. The new USMCA includes three key changes in the requirements for automobiles to qualify for a regional tariff exemption (Campbell 2018; Zumbrun 2018b). First, the rules of origin for autos have been stiffened to require 75 percent North American content, up from the original 62.5 percent. Second, more of the steel and aluminum used in automobiles has to be sourced from North American producers. Third, as much as 40 to 45 percent of the value of a finished car must be produced by workers earning a minimum of $16 per hour. This wage is at least four times more than what most Mexican workers currently earn in the automotive sector but far below what US and Canadian auto workers earn. Hence, the intention of this last provision is to force auto companies to either pay their Mexican workers a much higher wage or shift some of their production, especially of parts and components, to the United States or Canada.

Although the intention of these provisions is, evidently, to induce more automotive and metal production in the United States, the actual impact is far from certain. The vast majority of cars produced in Mexico already meet the 75 percent regional content threshold and companies have several years to reach this target, but meeting the minimum wage requirement could require some realignment of regional supply chains (Fickling and Trivedi 2018). Production costs would be likely to rise because of higher costs for labor, steel, and other inputs, which could make North American cars less competitive in global markets and more expensive for US, Mexican, and Canadian consumers. Nevertheless, some auto workers could gain either higher wages (in Mexico) or more jobs (in the United States or Canada) if the minimum wage requirement proves to be effective.

However, rules of origin and similar restrictions are a blunt and sometimes ineffective tool for compelling regional production within a trading bloc. If higher requirements for regional content and wages would raise production costs too high, automobile companies could choose to ignore USMCA tariff preferences altogether and bring cars into the United States under the **most-favored nation (MFN) tariff** of 2.5 percent under World Trade Organization (WTO) rules. This low tariff rate applies to all imported automobiles (although not to trucks and other larger vehicles), regardless of where they are produced, as long as they are not covered by USMCA or another preferential trade agreement. In a worst-case scenario, imposing excessive restrictions to qualify for USMCA preferences in automobiles could drive some auto producers to shift their operations out of North America and export to the US market from other locations while paying the 2.5 percent MFN tariff.

However, Lighthizer and other Trump trade officials have anticipated this problem, for which they have been considering a potential remedy: the imposition of a 25 percent tariff on all automobile imports using the same "national security" loophole in the US trade laws that they have already exploited for tariffs on steel and aluminum imports. The national security provision (Section 232 of the Trade Expansion Act of 1962) gives the president complete discretion to impose tariffs or other trade restrictions, even if his claims of a national security threat from the imports are not credible. Reportedly, Canada and Mexico were able to negotiate "side agreements" to USMCA that will exempt their automotive exports from such possible new tariffs but only up to certain quotas (quantitative limits) linked to their previous export levels. The case of steel remains a thorny one, as the new agreement did not eliminate the tariffs imposed by the Trump administration, while Mexico and Canada maintain that their exports of these products cannot be a threat to US security.

OTHER OUTCOMES IN THE NEW TRADE AGREEMENT

One of the most controversial elements of the original NAFTA was the strong enforcement mechanism it created for property rights of foreign investors. The "expropriation" clause in chapter 11 of NAFTA was interpreted broadly as prohibiting not merely the outright nationalization of foreign-owned assets but also any types of regulations (e.g., environmental laws) that could reduce potential corporate profits. This provision thus allowed foreign companies to claim property rights that are not recognized for domestic business firms in the laws of any of the member countries. Furthermore, chapter 11 created the **investor-state dispute settlement (ISDS)** system, which allowed foreign corporations to sue federal, state/provincial, or local governments before special panels of "experts" appointed to enforce these broadly defined property rights. Critics have argued that ISDS has a chilling effect on governments that might wish to adopt beneficial social or environmental regulations because of the constant threat of costly ISDS lawsuits.[7]

USTR Lighthizer made weakening ISDS a priority in the NAFTA renegotiation, not because he likes social and environmental regulations, but because he views ISDS as creating "political risk insurance for outsourcing" that implicitly subsidizes foreign companies that invest in Mexico (Miller 2018). Under USMCA, ISDS is abolished entirely for the United States and Canada, which chose to "opt out" in the negotiations. For Mexico, USMCA abolishes ISDS in general but keeps it in place for certain specific sectors such as energy and infrastructure (Zumbrun 2018b); ISDS would no longer apply to manufacturing industries in Mexico (Bernstein 2018). However, there may be less to the abolition of ISDS than meets the eye. Mexico has already adopted intellectual property rights and guarantees for foreign investors that meet NAFTA standards, and Mexico is keeping those in place precisely to reassure foreign corporations doing business in the country.

The abolition of ISDS for most industries could have a beneficial and unintended side effect: it could allow governments to adopt more legitimate social and environmental protections for their citizens without fear of ISDS complaints. Interestingly, the weakening of ISDS has been welcomed by US labor unions and progressive activists and opposed by the corporate interests that usually support trade agreements (see Bernstein 2018; Zumbrun 2018a; Zumbrun and Whelan 2018).

The Canadian, Mexican, and US negotiators also agreed that USMCA will have a term of 16 years, with a review to be conducted after 6 years leading to possible renewal for another 16 years. This provision represents a compromise over the USTR's original demand that the agreement would face "sunset" (abolition) every 5 years unless it would be renegotiated again and again (Harrup, Whelan, and Vieira 2018). The 16-year term and 6-year review process will allow business firms to do more long-term planning for their North American operations, compared to the 5-year sunset approach. However, the Trump administration hopes that even a 16-year horizon for USMCA—coupled with its other protectionist policies—could be an inducement for long-term investors interested in the US market to locate new plants there instead of in Mexico.

Instituting a process for periodically reviewing and revising USMCA is potentially a valuable change; one of the weaknesses of NAFTA was that it contained no procedures for amendment or updating. The Mexican and Canadian governments could welcome an opportunity to renegotiate USMCA after 2024, when the United States might have a new administration that could be less protectionist and belligerent than the Trump team, but even the extended 16-year sunset provision is one that Mexico and Canada accepted only reluctantly because of the uncertainty it could generate in the future.

The USTR (2017) originally demanded the complete elimination of NAFTA's chapter 19 dispute settlement process, which applied to alleged violations of NAFTA's trade provisions or other trade policies adopted by the three member countries. However, thanks to pressure from Canada in the final stages of the renegotiation, chapter 19 remains in place in the new USMCA. USMCA also includes new labor rights provisions, one of which would require firms to allow free elections for union representation, thus inhibiting the formation of the company-organized unions that are commonly found in Mexican export industries (see Bernstein 2018; Zumbrun 2018a). This is in line with International Labour Organization (ILO) convention 098, recently signed for the first time by the Mexican government, and fully in tune with the labor market reforms approved by Mexican president Andrés Manuel López Obrador. Measures to strengthen the enforcement of these labor rights provisions were negotiated by the USTR in 2019 in order to win approval of USMCA by Democrats in the US House of Representatives. However, the United States frequently violates labor rights too, for example, through so-called right-to-work laws that impede labor union organization in some states. It would be a greater step forward if USMCA included enhanced and enforceable labor rights provisions that would protect workers in all three countries, not just in Mexico.

An additional requirement imposed by the United States in USMCA is the prohibition of entering into trade negotiations or agreements with nonmarket economies, which is a thinly disguised veil for blocking Canada and Mexico from reaching separate trade deals with China.

WHAT KINDS OF ECONOMIC POLICIES ARE REALLY NEEDED?

What Mexico signed up for in NAFTA was a trade-and-investment agreement that would grant it preferential access to the US market in exchange for adopting US-style, market-oriented reforms; indeed, a key purpose of the agreement was to lock in those reforms, thereby enhancing foreign investors' confidence in Mexico. Ironically, it is now the United States, under the Trump administration, that has sought to renege on those commitments.

Remarkably, however, the United States is likely to gain very little from the Trump administration's trade policies—not only the new USMCA, but also the many tariffs imposed on imports of steel, aluminum, and numerous products from China. At most, this greater US protectionism can perhaps restore a few hundred thousand manufacturing jobs in sectors like steel and automobiles, but this would be a drop in the bucket in a country where the labor force totals around 160 million workers and tens of millions have lost jobs in the Covid-19 crisis. In a global economy that has fundamentally changed, a panoply of tariffs cannot re-create the industrial structure or job profile of past decades. Moreover, higher tariff barriers and more restrictive rules of origin can only make production that is shifted to the United States more costly and hence less competitive relative to other countries outside North America—especially by increasing costs in industries that use imported inputs. In addition, the Trump policies ignore the fact that if firms are forced to produce more goods in the United States, they will probably do so with more automated technologies that will not create the large numbers of jobs that existed in the past. Furthermore, Trump's protectionist trade policies have invited other countries like China and the European Union (EU) to retaliate by imposing tariffs on US exports, which hurt other US industries (such as motorcycles).

Moreover, Trump's protectionism is not accompanied by any coherent strategy for US industrial revitalization. Aside from imposing tariffs and renegotiating NAFTA and other trade agreements, the only other policies the Trump administration has instituted are lower tax rates for corporations and wealthy households, all of whom were already flush with cash, plus deregulation in every conceivable domain (labor standards, consumer safety, environmental protection, and financial regulation). This approach is at best a recipe for the creation of small numbers of low-wage jobs under unsafe working conditions, with destructive environmental and health side effects and significant risks of sparking future crises.

A true US industrial revitalization would require the exact opposite of the Trump administration's domestic policies. The government would have to plow significant resources into technological research, scientific education, and worker training. It would need to make massive public investments in infrastructure to create jobs in the present and provide for efficient public goods, such as transportation and communication networks, in the future. The United States also needs to address global warming by developing solar and wind power instead of promoting coal and oil production. The federal government needs to return to a more progressive income tax system and take other measures, including raising the minimum wage and stepping up anti-trust enforcement, to help reverse the long-term slide into worsened inequality. Taken together, these kinds of policies would create far more employment, put much more upward pressure on wages, and make US industries far more competitive than Trump's tariffs or the new USMCA.

On the Mexican side, since the export-led growth strategy founded on NAFTA has failed to promote rapid enough domestic growth to achieve convergence with the United States, Mexico needs to rebalance its strategic approach by placing relatively more emphasis on the internal market—without abandoning exports, of course. Strengthening the internal market in Mexico requires, above all, a major fiscal reform aimed at a significant redistribution of income to bolster the purchasing power of workers and the emerging middle class. This reform is also urgently needed to increase public investment in infrastructure and expenditures on basic social needs, such as education, health, and sanitation (Moreno-Brid 2013). There is consensus that such a fiscal reform is long overdue in order to increase the government's tax revenue, fortify its capacity to implement countercyclical policies, and make the whole budgetary system more progressive so that it offsets, rather than exacerbates, inequality (Grupo Nuevo Curso de Desarrollo 2017; Cordera and Provencio 2020). In addition, Mexican monetary policy needs to shift from an exclusive and excessive obsession with inflation to a more pro-investment and pro-growth stance, especially by preventing the peso from becoming overvalued.

Thus, most of the economic measures that both countries need to stimulate high and sustained economic growth are not trade policies. For example, both countries need to raise their minimum wages to reduce poverty and inequality and bolster consumer demand. Mexico actually adopted a policy of increasing its minimum wage in real terms in the last years of the administration of President Enrique Peña Nieto (2012–18). Subsequently, López Obrador supported a minimum wage policy designed to guarantee any employed worker an income that covers the cost of a basket of basic goods for herself and one family dependent. However, the United States has not increased its minimum wage under Trump, in spite of a massive campaign to raise it to $15 per hour.

USMCA does include requirements for enhanced rights of labor union organizing, which the López Obrador administration wanted to enact anyway. But for a trade agreement to really contribute to economic development throughout North America, it would need to be accompanied by the creation of an adequately funded regional development bank that could invest in industries and education in disadvantaged regions of all three countries. In order to effectively rein in China's export-promotion policies—which have damaged Mexican exports as well as US labor (see Gallagher, Moreno-Brid, and Porzecanksi 2008; Autor, Dorn, and Hanson 2016)—all three USMCA members would have to work cooperatively with each other and with other key trading partners, such as the EU, to negotiate with China or file WTO complaints against it. But in the end, all three North American nations need to make their own economies more equitable and competitive mainly through their own domestic efforts. The transformation of NAFTA into USMCA can only make a small contribution in this process, for better or for worse.

The enactment of USMCA has lessened the enormous uncertainty that Trump had created about the future of trade in the region (some uncertainty remains because of Trump's proclivity to impose new tariffs and other barriers). Nothing more, and nothing less. USMCA—like NAFTA decades ago—will not be the philosopher's stone that by itself will remove the key constraints binding long-term economic development and growth in the three countries. The fault or future is not in the stars or in trade policy. It lies elsewhere, in the still failed quest to design and implement an overall agenda for inclusive development and sustained long-term economic expansion. Unfortunately for Mexico, the

López Obrador administration so far has not put in place an agenda that would help put the Mexican economy on a dynamic path of environmentally sustainable and inclusive long-term growth. In fact, with the exception of the minimum wage and other labor-market policies, his administration is largely following the same neoliberal agenda that has marked Mexico's policy making since the launch of market reforms in the mid-1980s.

An active industrial policy is not in the agenda. Neither is a progressive fiscal reform or an initiative toward the creation of a system of universal social protection. Monetary policy remains focused on inflation targeting, while fiscal policy is committed to the most strict austerity the country has seen in decades. Indeed, as of mid-2020, the Ministry of Finance is aiming to cut expenditures, not to incur more public debt, and to register a primary budget surplus even in the midst of the most adverse economic shock that Mexico has experienced in decades, which has plunged the economy into the harshest recession in living memory.

Instead of removing the obstacles that have hindered Mexico's sustainable economic and social development, the present government may be making some of these restrictions even more binding. We have yet to see whether López Obrador will soon change policy course and forge a revitalized social pact with key economic and political actors in favor of a new agenda for sustainable and inclusive development and rapid and persistent economic expansion. In the case of the United States, the panorama appears even more complicated. Our hopes for a brighter, more inclusive future lie much more in the results of the 2020 presidential election than in any measures the Trump administration may undertake.

Suggested Reading

Blecker, R. A. 2016. Integration, productivity, and inclusion in Mexico: A macro perspective. In Alejandro Foxley and Barbara Stallings, eds., *Innovation and Inclusion in Latin America: Strategies to Avoid the Middle Income Trap,* 175–204. New York: Palgrave Macmillan.

———. 2019. NAFTA. In Robert E. Looney, ed., *Handbook of International Trade Agreements: Country, Regional and Global Approaches,* 147–65. Abingdon: Routledge.

Dussel Peters, E., and K. P. Gallagher. 2013. NAFTA's uninvited guest: China and the disintegration of North American trade. *CEPAL Review* 110: 83–108.

Moreno-Brid, J. C., R. A. Blecker, I. Salat, and J. Sanchez. 2018. Modernización del TLCAN y sus implicaciones para el desarrollo de la economía mexicana [Modernization of NAFTA and its implications for the development of the Mexican economy]. *Revista de Economía Mexicana, Anuario UNAM* 3(3): 249–98.

Moreno-Brid, J. C., and K. Gallagher. 2020. Mexico's road to a green new deal. *NACLA Report on the Americas* 52(2): 152–57.

Moreno-Brid, J. C., and J. Ros. 2009. *Development and Growth in the Mexican Economy: A Historical Perspective.* New York: Oxford University Press.

PART FOUR

Racial Politics

CHAPTER 13

What Is the Historical and Political Context for Trump's Nativist Appeal?

DAVID MONTEJANO

The unexpected presidential election of Donald J. Trump, wealthy businessman and reality TV celebrity, was a shocking event. Shocking because all his character flaws—misogynist, racist, narcissist, demagogue—were well known to the electorate. Shocking because, after eight years of President Barack Obama's tenure, many believed that we were in a "postracial" society. Especially shocking to Latinos because Trump regularly denounced Mexican immigrants as rapists and criminals and promised to build an immense "beautiful" wall along the southern border. The anti-Mexican theme clearly resonated among a critical element of the American electorate. "Build the Wall" became a favorite chant at his campaign rallies used to arouse his supporters.

This chapter explores the rise of Trump and places his nativist worldview in historical and political context. However startling, Trump's anti-Mexican rhetoric and white nativist campaign have a long historical lineage. This chapter outlines the conditions under which such nativist politics have surfaced and includes a discussion of the scholarly roots of "national security" literature that has informed the slogan, "Make America Great Again." Although Trump is reputed to not read books, the arguments of key conservative intellectuals have clearly influenced not only his views of immigration and the border but also the way these subjects are discussed in the general political arena, where success or defeat determines whether exclusionary or inclusionary policies are implemented.

NATION BUILDING AND NATIONAL IDENTITY

Among the many traditions and norms that Trump has repudiated or challenged is the immigrant theme embodied in the Statue of Liberty, that this country is a "nation of immigrants" that welcomes the "downtrodden." Trump's **restrictionist politics**—banning Muslims, separating families at the border, narrowing the grounds for asylum petitioners, and so on—signify a sharp repudiation of the American immigrant tradition. This immigrant tale has been an integral part of the national narrative: it conveyed a promise of inclusion based on hard work and ambition; it said that achieving the "American dream" was possible. But Trump has reminded us that the immigrant story has not been the totality of the American experience, that there is a darker side to American history.

Most pundits and scholars who comment on the immigrant situation assume that the nation has had preformed, fixed boundaries into which poured immigrants who eventually melted into an American stock. There is no examination of the nation-building experience itself, a history that involved Indian wars, plantation slavery, wars with Mexico and Spain, and expansion across the continent to California and eventually to Puerto Rico, Hawaii, and the Philippines. That history is one of **Manifest Destiny**—the nineteenth-century belief that the United States was destined to occupy the North American continent all the way to the Pacific. This westward expansion was built on the conquests of people with different cultures and colored skin—reds, blacks, browns, and yellows—which in time fused "whiteness" with American national identity. Although the population of the country has always been diverse, the dominant national image has been that of an Anglo-Saxon Protestant country.

Immigration, of course, has been a basic element of the nation-building experience, but immigrants generally adapted to the established ways of their new world. The massive waves of European and Mexican immigrants of the twentieth century assimilated the cultural lore and political lessons of the nineteenth century, even as they put in place a contemporary modern economy. Assimilation and amalgamation occurred but along ethnic-racial lines. Thus, for most of the twentieth century, "American" in the Southwest generally meant "white," an identity that melted various European groups (German, Irish, Polish, Italian, Jewish) into one, while "Mexican" likewise referred to race but not to citizenship. Trump reminded us that this folk association holds in the twenty-first century when he accused the federal judge presiding over a lawsuit against Trump University of bias because he was a

Mexican. The judge, Gonzalo Curiel, was born and raised in Indiana. Trump's characterization was a stark reminder that "melting" for Latinos, even the most successful, might not be possible. In Trump's eyes, "once a Mexican, always a Mexican."

In the case of the Chicano or Mexican American experience, any historical assessment must recognize its nineteenth-century origins in the Mexican-American War (1846–48) and the **annexation of northern Mexico**—which today includes California, New Mexico, Arizona, Utah, Nevada, and parts of Wyoming and Colorado and Texas. Ever since then, the Mexican presence has raised questions and anxieties about what is to be done with them. What was to be done with the 80,000 to 100,000 Mexicans left in the annexed territories? At both the Texas and California constitutional conventions, some worry was voiced about whether Mexicans should be allowed the right to vote. New Mexico, where most annexed Mexicans resided, was maintained as a colonial territory (much like Puerto Rico today) and not accorded statehood until 1920 because of concerns about its unassimilated Mexican population. In Texas, there were legal attempts to deny Mexican Americans the right to vote because of their indigenous background, but these were defeated because of the Treaty of Guadalupe Hidalgo, which ended the Mexican-American War and protected the citizenship rights of Mexicans in the United States. American citizenship for Mexican Americans has always been contested and ambiguous (see, e.g., Montejano 1987; Gomez 2007; Almaguer 1994).

MEXICAN IMMIGRATION AND NATIVISM

Mexican immigration did not raise serious alarms until the 1920s. A post–World War I increase in immigration from southern and eastern Europe, fear of the Bolshevik Revolution and anarchist violence, and anxiety about immorality and disorder in the country laid the foundation for a resurgent white nativist movement. The 1920s witnessed the rebirth of the Ku Klux Klan and the rise of anti-immigrant sentiment that moved Congress to severely limit eastern and southern European immigration. Remarkably, Mexican immigration escaped restriction because of the intervention of influential southwestern growers. Mexican labor was seen as essential for agriculture and other industry, but its presence nonetheless sparked bouts of nativist hysteria. In the late 1920s, warnings about the dire consequences of Mexican immigration appeared regularly in the popular and academic literature. Some even envisioned an ominous clash between blacks and Mexicans for "second place" in Anglo-American society. During the Great Depression that followed, such fears and claims about grave social problems gained traction. In the 1930s, approximately three million Mexicans and Mexican Americans were "repatriated" (i.e., deported) to Mexico.

Then in the 1940s, in order to make up for the labor shortages stemming from World War II, the US and Mexican governments created the Bracero Program for temporary guest workers. The program, which at its height saw an annual influx of 200,000 braceros (farm laborers) in the country, was renewed through 1964. When the recession of the early 1950s set off another panic about the "wetback problem," the Immigration and Naturalization Services (INS) agency launched Operation Wetback, the largest mass deportation sweep in American history—netting up to 1.3 million undocumented immigrants during a three-year period. Since many of those rounded up were then simply "enrolled" in the Bracero Program, Operation Wetback might be seen as political ploy meant to placate an anxious American public (Hernández 2010).

In sum, the story of Mexican immigrants and their Mexican American relatives has been one of periodic recruitment and expulsion. The practice of relaxing borders during prosperous times and tightening them during hard times explains much of the history of Mexican immigration to this country. This history also highlights the contradiction of needing Mexican labor but not wanting to grant Mexican immigrants citizenship or permanent residency.

A NATIONAL SECURITY NARRATIVE

Not surprisingly, those advocating immigration restriction and deportation often cite national security interests. In 1975, for example, Immigration Commissioner Leonard Chapman, former commandant of the Marine Corps, warned of "a vast and silent invasion of illegal aliens" numbering some 12 million (quoted in Langewiesche 1992). In 1978, former CIA director William Colby asserted that Mexico was a far greater threat than the Soviet Union, predicting an additional twenty million illegal aliens in the country by 2000 (Sheer 1978). Southwestern governors have also sounded the alarm. In 1983, Bruce Babbit of Arizona commented, "In the War of 1848, we annexed the Southwest and now the Mexicans are taking it back" (quoted in Geyer 1983). Babbit voiced concern, now that the border had dissolved in real terms, about what this meant for cultural levels in education—and for birth control!

In 1985, Richard Lamm of Colorado issued similar warnings in a more strident tone. Speaking of blacks and Hispanics, Lamm said, "We are heading for an America in which we will have two angry, under-utilized and under-educated, frustrated, resentful, jealous, and volatile minority groups existing unassimilated and unintegrated without our borders" (Lamm 1985). Governor Lamm urged that we regain control of our border and our inner cities. These warnings by government officials and politicians never made any distinctions between American citizens of Mexican descendent and immigrants—both were brown and Latino.

In the 1990s the fin-de-siècle assessments of the country manifested much concern and even fear about this growing Latino presence. An April 1990 issue of *Time* put the matter bluntly: "What will the U.S. be like when whites are no longer the majority?" (America's changing colors 1990). The question betrayed an anxiety over whose history, values, language, and identity will count in the future. A May 1992 *Atlantic Monthly* analysis of the consequences of large-scale Mexican immigration concluded that "these newcomers may indeed be the ones we cannot accommodate" and noted that the border could be sealed "with a large-scale deployment of the U.S. armed forces and the creation of free-fire zones. It would not require much killing: the Soviets sealed their borders for decades without an excessive expenditure of ammunition. The simple fact that there existed a systematic policy of shooting illegal immigrants would deter most Mexicans" (Langewiesche 1992). Russian-inspired ideas about border control have been floating around long before Donald Trump advocated them. In fact, the sealing of the border began in earnest in the 1990s.

In September 1993 the Border Patrol, in an experiment, demonstrated that the El Paso–Juárez border could be sealed with a massive show of force. In Operation Blockade (later renamed Operation Hold the Line), four hundred agents were stationed along the Rio Grande from Ysleta to Sunland Park, a distance of twenty miles, or twenty agents per mile. One El Paso resident with relatives in Juárez commented, "If it [the blockade] continues, I guess I'll know what people in east and west Germany felt like when families were separated by the Berlin Wall" (Operation Blockade 1993) The deployment dramatically reduced undocumented day traffic in El Paso. Soon California politicians clamored for a similar blockade along their border with Mexico. Operation Gatekeeper in San Diego and Operation Safeguard in Arizona were launched in response. The Border Patrol strategy was to block entry along the urban zones and use the Sonoran Desert as a natural barrier (Montejano 1999).

THE QUESTION OF MEXICO

Add to this domestic scenario the question of Mexican political stability and economic development, especially as these affect emigration to the United States. Unfortunately, violence within Mexico, much of it drug related, has raised the question of whether Mexico can be considered "a failed state." The tragic and much-publicized stories of the disappearances of women in Juárez, of the kidnapping and massacre of forty-three college students in southern Mexico, and of the assassinations of journalists throughout the country suggest that Mexican society is under considerable strain. The symptoms and causes for such instability include ingrained government corruption, poverty and repression, and emigration.

Given the attention that US national security personnel have given to the Mexican immigrant population, it should not be surprising that they have also considered options for dealing with a failed Mexican state. In 1996, Casper Weinberger, former secretary of defense under President Ronald Reagan, published a book titled *The Next War* that described one such option for Mexico. The book was a collection of, as Weinberger put it, "literary war games, developed in the spirit of the Pentagon's computerized scenarios" (Weinberger and Schweizer 1996, iv). The exercises were meant to identify the weaponry and equipment needed to accomplish the mission of neutralizing any given national security threat.

The hypothetical Mexican crisis unfolds with the assassination of a pro-American president who had been clamping down on corruption and the drug trade. In the following turmoil, a charismatic university professor, "trained by Jesuits," rides to power on a nationalist, "anti-gringo" platform. The source of his campaign funds is a mystery. The new president nationalizes the banking and insurance industry and drives the country to economic collapse, which creates hyperinflation and food shortages. He then predictably strengthens the army to suppress dissent and attempts to accommodate the drug cartels, which turn out to be his primary campaign source. Millions of Mexicans flee northward to escape the chaos.

In this hypothetical scenario, the United States responds by deploying sixty thousand troops along the US-Mexico border, but they cannot contain the exodus. Social services from San Diego to Brownsville are stretched thin, and there are reports of a tuberculous outbreak in El Paso. The drug wars spill over to the Southwest and the US president and his national security advisers decide that enough is enough. The United States invades Mexico to bring peace and tranquillity to the country but ultimately fails to capture the Mexican president, who has escaped to the mountains of Zacatecas to wage guerrilla warfare. Weinberger's fantasy invasion ends with the prospect of a drawn-out guerrilla war.

The specter of the "next war" being waged in Mexico because of "an immigration emergency" was rehearsed by the Pentagon and a multi-agency government group in the 1990s, long before 9/11 and the ascendancy of Trump (see Dunn 1996).

SCAPEGOATING IN ELECTORAL POLITICS

The twentieth-century experience points to the close association between economic hard times (perceived or real), anti-Mexican sentiment, and exclusionary policies. The link between domestic economic difficulties and a rise in racial and ethnic tensions is well established. What is needed to trigger the link, however, is a public campaign that blames Mexico and Mexicans for the hard times and the threats to national security. This takes place in the electoral arena, where political parties and candidates identify problems and offer solutions. There are any number of negative images about Mexicans—their criminality, laziness, poverty, and so forth—that can be weaponized in a close election.

In a winner-take-all electoral contest, there always exists the temptation to appeal to race—race baiting—if the strategy has a chance of success. Southern politicians perfected the method of finding a bogeyman—communists, labor racketeers, integrationists, "uppity Negroes"—and then claiming to be saviors. Beginning with Arizona senator Barry Goldwater's presidential campaign in 1964, the Republican Party sought to capitalize on the white backlash to the civil rights movement and adopted this southern approach as their national strategy. Although Goldwater did not win against incumbent Lyndon Johnson, the next Republican presidential candidate, Richard Nixon, used this **Southern Strategy** successfully and was elected in 1968. This provided the basis for an explicit statement on the matter by the Republican theorist Kevin Phillips. Phillips's *The Emerging Republican Majority* (1969) became the handbook on how to encourage racial polarization along party lines without appearing to be racist. The strategy proved successful in the victorious presidential campaigns of Reagan in 1980 and 1984, and the 1988 Bush campaign infamous for its prison furlough ad that included an image of Willie Horton to play on the fear of African American criminality.

Until Trump's presidency, most of the race baiting and dog whistling had been directed at African Americans, with Latinos occupying an ambiguous place in Republican thinking. Economic conservatives "liked" Latinos.

Reagan had praised immigrants for their work ethic, and the George Bush–Jim Baker wing of the GOP wished to recruit Hispanics, who were seen as receptive to a "family values" platform. On the other hand, cultural conservatives—the English-only, anti-affirmative action, fundamentalist wing of the party—readily identified Latinos as un-American.

This division of opinion between economic and cultural conservatives flared into the open in the 1990s over the question of immigration and free trade. In 1992 presidential candidate Pat Buchanan explicitly opposed immigration that "diluted" America's European heritage and called for tightening the US-Mexico border. The unease of some Republicans with "Hispanics" now surfaced publicly. Describing Hispanics as a "strange anti-nation" within the United States, Buchanan blasted Republican courtship of Hispanics, noting that "Republican success with Hispanics, as with other minorities, is often at the expense of conservative principles" (Buchanan 2007, p.44). The Republican establishment was able to contain its internal divisions through the George W. Bush years.

After the presidential election of Barack Obama in 2008, an election that Mitt Romney lost even though he won 61 percent of the white vote, the party leadership decided to embark on a campaign to recruit conservative Hispanics into the fold. Trump's campaign completely upended such thinking. In a field of Republican candidates who hoped to appeal to a rising Hispanic electorate, Trump was alone in courting Republicans "who didn't want the party to remake itself, who wanted to be told that a wall could be built and things could go back to the way they were" (Klein 2018). Trump's mix of economic populism and deliberate racial polarization was thought to be demographically doomed, but instead it won him precisely the midwestern white voters who had been overlooked in previous elections. His description of a country overrun by Mexican criminals and MS-13 gang members provided an ideal foil for his demagoguery.

There is, of course, no need for racist scapegoating to be limited to a particular minority or to be contained within one political party, especially if this results in electoral success. The state of California in the early 1990s provides an excellent case in point.

A CASE IN POINT: CALIFORNIA, 1994

In California, the rise in anti-Mexican sentiment had been evident for some time. In San Diego County the most spectacular example of Mexican bashing had been the Light Up the Border campaign, dating to

November 1989, which attracted more than a thousand people who parked at sundown and trained their headlights on the border. As the California economy worsened in the early 1990s and unemployment reached near 10 percent, "citizen groups" began to spring up throughout the state to protest "street hiring" and to urge the INS to conduct raids. Three quarters of Californians, according to the 1992 Roper poll, believed that the state had too many immigrants, that they were a financial burden, and that steps should be taken to limit the population. Incumbent governor Pete Wilson, up for reelection in 1994 and with one of the lowest popular ratings in memory, sensed a winning issue. As the former mayor of San Diego, Wilson had been considered a moderate Republican. But now he cynically blamed immigrants for the state's budget difficulties and for problems with the schools, hospitals, and community services. Wilson and **Proposition 187**, a ballot measure championed by Wilson to deny educational and health benefits to "illegal immigrants," coasted to easy victories (Montejano 1999).

In 1994, however, there was little difference between "conservative" Republican and "progressive" Democrat on the question of immigration. During his campaign, Governor Wilson had called for a constitutional amendment that would deny citizenship to US-born children of illegal immigrants. In response, US Senator Barbara Boxer, a Democrat, called for the stationing of National Guard troops along the border. Other Republican and Democratic notables joined in as each side attempted to outdo the other in calling for the closing of the border. The top politicians of both parties engaged in Willie Horton politics by making undocumented immigration the central issue in the elections of 1994.

As the result of this gubernatorial campaign, alarmist anti-immigrant rhetoric became commonsense political discourse. Equally troubling was the manner in which anti-immigrant sentiment spurred other ballot initiatives that appealed to the majority of white voters. In 1995–96, driven by the need to galvanize support for a presidential bid, Governor Wilson led a successful campaign to pass **Proposition 209**, which banned affirmative action policies in the state. In 1998, **Proposition 227** banning bilingual education in public schools passed. Like Proposition 187, Proposition 227 had been the major plank of a high-profile gubernatorial campaign.

Basically Trump did to the nation what Wilson did to California in the 1990s. Prepping the ground was the rise of the right-wing media, led by Fox News, that constantly raised alarms about securing the border. The attack of 9/11 and subsequent "war on terror" also heightened a sense of national vulnerability to foreign threats. Trump tapped into these anxieties and cast himself as a savior. His campaign followed the Phillips handbook—except that dog whistles were now bombastic chants of "Build the Wall."

MAKING AMERICA GREAT (AND WHITE) AGAIN

Trump's campaign slogan, "Make America Great Again," was based on two premises: the country was in economic decline, and the country was threatened by lax immigration and border controls. Trump the performer was effective in persuading his audience that this was the case, often "frightening" them, according to one observer (Ganz 2018). Then evoking the urgency posed by such decline and insecurity, Trump promised to deal with both. Indeed, at the core of Trump's worldview, both were linked. The national decline was due as much to the presence of Mexican immigrants as to trade deficits and ill-conceived trade policies. The decline of America was cultural and racial as well as economic.

Again, Trump's ideas about these matters were not novel. The question of whether the United States is in a period of decline has been discussed so extensively that the literature has been dubbed the "declinist school." One of its most prominent advocates has been the historian Paul Kennedy. In his 1987 best seller, *The Rise and Fall of Great Powers*, Kennedy links the decline with the "browning" of the country. Kennedy warns that high birthrates among American minorities and the loss of well-paying manufacturing jobs make it "unwise to assume that the prevailing norms of the American political economy . . . would be maintained if the nation entered a period of sustained economic difficulty" (535). In his sequel, *Preparing for the 21st Century* (1993), Kennedy is more explicit about the matter. Describing the implications of the "browning" of America, Kennedy points out, "The mass migration at the moment is only the tip of the iceberg. We have to educate ourselves and our children to understand why there is going to be trouble" (312).

The most prominent alarmist pronouncement about the danger of America's "browning" was that of Samuel P. Huntington in 2004. Huntington, a Harvard professor and a policy analyst with direct ties to the National Security Council, gained considerable recognition with his best-selling book, *The Clash of Civilizations and the Remaking of the World Order* (1996). With Gulf War I as his backdrop, Huntington forecast a "clash of civilizations" between the Muslim world and the Western one. The events of 9/11 made Huntington appear to be prophetic. If *The Clash of Civilizations* was Huntington's take on the external threat faced by the United States, *Who Are We?* was his take on the internal threat faced by the country, a threat posed by Latinos and more specifically Mexicans (Huntington 2004b). Huntington was the intellectual who linked Muslims and Mexicans as threats to the security of the United States.

One point that is especially intriguing in both Kennedy and Huntington is their commentary, in Kennedy's words, that the "prevailing norms of the American political economy" might not be maintained in a period of economic decline and ongoing "browning." Huntington also describes an "exclusivist" scenario in which a movement of "native white Americans" revives an America that excludes and suppresses those who are not white or European. He states ominously, "As the racial balance continues to shift *and more Hispanics become citizens and politically active, white groups may look for other means* of protecting their interests" (Huntington 2004a, 41; my emphasis). He calls this "a possible and plausible response" that with "serious economic down turns and hardship could be highly probable" (41). Was Huntington preparing us for a white nativist backlash? Is this Charlottesville?

In sum, the ideas behind the slogan "Make America Great Again" have been circulating in conservative circles for some time. The promise that Trump offers to his supporters is not just economic prosperity, but a nation protected from brown-skinned immigration.

A CONCLUDING NOTE

Historically the pattern is evident: in times of perceived economic duress, nativism and racism rise. Such sentiments, while always expressed by a few groups, are afforded legitimacy by politicians attempting to capitalize on white public discontent. Unthinkable policies become conceivable, and people of color, whether native born or immigrants, become transformed into scapegoats for a variety of social ills. Since the early twentieth century, restrictionist or anti-immigrant interest groups have been attempting to catalyze public support for their nativist ideas in the political arena. It is in this arena that candidates and political parties generate support for race relations policies that may be either inclusionary or exclusionary. Election outcomes determine which direction society will take.

Which way for the future? Exclusion or inclusion? The success of Trump's explicitly anti-immigrant and anti-Mexican campaign has clearly upended Republican initiatives to reach out to Hispanics. "Build the Wall," unfortunately, will be a chant that we will be hearing repeatedly for the foreseeable future. Expect other campaigns to rally around more border control and to scapegoat immigrants for various domestic evils. Moreover, as the California experience demonstrated, anti-immigrant sentiment can easily morph into other so-called patriotic campaigns.

But the California experience also reveals the folly of demonizing the Mexican community, as Governor Pete Wilson and the Republican Party did in the 1990s. As the sociologists David Hayes-Bautista, Werner Schink, and Jorge Chapa noted then, even if all Mexican immigration was stopped, Mexican Americans were bound to become the majority in the California population (Hayes-Bautista, Schink, and Chapa 1988). By 2017 Hispanics represented the largest demographic group in California, over 39 percent of the population. Non-Hispanic whites came in second at approximately 37 percent. The consequences are clear. A growing and galvanized Mexican American electorate undergirds a dominant Democratic Party, to the extent that today the Republican Party has virtually no influence in California state policy.

The California experience looms large in the minds of nervous Republicans. In an effort to contain minority political participation, the Republican Party and Trump have placed considerable emphases on voter fraud and citizenship requirements. However, it may already be too late, if one looks at Texas. In Texas, Latinos are on the cusp of becoming the largest racial-ethnic group in a few years (2022). The median age of Anglos is forty-two, compared to twenty-nine for Latinos. Approximately two hundred thousand young Latinos reach voting age and become eligible to vote each year (Miller 2018; Saenz 2018; Tavernise 2018). In other words, the "browning" of America, so feared by conservative commentators and politicians, has already occurred. Donald J. Trump may have been the last gasp of a nativist white electorate. Perhaps it is somewhat fitting that white nativism ends its reign with a clownish buffoon.

Suggested Reading

Douthat, R. 2018. The white strategy: Trump's winning coalition and its weaknesses. *New York Times,* August 11. Available at https://www.nytimes.com/2018/08/11/opinion/sunday/the-white-strategy.html.

Hayes-Bautista, D. E. 2004. *La Nueva California: Latinos in the Golden State.* Berkeley: University of California Press.

Omi, M., and H. Winant. [1986] 2015. *Racial Formation in the United States.* 3rd ed. New York: Routledge.

Tarpley, W. G. 1996. The future according to London (book review of C. Weinberger and P. Schweizer, *The Next War*). *Executive Intelligence Review* 23(49): 64–67. Available at https://larouchepub.com/eiw/public/1996/eirv23n49-19961206/eirv23n49-19961206_064-the_future_according_to_london.pdf.

Yee, V., K. David, and J. K. Patel. 2017. Here's the reality about illegal immigrants in the United States. *New York Times,* March 6. Available at www.nytimes.com/interactive/2017/03/06/us/politics/undocumented-illegal-immigrants.html.

CHAPTER 14

How Has the New Mexico-US Relationship Affected Mexican Nationalism?

REGINA MARTÍNEZ CASAS AND
RAFAEL ELÍAS LÓPEZ ARELLANO

In 1813, José María Morelos y Pavón, as part of the complex task of creating an independent nation out of what had been a territory of the Spanish crown for almost three hundred years, composed a document outlining the organization of government titled, *Sentimientos de la Nación* (Feelings of a nation). This established the guidelines for the separation of powers and enumerated the principles that should govern the fledgling Mexican nation, among which was the need to strengthen national identity and to beware of immigration. The tenth article states in part, "Foreigners are not to be admitted, unless they are artisans capable of instructing and free of all suspicion." The need to strengthen a sense of nation based on definitions of *self* and *other,* also understood as the *desirable* and the *undesirable,* has been evident in narratives since Mexican independence and has contributed to the creation of Mexican identity. In various moments, the threat—real or symbolic—of invasion, aggressions, or other factors that put the integrity of the nation at risk has prompted different expressions that seek to strengthen nationalist feelings and bolster social cohesion. In this chapter, we present a new dynamic for the expression of national integrity given the new relationship that was ushered in with Donald Trump's rise to power as president of the United States. From the start of the electoral process, Mexico and Mexicans became a recurrent theme in explaining the majority of North America's economic woes. In response, Mexico has developed defensive strategies, with arguments that appeal to the importance of the binational relationship. This has generated a rather exhausting rhetorical pendulum of estrangement and attempts at rapprochement in the discourse of both countries. The lack of coherence in what is said, primarily by President Trump, generates tensions and contradictions that have eroded the binational relationship.

SPEECH GENRES AND SOCIAL POWER

The configuration of **speech genres** occurs from statements by subjects in concrete contexts of interaction, reflecting the specific conditions and concrete objectives of actors and characterized by thematic content, linguistic style, and composition. In exploring a concrete type of statement from this perspective, the publication of messages on **Twitter** is a new form of interaction not undertaken face-to-face but rather via a digital platform that offers a certain degree of anonymity or interactive distance: messages are directed at unspecified recipients (see Bakhtin [1979] 2008). We understand **discourse** as a resource of social power, which has consequences. These consequences are measured in what theorists of **speech acts** (a technical term that refers to particular communicative interactions) define as **illocutionary force,** that is, the real and immediate impact of a statement on the recipient. Speech can be narrations charged with emotions, particularly nationalist discourses. As Bhabha writes, "For the nation, as a form of cultural *elaboration* . . . , is an agency of *ambivalent* narration that holds culture at its most productive position, as a force for 'subordination, fracturing, diffusing, reproducing, as much as producing, creating, forcing, guiding'" (1990, 3–4; original emphasis). Thus our theoretical approach aims to consider speech genres in their emotional dimension and in association with exercised and reproduced forms of concrete power (Duranti 1997).

TENSION BETWEEN NEIGHBORS: CONFLICTS
PAST AND PRESENT

Within the arena of emotionally charged speech, various researchers of **Mexican nationalism** have suggested that a tension exists between a national construction based on cultural features—the indigenous past, cultural wealth—and the conflictive relationship with other nations, particularly the United States (Brading 1955; Lomnitz 2010, 2016). The tension between Mexico and the United States, dating back more than a century, has been expressed in discordant feelings regarding the loss of territory, US political intervention in the Mexican Revolution, and subsequent economic interventions that intensified toward the end of the twentieth century and continue to this day (Meyer 2006). Given this, it is critical to refer briefly to some antecedents and to highlight certain contexts and junctures that have marked the two countries' relationship as neighbors, with the aim of explaining the significant shift in the form of communication between them, from formal diplomacy to Twitter messages. Such has been the nature of much of the discussion between government officials, including the presidents of both countries who, in other times, would have resorted to diplomatic protocols.

Mexico has intermittently formed part of the nationalist discourse in the United States. Notably, its presence in national discussions diminished to the point of almost disappearing following the September 2001 attacks. However, this did not mean a warming of the bilateral relationship. On the contrary, the effects of NAFTA, migration flows, and growing economic interdependence meant a more intense relationship between the two countries. Nevertheless, the absence of mutual insults, encouraged by the neoliberal policies implemented by Mexican authorities, gave rise to a resignification of the relationship within the public sphere. Cultural exchanges and the *Mexicanization* of daily practices, such as food and art, became more prevalent. This changed dramatically with Donald Trump's presidential candidacy in 2015. Mexico suddenly became a constant feature in a campaign marked by **nationalist stereotypes** that did not cease, even after he had won the election. On the contrary, they have increased and have become part of President Trump's daily communication agenda. Initially, the Mexican government responded with silence, but as the indignation of the Mexican population on both sides of the border increased, Mexican authorities began responding in an increasingly emotive manner. This intensified when Andrés Manuel López Obrador began his presidential campaign in 2018, during which he promised to respond to all of President Trump's messages. However, as we will show, as president, he has had to submit to the necessity of developing a good binational relationship.

The first Twitter messages that we identified in the construction of new nationalistic feelings have an almost anecdotal origin. On February 22, 2015, President Peña Nieto congratulated Mexican filmmakers for their Oscars, mentioning one in a particular tweet: "Alejandro González Iñárritu, what a well-deserved recognition of your work, devotion and talent. Congratulations! Mexico celebrates with you."[1] The triumph of the filmmakers was presented as the artistic and cultural achievement of all Mexicans.

In response, Donald Trump, then still a businessman with aspirations of becoming a presidential candidate, tweeted, "The Oscars are a sad joke, very much like our President. So many things are wrong!"[2] Later in the week, he revisited the issue: "The Oscars were a great night for Mexico & why not—they are ripping off the US more than almost any other nation."[3]

In a narrative that progressed from discrediting the awards to criticizing the economy and, later in the day, to denouncing Mexican institutions as part of a corrupt system and threatening, he posted on Twitter, "The Mexican legal system is corrupt, as is much of Mexico. Pay me the money that is owed me now—and stop sending criminals over our border."[4] On February 25, he referred to reactions in Mexico and justified his position by arguing that the United States was being scammed.[5] The first major issue that became a permanent feature of his campaign, via Twitter, was the need to build a wall along the border, to be paid for by Mexico.

THE BORDER WALL

In August 2016, as the Republican Party candidate, Trump highlighted labor issues and complained of a large-scale relocation of employment in industrial manufacturing to Mexico, promising that this would end once he won the election.[6] Following these declarations, the Republican candidate met with President Peña Nieto and expressed his enthusiasm for the meeting.[7] The Mexican president explained that he had invited all the US presidential candidates to discuss the bilateral relationship and commented, "At the beginning of the conversation with Donald Trump I made it clear that Mexico would not pay for the wall.... From there, the conversation moved on to other issues and proceeded in a respectful manner."[8]

However, President Peña Nieto wrote, "I regret and condemn the decision by the USA to continue building a wall that, rather than uniting us, divides us.... Mexico offers and demands respect, as the fully sovereign nation that we are."[9] It is notable that instead of responding as dictated by the protocols of the binational relationship, Mexico chose to respond to candidate Trump via social media, using the same message register. This provoked an aggressive reply: "The U.S. has a 60-billion-dollar trade deficit with Mexico. It has been a one-sided deal from the beginning of NAFTA with massive numbers of jobs and companies lost. If Mexico is unwilling to pay for the badly needed wall, then it would be better to cancel the upcoming meeting."[10] Mexico's response was decisive. In his next tweet, Peña Nieto canceled a scheduled meeting: "We informed the White House this morning that I would not attend a working meeting programmed for next week with @POTUS." He added, "Mexico reiterates its willingness to work with the United States to reach agreements that favour both nations."[11] Trump responded, "Mexico has taken advantage of the U.S. for long enough. Massive trade deficits & little help on the very weak border must change, NOW!"[12]

In June 2017, President Trump once again referred to the wall: "Mexico was just ranked the second deadliest country in the world, after only Syria. Drug trade is largely the cause. We will BUILD THE WALL!"[13] This time, the response was an official statement: "In order to be effective, we should stop blaming each other. We hope to continue working with the United States government in combatting illegal drugs, based on the principles of shared responsibility, teamwork and mutual trust."[14] By making an official statement rather than sending a Twitter message, Mexican authorities changed the channel of communication. In addition, the author of the message was different: the response did not come from the president but from his foreign minister.

Trump's first messages of 2018—now as president of the United States—were emphatic. He reaffirmed his position on building a wall and how it was to be financed: "The Wall will be paid for, directly or indirectly, or through longer term reimbursement, by Mexico, which has a ridiculous $71 billion dollar trade surplus with the U.S. The $20 billion dollar Wall is 'peanuts' compared to what Mexico makes from the U.S. NAFTA is a bad joke!" In another tweet on the same day, he added, "We need the Wall for the safety and security of our country. We need the Wall to help stop the massive inflow of drugs from Mexico, now rated the number one most dangerous country in the world. If there is no Wall, there is no Deal!"[15]

In the context of messages regarding the building of the wall and drug trafficking, the Foreign Minister Videgaray Caso resorted to Twitter: "We reiterate what we have said on various occasions: Mexico will not pay, in any way, for a wall along the border on United States' territory. This resolution is not part of a Mexican negotiation strategy, but rather a principle of sovereignty and national dignity."[16]

In March, Trump returned to the issue of the US trade deficit: "We have large trade deficits with Mexico and Canada. NAFTA, which is under renegotiation right now, has been a bad deal for U.S.A. Massive relocation of companies & jobs. Tariffs on Steel and Aluminium will only come off if new & fair NAFTA agreement is signed. Also, Canada must ... treat our farmers much better. Highly restrictive. Mexico must do much more on stopping drugs from pouring into the U.S. They have not done what needs to be done. Millions of people addicted and dying."[17]

MIGRATION AND THE ISSUE OF *OTHERNESS*

In April, Trump lashed out at the Democratic Party: "Border Patrol Agents are not allowed to properly do their job at the Border because of ridiculous liberal (Democrat) laws like Catch & Release. Getting more dangerous. 'Caravans' coming. Republicans must go to Nuclear Option to pass tough laws NOW. NO MORE DACA DEAL!" In another Tweet, he added, "Mexico is doing very little, if not NOTHING, at stopping people from flowing into Mexico through their Southern Border, and then into the U.S. They laugh at our dumb immigration laws. They must stop the big drug and people flows, or I will stop their cash cow, NAFTA. NEED WALL!"[18] Simultaneously, the civil organization People Without Borders organized a migrant caravan of more than a thousand Central Americans that would cross Mexico and seek asylum in the United States.

The next day, Trump spoke of migration regulation: "Mexico has the absolute power not to let these large 'Caravans' of people enter their country. They must stop them at their Northern Border, which they can do because their border laws work, not allow them to pass through into our country, which has no effective border laws."[19] He then demanded border control legislation from the US Congress in order to prevent the massive entry of people and drugs. Just one day later, he insisted, "The big Caravan of People from Honduras, now coming across Mexico and heading to our 'Weak Laws' Border, had better be stopped before it gets there. Cash cow NAFTA is in play, as is foreign aid to Honduras and the countries that allow this to happen. Congress MUST ACT NOW!"[20]

President Peña Nieto responded, "Something that brings together and unites absolutely all Mexicans is our certainty that nothing and no one stands above the dignity of Mexico."[21] He elaborated in a widely circulated Twitter video: "If your recent declarations derive from a frustration with internal policy or laws or with your congress, deal with them, not the Mexicans. . . . The Mexican government has directed its efforts at building an institutional relationship of mutual respect and benefit for both nations. . . . [I]f you would like to come to agreements with Mexico, we are ready. As we have demonstrated until now, we are always prepared to dialogue with seriousness, in good faith and in a constructive spirit."[22]

In July, Trump's tweets dealt with border security. On July 31, he wrote, "One of the reasons we need Great Border Security is that Mexico's murder rate in 2017 increased by 27% to 31,174 people killed, a record! The Democrats want Open Borders. I want Maximum Border Security and respect for ICE and our great Law Enforcement Professionals!"[23] In October, he referred to US economic aid to Central America: "In addition to stopping all payments to these countries, which seem to have almost no control over their population, I must, in the strongest of terms, ask Mexico to stop this onslaught—and if unable to do so I will call up the U.S. Military and CLOSE OUR SOUTHERN BORDER!"[24] President Peña Nieto responded, "@SEGOB_mxand @SRE_mx have been instructed to maintain dialogue with the #CaravanaMigrante in order to guarantee safe conditions and an orderly migration respectful of the legal framework and human rights."[25] A few days later, Trump complained of Mexico's inability to detain the migrant caravan. The caravan, the wall, and migration continued to be issues in his tweets: "Despite the large Caravans that WERE forming and heading to our Country, people have not been able to get through our newly built Walls, makeshift Walls & Fences, or Border Patrol Officers & Military. They are now staying in Mexico or going back to their original countries."[26]

When Andrés Manuel López Obrador assumed the presidency of Mexico, he immediately tweeted, "Today I spoke with President Donald Trump. We dealt with the issue of migration in a respectful and friendly manner and discussed the possibility of applying a joint program for development and job creation in Central America and in our own country."[27] The new head of the National Immigration Institute added, "Migration should not be stigmatized. The one who championed denouncing the caravan and immigration as criminals was President Trump during the recent election campaign, just like he did for his presidential campaign, in which the bad guys were the Mexicans" (Guillen López 2018). The controversial issue in this situation was the suggestion that given the impossibility of entering the United States, members of the caravans would be returned to their countries of origin.

Regarding migration policy, Trump indicated, "Mexico is doing NOTHING to stop the Caravan which is now fully formed and heading to the United States. We stopped the last two—many are still in Mexico but can't get through our Wall, but it takes a lot of Border Agents if there is no Wall. Not easy!"[28] The messages became more aggressive: "Without a Wall there cannot be safety and security at the Border or for the U.S.A. BUILD THE WALL AND CRIME WILL FALL!"[29] He then referred to the possibility of closing the border: "Mexico has for many years made a fortune off of the U.S., far greater than Border Costs. If Mexico doesn't immediately stop ALL illegal immigration coming into the United States through our Southern Border, I will be CLOSING."[30]

President López Obrador responded to this while at an event to deliver social programs: "We are not going to fight, peace and love, or do you all want me to answer . . . put up your hands those who think we should act prudently . . . these are my people" (López Obrador 2019). *El Diario* quoted López Obrador, "We have said to President Trump that the best way of confronting the issue of migration is to create employment and better living conditions in Central America and in Mexico, and that is the way to solve the problem, there is no other" (EFE/GETY 2019). The same day, the foreign minister, M. Ebrard, tweeted, "Mexico will not respond to threats. We are a great neighbor. The million and a half North Americans who have chosen our country as their home can attest to that. . . . For them, we are also the best neighbor they could have."[31]

While at the end of March Trump was accusing Mexico of not doing anything to control migration, he began April by congratulating the country for the detentions they were carrying out: "After many years (decades), Mexico is apprehending large numbers of people at their Southern Border."[32] In another message, he commented, "The Crazed and Dishonest Washington Post again purposely got it wrong. Mexico, for the first time in decades, is meaningfully apprehending illegals at THEIR Southern Border, before the long march up to the U.S. This is great and the way it should be. The big flow will stop."[33] The next day he tweeted, "We have redeployed 750 agents at the Southern Border's specific Ports of Entry in order to help with the large scale surge of illegal migrants trying to make their way into the United States. This will cause traffic & commercial delays until such time as Mexico is able to use."[34] This did indeed affect traffic and binational trade. Just days later, Trump did an about-face: "I . . . never ordered anyone to close our Southern Border (although I have the absolute right to do so, and may if Mexico does not apprehend the illegals coming to our Border). . . . It is all Fake & Corrupt News!"[35]

FINAL CONSIDERATIONS

From campaign promises to the order to begin construction of a border wall, President Trump's rhetoric on containing immigration at the Mexican border, mainly via Twitter, and thus preventing the entry of undesired people into the United States, has provoked the resurgence of nationalist sentiments in both countries. Xenophobic comments, offensive to Mexicans, are replicated daily against the Central American population—the other Mexico, as Trump refers to it—on social networks and are reminiscent of Morelos's warning of the danger of invasion by foreigners to national integrity. Both nationalist narratives appear to converge, but their origins are very different. Mexican nationalism of the nineteenth century arose in defense of its sovereignty and the territory it lost to foreign armies. US nationalism has arisen partly in response to the incursion of Mexico and Mexicans into the United States, for example, US reliance on unskilled labor from Mexico, the browning of the US population, and Mexican influences on food and culture.

The criminalization of immigration has been a constant feature of the rhetoric justifying a series of political decisions that have managed to build an imaginary border wall between the two countries. Mexico's migration policies have been strongly influenced by Trump's messages. The blockages of both people and merchandise at border crossings have put pressure on the decision making of the Mexican government, though President López Obrador has attempted to avoid direct confrontation. The illocutionary force acquired by Trump's messages has been surprising, as evidenced in Mexico's response mechanisms. If at any point it was thought that the 2018 Mexican elections were influenced by the need for political leadership that could generate a new nationalism to protect it from attacks, this is now in question. López Obrador bets on public speech. Every morning, in long press conferences, he defines the communication agenda of the country and instructs the decision making of various social and political actors. These press conferences inform the public about the actions officials will take in relation to larger national issues, among them migration and the relationship with the United States, using long explanations directed to journalists and, through them, to the whole of Mexican society.

In contrast, President Trump continues to bet on a new speech registry, short, emotive, and massive, that has shown itself to be extremely effective, both within the United States and in defining the US relationship with the rest of the world, especially with Mexico.

Suggested Reading

Bassets, M. 2017. Trump promete que México pagará el muro "de una manera u otra" [Trump promises that Mexico will pay for the wall "one way or another"]. *El País,* January 26. Available at https://elpais.com/internacional/2017/01/25/estados_unidos/1485364719_634723.html.

Chicago Sun Times. 2018. Mexico's foreign minister to Trump on Twitter: "We will NEVER pay for a wall." August 28. Available at https://chicago.suntimes.com/immigration/luis-videgaray-caso-donald-trump-enrique-pena-nieto-mexico-border-wall/.

Jackson, L. 2017. Twitter diplomacy: How Trump is using social media to spur a crisis with Mexico. *The Conversation,* January 27. Available at http://theconversation.com/twitter-diplomacy-how-trump-is-using-social-media-to-spur-a-crisis-with-mexico-71981.

Linthicum, K. 2018. Los tweets de Trump contra México, más ficción que realidad [Trump's tweets against Mexico, more fiction than reality]. *Los Ángeles Times,* April 2. Available at www.latimes.com/espanol/eeuu/la-es-los-tweets-de-trump-contra-mexico-mas-ficcion-que-realidad-20180402-story.html.

Nájar, A. 2019. Cierre de frontera México—EE.UU.: AMLO responde a las amenazas de Trump de clausurar la frontera con "amor y paz" [Mexico-U.S. border closure: AMLO responds to Trump's threats to close the border with "love and peace"]. BBC News, April 3. Available at www.bbc.com/mundo/noticias-america-latina-47796427.

Santiago, L., and C. E. Shoichet. 2018. Trump says caravan migrants are turning back. Mexico says most are still at the border. CNN World, December 11. Available at https://edition.cnn.com/2018/12/11/americas/mexico-caravan-trump/index.html.

Tourliere, M. 2018. Trump tuitea y México obedece [Trump tweets and Mexico obeys]. *Proceso,* 2190, October 20, 6–14.

CHAPTER 15

What Are the Social Consequences of Immigrant Scapegoating by Political Elites?

RENÉ D. FLORES

On June 16, 2015, Donald Trump announced he was running for president of the United States of America at a campaign rally at the New York City Trump Tower. Up until that point, the Republican National Committee (2013) blamed hardline stances on immigration for Mitt Romney's loss to Barack Obama in 2012, especially Romney's call for the "self-deportation" of undocumented immigrants. Indeed, Romney obtained only 27 percent of the Hispanic vote. Nevertheless, in 2015 Trump broke with the party line by bringing immigration into the forefront in his announcement speech. He said:

> When Mexico sends its people, they're not sending their best. They're not sending you.... They're sending people that have lots of problems, and they're bringing those problems with [them]. They're bringing drugs. They're bringing crime. They're rapists. And some, I assume, are good people. But I speak to border guards and they tell us what we're getting. And it only makes common sense. It only makes common sense. They're sending us not the right people. It's coming from more than Mexico. It's coming from all over South and Latin America, and it's coming probably—probably—from the Middle East.

Trump's speech, which was widely covered by the media, proved influential. Eventually, all the other Republican candidates, with the exception of Jeb Bush, took a hardline approach to immigration. Though some expected Trump to become more conciliatory after winning the election, as president he continued to scapegoat immigrants, promising to build a "big, beautiful wall" that would "save taxpayers hundreds of billions of dollars by reducing crime, drug flow, welfare fraud, and burdens on schools and hospitals" (Trump 2018).

Given Trump's position at the top of the country's political power structure and his nearly unfettered access to the media, this chapter explores the intended and unintended consequences that the targeting of immigrants has set in motion by politicians in California, Florida, and Pennsylvania. It concludes by providing some evidence of the short-term consequences of Trump's rhetoric and by trying to predict some of its long-term consequences at the national level.

PERSPECTIVES ON POLITICAL RHETORIC

Can the xenophobic nationalism of nativist political elites affect public sentiment toward immigrants and ethnic minorities? One theory—the **symbolic politics perspective**—suggests yes, that elite statements may shape public views of targeted groups. From this perspective, individuals acquire affective predispositions such as ethnocentrism, racial attitudes, and altruism through socialization early in life. These predispositions guide attitudes toward social and political issues (Easton and Dennis 1969; Hyman 1959; Sears 1993). When promoting divisive public policies, politicians use symbolic language that implicitly identifies social groups, such as racial minorities, immigrants, and poor families, as the source of social ailments (Beckett 1997; Calavita 1996; Edelman 1977). When these symbolic appeals connect with people's emotional predispositions, the general public will often rally around punitive policies that target specific groups (Sears 1993) and may even shape public views of these groups (Calavita 1996; Chavez 2001, 2008; Santa Ana 2002).

However, previous studies have not firmly established whether politicians who advocate restrictionist *immigration* policies are *causing* or merely *echoing* public opinion. It is certainly plausible that politicians' statements could have an independent effect on public opinion toward minorities, but it is equally possible that they merely reflect the views of the general population by adopting anti-minority stances.

SOCIAL EFFECTS OF IMMIGRANT SCAPEGOATING: PENNSYLVANIA

To anticipate the effects of Trump's nativist rhetoric, in this chapter I examine previous examples of political elites scapegoating immigrants in the United States. The targeting of immigrants by political elites typically produces a mix of social effects, which vary by their intentionality (*are effects intended or unintended by nativist elites?*) and their durability (*are the social consequences short or long term?*). The long-standing conflict between immigrants and the political elites of the city of Hazleton, Pennsylvania, illustrates some of these processes.

Hazleton is a working-class city of about 25,000 largely populated by the descendants of Southern and Eastern European miners. In 2006, Hazleton made international headlines by passing the **Illegal Immigration Relief Act (IIRA)**, a strict immigration ordinance that fined employers and landlords of undocumented immigrants and established English as the official language of the local government (Longazel 2013). Lou Barletta, Hazleton's mayor and the law's chief proponent, became a fixture on national news blaming Latino immigrants for bringing crime, abusing social services, and undermining Hazleton's quality of life.

I conducted interviews with Hazleton residents during two time periods, the summers of 2007 and 2011 (Flores 2014). My goal was to understand how these elite-led processes were shaping Hazleton's social environment and examine the short- and medium-term social ramifications of the law for both immigrants and natives.

Since the city's founding, the population of Hazelton had been overwhelmingly non-Hispanic white. This began changing in the late 1990s, as an influx of Hispanic immigrants began settling in the area. By 2000, Hispanics amounted to 4.9 percent of the city's population (most of whom originated from the Dominican Republic), and African Americans were 1.1 percent (see **table 15.1**). Many of the new Dominican arrivals moved from urban areas in New York and New Jersey and were lured by the area's affordable housing prices and the availability of service and light-manufacturing jobs (Longazel 2013).

The IIRA was proposed following two high-profile crimes allegedly involving Dominican immigrants. In an open letter to local residents, Mayor Barletta claimed that "illegal immigrants" were "destroying our neighborhoods and diminishing our overall quality of life" by bringing crime, overcrowding classrooms, and using up social services (Flores 2014). Barletta then promised that he would "get rid of the illegal people" by importing the IIRA, which had been originally created but rejected in Escondido, California (Jordan 2006). "It's this simple," the mayor argued, "they must leave" (Powell and García 2006).

The American Civil Liberties Union (ACLU) sued the city of Hazleton to stop the implementation of the IIRA, and the ordinance was not

TABLE 15.1. ETHNIC AND RACIAL COMPOSITION OF HAZLETON, PA, 2000–2010

	2000		2005–7		2010	
	N	%	N	%	N	%
Total Population	23,329	100	21,980	100	25,340	100
Non-Hispanic or Latino	22,197	95.1	17,864	81.2	15,886	62.7
Non-Hispanic white	21,741	93.2	17,200	78.2	14,955	59.0
Non-Hispanic black	248	1.1	635	2.8	497	2.0
Hispanic or Latino (of any race)	1,132	4.9	4116	18.7	9,454	37.3
Mexican	159	0.7	224	1.0	886	3.5
Puerto Rican	271	1.2	706	3.2	1,699	6.7
Cuban	11	0	11	0.1	48	0.2
Other Hispanic or Latino	691	3	3,175	14.4	6,821	26.9

SOURCE: US Census; 2005–7 figures are based on American Community Survey 3-Year Estimates.

formally implemented. Nevertheless, its proposal had immediate consequences. As figure 15.1 shows, the publication of immigration-related stories in the local paper, the *Standard-Speaker*, increased by 400 percent the year the ordinance was approved, from 23 stories in 2005 to 92 in 2006. Such articles often reproduced the view of Hazleton's political elites that immigrants were negatively affecting the town, especially in regard to crime and violence. Indeed, figure 15.1 shows that the number of local newspaper articles linking immigrants with crime had a statistically significant increase of more than 10 percent in 2006.[1] Despite the media's increased focus on crime, as the figure also shows, both property and violent crime rates had remained relatively stable since 1999. Further, undocumented immigrants were involved in only twenty felonies between 2000 and 2006 (Longazel 2013).

Based on the qualitative data I collected, I found that the ordinance proposal and the accompanying nativist elite rhetoric led to several short-term social consequences in Hazleton. Some of them were intended by local elites, such as the departure of a few Hispanic families who became afraid of the polarized social climate. Further, Mayor Barletta's local popularity increased. This happened at a time when he was facing a tough reelection challenge by an even more outspoken anti-immigrant politician named Mike Marsicano (Flores 2014).

At the same time, this nativist push also had some consequences that were not entirely anticipated by local elites. Instead of pacifying the local population, as some local leaders had expected, the law and the discourse surrounding it further incensed locals and increased

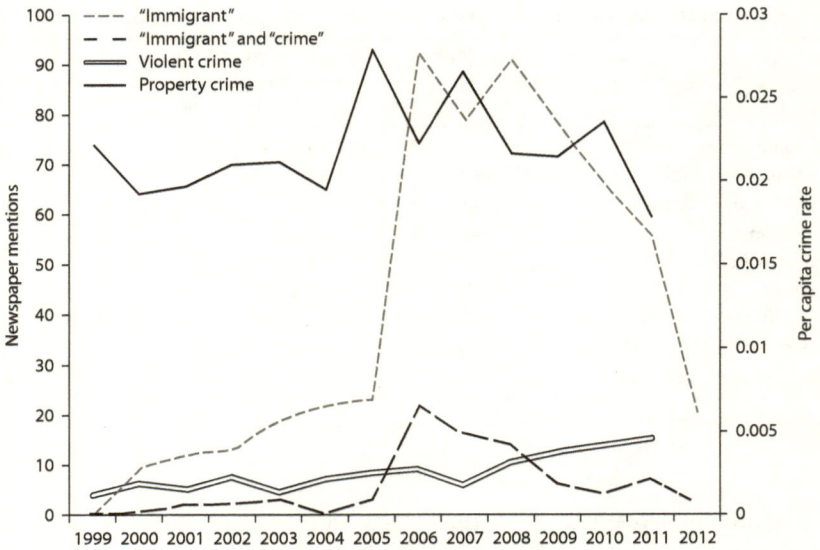

FIGURE 15.1. Newspaper Coverage and Crime Rates in Hazleton, PA, 1999–2012.

Note: The line labeled "Immigrant" indicates the number of articles related to immigrants published by Hazleton's local newspaper, the *Standard-Speaker*. The line labeled "Immigrant and crime" shows the number of articles that linked immigrants with crime. On the right axis, the lines labeled "Violent crime" and "Property crime" represent the per capita violent and property crime rates, respectively, in Hazleton. Sources: Uniform Crime Reporting (FBI); *Standard-Speaker*.

anti-immigrant activism (Flores 2014). After the ordinance was made public, local residents formed several anti-immigrant groups, including Voices of the People (Fennick 2007). This law also led to multiple town hall meetings, rallies, and anti-immigrant demonstrations (Birkbeck 2007).

Another unintended consequence of this elite effort was that ethnic boundaries between immigrants and natives hardened. Tony, a thirty-nine-year-old first-generation Dominican immigrant, moved to Hazleton from New York City in 2001 after he lost his job during the city's post-9/11 economic downturn. He remembers being welcomed by his native white neighbors when his family moved to Hazelton. "I moved twice [within town] and my neighbors welcomed me with a cake. But after the ordinance [was proposed] everything changed. The same people that would bring you a cake before now look at you with suspicion wondering if you are illegal, and if you are, it doesn't matter if they already know you, you become a criminal." Tony's story reflects the common belief among Hispanics that local views of Hispanics had significantly hardened even among some native whites they had previously befriended (Flores 2014).

The ordinance also cemented the local perception that most Hispanic immigrants did not have legal documents. Though prior to the ordinance locals suspected some Hispanics of being undocumented, especially those who spoke Spanish, suspicion intensified during the ordinance debates. According to a middle-aged Peruvian immigrant, "After the ordinance [was proposed], all Hispanics became illegal" in the eyes of non-Hispanic white residents.

Hazleton elites' decision to push for the ordinance by portraying local immigrants as a growing menace had another unintended consequence: it colored natives' perceptions of the town itself. Despite relatively low crime levels, most of my non-Hispanic white informants in 2007 believed that Hazleton was under siege by criminals. While some residents acknowledged that the area had a long connection with organized crime,[2] most believed that, as city officials argued, Hispanic immigrants were laying siege to what used to be a "quiet little town" (Tarone 2006). A sixty-one-year-old local woman attending a pro-ordinance rally in 2007 told the local newspaper, "If it wasn't for him [Mayor Barletta] the city would be overrun with guns and gangs. This used to be a quiet city; now you can't leave your doors open" (Birkbeck 2007).

In reality, local per capita crime rates had remained stable over the years in spite of the city's demographic changes (see figure 15.1). However, Shannon, a twenty-eight-year-old non-Hispanic white single mother whose family moved from New Jersey in the late 1980s because of the area's affordable housing, answered the question about how she liked living in Hazleton with the response, "Have you looked at the paper? The Mayor is trying to help but it is freaking unsafe around here. That's why I'm getting a license to carry [a gun]. Having a 3-year-old with me all the time, I can't take chances." Her boyfriend had recently acquired a handgun out of security concerns (Flores 2014).

How durable were these social consequences? To examine this question, I returned to Hazleton in 2011. Mayor Barletta was elected to State Congress in 2010 after he gained nationwide notoriety through the IIRA. Somewhat surprisingly, my local informants consistently told me that ethnic tensions had declined considerably. In addition, as figure 15.1 shows, the local newspaper published fewer stories linking immigrants with crime over time after an all-time peak in 2006 (the year the IIRA was proposed). In the intervening years, Hazleton experienced a dramatic demographic transformation that may have contributed to the perceived decline in ethnic animosity. Table 15.1 shows that despite Barletta's expectation that Hispanics would flee due to the IIRA (Barry 2006), the Hispanic population had grown to 37.3 percent of the total Hazleton population by 2010 from less than 5 percent in 2000.

These changing demographic realities were slowly altering Hazleton's political landscape. Some Hispanic residents believed that local politicians were increasingly reluctant to antagonize the Latino community because of its growing political muscle. A middle-class Hispanic immigrant told me, "I think the [Latino] community grew too much for them to come out against us. Politicians want to get elected and they know that they need Latinos' support. They know it." In the wake of the IIRA proposal, several Latino candidates ran for public office. Though none of them was successful, there was increasing local recognition of the potential political power of Hispanic residents and of the fact that Latinos could eventually "elect their own Spanish mayor just like Italians did," as an Italian American politician put it (Flores 2014).

SCAPEGOATING AND REACTIVE ETHNICITY: FLORIDA

Was the short-term increase in anxiety and perceived insecurity a phenomenon restricted to Hazleton, or was it also found in other communities that proposed similar anti-immigrant policies?

The Hazleton findings highlight the unpredictability and diversity of the social changes brought about by the scapegoating of immigrants by elites. Another unexpected outcome of scapegoating is the emergence of **reactive ethnicity** among targeted immigrant communities. Reactive ethnicity can be defined as ethnic militancy in reaction to perceived discrimination by the mainstream (Haller, Portes, and Lynch 2011). External attacks often increase internal solidarity among the targeted group. They also energize ethnic identities and help define and strengthen the boundaries of the group itself (Coser [1956] 1998). Attacks foment a feeling of "we" among the attacked, a sense of groupness (Brubaker 2002). This newly acquired group consciousness may then become politicized to respond to external threats. In some cases, the newly energized minority group may even displace the very nativist forces that had targeted it.

An early example of reactive ethnicity came about during the Mariel boatlift in the early 1980s in Miami, Florida. The Mariel boatlift was a mass emigration of Cubans, who traveled from Cuba's Mariel Harbor to the United States between April and October 1980. The Cuban government announced that it would allow anyone to leave the island after approximately ten thousand Cubans tried to gain asylum by taking refuge on the grounds of the Peruvian embassy. The arrival of the refugees in the United States became a thorny issue for US president Jimmy Carter, especially after Castro announced that a number of them had been released from Cuban jails and mental health facilities (Engstrom 1997). Both governments agreed to end the Mariel boatlift in October 1980. A total of 124,769 Cubans reached Florida through this boatlift.

Prior to the arrival of Marielitos, the Cuban community in Miami, composed mostly of political exiles who had fled the Castro regime, was well regarded by "Anglos" (non-Hispanic whites). Many Cubans occupied important positions in Anglo businesses and associations and were often portrayed as a "model" minority. At that time, the majority of the Cuban American community was outward oriented. Instead of being involved in local Miami politics, they were mostly concerned with undermining the Castro regime in Cuba. Occasional forays into local politics were criticized by community members as detracting from this goal (Portes and Stepick 1993).

Cuban Americans warmly received the first wave of Mariel refugees by sending volunteers and resources to meet their newly arrived countrymen. However, the Anglo community in Miami grew uneasy since it feared that growing numbers of Cubans would threaten its hegemony over the local power structure. As the voice of the Anglo establishment, the *Miami Herald* opposed the relocation of Mariel refugees in a series of editorials and by publishing unflattering news stories about Marielitos. The stories often focused on crimes allegedly committed by the newcomers. They failed to influence Carter's policies on the refugees, but they did shape how Marielitos were perceived by Anglo society and even Cuban Americans, who began to distance themselves from the newcomers. Nevertheless, increasingly, Anglos began painting all Cubans with the same brush. By 1982, surveys reported that "Cubans" were the least favored group by native whites. Fifty-nine percent of US residents believed "Cubans" had been bad for the country, the worst score among all ethnic and racial groups (Portes and Stepick 1993, 31).

In response to Mariel, a grassroots movement of native whites began pushing for an English-only, anti-bilingualism measure. Their goal was to prohibit local governments from funding programs or activities in a language other than English. This movement claimed that Cubans were not assimilating as prior groups had but that they "expected America to adapt to them." Cuban Americans were shocked when local residents overwhelmingly voted for the referendum. "[It] was a slap in our face," a Cuban American Dade County official said. "People began to feel 'more Cuban than anyone.' There was anger at the insult, but no organization yet" (Portes and Stepick 1993).

In the face of this growing stigmatization, Cuban Americans turned their attention inward. They responded to strong outside animosity by undergoing a process of reactive formation: they sought to redefine the situation in terms more favorable to their own self-image and their role in the community. They organized several organizations, including Facts about Cuban Exiles (FACE) and the Cuban-American National Foundation (CANF), to push for a counternarrative that focused on the positive contributions of Cuban immigrants to Florida and the United States in general. In this way, the emergence of ethnicity among Cubans was "reactive" since it was activated by Anglos' attempt to reassert their hegemony (Portes and Stepick 1993).

Cubans' push for increased political representation was successful. Before the referendum, there were few Cuban elected officials. By mid-decade, however, the mayors of the most important southern Florida communities including Miami were Cuban born. Today, the political power of Cuban Americans is well established, and it has expanded beyond Florida. There are currently three powerful Cuban Americans in the US Senate: Marco Rubio (R) from Florida, Ted Cruz (R) from Texas, and Bob Menendez (D) from New Jersey.

This increased representation has had direct public policy consequences. When the "Anti-bilingual" referendum was approved in Miami, the Dade County Commission was majority Anglo. By 1993, a shift in power had occurred. The new commission had six Hispanic, four black, and three Anglo members. One of their first actions was to unanimously repeal the referendum. In explaining this decision, Commissioner Miguel Diaz de la Portilla, a son of Cuban immigrants who represented the Metro Dade area, said that the ordinance was written in a climate of hate and fear. "It excludes people," he said. "What is the American culture? Who's going to define it? We're a country of immigrants" (Associated Press 1993).

Indeed, though Cuban Americans tend to lean Republican, Cuban American politicians have at times supported pro-immigrant policies, including a sanctuary city law passed by the city of Miami (though it was later repealed under pressure from the Trump administration) (Associated Press 2017).

SCAPEGOATING AND BACKLASH: CALIFORNIA

The same pattern of short-term political gains but long-term losses for elites who rely on immigrant scapegoating can be found in more progressive states like California. A similar process of reactive ethnicity emerged in California among the Latino community after restrictionist groups introduced the "Save Our State" (SOS) ballot initiative, also known as Proposition 187, in 1994. This initiative was designed to establish a state-run citizenship screening system to prevent undocumented immigrants from accessing nonemergency health care, public education, and other services in California (Alvarez and Butterfield 2000). The proponents of Proposition 187 deployed metaphors and images portraying immigrants as abusing social services and as "stretching the [welfare] system beyond capacity" (Calavita 1996, 298). These images resonated with popular concerns over government's budget deficits in the context of the increasingly dire economic conditions faced by many US workers, including declining wages and heightened job insecurity (Calavita 1996). When the vote came, California voters overwhelmingly approved it. Besides encouraging popular support for Proposition 187, California politicians' use of threatening metaphors like "brown tide rising," "army of invaders," and "burdens" to describe Latino immigrants may have hardened popular views of Latinos (Chavez 2001, 2008; Santa Ana 2002).

Interestingly, Proposition 187 in California followed a pattern similar to the anti-immigrant initiatives introduced by Anglo elites in Florida in the early 1980s. While an electorate that came to see Latino immigrants with suspicion approved the ballot, it also generated internal solidarity among the Latino community. In addition, much like in Hazleton and Miami, it led to the emergence of Latino leaders who sought to counter the prevailing negative narratives of immigrants and tried to politically mobilize Latinos along newly charged ethnic lines. Some of these newly minted Latino activists would eventually occupy high-level positions within California government. Kevin De León, a Guatemalan American who became the first Latino leader of the state senate in more than a century, helped organize the state's largest protest against Proposition 187. "I cut my teeth politically organizing against Prop 187 because my values were offended," De León later said. "Politicians—both Republicans and Democrats—were scapegoating immigrants for every political and social and economic ill" (Hart 2018).

Despite the humbler socioeconomic background of Latinos in California relative to Cuban Americans in Florida (Portes and Rumbaut 2001), their representation levels have grown significantly since Proposition 187. Today they constitute nearly 40 percent of California's population, surpassing the white, non-Latino population, and they now make up 20 percent of the Legislature (Romero 2016). The energizing of Latino voters has shifted the state's political landscape. With the exception of Governor Arnold Schwarzenegger, no other Republican politician has won a California gubernatorial, senatorial, or presidential election since 1994.

In the post–Proposition 187 period, a wave of powerful Latino leaders has emerged, including the last two mayors of Los Angeles, Antonio Villaraigoza and Eric Garcetti; former Lieutenant Governor Cruz Bustamante; and Anthony Rendón, a Democrat representing California's 63rd Assembly District, who is the current speaker of the Assembly. California Latino politicians have had a significant impact on public policies. Indeed, on the twentieth anniversary of Proposition 187's passage, De León's Senate Bill 396 erased Proposition 187's language from the books (Hart 2018). California is now at the forefront of expanding rights and services to undocumented immigrants. A 2017 state law declared California a sanctuary state for undocumented immigrants. In addition, the state allows these immigrants to obtain driver's licenses and also provides some health care services and legal assistance for them (Romero 2016).

From being one of the most regressive states on immigration, California now is at the forefront of expanding the rights of its undocumented residents, openly defying the restrictionist immigration policies of the Trump administration.

ANTI-IMMIGRANT RHETORIC GOES NATIONAL: IS THERE A TRUMP EFFECT?

Trump's use of harsh anti-immigrant rhetoric as a political weapon is not without precedents. Politicians in the past have embraced similar rhetoric against Cuban immigrants in Florida, Dominicans in Pennsylvania, and Mexicans in California. In all of these cases we see similar patterns. The threatening themes used by nativist politicians strike a nerve among a significant portion of the majority group, leading to short-term political victories for these political entrepreneurs. At the same time, the scapegoating of immigrants by political elites can set in motion a series of social processes far beyond their control. In the short term, ethnic boundaries around the targeted group may harden and anti-immigrant activism may increase. However, this may promote solidarity within the minority group, which may trigger political mobilization in the long term. This political mobilization, an example of reactive ethnicity, could eventually threaten nativists' grip on political power.

Will Trump nativist rhetoric lead to similar social outcomes? Journalists have claimed that Trump's rhetoric energized white supremacists and hardened public attitudes toward immigrants (Burke 2016; Carroll 2016; Haberman 2016). Further, actual violence has been directly linked to Trump's rhetoric (Fox 2015). It is not entirely clear whether these reported incidents were isolated cases.

In a recent paper, I find that in the short term Trump's nativist rhetoric may be consequential. More specifically, I find experimental evidence that exposure to Donald Trump's anti-immigrant rhetoric leads to expressing more negative views of immigrants in surveys (Flores 2018). Such negative effects, however, are concentrated among Republicans and individuals without college degrees.

In addition, I find that these effects are ephemeral. They dissipate within days. The temporality of these effects implies that to keep the population in a constant state of excitement, anti-immigrant politicians need to constantly repeat their restrictionist messages, as Trump himself does in his rallies and on Twitter. Last, I find that these effects are not author-dependent. Statements by politicians were not more impactful than statements by local residents. This suggests that the power of elite rhetoric primarily lies in its capacity to reach the masses via the news media.

Previous scholars have argued that elite statements that are explicitly racial in nature, like Trump's speech on immigration, may fail to have attitudinal effects because explicit racist views are no longer socially acceptable (Bonilla-Silva 2003; Mendelberg 2001). Their argument is that since being openly racist is no longer socially acceptable, nativist politicians had to use covert language to send racial messages to activate voters' racial resentment. Nevertheless, Trump's rise suggests that immigration statements may be an exception. Immigrants' contested legality may allow critics to explicitly target them without seemingly violating anti-racist social norms. Undocumented immigrants may be perceived by natives to be outside of the polity and hence not deserving of "civil rights" (Waters and Kasinitz 2015).

Will Trump's nativist push have similar long-term effects as prior nativist efforts? Based on prior experiences, we can expect several social effects. First, Trump may be aiding in the racialization of US Latinos and Muslims as nonwhite groups. The racial status of these groups has historically been uncertain as they have moved in and out of whiteness (Maghbouleh 2017; Lopez 1997). Nonetheless, Trump's constant attacks on these groups may reinforce group stereotypes and more firmly place them on the nonwhite side of the "color" line as racialized minorities.

Second, Trump's activities may be redrawing ethnic boundaries and reshaping ethnic identities in the United States. Trump has made scathing remarks about Mexicans, Puerto Ricans, Salvadorans, and South Americans (Segarra 2017; Trump 2015). In doing so, he may be activating a process of reactive ethnicity among Latinos. His nativist rhetoric could be weakening intra-Latino boundaries and promoting stronger pan-ethnic identification among Latinos in general. A newly emboldened and politicized Latino group may spell trouble for nativist politicians.

Some Republican strategists have urged their party members to tone down nativist rhetoric to avoid alienating Hispanic voters (Rove 2013). Though this may be a sensible long-term strategy, the temptation for conservative politicians to exploit racial and ethnic anxieties is high, especially given Trump's apparent gains, at least in the short term, using this strategy. This may create a vicious circle. In response to this rhetoric, minorities seem to be coalescing around the Democratic Party. This, however, may only further exacerbate this process. To the extent that conservative politicians perceive immigrants and ethnic and racial minorities as solid Democratic constituencies, stoking racial resentment among whites may continue to be a tempting political strategy for them.

Suggested Reading

Alba, R., and V. Nee. 2009. *Remaking the American Mainstream: Assimilation and Contemporary Immigration.* Cambridge, MA: Harvard University Press.

Bonilla-Silva, E. 2017. *Racism without Racists: Color-Blind Racism and the Persistence of Racial Inequality in America.* Lanham, MD: Rowman & Littlefield.

Massey, D., and M. Sánchez. 2010. *Brokered Boundaries: Creating Immigrant Identity in Anti-Immigrant Times.* New York: Russell Sage Foundation.

CHAPTER 16

How Do Latinos Respond to Anti-Immigrant Politics?

GARY SEGURA, MATT BARRETO, AND ANGELA E. GUTIERREZ

While evidence from California suggests that group threat mobilizes Latinos, nationally there has never been a test case for this theory. In 2016, the Donald Trump campaign provided a clear case of group threat through his divisive rhetoric and policy proposals targeting Mexican Americans and immigrants. In this chapter, we present evidence using the **2016 Collaborative Multi-Racial Post-Election Survey (CMPS)** data to show that Latino voters were politically motivated by Trump's anti-Latino rhetoric. These data also show that Latino voters who perceive Latinos as a panethnic racialized group and feel a sense of immigrant-linked fate are more likely to hold negative views of, and feel angry toward, the Republican presidential candidate during the 2016 election. In this chapter, we also present evidence that Latino voters who were angry were more likely to engage in political activities during the 2016 election. The findings hold for US-born Latinos, as well as among non-Mexican Latinos who felt similarly targeted by Trump's rhetoric and proposals.

RACIALIZED PANETHNICITY: A POLITICIZED IDENTITY

While the majority of Latinos are classified racially as white, the panethnic category "Latino/Hispanic" was adopted by the US government in 1970 as a way to distinguish people of Latin American origin (Mora 2014). Scholars have long debated the appropriateness of panethnic identifiers to categorize such a diverse group, arguing in some instances that they will be able to assimilate into whiteness and in other instances that the group itself is too diverse for the panethnic term to hold meaning (Citrin and Sears 2014; Perlmann 2005; Beltrán 2010). Whether or not people ascribe to panethnic identities is a valid question given that racially the majority of Latinos in the United States are classified as white and may more strongly identify with their national origin. This issue is exacerbated when we consider intragroup discrimination on the basis of national origin and assimilation in the United States (Lavariega Monforti and Sanchez 2010). However, we argue that the racialization of Latinos in the United States will serve to increase the salience and significance of their **panethnic identity**.

Despite the relative newness of the Latino/Hispanic category, discrimination faced by all Latinos in the United States has been recorded throughout its history. These different ethnic groups have faced a common history of **racialization** in the United States since the 1800s. Whether discussing urban renewal projects in New York City, which purged a large portion of the Puerto Rican community from the area, or English-only efforts in Dade County, Florida, aimed at the growing Cuban American population, or school segregation and the disenfranchisement of Mexican Americans in the Southwest, the common experience among these Latino ethnic groups is their marginalized status in the United States (Sanchez 2007; Arington 1990; Ortiz and Telles 2012; Padilla 1985). Scholars have found that due to a long history of racial inequality and discrimination, the racialization of Mexican Americans and other **national-origin groups**—Cuban, Dominican, Salvadoran, Brazilian, or Columbian Americans, for example—does not end after initial migration and assimilation but instead spans generations (Telles and Ortiz 2008; Rumbaut 2009). Thus, while the panethnic nomenclature may be uniquely American, newer immigrant arrivals from Latin America recognize the poor treatment of Latinos in the United States (Portes and Bach 1985).

As immigrants come to the United States, they are exposed to the racial frame that structures the US social hierarchy. Immigrants come to realize that these panethnic identities are in fact racialized by the broader US society and learn their position in the hierarchical structure (Valdez 2016). We argue that Latinos in the United States have come to understand that the broader American society largely does not view Latin American countries distinctly and that discrimination is likely to occur no matter the country of origin. Because of the racial hierarchy in the United States, members from other groups racialize Latinos into one amorphous group (Masuoka and Junn 2013; Valdez 2016), and because of this racialized identity, Latinos are more likely to view themselves as similar in status and as members of the same panethnic group. We do not deny that Latinos have an affinity for their national-origin group, but we believe that panethnic identity has been racialized by US society.

This is supported by data from the 2016 Collaborative Multi-Racial Post-Election Survey (CMPS). This online survey was conducted from December 3, 2016, to February 15, 2017. It was available in multiple languages, including English and Spanish. Among its 10,145 respondents were 3,003 Latinos. The Latino sample includes both registered and nonregistered voters, thus allowing a more thorough examination of the impact of anti-Latino and anti-immigrant rhetoric on nonvoters and those who may have engaged in other forms of nonelectoral participation.

In this survey, respondents were asked how much being Latino/Hispanic is an important part of how they see themselves. Fifty-five percent of respondents said it was very important, with an additional 32 percent stating that it was somewhat important. Only 13 percent of all respondents claimed being Latino was not very, or not at all, important to how they viewed themselves.

How respondents view and interpret their racialized identity is important to disentangling the behavior of Latino voters in the 2016 election. In their work on direct and indirect xenophobic attacks, Sergio Garcia-Rios, Francisco Pedraza, and Bryan Wilcox-Archuleta (2018) theorize about the novel concept of an **identity portfolio.** They argue that individuals contain a portfolio under which multiple identities are stored and used in the political decision-making process. Based on **social identity theory,** whereby a person's sense of self is based on belonging to a particular group, Garcia-Rios, Pedraza, and Wilcox-Archuleta (2018) argue that social identities that are more salient to individuals are more easily politicized via hostile rhetoric than less salient identities (see also Tajfel and Turner 1979).

They find that high-identifying Mexican Americans dislike Trump when compared to low identifiers and other national-origin groups (Garcia-Rios, Pedraza, and Wilcox-Archuleta 2018). Similar to national-origin group identity, Latinos may hear Trump's rhetoric and respond to the xenophobic attack not as Mexican Americans or Cuban Americans but as racialized Latino/Hispanics. Thus, by starting his presidential bid with a xenophobic attack against Mexican American immigrants and those who enter the United States via the southern border, Trump angered and provoked a much larger community in the United States.

We hypothesize that Latinos who have developed a **racialized panethnic identity** were angered by Trump's rhetoric and were more likely to view him unfavorably. This racialized identity is particularly important in 2016 when individuals may feel that their membership in the broader US society is being questioned. Furthermore, not only are Latinos in the United States racialized by their skin color, language, and culture, but Donald Trump's attack against immigrants particularly resonates with the Latino population because of their more recent immigrant history. Studies have argued that immigrant status has become one of the key factors in racializing immigrants (Cobas, Duany, and Feagin 2016). Immigration is a serious issue for many Latinos given that 67 percent of registered Latino voters personally know someone who is undocumented (Barreto and Segura 2014). The number of Latinos who would be impacted by changes to immigration policy extends well beyond the foreign-born Mexican American population. While 35 percent of Mexican Americans are immigrant, first-generation immigrants comprise a greater percentage of other Latin American nationalities.

We hypothesize that due to anti-immigrant attacks, Latino identity will gain primacy not only by the most threatened national-origin group but also by Latinos of all nationalities who feel a connection to this identity. To operationalize a racialized panethnic identity, we focus on two measures, feelings of racialized discrimination toward Latinos in the United States broadly and a new measure we call **immigrant-linked fate.** Because the measures for panethnic and national-origin identities are so highly correlated, we opted to use the items that we believe are most likely to capture the racialized nature of panethnicity. We argue that racialized identity and immigrant-linked fate were made salient in the 2016 election, and those with high levels of immigrant-linked fate and racialized discrimination are most likely to hold an unfavorable view of the Republican candidate. We suspect that these two variables may work independently of one another, but when high levels of both are present, we may see a greater dislike for the Republican candidate. We also expect that Latinos who view Trump unfavorably are more likely to feel angry about the 2016 election and mobilize during the 2016 campaign.

GROUP THREAT, GROUP ANGER

While Trump's rhetoric may stoke fear and anger among Latinos, the type of rhetoric espoused by Trump in the 2016 election is not new to American politics (Pedraza and Osorio 2017; Santa Ana 2017). Prior to the 2016 presidential election there were other opportunities to study how Latinos respond to threat. In the early 1990s in California, Latinos faced political threat with Propositions 187, 209, and 227 (Hajnal and Baldassare 2001; HoSang 2010).[1] In December 2005, Latinos were once again faced with political threat, this time at the national level, when the Sensenbrenner Bill (HR 4437), passed the US House. This bill if passed by Congress would have made it a felony to be undocumented in the United States. The response was strong not only among Mexicans, who make up the largest portion of the Latino population in the United States, but also among other groups of Latin American origin (Barreto et al. 2009). Many took to the streets to protest the bill. Activists helped mobilize cities in the form of mass protest demonstrations (Ramirez 2013; Zepeda-Milan 2017). But few researchers have been able to measure the ways Latinos responded to political threat outside of protest. Our aim is to examine a host of different types of political participation activities to see if the response to threat goes beyond the scope of a few activities to a broader range of political mobilization.

An important aspect to consider is that emotional responses to threatening rhetoric can play an instrumental role in motivating individuals to either engage with or disengage from the political process. Theories on emotion have hypothesized that people often respond via habit when in predictable situations, but when unexpected events arise, individuals are often alert and may respond with anxiety and fear (Marcus, Neuman, and MacKuen 2000; Neuman et al., 2007). Anger arises in response to a negative event, which is caused by a specific agent viewed as unjust or illegitimate, thus eliciting a different response (Huddy, Feldman, and Cassese 2007; Valentino et al. 2008). Conducting experiments on emotional cues and behavioral responses, Nicholas Valentino et al. (2011) found that anger is likely to increase all forms of political participation while other emotions like fear are inconsistent in increasing political participation. Given Trump's rhetoric in the 2016 election, we might expect that many Latino voters would feel anger about his comments and his racialized language regarding Latinos, which would lead to an increase in political participation.

We hypothesize that Latinos who recognize the racialized structure in the United States and hold a strong sense of immigrant-linked fate will hold more unfavorable opinions about Trump. Furthermore, we expect that people who dislike Trump particularly because of his rhetoric will be angrier in the 2016 election. Those who are angry because of the anti-Latino, anti-immigrant rhetoric should also be more likely to participate during the 2016 election. We expect that state context will have little bearing on Trump favorability and mobilization and anticipate that dislike for Trump and mobilization will not be limited to Mexican Americans but will be consistent across all national-origin groups and generations.

DATA AND RESULTS: RACISM AND IMMIGRANT-LINKED FATE

In order to examine our hypotheses, we relied on the 2016 Collaborative Multi-Racial Post-Election Survey. First, we constructed a racism scale out of two questions on the CMPS: "How much of a problem do you think discrimination is in preventing Latinos in general from succeeding in America?" and "How much discrimination is there in the United States today against Latinos?" These help us capture perceived economic and social discrimination toward Latinos in American society today.[2] Table 16.1 displays the frequencies of the racism scale by national-origin group. Second, we rely on an immigrant-linked fate item on the survey to capture whether or not respondents believed that what happens generally to immigrants in this country will have something to do with what happens in their lives. This is the first time that this question has been asked on a survey, but given that immigration has a lot to do with the position of Latinos in the racial hierarchy, we expect that immigrant-linked fate is a strong component of a racialized Latino identity. Our two key independent variables are moderately and positively correlated[3] but not so much so that we are concerned about losing statistical power.

DATA AND RESULTS: TRUMP FAVORABILITY

The results indicate that the racism scale and immigrant-linked fate are strongly correlated with negative attitudes toward Trump (**table 16.2**). We also find that compared to first-generation respondents, being a second-generation Latino is correlated with a more negative view of Trump, but third-generation Latinos appear to hold more favorable views of Trump when compared to first-generation respondents. This suggests that opposition to Trump is strongest among those closer to the immigrant experience. However, we find that individuals who are fourth generation and beyond are not distinguishable in their views of Trump when compared to first-generation Latinos, so perhaps the third-

TABLE 16.1 SUMMARY OF RESPONSE TO THE RACISM SCALE ITEMS BY NATIONAL ORIGIN GROUP

Racism Scale	Cuban	Mexican	Puerto Tican	South American	Central American	Dominican	Other Ethnic
0	14	0	0	2	1	1	1
0.25	5	2	4	5	2	2	7
0.5	7	7	7	13	11	17	12
0.75	14	8	9	9	7	8	9
1	9	10	13	7	13	6	10
1.25	19	15	24	24	24	21	21
1.5	17	22	18	17	14	23	20
1.75	11	23	19	17	23	19	14
2	4	13	7	5	4	2	6
Total	100%	100%	100%	100%	100%	100%	100%

generation respondents may be distinct in their greater levels of support for Trump.

As expected, Democrats and Independents hold less favorable views of Trump than Republicans. In addition, being more ideologically conservative and Evangelical is correlated with holding a more favorable view of Trump. When looking at how support for Trump changes by national origin, we find that being of Central American or Cuban origin is correlated with holding a more positive view of Trump when compared to Mexican Americans. However, we find no effect among other national-origin groups. This might be expected for Cubans given that they are known to lean Republican, but we are unsure why we see this correlation for Central Americans. It might be because close to 50 percent of the Central American sample was born in the United States. We further find that Trump favorability is uncorrelated with living in any particular state.

To better understand the nuances of location, national origin, and generation, we ran several additional interaction models for both Trump favorability and political participation. Since the correlation of racism scale and Trump favorability is strongest, we chose to run interactions with the racism scale and state, national origin, and generation variables. **Figure 16.1**, top image, displays the predicted probability of viewing Trump very unfavorably when state is interacted with the racism scale. We find that when individuals rank the lowest on the racism index, their probability of viewing Trump very unfavorably ranges from about 32 percent in California to 43 percent in New York and New

TABLE 16.2 RACISM SCALE AND IMMIGRANT-LINKED THREAT

	Trump Favorability	Anger	Anger	Participation
Immigrant Linked Fate	−0.168*** (0.033)	0.111*** (0.032)		
Racism Scale	−0.857*** (0.097)	0.798*** (0.106)		
Reverse Trump Favorability		0.497*** (0.054)	0.590*** (0.053)	
Feeling angry during election				0.431*** (0.051)
Racism most important issue	−0.718*** (0.135)	0.301* (0.118)	0.432*** (0.115)	−0.017 (0.066)
Second generation	−0.298* (0.113)	0.456*** (0.114)	0.319*** (0.111)	0.301*** (0.063)
Third generation	0.345* (0.158)	0.546** (0.173)	0.422* (0.170)	0.521** (0.088)
Fourth Generation +	−0.226 (0.152)	0.301 (0.156)	0.058 (0.150)	0.303*** (0.089)
Uses Spanish Language	−0.092* (0.041)	−0.137* (0.042)	−0.092* (0.041)	0.128*** (0.024)
Democrat	−1.837*** (0.126)	0.091 (0.149)	0.199 (0.145)	0.065 (0.078)
Independent	−1.347*** (0.123)	−0.215 (0.149)	−0.230 (0.145)	−0.256** (0.083)
Ideology	0.246*** (0.045)	−0.029 (0.046)	−0.059 (0.044)	−0.195** (0.026)
Internal Efficacy	0.017 (0.038)	−0.129** (0.039)	−0.170** (0.038)	0.042* (0.021)
Economy Worse	−0.189*** (0.038)	0.036 (0.036)	0.048 (0.035)	−0.057*** (0.020)
Cuban	0.604** (0.223)	0.154 (0.267)	−0.068 (0.255)	0.166 (0.129)
Puerto Rican	−0.142 (0.165)	−0.358* (0.163)	−0.478** (0.160)	0.159 (0.088)
Dominican	−0.036 (0.255)	−0.588** (0.268)	−0.822** (0.261)	−0.076 (0.154)
Central American	0.334* (0.153)	−0.095 (0.161)	−0.242 (0.157)	−0.134 (0.094)
South American	0.215 (0.194)	−0.181 (0.205)	−0.384 (0.199)	0.266** (0.100)
Spanish\Other	0.134 (0.202)	0.117 (0.213)	0.066 (0.209)	−0.003 (0.117)
Arizona	−0.256 (0.252)	−0.424 (0.236)	−0.331 (0.231)	−0.232 (0.143)
Texas	0.042 (0.123)	−0.064 (0.122)	−0.105 (0.119)	−0.377*** (0.076)
Florida	0.271 (0.175)	−0.147 (0.181)	−0.106 (0.178)	−0.156 (0.097)
New York & New Jersey	0.117 (0.174)	−0.057 (0.171)	−0.055 (0.168)	−0.274*** (0.097)[i]
All other states	0.046 (0.117)	−0.135 (0.119)	−0.124 (0.116)	−0.129* (0.065)

Evangelical	0.592*** (0.105)	-0.123 (0.113)	-0.109 (0.109)	0.181** (0.062)
Education	-0.061 (0.040)	0.043 (0.040)	0.079* (0.039)	0.209*** (0.022)
Income	-0.021 (0.017)	0.083*** (0.017)	0.077*** (0.017)	0.043*** (0.009)
Age	-0.015*** (0.003)	-0.002 (0.003)	-0.005 (0.003)	0.003 (0.002)
Female	-0.396*** (0.088)	0.594*** (0.090)	0.606*** (0.087)	-0.283*** (0.051)
Constant		-3.196*** (0.365)	-2.035*** (0.334)	-1.448*** (0.177)
Observations	2,834	2,912	2,912	2,997
Log Likelihood				-3,028.015
Akaike Int. Crit.				6,112.030

NOTE: *p<0.05; **p<0.01; ***p<0.0

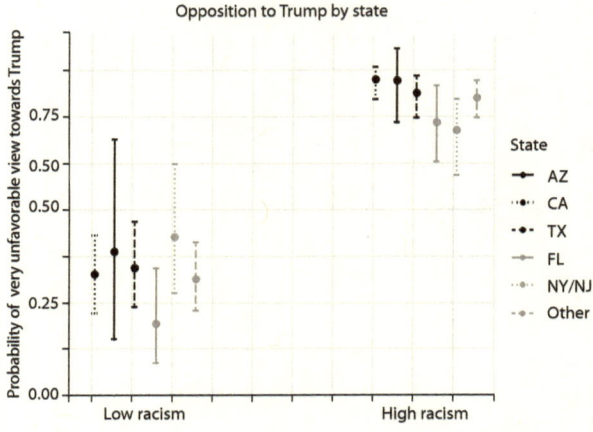
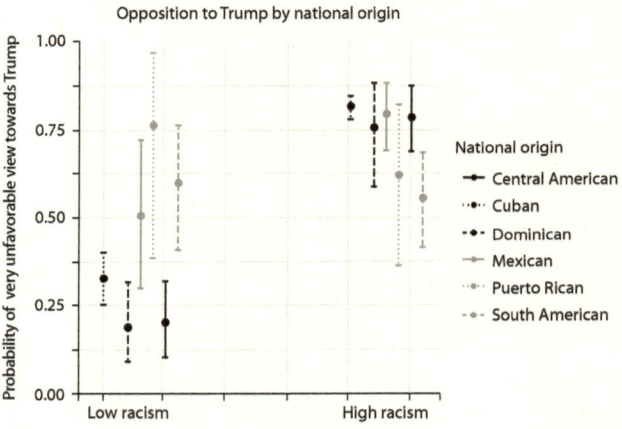
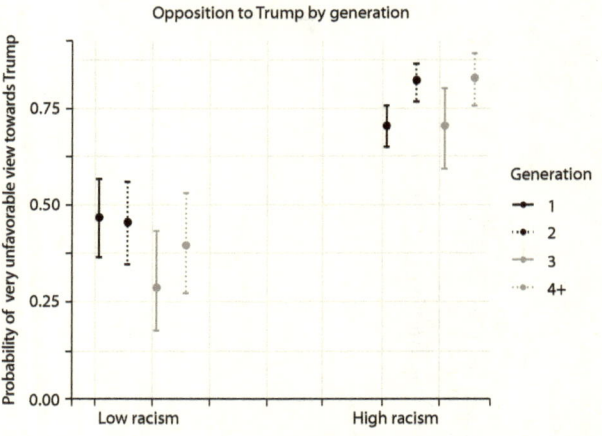

FIGURE 16.1. Trump Favorability Interaction Models.

Jersey. The point estimates and confidence bands are all close together, indicating that a dislike for Trump is not unique to any particular state. When we set our racism index to the highest level, we find that the predicted probabilities of viewing Trump very unfavorably dramatically increase in every state. Predicted probability point estimates for viewing Trump very unfavorably range from 70 percent in New York and New Jersey to 84 percent in Arizona and California.

The middle image of figure 16.1 displays the predicted probability of viewing Trump very unfavorably when we interact national-origin groups with the racism index. As with the previous models, a higher score on the racism index is associated with a higher probability of viewing Trump very unfavorably. One notable exception is among respondents of South American origin.[4] For our South American respondents, a high value on the racism index is associated with a lower probability of viewing Trump very unfavorably. Conversely, a low value on the racism index is associated with a high probability of viewing Trump unfavorably. South Americans who score the lowest on the racism index have a 60 percent predicted probability of viewing Trump very unfavorably, while those who view racism as a problem the most have only a 55 percent predicted probability of viewing Trump very unfavorably. It seems that for South Americans opposition to Trump has more to do with attacking immigrants and feeling a connection to immigrants than with racism in American society itself. The racism scale provides little movement for Cuban Americans, but for all of the other national-origin groups, we see a slight shift upward in the predicted probability of viewing Trump unfavorably.

The bottom image in figure 16.1 displays the results of the interaction between the racism scale and generation. The results indicate that perceiving high levels of racialized discrimination is associated with higher levels of dislike for Donald Trump among all generations. Our findings show that racialized discrimination played a key factor in shaping opposition to Trump. Respondents move from possibly viewing Trump unfavorably to almost certainly holding a negative view of Trump as perceptions of racialized discrimination increase.

For our anger models, instead of relying on immigrant-linked fate and the racism index (already strongly correlated with Trump favorability), we used a reverse coded Trump favorability variable as our key predictor for feeling angry during the 2016 election. **Figure 16.2** displays the marginal effect of each coefficient on the predicted probability of being angry often or always during the 2016 election. We find that

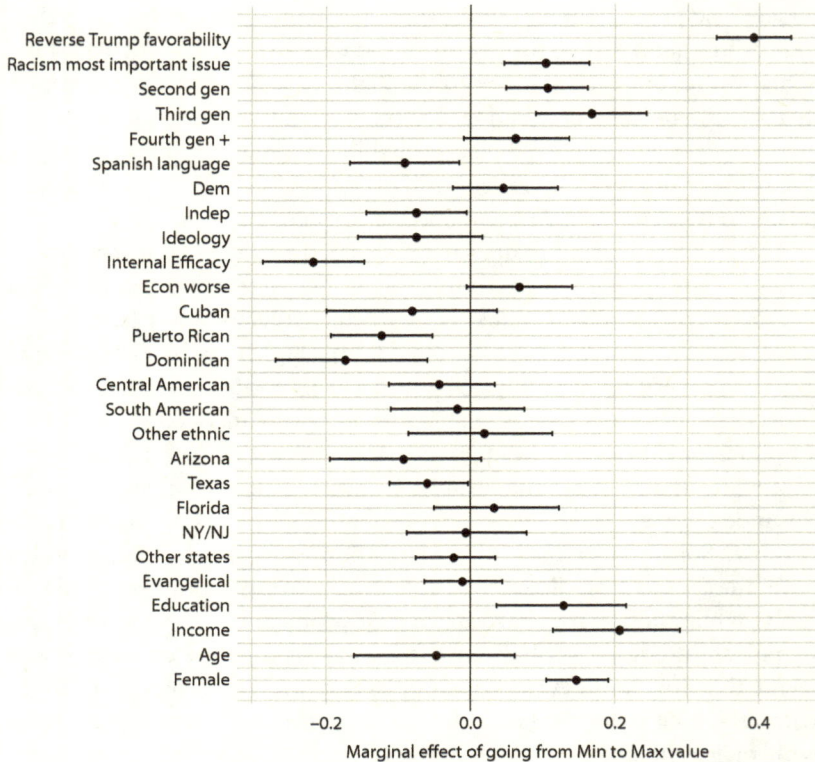

FIGURE 16.2. Changes in Probability of Being Angry Often or All the Time during the 2016 Election.

when compared to all of the other independent variables, disliking Trump is associated with the largest increase in probability of feeling angry during the 2016 election.

To better understand this relationship, **figure 16.3** displays the predicted probability of being angry often or always during the 2016 election by how much respondents dislike Trump. Having a very favorable view of Trump is associated with a 20 percent predicted probability of feeling angry often or always during the 2016 election. Those who have a very unfavorable view of Trump are associated with a 60 percent probability.

DATA AND RESULTS: POLITICAL PARTICIPATION

Next, we look at what motivated political participation. Our hypothesis is that Trump angered many Latino voters, and this anger is associ-

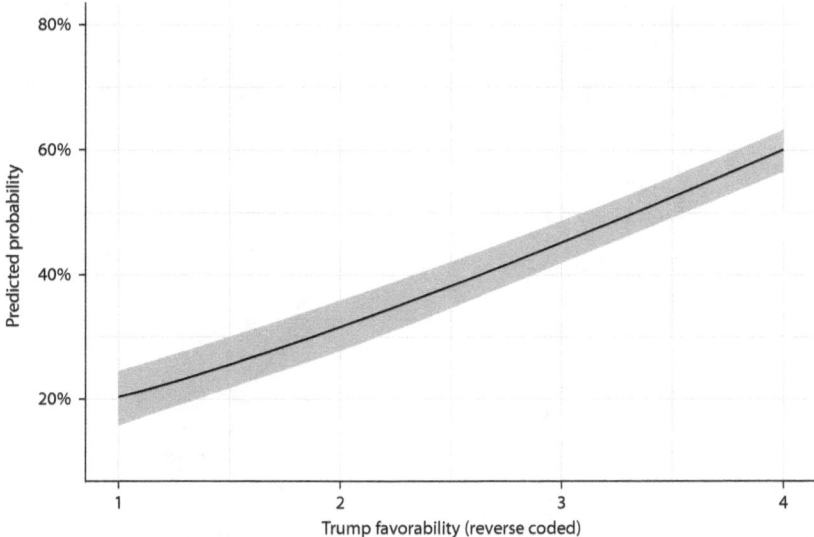

FIGURE 16.3. Predicted Probability of Being Angry Often or Always during the 2016 Election.

ated with an increase in political participation. Our political participation variable is the sum of engaging in the five following political activities: (1) working for a political campaign; (2) donating money to a political party or campaign; (3) being a member of a civic group; (4) contacting government officials; and (5) engaging in political protest.[5] The results from the political participation model can be found in table 16.2. We find that feeling angry during the 2016 election is positively correlated with engaging in political activities.

We again ran three additional interaction models to see if anger influences political participation differently when interacted with location, national origin, and generation. The first image in **figure 16.4** presents the predicted count when anger is set to the lowest and highest values in each state. We find that anger works similarly in all states. Those who are angry are more likely to participate. This effect is strongest in Florida, where the count of actions increases from a 0.35 to 0.90.

Similarly, we find that when we interact anger with national origin, anger is positively correlated with political participation. We find that anger is especially strong and statistically significant for Dominican Americans. Dominican Americans who are low on the anger scale have

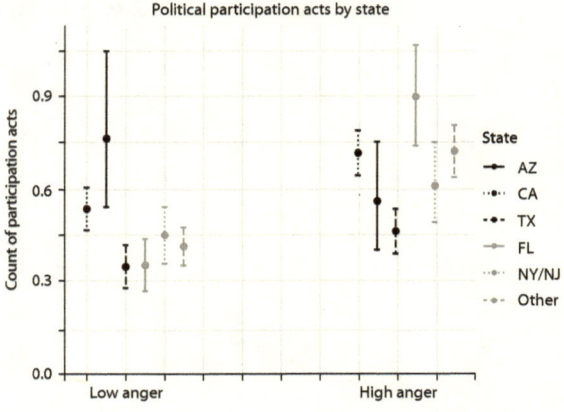
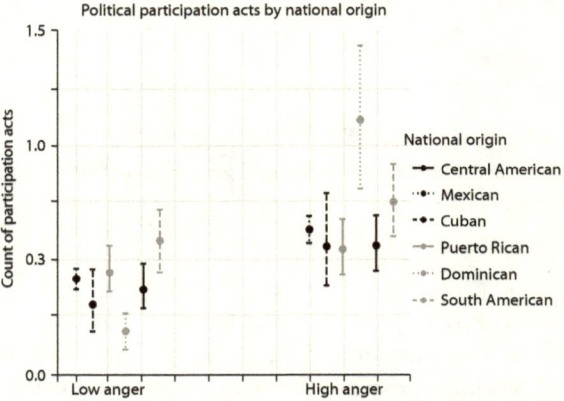
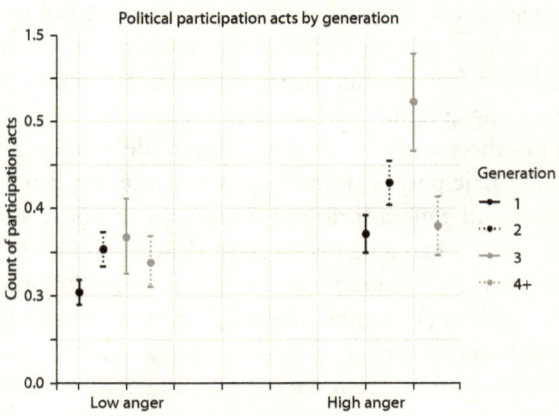

FIGURE 16.4. Political Participation Models by State, National Origin, and Generation with Displays of the Marginal Effect of Going from the Lowest Value of Each Coefficient to the Highest Value while Holding All Other Variables at Their Mean.

a predicted count estimate of 0.18, but when Dominican Americans are high on the anger scale, their predicted count increases to 1.11.

Our final interaction in the last column of figure 16.4 displays the predicted count of political participation acts a person engages in when anger is interacted with generation. Once again we find that anger positively correlated with political participation and that it is especially strong among third-generation respondents. When anger is set at its lowest value the predicted count of high cost political action is 0.5, but when anger is set to its highest value the predicted count increases to 0.96. The effect of anger is not very strong among first-generation respondents, but this may be related to the fact that they were not born in the United States, potentially making them more hesitant to participate. Our findings suggest that anger is an effective mobilizer, which is strongly correlated with an increase in political participation in almost every state, across ethnicities, and spanning multiple generations.

CONCLUSION AND DISCUSSION

In this chapter, we aimed to empirically examine the claim that group threat drove Latino attitudes and political behavior in the 2016 election. We argued that while the focus of the campaign rhetoric coming from Donald Trump was primarily Mexican Americans and immigrants, Latinos of other national origins and other subgroups also felt under attack. Despite the diversity of the Latino population, Latinos share a common racialized group. Without a doubt, in the social hierarchy these same racialization processes deem Latinos as outsiders, regardless of the vast heterogeneity among them.

Extant research has shown compelling evidence that anti-immigrant and anti-Latino rhetoric as well as a threatening political context influenced Latino partisanship, drove naturalization, and heightened turnout among Latinos in California in the 1990s. More recent work has also shown evidence of how threat has driven Latinos to engage in protests and rallies. This work has shown that the Sensenbrenner bill in the mid-2000s triggered massive protests by Latinos, and other immigrants, who fought for their dignity and humanity in the face of an extremely hostile political context (Zepeda-Milan 2017). Despite the fact that the protesters who took part in the 2006 marches chanted "Today We March, Tomorrow We Vote," the spillover effects into other types of engagement were difficult to assess. The anti-immigrant and anti-Mexican presidential campaign carried out by Donald Trump in 2016 presented itself as a case of national group threat to the Latino community. Here we have examined how this particular case drove favorability and participation among Latinos. We found that perceptions of racialized discrimination toward Latinos as well as immigrant-linked fate shaped Trump's low favorability among Latinos. We found that this held across the board for Latinos of various national origins, in multiple state contexts, and across generational status, supporting our argument that the anti-Mexican and anti-immigrant threats from the presidential campaign and Donald Trump increased the saliency of a racialized Latino immigrant identity.

Furthermore, the finding revealed that Latinos who share an immigrant-linked fate and those who felt that Latinos are racialized were more likely to feel angry during the 2016 election. We also found that those who were angry were particularly mobilized as they felt strongly connected to the immigrant community. Once again, regardless of generational status, national origin, or state of residency, Latinos were eager to participate in various ways because they recognized that they were connected to their immigrant counterparts. Our results suggest that Trump's rhetoric reduced his favorability among Latinos and angered members of the Latino community, further mobilizing Latino voters.

Our work has several implications for future research. First, it suggests that despite the increasing heterogeneity and diversity within the Latino community, there are many things that continue to bind and bring together this community into a cohesive group with political priorities and a political agenda. The way in which members of this community are racialized and treated by others in America suggests that the "Latino" label will continue to have repercussions for decades to come. Second, the findings here show evidence that a nationwide political threat drives favorability and results in greater levels of engagement for Latinos. However, future work must investigate whether or not hostility and threat always result in greater levels of engagement among members of marginalized communities. But what is clear from our findings is that threat can be mobilizing across a broad spectrum, further unifying and politicizing what it means to be Latino.

Suggested Reading

Abrajano, M., and Z. L. Hajnal. 2015. *White Backlash: Immigration, Race, and American Politics*. Princeton, NJ: Princeton University Press.

Barreto, M. A., and G. M. Segura. 2014. *Latino America: How America's Most Dynamic Population Is Poised to Transform the Politics of the Nation*. New York: Public Affairs.

Cobas, J. A., J. Duany, and J. R. Feagin. 2016. *How the United States Racializes Latinos: White Hegemony and Its Consequences*. New York: Routledge.

Garcia-Rios, S., F. Pedraza, and B. Wilcox-Archuleta. 2019. Direct and indirect xenophobic attacks: Unpacking portfolios of identity. *Political Behavior* 41(3): 633–56.

CHAPTER 17

Anti-Immigrant Backlash: Is There a Path Forward?

ZOLTAN L. HAJNAL

America, the land of immigrants, appears now to be the land of an **anti-immigrant backlash**. At the national level, that backlash and the role that Donald Trump has played in it are well known. But the Trump story—as fascinating and menacing as it is—is only a part of the immigrant backlash story. Activities at the state level have been just as important and perhaps just as threatening. This chapter examines the immigrant backlash at the state level. We know that state legislatures have become increasingly central to immigration policy, but we know less about the contours of those state-level policies. Is the backlash at the state level as broad and as severe as what we see at the national level? And equally important, are there any positive developments that can be copied? In particular, are there any lessons from states like California, which was once at the forefront of the anti-immigrant backlash and may now be at the vanguard of pro-immigrant policy making? Finally, is there anything immigrants themselves can do to deter or overcome the backlash? Ultimately this chapter presents a mixed picture. The data show that where there is mass in-immigration and a larger concentration of Latinos, the policy backlash is severe. In these states, policy has moved sharply in a more regressive and punitive way. But there are also some signs of positive and inclusive steps. The evidence shows that once the Latino population becomes large enough and crosses a demographic threshold, politics and policy begin to shift back toward inclusion and generosity.

A BROADER ANTI-IMMIGRANT BACKLASH?
WHAT WE KNOW

Immigration has traditionally been the purview of the federal government, but in the past two and a half decades, states have become increasingly active on the immigration front. Since 1992 states have passed over three thousand bills that explicitly deal with immigration (NCSL 2018). Although systematic analysis of the thousands of state-level laws addressing immigration has been limited, several relatively clear patterns have emerged.

First, the laws passed by state legislatures are diverse, with some offering tangible benefits to immigrants and others seeking to target and penalize different segments of the immigrant population. One study found that between 2005 and 2011, "welcoming" laws were slightly more common than "hostile" laws (Monogan 2013). The fact that some states are passing measures that seek to aid immigrants and foster their assimilation certainly raises hope for an end to the backlash. Also hidden beneath the overall pattern is considerable variation within states. Some states have moved in a decidedly anti-immigrant direction over time, while others like California have shifted very clearly from an anti-immigrant policy stance to a much more pro-immigrant policy output. That variation also suggests that there may be some lessons about how to shift from more exclusive to more inclusive policies.

Second, a closer look at the substance of these laws reveals that their net impact is clearly negative. Although the number of "welcoming" laws outnumbers the number of "hostile" laws over much of this period, further research shows that the majority of "welcoming" bills that are passed are largely symbolic with little or no tangible resources attached (Monogan 2013; see also Rivera 2015). By contrast, the clear majority of anti-immigrant laws have a major substantive impact. Of all the laws "affecting many immigrants in a substantial way," just under 60 percent negatively impact immigrants (Rivera 2015). During this period states have done everything from reducing or eliminating immigrants' access to public services in education, health, and welfare to allowing the police to target individuals suspected of being undocumented. In sum, there has been a clear anti-immigrant bent to state-level policy making on immigration. The anti-immigrant backlash is very real.

Third, and perhaps most important, analysis across states reveals a clear pattern to these measures. It is the states with the largest Latino populations that have been the most active and the most aggressive

(Rivera 2015). Texas, perhaps more than any other state, exemplifies this pattern. As one of the states with both the higher share of Latinos and the largest number of undocumented residents, it passed seven anti-immigrant laws between 2007 and 2009, including measures to detect and deter undocumented use of the state Medicaid program, reducing eligibility for the state's Child Health Care Program, and requiring private companies that work with the state to demonstrate that they do not employ unauthorized workers.

On the other end of the spectrum, the ten states with the smallest Latino populations passed on average only two anti-immigrant laws over the same period. Instead states with few immigrants and Latinos tended to pass more pro-immigrant legislation. Vermont, for example, expanded welfare eligibility, New Hampshire passed stiffer penalties for cross-border sexual and labor exploitation, and Montana passed a measure opposing implementation of the federal REAL ID Act. In fact, eight of the ten states with the smallest Latino population passed more pro-immigrant bills than anti-immigrant bills. At least in terms of explicit measures that directly and explicitly target immigrants, there is a real backlash, and that backlash is most pronounced where the Latino population is largest and most visible.

These patterns are important, but they may actually be understating the influence of immigration on policy. Almost all of the research to date looks at policies that are *explicitly* focused on immigrants.[1] That focus on explicit immigration policies ignores a broad range of critical policy areas like education, welfare, crime, health, and taxes that are only *implicitly* tied to immigration. Policies that defund schools or that criminalize certain behaviors may not be explicitly focused on immigrants but may nonetheless have massive impacts on the immigrant community. If Americans are thinking about immigrants or Latinos when they decide whether or not to fund schools, to be lenient to criminal offenders, or to raise taxes, the backlash could be very broad.

This broad anti-immigrant backlash may, however, not be the entire story. Another goal of this chapter is to examine the role that *immigrants* themselves play in this process. One of the implications of the argument so far is that immigrants can do little on their own to affect change. Up to this point, the only role that the immigrant population can play is to spark a white reaction. The mere presence of immigrants changes the attitudes and actions of the rest of America. That is an important part of the story—especially considering that white Americans make up the vast majority of the voting population.

But it is far from the entire story. There is another side of the equation: the role that racial and ethnic minorities play in American politics. In fact, this chapter argues that immigrants have some agency in the policy process. While the immigrant backlash is a powerful force, given sufficient numbers immigrants can begin to overwhelm that force. Once the size of the immigrant population passes a certain threshold, immigrants should be able to mobilize to influence policy outcomes, and policy should begin to shift back to the left. The end result is that the relationship between **immigrant context** and policy should be a curvilinear one.

MEASURING IMMIGRANT CONTEXT

There are all sorts of different ways one could measure immigrant context. The natural choice is likely to be the percent foreign born of each state. But that may not be the population that white Americans are most likely to notice and react to. Indeed, the data show very clearly that white Americans tend to hold very different attitudes toward different groups of immigrants. On the one hand, Asian Americans are seen as the model minority—hardworking, intelligent, and productive (Lee 2000). In sharp contrast, the other large immigrant-based group, Latinos, is characterized through **stereotypes** as undocumented, not paying taxes, prone to welfare, predisposed to violence, and generally a burden (Bobo and Johnson 2000). Opinions about the Asian Americans and Latinos certainly vary across individual white Americans, but if there is an **immigrant threat** in the minds of white America, it is likely to be focused squarely on the Latino population. As the most visible sign of all the supposed problems with the immigrant population and as the most potentially threatening element of the immigrant population, it is the Latino population that is likely to drive white reactions and thus state policies. As such, the analysis that follows centers on the broader Latino population to measure the immigrant threat.

EVIDENCE OF A BROADER POLICY BACKLASH

The question then becomes, is there a policy backlash in states with larger Latino populations? Do larger concentrations of Latinos lead to policies that are more regressive, more punitive, and less generous? As I show, the answer is clear. States with more Latinos tend to redistribute less and punish more.

TABLE 17.1 GOVERNMENT POLICY IN HEAVILY LATINO STATES IS MORE REGRESSIVE (SHARE OF ALL STATE SPENDING)

Spending	States with a Small Latino Population	States with a Large Latino Population	Proportional Difference in Spending
Health care	3.7%	2.5%	−32%
Corrections	3.9%	4.7%	+21%
Education	25.8%	24.8%	−4%
Taxation			
Sales tax	27.5%	36.4%	+32%
Property tax	5.8%	1.3%	−78%

The initial test is a simple one. **Table 17.1** compares state spending in three policy areas—health, prisons, and education—in states with large Latino populations to spending in states with small Latino populations. The analysis centers on the *proportion* of the state budget to neutralize variations that occur because one state is richer than another.[2] On the face of it, health, prisons, and education are not about immigration and the immigration threat, but these "nonracial" policies could very much be driven by attitudes toward immigrant or Latino groups—especially in states where many, if not most, of the people impacted by the policies are Latinos and immigrants. In two of the three policy areas—health and prisons—there is a sharp difference between spending in states with large Latino populations and in states with relatively small Latino populations.[3]

Just as a **racial threat theory** would predict, majorities that feel threatened by minority populations impose on them harsher political, social, and economic burdens. So in states with a large Latino population that could benefit from public services, Medicaid funding is significantly lower. Specifically, Medicaid falls from 3.7 percent of the budget in states with relatively few Latinos to 2.5 percent of the budget in states with large numbers of Latino. At first glance, that might seem like a small drop, but as the third column of table 17.1 illustrates, it actually represents a pretty sizable shift in spending. Heavily Latino states spend 32 percent less on Medicaid than states with few Latinos.

Also as expected, the pattern is exactly the opposite for spending on criminal justice. In states where Latinos represent a large share of the population and could be the target of tougher laws and harsher sentences, spending on prisons is substantially higher. Heavily Latino states spend 4.7 percent of their budgets on prisons, while states with small

Latino populations spend only 3.9 percent of their budgets in the same way. Again that difference might at first seem small, but it represents a 21 percent increase in the share of the budget going to prisons.

The third policy area, education, also fits the pattern, but here the differences are small no matter how one looks at it. States with larger Latino populations spend less—but only 4 percent less—on education. At least judging by this first test, there is no major difference in education spending between states with differing Latino population shares. Other more rigorous tests, however, reveal a robust relationship.

How governments spend their money is only half of the fiscal story. Without taxes and fees, there can be no public services. State governments also have to make weighty decisions about how they raise their revenues. On this front, tax decisions are the most important. States can choose to raise revenue through more progressive taxes like property taxes or they can favor more regressive means like sales taxes. Regressive taxes like sales taxes will fall most heavily on immigrants, Latinos, and the poor, for whom retail sales represent a large share of their spending. By contrast, progressive taxes like property taxes will benefit those on the lower end of the spectrum because they generally do not own property. Thus, the extent to which states favor sales over property taxes could say a lot about who they seek to penalize and who they seek to benefit.[4]

What tax patterns do say is very clear. States that are heavily Latino tend to raise much more of their revenue through regressive sales taxes and much less of their revenue through progressive property taxes. The differences are substantial. There is, in fact, a 32 percent increase in the share of revenue raised through sales taxes in states where Latinos represent a large share of the population. Likewise, there is a 78 percent decrease in the share of revenue raised through progressive property taxes in those same states (compared to states with small Latino population shares).

It is also worth noting that these patterns fit with the related research on welfare. Existing studies have found a close link between racial diversity and state welfare policy (Fellowes and Rowe 2004; Soss, Fording, and Schram 2008; Hero and Preuhs 2006). Welfare benefit levels tend to be lower in states with lots of minorities where the perceived threat is the greatest and where much of the resources would not be going to fellow white Americans (Hero and Preuhs 2006).

The overall pattern is fairly clear. States with larger Latino populations tend to spend and tax in ways that appear to target the Latino community and benefit other more advantaged segments of the population. That means less spending on public services when Latinos could be the beneficiaries and more on criminal justice when Latinos could be the target. It also means higher taxes on the poor and lower taxes on the rich in heavily Latino states. All of this differs in states with smaller Latino populations where public services are more generous and taxes are more progressive. In short, the size of the Latino population very much appears to shape how states raise and spend their money.

A MORE DEFINITIVE TEST OF THE RACIAL THREAT STORY

After adjusting for other possible factors that might shape state government spending and taxation—such as the share of citizens identifying as conservative, the share of state legislators who are Republican, the unemployment rate, median household income, the professionalization of the legislature, and several demographic factors, including the proportion of residents with a bachelor's degree and the share of residents who are African American and Asian American—the same racial threat story emerges. All else being equal, states with larger Latino populations are significantly less likely to spend money on education, significantly less likely to provide Medicaid, and significantly more likely to devote money to prisons. Controlling for this more complex range of factors also confirms the link between Latino population share and tax policy.[5] States with more Latinos rely more heavily on regressive taxes and utilize progressive taxes much less often.

All of this indicates that America's increasingly diverse population is generating a real, wide-ranging backlash. As the Latino population grows, Americans become less willing to invest in public services like education, health, and welfare and more willing to fund prisons. In other words, when the policy is more apt to impact Latinos, benefits decline and punishment increases.

THE OTHER SIDE OF THE BACKLASH EQUATION: THE ROLE IMMIGRANTS CAN PLAY

The conclusions so far suggest that Latinos are really just a pawn in a game played by the rest of the American population. Are Latinos really without any agency in the policy world? What about California where 23 percent of state legislators are Latino or New Mexico where 40 percent of the eligible voter population is Hispanic? Do Latino num-

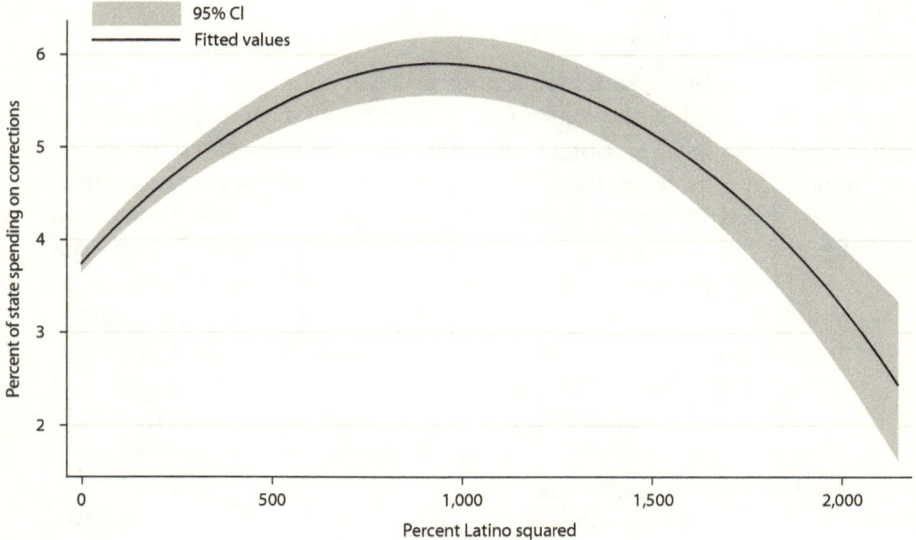

FIGURE 17.1. Effect of Latino Context on Corrections Spending.

bers eventually matter? Can Latinos begin to assert themselves when they grow sufficiently large in number?

One can test this more complex model by looking at how spending changes as the Latino population nears a majority. That test confirms that Latinos do play a role in the policy world and that they can begin to decide their own fates when their numbers are sufficient.[6] **Figure 17.1** illustrates the relationship between Latino population share and spending on corrections. The figure shows that growth in the Latino population first leads to a rise in the proportion of state funds that go to corrections, but as Latinos become a larger and larger share of the state, the amount of corrections spending declines substantially.[7] Once Latinos pass a particular threshold, Latino population growth begins to be associated with increasingly liberal corrections policies. In other words, the Latino population serves as more than just a threat to the rest of the community.

Similar curvilinear effects are also found on education spending as well as tax policy. Latinos themselves appear to have an impact on policy. If Latinos grow to a third of the national population and become large majorities in many states, as they are expected to do by the middle of the twenty-first century, then they might have much more of a say than they do now and state policies might look very different from what they do now.

THE CALIFORNIA LESSON

California's history with immigration and its policy response aptly illustrate this complex relationship. As one of the first states to face large-scale Latino immigration, California was one of the first to try to actively impose restrictions on services to undocumented immigrants, as evidenced by the now-infamous Proposition 187. With Proposition 187, the "Save Our State" initiative of 1994, the voters of California overwhelmingly passed a measure that sought to exclude undocumented immigrants from access to a range of public services. That omnibus anti-immigrant legislation was quickly followed by passage of Proposition 209, a measure that outlawed affirmative action in the state, and Proposition 227, a measure that sought to enshrine English as the state's official language and end bilingual education. Many other states followed suit. But California was the first.

During this period, policy on immigration, education, and corrections shifted decidedly to the right. California fell from among the top half of all states in per pupil education funding in 1980 when whites represented the overwhelming majority of schoolchildren to near the bottom (44th place) in 2009 when Latinos were the single largest racial/ethnic group among school age children (California Department of Finance 2019). Likewise, corrections funding more than tripled as a proportion of the budget, from only about 2.9 percent in 1980 to well over 10 percent in 2005 (California Department of Finance 2019).

As the Latino population has grown and amassed enough influence to be an important part of the state's Democratic majority, policy has once again shifted to the left. With the active support of Latinos, who now account for 38 percent of the population, and with the strong backing of Latino legislators, who now hold 23 percent of the seats in the state legislature, a series of pro-immigrant measures has passed the legislature. This includes measures offering undocumented immigrants in-state tuition, drivers' licenses, and the opportunity to practice law. Education and corrections funding are also now slowly following suit. In the past few years, state education funding has already seen a slight but noticeable uptick. With voters passing Proposition 30, a tax measure that is expected to raise billions for K–12 education, the state is likely to see even more growth in education spending. On the other end of the spectrum, corrections funding has dropped markedly and the state has initiated a number of steps to gain early release of prisoners. Also, it has shifted efforts from imprisonment to greater rehabilitation.

A range of different factors has contributed to these policy changes in California, but Latino context and the immigrant threat narrative appear to be an important part of the story.

CONCLUSION

America's anti-immigrant backlash has consequences far and wide. Those consequences are not just national—where Donald Trump's administration has targeted immigrants time and again. The consequences extend to state-level politics and policies as well. The pattern across states is clear. A large Latino population sparks a racial threat and a backlash that lead to decreased funding for education, a larger criminal justice apparatus, and a more regressive taxation system. All of this could have very real and very negative consequences. Latinos already lag far behind whites and Asian Americans in nearly every indicator of educational performance (graduate rates, standardized test scores, etc.) and are already greatly overrepresented in the criminal justice system, so the decision to reduce education funding and increase corrections funding in states with a large Latino community may exacerbate the problem even further. This rightward policy shift also runs counter to the preferences of the majority of the Latino population (Fraga et al. 2012). As Latinos grow in number, they get less and less of what they want.

For many, this is not at all surprising. Many have suspected that immigration and the growing Latino population are generating a harsh reaction. Trump's campaign did little to quell those suspicions. The Republican Party has actively employed the immigrant threat narrative to try to attract more white voters and shift the partisan balance of power in their favor (Hajnal and Rivera 2014; Abrajano and Hajnal 2015).

What is novel here is seeing just how wide ranging these consequences are. In a political era in which many claim that the significance of race has faded, larger concentrations of Latinos are leading what appears to be a fundamental reordering of political preferences. States are reacting to immigrant arrivals not simply by making laws that explicitly target immigrants but also and more fundamentally by changing the core priorities of state government across a broad range of ostensibly nonracial policies like education, health, criminal justice, and taxes. The patterns illustrated in this chapter suggest that the nation's increasingly diverse population is having a profound impact on the politics of America. Who wins and who loses in the battle over state policy is very much a function of racial context and racial threat.

This story is not, however, a purely negative one. Latinos, despite all of the barriers they face, also have some agency and are able to shift policy in a pro-Latino direction if their numbers are large enough. If the census's population projections are correct and whites lose their majority status in a few decades, then this emerging pattern bodes well for Latinos and the immigrant population over the long term. We may experience more anxiety, more conflict, and more backlash in the near term. But over the longer term, the influence of Latinos and other minorities should only grow more pronounced and policy should become more aligned with their preferences.

Suggested Reading

Abrajano, M., and Z. Hajnal. 2015. *White Backlash: Race, Immigration, and Party Politics*. Princeton, NJ: Princeton University Press.

Griffin, R., and R. Texiera. 2017. The story of Trump's appeal: A portrait of Trump voters. Democracy Fund, Voter Study Group. Available at www.voterstudygroup.org/publication/story-of-trumps-appeal.

Gulasekaram, P., and S. K. Ramakrishnan. 2015. *The New Immigration Federalism*. New York: Cambridge University Press.

Hainmueller, J., and D. Hopkins. 2014. Public attitudes toward immigration. *Annual Review of Political Science* 17: 1–25.

Haynes, C., J. Merolla, and S. K. Ramakrishnan. 2016. *Framing immigrants: News Coverage, Public Opinion, and Policy*. New York: Russell Sage Foundation.

Perez, E. O. 2016. *Unspoken Politics: Implicit Attitudes and Political Thinking*. New York: Cambridge University Press.

Schildkraut, D. 2005. *Press "One" for English: Language Policy, Public Opinion, and American Identity*. Princeton, NJ: Princeton University Press.

Valentino, N., T. Brader, and A. E. Jardina. 2013. The antecedents of immigration opinion among U.S. whites: General ethnocentrism or media priming of Latino attitudes? *Political Psychology* 34: 149–66.

Acronyms

ACA	Affordable Care Act
ACS	American Community Survey
AGR	Annual average growth rate
AMIA	Asociación Mexicana de la Industria Automotriz / Mexican Association of the Automotive Industry
AMLO	Andrés Manuel López Obrador, president of Mexico
ASERCA	Agencia de Servicios a la Comercialización y Desarrollo de Mercados Agropecuarios / Support and Services to Agricultural Marketing
BANXICO	Bank of Mexico
BIE	Banco de Información Económica / Repository of Economic Information
CAIP DEA	Community Adjustment and Investment Program Designated Eligible Areas
CAR	Center for Automotive Research
CEDRSSA	Colección Estudios e Investigaciones, Centro de Estudios para el Desarrollo Rural Sustentable y Soberanía Alimentara / Collection for Study and Research, Center for the Study of Sustainable Rural Development and Food Sovereignty
CEFP	Centro de Estudios de Finanzas Públicas / Center for Public Finance Studies
CEPAL	Comisión Económica para América Latina y el Caribe / Economic Commission for Latin America and the Caribbean

CESS	Congressional Election Sample Survey
CGE	Computable general equilibrium model
CIDE	Centro de Investigación y Docencia Económicas/Center for Research and Teaching in Economics
CIR	Comprehensive immigration reform
CKD	Completely Knocked Down (Automotive)
CMPS	Collaborative Multi-Racial Post-Election Survey
CONAPO	Consejo Nacional de Población/National Population Council
CONASAMI	Comisión Nacional de Salarios Mínimos/National Commission of Minimum Wages
CPS	Current Population Survey, a joint effort of monthly data collection between the US Bureau of Labor Statistics and the US Census Bureau. It collects information on different socioeconomic variables like country of origin and wages and employment, among many others.
CZs	Commuting zones
DACA	Deferred Action for Childhood Arrivals
DEA	Designated Eligible Areas
DHS	Department of Homeland Security
DNC	Democratic National Committee, leadership committee of the Democratic Party
EMIF	Encuesta sobre Migración en la Frontera Norte de México/Border Survey of Mexican Migrants
ENE	Encuesta Nacional de Empleo/National Survey of Employment
ENEU	Encuesta Nacional de Ocupación y Empleo Urbano/National Survey of Urban Employment. Collects information on wages and employment for the urban areas of Mexico. It was discontinued in 2004 after ENOE started.
ENOE	Encuesta Nacional de Ocupación y Empleo/National Survey of Occupation and Employment. Collects information on wages and employment for a representative sample of urban and rural areas of Mexico.
EPI	Economic Policy Institute
EPN	Enrique Peña Nieto, former president of Mexico
EU	European Union
FDI	Foreign direct investment
GDP	Gross domestic product
GMS	Genetically modified seeds

List of Acronyms

GOP	Grand Old Party, nickname for Republican Party
ICE	Immigration and Customs Enforcement
ICT	Information and communication technology
IDB	Inter-American Development Bank
IIRA	Illegal Immigration Relief Act (Pennsylvania, 2006)
ILO	International Labor Organization
ILOSTAT	ILO Department of Statistics
IMMEX	Manufacturing, Maquiladora, and Export Services
INA	Industria Nacional de Autopartes/National Auto Parts Industry
INEGI	Instituto Nacional de Estadisticas y Geografía/National Institute of Statistics, Geography, and Informatics. Conducts the Mexican population census, economic census, and agricultural and job census, as well as other surveys for statistical and geographic information in Mexico.
IPUMS	Integrated Public Use Microdata Series. Collects census and survey data worldwide for research and analysis.
IRCA	Immigration Reform and Control Act (1986)
ISDS	Investor-state dispute settlement
LASANTI	Los Angeles–San Diego–Tijuana
LPR	Legal permanent resident
MAGA	Make America Great Again. Trump campaign slogan.
MAI	Mexican Automotive Industry
MFN	Most favored nation
MMP	Mexican Migration Project
MTC	Monterrey Technology Center
NADBank	North American Development Bank
NADB CAIP	North American Development Bank Community Adjustment and Investment Program
NAFTA	North American Free Trade Agreement
NAS	National Academy of Sciences
NBER	National Bureau of Economic Research
OEM	Original equipment manufacturer (Automotive)
OICA	Organización Internacional de Fabricantes de Automóviles/International Organization for Automobile Manufacturers

POTUS	President of the United States
PPP	Purchasing power parity
PROCAMPO	Programa de Apoyos Directos al Campo/ Program for Direct Support to Rural Areas
RDA	Rural development advance
RNC	Republican National Committee. Leadership committee of the Republican Party.
SBA	Small Business Association
SBO	Survey of Business Owners and Self-Employed
SIACON	Sistema de Información Agroalimentaria de Consulta/Agrifood Information Consulting System
SIAP	Servicio de Información Agroalimentaria y Pesquera/Agriculture and Fisheries Information System
SIPP	Survey of Income and Program Participation
SOS	"Save Our State" Initiative, Proposition 187 (California, 1994). Ballot initiative to deny health care to undocumented migrants.
STPS	Secretaría del Trabajo y Previsión Social—Gobierno de México/Ministry of Labor and Social Welfare, Government of Mexico
TAA	Transitional Adjustment Assistance
TPP	Trans-Pacific Partnership Act
UCLA NAID	University of California, Los Angeles, North American Integration and Development Center
USMCA	United States-Mexico-Canada Agreement
USTR	United States Trade Representative
VAM	Vehículos Automotrices Mexicanos/Mexican Automotive Vehicles
WISER	World Institute for Strategic Economic Research
WTO	World Trade Organization

Notes

INTRODUCTION

1. See Badkern 2012: "Mexican immigrants contribute 4 percent of total U.S. GDP. Including second and third generation Mexicans, their contribution rises to 8 percent." Based on 2011 BBVA data, 4 percent comes to $600 billion; if raised to 8 percent, that is a $1.2 trillion contribution to the approximately $15 trillion US GDP. See also Schink and Hayes-Bautista 2017; Huertas and Kierkegards 2019.

2. Huntington 2004, 30.

CHAPTER 1

1. The *Wall Street Journal*'s Bob Davis and Jon Hilsenrath (2016) have gone further in helping to validate Trump's narrative with weak correlations. Extrapolating from a well-known research paper's (Autor, Dorn, and Hanson 2016) narrow analysis of the "trade exposure" caused by Chinese imports on some economic sectors in some parts of the country, they attribute a wide array of the US economy's shortcomings to trade with China and Trump's support in these parts of the country. They report that "in this year's Republican presidential primary races, Mr. Trump won 89 of the 100 counties most affected by competition from China" (Davis and Hilsenrath 2016).

2. Trade sectors include, for example, agricultural products; forest products; electronic products; chemical products; energy products; minerals and metals; textiles, apparel, and footwear; machinery; and transportation equipment.

3. We used ordinary least squared (OLS) regression data analysis models to capture the separate effect of individual variables for predicting Trump support. For robustness, we added the roughly 1,150 small counties that did not have trade data and assigned them values of 0, for both the macro and micro

analyses. In addition, we control for county population and cluster by state. We also modeled independent variables such as immigration in various ways—% total or Hispanic immigrants, % total, Hispanic or Mexican non-naturalized immigrants, or % recent total, Hispanic or Mexican immigrants—and the results were similar.

4. WISER data is available for imports at the national level by sector.

5. Inferring individual behavior from macro or county level analysis is problematic and often referred to as "ecological inference." Rather, individual behavior is better assessed by micro level analysis, as seen in table 1.2.

6. The question on TPP was the only one regarding trade agreements, and it was worded, "If you were in Congress would you vote FOR or AGAINST each of the following? Trans-Pacific Partnership Act Free trade agreement among 12 Pacific nations (Australia, Brunei, Canada, Chile, Japan, Malaysia, Mexico, New Zealand, Peru, Singapore, and the U.S.)."

7. In table 1.1, we used OLS regression data analysis models.

8. In tables 1.2 and 1.3, we used hierarchical logit regression data analysis models to examine macro responses with binary variables. We present coefficients, standard errors, and significance tests for our four models. Model 1 is our baseline model and includes levels of recent immigration, Mexican imports, and population size. Model 2 adds demographic variables to the Model 1 variables, and Model 3 adds only the economic variables. Model 4, the full model, includes all the variables. Models 1 and 4 show the effect of trade and immigration.

CHAPTER 3

1. For detailed data on each of the five features and further information, see Giorguli, García-Guerrero, and Masferrer 2016; Giorguli and Angoa 2019.

CHAPTER 4

1. Numbers based on US Census Bureau reported in an analysis by the Pew Research Center (2015).

2. Hanson, Liu, and McIntosh 2017; Villarreal 2014; Massey, Durand, and Pren 2014.

3. Northbound flows to the United States refer to survey respondents who are Mexican-born individuals 15 years of age or older, arriving at Mexico's northern border region, who reported that they intend to cross to the United States and are not residents of Mexican border cities or the United States.

4. Author's calculations based on fertility rate data from the World Bank, https://data.worldbank.org/.

5. The threshold argument was set out in Espenshade 1994.

CHAPTER 5

1. See www.migrationpolicy.org/article/family-separation-and-zero-tolerance-policies-rolled-out-stem-unwanted-migrants-may-face; www.nytimes.com/2018/11/08/us/politics/trump-asylum-seekers-executive-order.html; www.washington

post.com/world/national-security/at-the-us-border-asylum-seekers-fleeing-violence-are-told-to-come-back-later/2018/06/12/79a12718-6e4d-11e8-afd5-778aca903bbe_story.html?utm_term=.0fa1679e2af6.

2. See also www.pbs.org/wgbh/nova/next/body/psychological-damage-inflicted-by-parent-child-separation-is-deep-long-lasting/.

3. See www.gob.mx/tramites/ficha/afiliacion-al-seguro-popular-en-tu-localidad/CNPSS179.

CHAPTER 6

1. Instituto Nacional de Estatísticas y Geografía (INEGI) and Gobierno de Baja California, *Anuario estadístico y geográfico de Baja California, 2016* [Statistical and geographic yearbook of Baja California, 2016], figure 6.18. Retrieved from http://internet.contenidos.inegi.org.mx/contenidos/Productos/prod_serv/contenidos/espanol/bvinegi/productos/nueva_estruc/anuarios_2016/702825083663.pdf.

2. Our calculations based on U.S. Census Current Population Survey for these California counties: Los Angeles, Orange, San Bernardino, San Diego, and Riverside.

3. For a description of the Civil Rights Project, see https://civilrightsproject.ucla.edu/.

4. This survey was designed and implemented through a collaboration between researchers at the University of California, San Diego; the Universidad Autónoma de Baja California; the University of California, Los Angeles; and El Colegio de la Frontera Norte and involved fieldwork by many UABC and UCSD students.

CHAPTER 7

1. Taking into account differences in the cost of living reduces this difference somewhat, of course. Clemens, Montenegro, and Pritchett (2008) estimate that the average low-skilled worker earns 2.5 times more in the United States than in Mexico when controlling for differences in the cost of living.

2. See Krogstad, Passell, and Cohn 2017.

3. We use data from the 1996–2004 March Current Population Survey Annual Social and Economic Supplement and the 2005–2014 American Community Survey from, respectively, King et al. 2010 and Ruggles et al. 2015.

4. For a more detailed explanation of the methodology, see Orrenius and Zavodny 2016. Of particular note, we adjust our estimates upward by 20 percent to account for the likely undercount of unauthorized immigrants. We believe this is a conservative adjustment for newly arrived Mexican workers who are unauthorized. See Hanson 2006; Baker and Rytina 2013; Warren and Warren 2013; Warren 2014; and Genoni et al. 2017 for estimates of undercount rates. Our adjustment also helps correct for estimates of the migrant flow that are not likely to capture immigrant workers who overstay or otherwise violate the terms of a visa and are therefore newly unauthorized workers, although not new entrants to the United States.

5. See Orrenius and Zavodny 2016 for earlier studies using this technique.

6. These estimates are created by applying our SIPP probability model to the CPS and ACS data on all Mexican immigrant workers.

7. The total Mexican-born population in the United States has been falling since 2007, with the number of arrivals declining and the number of migrants returning to Mexico rising (Gonzalez-Barrera 2015). The rate of population growth was slowing even before the Great Recession. Chiquiar and Salcedo (2013) estimate that net migration inflows (legal and illegal) from Mexico averaged 277,000 per year during 2000–2007, down from 466,000 annually during 1990–2000.

8. The average estimate across our three methods is shown.

9. The apprehensions data are from www.cbp.gov/sites/default/files/documents/BP%20Total%20Apps%2C%20Mexico%2C%20OTM%20FY2000-FY2015.pdf for 2000–2014 and www.cbp.gov/sites/default/files/documents/BP%20Southwest%20Border%20Sector%2A for 1996–99; the latter data are all nationalities, not just Mexicans; Mexicans were the vast majority of apprehended entrants during that period. The apprehensions data are by fiscal year.

10. The US wage is the annual average weekly wage from the Bureau of Labor Statistics (BLS) payroll employment survey, deflated using the CPI-W; US construction permits are annual permits issued for single-family privately owned structures; US employment is seasonally adjusted total nonfarm December payroll employment from the BLS. The Mexican real wage is from Organization for Economic Cooperation and Development (OECD) measures of annual wages for full-time workers, deflated using the Mexican Consumer Price Index (CPI); Mexico total employment is also from OECD measures of average annual employment (formal and informal sectors).

11. The construction permits estimated coefficient is negative and statistically significant at the 10 percent level when included in the third column specification but is not shown here to conserve space.

12. Mexican exports to the United States and Canada are from the International Monetary Fund and are expressed in real (2014) dollars.

13. Significance levels are lower if we use contemporaneous measures of economic conditions, suggesting that migrants make their decisions based on economic conditions in the recent past.

14. Border Patrol staffing is from www.cbp.gov/sites/default/files/documents/BP%20Staffing%20FY1992-FY2015.pdf. Relative cohort size is calculated using data on Mexican births from the World Development Indicators (http://databank.worldbank.org/data/reports.aspx?source=health-nutrition-and-population-statistics:-population-estimates-and-projections#) and on US-born high school dropouts as calculated from the CPS and ACS data.

15. Seasonality and part-time employment make it difficult to measure agriculture sector jobs on an annual basis. There are sectors within agriculture where dependence on unauthorized labor is much higher than that suggested by the ACS data presented here. For example, unauthorized immigrants are estimated to make up at least half of all crop workers (Martin 2018).

CHAPTER 9

1. While the 1986 IRCA and 1990 legislations legalized undocumented stock, future migration flows were left at very low levels. The 1996 law (IIRIRA) and subsequent post-9/11 legislation such as the Secure Fence Act of 2006 signaled a further restriction on legal migration as well as the rapid buildup of border enforcement and deportation expenditures.
2. See USTR 2017.
3. See McDonald, Thierfelder, and Robinson 2007 and McDonald and Thierfelder 2016 for a description of the model. It is based on the GTAP data set, as are virtually all global CGE trade models. See Ianchovichina and Walmsley 2012 for a description of the GTAP data.
4. Out-migration from southeastern Mexico and Central America is still rising, but net migration from Mexico as a whole is negative.
5. The period of rising and falling population growth related to family migrations from the high-birthrate countryside to the lower birthrates in cities or across borders.
6. Robinson et al. 1993. A working paper version came out as Robinson et al. 1991. Shortly thereafter, Levy and Sweder von Wijnbergen (1992) found similar results.
7. A trade bloc can be defined as a group of countries that has higher within-bloc trade shares of member countries than with countries outside the bloc.
8. Named after W. Arthur Lewis, who developed the model and won the Nobel Prize in economics in 1979 for his work.
9. The process also involves an expansion of the urban informal sector, which dampens the transition and can provide a continuing source of surplus labor and potential migrants. See Fields 2004.
10. Card 1990; Borjas 2015; Peri and Yasenov 2015. The debate was mostly focused on the low-wage immigrant labor market, and did not consider the benefits of migration to the US economy as a whole. Other studies, discussed below, indicate that immigrant and native workers are largely complementary, not competitive, in labor markets.
11. Hinojosa-Ojeda 1994, 2002. See Hinojosa 2019 for a 25-year restrospective on the impact of the North American Development Bank, particularly the US CAIP designed to address community employment and adjustment. While the NADBank Charter called for a Mexican CAIP to address labor adjustment issues related to community investments to address the root causes of migration, it was never established and the funds for its creation have never been accounted for.
12. Yúnez-Naude, Villanueva, and Serrano 2012. These programs grew to represent the largest Mexican government conditional cash transfer programs, emulated worldwide, but which for the most part ignored a community investment focus to address the root causes of out-migration.
13. See Trade Adjustment Assistance database, www.citizen.org/trade-adjustment-assistance-database; Robert 2011.
14. See Cuecuecha and Scott 2010.
15. See chapter 7, by Orrenius and Zavodny, and chapter 10, by Yúnez-Naude, Mora-Rivera, and Govea-Vargas, in this volume.
16. See chapter 2, by Massey, in this volume.

CHAPTER 10

1. E.g., from an annual average of 18.1 million metric tons (m.t.) during 1980–1993 to 30.5 million during 1994–2016 (Yúnez-Naude, Dyer, and Hernández-Solano 2020).

2. Our own estimates in 2016 pesos based on data from the Instituto Nacional de Estadística y Geografía (INEGI 2017). Berries can be added to the listed fruits. No disaggregated official data are available for these fruits. However, field observations in the states of Jalisco and Michoacán indicate a pronounced growth of employment and of berry production for the US market.

3. No consistent yearly time series data were found beginning in 1980 or 1990. The reported data source for 1999 to 2015 is for foreign trade (SIAP 2017b); also for exports, below. The translation of figures to constant pesos used the Bank of Mexico's price index (SIE 2017) and data from INEGI 2017.

4. The ratio of exports to output went from 0.11 in 1999–2007 to 0.74 in 2008–14 for avocados, 0.09 to 0.26 for citrus, and 0.12 to 0.75 for tomatoes (Yúnez-Naude and Hernández-Solano 2018).

5. Between 1999–2007 and 2008–14, the ratio of imports to output went from 0.2 to 0.34 for corn, 2.93 to 6.1 for rice, 0.67 to 0.92 for wheat, 0.45 to 0.24 for sorghum, 36.7 to 20 for soybeans, and 0.12 to 0.14 for barley (Yúnez-Naude and Hernández-Solano 2018).

6. Trade diversion occurs when a free trade agreement's (FTA's) trade flows with the rest of the world are smaller prior to the FTA formation (Lederman, Maloney, and Servén 2004). Official published data on Mexico-US imports and exports currently cover only from 2003 to 2015.

7. Rain-fed land in corn has contracted—almost constantly since the turn of the present century. Cropland in corn has shifted again toward irrigated areas, with higher yields in northern Mexico (Dyer et al. 2018). From 1994 to 2016 the annual average growth rate (AGR) of corn production in Mexico was 3.6 percent in volume and 1.2 percent in value at constant 2016 pesos, and corn production in both rain-fed and irrigated land also increased: in volume by an AGR of 2.9 and 3 percent and in value by 1 and 1.3 percent, respectively (the estimates are from data from Agriculture and Fisheries Information Services [SIAP 2017a]).

8. Based on figure 10.1, it can be argued that in practice full market access of corn exports from the United States began in 1994 since the government of Mexico did not charge the agreed tariffs in NAFTA negotiations when corn imports exceeded the established quota.

9. Recent changes in the value of field crop production in Mexico cannot be attributed to agricultural policy since they can be largely explained by the evolution of prices (Dyer et al. 2018).

CHAPTER 11

1. It is important to note that a methodological problem exists that results in an overestimation of FDI from the United States. That is, this FDI does not necessarily mean that the companies are American. Many non-American OEMs

and Tier Ones have subsidiaries in the United States, and for the subsidiaries in Mexico, the head offices are often to be found in the United States.

2. In the framework of the seventh round of negotiations, Trump wants to elevate the rules of origin of auto parts from between 50 and 62.5 percent (the current rate) to between 72.5 and 85 percent. To make matters worse, in January 2018, fiscal reforms came into effect that seek to repatriate investments established in Mexico, specifically in the automotive sector, through attractive fiscal benefits. The information technology for companies decreased from 35 to 21 percent. Furthermore, on March 8, 2018, the United States imposed tariffs of 25 and 10 percent on imported steel and aluminum. Although Mexico was exempted, this may result in rising costs given that 13 percent of world steel production goes to the automotive industry and trade in this product is global, as is that of the MAI.

3. It is notable that regarding the FDI from the United States, more is directed to auto parts than to assembly, except in 2013 and 2017. This may be explained by the two models of agglomeration that exist in the country (the satellite companies around the OEMs, on the one hand, and the maquiladora [foreign-owned] companies, on the other), although there is more and more commercial and noncommercial interaction between both models and although in both cases the supply can be directed to plants established both in Mexico and abroad.

4. Data from Ramon Alvarez, general director of the National Auto Parts Industry, January 18, 2018 (telephone interview).

5. Wages in the MAI are very low compared to those paid in the United States, although within Mexico they are relatively high. Wages in the MAI pay more than 2 to 3 times the minimum wage, especially in OEMs. But in reality these MAI wages are very low due to their low purchasing power. Therefore, this issue was discussed at length in the recent NAFTA renegotiation.

CHAPTER 12

1. For a comprehensive retrospective on the expectations for NAFTA and its actual impact, see Blecker 2019.

2. However, these increases are measured in nominal dollars (not adjusted for inflation) and include significant double counting of intermediate goods used in producing exports. Econometric estimates in Romalis 2007 and Caliendo and Parro 2015 reveal that only a small part of those increases can be attributed to NAFTA tariff reductions.

3. Authors' calculations for 1980–93 and 1994–2016 based on data from World Bank, *World Development Indicators Database,* retrieved from https://datacatalog.worldbank.org/dataset/world-development-indicators.

4. Authors' calculations based on International Monetary Fund, *World Economic Outlook Database,* April 2018, retrieved from www.imf.org/external/pubs/ft/weo/2018/01/weodata/index.aspx.

5. Authors' calculations based on data from the *Mexican Censos Económicos* and *Encuesta Mensual de la Industria Manufacturera,* www.inegi.org.mx/, and US Bureau of Labor Statistics, www.bls.gov, downloaded August 8, 2017, and earlier. Details available on request.

6. The *total* increase in Mexico's manufacturing employment under NAFTA up to 2018 was about 900,000 (from 2.9 million in 1993 to 3.8 million in 2018), which is barely enough to cover the *average annual increase* in the country's labor force (working-age population) of about 950,000 since that time (data from Blecker 2014; updated from Instituto Nacional de Estadística y Geografía [INEGI], Encuesta Mensual de la Industria Manufacturera, retrieved from http://www.inegi.org.mx/sistemas/bie/).

7. See, e.g., Public Citizen 2018; Zepeda, Wise, and Gallagher 2009.

CHAPTER 14

1. (@EPN), February 22, 2015. Retrieved from https://twitter.com/epn/status/569721209929072640?s=21.

2. (@realDonaldTrump), February 15, 2015. Retrieved from https://twitter.com/realdonaldtrump/status/569730008945692672?s=21.

3. (@realDonaldTrump), February 24, 2015. Retrieved from https://twitter.com/realdonaldtrump/status/569730008945692672?s=21.

4. (@realDonaldTrump), February 24, 2015. Retrieved from https://twitter.com/realdonaldtrump/status/570384640281870337?s=21.

5. "So many people are angry at my comments on Mexico—but face it—Mexico is totally ripping off the US. Our politicians are dummies!" (@realDonaldTrump), February 25, 2015.

6. "Vast numbers of manufacturing jobs in Pennsylvania have moved to Mexico and other countries. That will end when I win!" (@realDonaldTrump), August 1, 2016.

7. "I have accepted the invitation of President Enrique Pena Nieto, of Mexico, and look very much forward to meeting him tomorrow." (@realDonaldTrump), August 30, 2016.

8. (@EPN), August 31, 2016. Retrieved from https://twitter.com/epn/status/771423919978913792?s=21.

9. (@EPN), January 25, 2017. Retrieved from https://twitter.com/epn/status/824447050066468865?s=21.

10. (@realDonaldTrump), January 26, 2017. Retrieved from https://twitter.com/realdonaldtrump/status/824616644370714627?s=21.

11. (@EPN), January 26, 2017. Retrieved from https://twitter.com/epn/status/824660333964824576?s=21.

12. (@realDonaldTrump), January 27, 2017. Retrieved from https://twitter.com/realdonaldtrump/status/824970003153842176?s=21.

13. (@realDonaldTrump), June 22, 2017. Retrieved from https://twitter.com/realdonaldtrump/status/878013639613186049?s=21.

14. L. Videgaray Caso, Official Statement, June 22, 2017. Retrieved from www.gob.mx/sre/prensa/mexico-reitera-su-posicion-sobre-la-relacion-bilateral-con-los-estados-unidos-de-america?state=published; for the statement in English, see https://goo.gl/6tCmDf. There were several publications with data that supported the argument, for example: "Mexico is far from being one of the most violent countries. Only in Latin America, countries such Honduras, Venezuela, Belize, Colombia and Brazil have homocide rates of 90.4, 53.7, 44.7,

30.8, and 25.2, respectively, for every 100,000 inhabitants, while in Mexico the rate is 16.4, well below several countries in the region." SR Press Release, June 22, 2017, available at www.gob.mx/sre/prensa/comunicado-de-prensa-113327.

15. (@realDonaldTrump), January 18, 2018. Retrieved from https://twitter.com/realdonaldtrump/status/953951365532876800?s=21 and https://twitter.com/realdonaldtrump/status/953979393180950528?s=21.

16. (@Lvidegaray), January 18, 2018. Retrieved from https://twitter.com/lvidegaray/status/954018280364109830?s=21.

17. (@realDonaldTrump), March 5, 2018. Retrieved from https://twitter.com/realdonaldtrump/status/970626966004162560?s=21.

18. (@realDonaldTrump), April 1, 2018. Retrieved from https://twitter.com/realdonaldtrump/status/980443810529533952?s=21 and https://twitter.com/realdonaldtrump/status/980451155548491777?s=21.

19. (@realDonaldTrump), April 2, 2018. Retrieved from https://twitter.com/realdonaldtrump/status/980762392303980544?s=21.

20. (@realDonaldTrump), April 3, 2018. Retrieved from https://twitter.com/realdonaldtrump/status/981121409807155200?s=21.

21. (@EPN), April 5, 2018. Retrieved from https://twitter.com/epn/status/981992980490862592?s=21.

22. (@EPN), April 5, 2018. https://m.youtube.com/watch?v=-NzOXHHBwLQ.

23. (@realDonaldTrump), July 31, 2018. Retrieved from https://twitter.com/realdonaldtrump/status/1024248479386923009?s=21.

24. (@realDonaldTrump), October 18, 2018. Retrieved from https://twitter.com/realdonaldtrump/status/1052885781675687936?s=21.

25. (@EPN), October 19, 2018. Retrieved from https://twitter.com/epn/status/1053487710244102144?s=21.

26. (@realDonaldTrump), December 11, 2018. Retrieved from https://twitter.com/realdonaldtrump/status/1072459097855938560?s=21.

27. (@lopezobrador), December 12, 2018. Retrieved from https://twitter.com/lopezobrador_/status/1073026515418402816?s=21.

28. (@realDonaldTrump), January 19, 2019. Retrieved from https://twitter.com/realdonaldtrump/status/1086626739835625474?s=21.

29. (@realDonaldTrump), January 24, 2019. Retrieved from https://twitter.com/realdonaldtrump/status/1088430717611245571?s=21.

30. (@realDonaldTrump), March 29, 2019. Retrieved from https://twitter.com/realdonaldtrump/status/1111653530316746752?s=21.

31. (@m_ebrard), March 29, 2019. Retrieved from https://twitter.com/m_ebrard/status/1111691032192782336?s=21.

32. (@realDonaldTrump), April 2, 2019. Retrieved from https://twitter.com/realdonaldtrump/status/1113089157683953665?s=21.

33. (@realDonaldTrump), April 5, 2019. Retrieved from https://twitter.com/realdonaldtrump/status/1114151754722156544?s=21.

34. (@realDonaldTrump), April 6, 2019. Retrieved from https://twitter.com/realdonaldtrump/status/1114672393773912064?s=21.

35. (@realDonaldTrump), April 13, 2019. Retrieved from https://twitter.com/realdonaldtrump/status/1117213859696267264?s=21.

CHAPTER 15

1. The total number of stories published in the *Standard-Speaker* linking immigrants with crime increased to 23.9 percent in 2006, from 13.0 percent in 2005.

2. Due to Hazleton's past connections with the Mafia, many locals referred to it as "Mob City" (Cooney 2010).

CHAPTER 16

1. California Proposition 187, also known as the "Save Our State (SOS)" initiative, was a 1994 ballot initiative to prohibit non-US citizens from benefiting from public services such as health care and public school education. The proposition also mandated the reporting of individuals suspected of being undocumented to the California State Attorney and US Immigration and Naturalization Services. Governor Pete Wilson was among its strongest supporters. This law was passed by California voters in a referendum and was later found to be unconstitutional in federal court. Proposition 209 (1996) was a ballot initiative that ended affirmative action in governmental programs, and Proposition 227 (1988) was a ballot initiative that limited bilingual education in public schools.

2. Given the richness of the CMPS, there were many discrimination and racism variables to choose from. The first item we include is, "How much of a problem do you think discrimination is in preventing Latinos in general from succeeding in America?" This is a 5-item question whose response ranges from not a problem at all to the primary problem. The second discrimination item we include asks, "How much discrimination is there in the United Stated today against Latinos?" This is also a 5-item question whose response ranges from none at all to a lot. Each variable was rescaled between zero and one, with zero indicating no perceived racism and one indicating the highest level of perceived racism. The two items were added, creating a scale that ranges from 0 to 2.

3. Each variable was rescaled between zero and one, with zero indicating no perceived racism and one indicating the highest level of perceived racism. The two items were added, creating a scale that ranges from 0 to 2. While the alpha for this scale is moderately strong (.66), we believe that these questions give us a more well rounded understanding of how respondents perceive racism toward Latinos in the United States today by including the traditional discrimination items measured in the extant literature (Sanchez 2007).

4. "South American" will be used to refer to individuals living in the United States who trace their ancestry to countries in South America.

5. Since our dependent variable is a count, we ran it as a poisson regression. We expect that anger is going to increase political engagement in all states, for all national-origin groups, and across all generations.

CHAPTER 17

1. Important exceptions are a study by Hopkins (2010) that finds that local tax rates are tied to growth in the local immigrant population and others that

look at the relationship between racial diversity and welfare policy (Fellowes and Rowe 2014; Soss, Fording, and Schram 2008).

2. However, in a series of robustness tests I also look at per capita spending in each area.

3. Specifically, I compare the top quarter of states based on the share of the population that identifies as Latino to the bottom quarter of states.

4. Aside from property and sales taxes, most other tax revenue comes from income taxes, which can range from regressive to progressive and are harder to characterize.

5. This pattern persists if we instead shift to an analysis of per capita spending, per pupil spending, or total dollars spent in each policy area.

6. Specifically, I find that the percent Latino squared term is statistically significant, indicating that there is a robust curvilinear effect to Latino population size.

7. Though the effect of Latino context on corrections spending is no longer statistically significant at larger values.

Glossary of Key Terms

AGRICULTURAL OUTPUT—measures the value of agricultural products that, free of intrabranch consumption, are produced during the accounting period and, before processing, are available for export and/or consumption. The measure of output refers to final output. In comparison to harvested output, this narrower concept excludes intrabranch consumption, whether by the producing farm or by a farm other than the producing farm, and, concerning crop products, losses between harvest and utilization/storage. *Chapter 10*

ANNEXATION OF NORTHERN MEXICO—areas awarded to the United States in the Treaty of Guadalupe Hidalgo at the conclusion of the Mexican-American War (1846–48), which today include California, New Mexico, Arizona, Utah, Nevada, and parts of Wyoming and Colorado and Texas. *Chapter 13*

ANNUAL INFLOW—new arrivals in a single year of unauthorized Mexican migrants. *Chapter 2; see also* **in-migration**

ANTI-IMMIGRANT BACKLASH—a series of actions by native-born Americans that target immigrants to discourage immigration and reduce the well-being of immigrants in America. *Chapter 17; see also* **white backlash**

ASERCA (AGENCIA DE SERVICIOS A LA COMERCIALIZACIÓN Y DESARROLLO DE MERCADOS AGROPECUARIOS / AGENCY FOR SUPPORT AND SERVICES TO AGRICULTURAL MARKETING)—the agency created in Mexico to support farmers while Mexico transitioned from state regulation of agriculture to an economic free-market orientation and trade liberalization under NAFTA. *Chapter 10; see also* **trade liberalization, neoliberalism, marketing supports**

ASYLUM CRISIS—the current situation of the US asylum system, reflected in the more than half a million cases pending resolution, the long waiting periods for people applying for asylum, and the insufficiency of the responsible government offices to respond in a timely and fair way to the pending applications. *Chapter 3*

AUTOMOTIVE VALUE CHAINS—the highly integrated systems for the production and sale of automotive vehicles: raw materials –> auto parts –> part suppliers –> assembly –> dealerships. These linked segments deal mainly with the importation and exportation of parts, components, and systems and are based on intra- and interfirm trade. *Chapter 11; see also* **value chains, global value chains**

BABY BOOM COHORT—in demographic terms, a cohort is a group that shares a particular characteristic. The baby boom cohort is the group of people represented by the marked increase in babies born between 1945 and 1965. *Chapter 8*

BACKWARD LINKAGES—the demand created for inputs produced by other industries, such as the steel and auto parts (brakes, windshields, etc.) used to produce finished automobiles. *Chapter 12*

BORDER ENFORCEMENT—the militarization of the US-Mexico border with increased Border Patrol as a result of restrictive immigration legislation. Apprehensions of undocumented migrants became the visible manifestation of a self-perpetuating cycle in which enforcement produced more apprehensions and more apprehensions justified more enforcement. *Chapter 2; see also* **immigration enforcement**

BORDER INDUSTRIALIZATION PROGRAM (1965)—a program that allowed for industrial production on the Mexican side of the border to enter the United States without paying tariffs. *Chapter 9*

BORDER SURVEY OF MEXICAN MIGRATION / ENCUESTA SOBRE MIGRACIÓN EN LA FRONTERA NORTE DE MÉXICO (EMIF)—the oldest continuous research program tracking original data on the number of people crossing the US-Mexico border legally or illegally. Conducted in Mexico by Mexican interviewers, the survey asks northbound respondents whether they are crossing into the United States legally or not. It is conducted at select border-crossing points and at airports in the interior of Mexico and offers a unique glimpse at the size and characteristics of migration in both directions across the border with data systematically assembled on a quarterly basis. Annual comparisons for the same quarter allow analyses that account for seasonal variations in the flow. The border survey is particularly valuable because the methodology has been repeated consistently over many years. *Chapter 4*

BRACERO PROGRAM—a temporary worker agreement between the United States and Mexico that authorized short-term work visas for Mexican farm laborers (braceros) for periods of seasonal employment. Originally negotiated as a temporary wartime arrangement in 1942 when there was a labor shortage, the Bracero Program was successively extended by Congress, with peak employment in the late 1950s. During the early 1960s it was scaled back and the agreement was canceled by Congress as of January 1, 1965. *Chapter 2; see also* **farm labor**

CENTRAL AMERICAN FLOWS—migrants leaving countries in Central America for the United States; the smallest population overall but one in five immigrants to the United States. New immigration from Central America has surpassed that of Mexico. *Chapter 3*

CIRCULAR MIGRATION—a pattern of migration wherein individuals go back and forth to the United States, spending a period of time working in the

United States and then returning to Mexico before coming back to the United States again. *Chapter 2*

COLLABORATIVE MULTI-RACIAL POST-ELECTION SURVEY (CMPS)—an online survey conducted from December 3, 2016, to February 15, 2017. Available in multiple languages, the survey encompassed 10,145 respondents, with oversamples of Asians, blacks, and Latinos. *Chapter 16*

COMMERCIAL FARMERS—agricultural producers producing for the market (in contrast to **subsistence farmers**). *Chapter 10*

CONTEXT OF RECEPTION—the way in which immigrants are perceived and received upon arrival in a new country. *Chapter 5*

CORN BIODIVERSITY—like other highly valued cultivated seeds, corn is conserved to preserve its biodiversity, either ex situ, by freezing them, or in situ, by traditional farmers in Mexico and in other developing countries. Through seed management different varieties of corn are cultivated according to agro-ecological conditions and quality for consumption. As corn is a major food staple, biodiversity conservation is fundamental to sustain development worldwide since, among others, biodiverse corn seeds are the basis for developing improved seeds. *Chapter 10*

DECOUPLED PAYMENTS—government cash transfers paid to producers that do not influence their production decisions or the use of specific factors of production. *Chapter 10*

DEMOGRAPHIC DYNAMICS—changes in the population composition of a country as reflected in the age structure, sex distribution, and territorial location of the population. They are the combination of the trends in mortality, fertility, and internal and international migration. *Chapter 3*

DEMOGRAPHIC TRANSITION—changes that evolve in a population around socio-economic factors like age, income, education, and birthrate; in the case of Mexico a fertility transition was caused by rapid fertility decline. *Chapter 2; see also* **fertility decline, fertility transition**

DEPENDENCY RATIOS—the result of dividing the number of children (under 15 years of age) and older population (65 and above) by the working-age population (15–64 years of age). The number of children and older people depends on the population of those of working age. *Chapter 3*

DEVELOPMENT POLICIES—government interventions to promote growth with equity and sustainability. *Chapter 10*

DISCOURSE—the largest unit of linguistic analysis; includes a whole communicative event (written and/or oral communication along with social practice) that creates knowledge and a sense of self and is a resource of social power. *Chapter 14*

DUAL CITIZENS—the population that has citizenship in two countries. *Chapter 3*

ECONOMIC CONVERGENCE—a process in which less developed countries, which have lower levels of per capita income and labor productivity, grow faster than the more advanced economies and catch up to the latter. *Chapter 12*

ECONOMIC INEQUALITY—the *relative income gaps* between different strata of the population, such as the top 1% and bottom 99%, or other breakdowns, such as workers with different degrees of education and skills. One measure of economic inequality is income inequality. Another is wage inequality. The disparity between a CEO, for example, and those with the lowest income is growing. A low minimum wage is usually an indicator of high poverty rates. The United States ranks third and Mexico second worst among the 30 **Organization for Economic Cooperation and Development (OECD)** countries with respect to income inequality. *Chapter 6*

EDUCATIONAL ATTAINMENT—level of education completed. High attainment includes some college education; low attainment is non-college-educated high school graduates; and very low levels of attainment include those who fail to finish high school. A low minimum wage is associated with a larger portion of the population with low and very low educational attainment. *Chapter 6*

EDUCATIONAL UPGRADING—increases in educational attainment. These increases began early in the twentieth century with the "high school completion" movement and continued after World War II with the expansion of public higher education, a benefit provided for veterans under the GI Bill. *Chapter 8*

EMPLOYMENT-BASED VISA PROGRAMS—visas and work permits for foreign workers. *Chapter 7*

FARM LABOR—people employed by a farm operator to assist with farmwork, including regular, seasonal, local, migratory, full-time, or part-time employment. *Chapter 10; see also* **Bracero Program, H2A visas**

FERTILITY DECLINE—a decline in the number of babies born into the population. In demographic terms, the fertility rate is a measure of the number of offspring born into the population. *Chapter 3*

FERTILITY TRANSITION—decrease in the total fertility rate (average number of children per women). In countries such as Mexico, the transition happened at a rapid pace (faster than in other regions such as Europe). For the Mexican case, the fertility rate decreased from close to 7 children per woman in 1970 to 2.2 in 2017. *Chapter 3*

FOREIGN DIRECT INVESTMENT (FDI)—the acquisition of a significant share of ownership in an enterprise located in a foreign country. Contrary to popular understanding, FDI does not necessarily entail investment in new production facilities; although this is one possible form, FDI can also involve simply buying an existing firm (or large numbers of shares in a firm) in another country, and it may occur in services or finance as well as in manufacturing. *Chapter 7*

GENETICALLY MODIFIED SEEDS (GMS)—designed to make a plant more resistant to rain, drought, pests, etc., by altering their genetic makeup to exhibit traits that are not naturally theirs. In general, genes are taken (copied) from one organism that shows a desired trait and transferred into the genetic code of another organism. *Chapter 10*

GLOBAL CHAINS—*see* **global value chains**

GLOBAL PRODUCTION CHAINS—*see* **global value chains**

GLOBAL SUPPLY CHAINS—*see* **global value chains**

GLOBAL VALUE CHAINS—highly integrated international links to supply, labor, and production in which the different stages of the production process are located across different countries. The integration into global production chains, sometimes called global supply or production chains, has expanded production levels and maintained great economic dynamism in spite of losses in the United States in manufacturing jobs (and the accompanying US trade deficit with Mexico). *Chapter 11; see also* **value chains, automotive value chains**

GLOBE MODEL—a computable general equilibrium (CGE) model constructed to include trade interactions on a worldwide scale. *Chapter 9*

GREAT RECESSION—sometimes referred to as the Great Recession of 2008. The Great Recession describes a period of economic decline in the United States between 2007 and 2010 that included severe increases in poverty and unemployment. It is the longest US downturn since World War II, as well as the most significant since the Great Depression. *Chapter 3*

GROUP THREAT—a theory that argues that larger concentrations of particular groups lead to greater feelings of threat and anxiety among another, usually the dominant, population. *Chapter 1; see also* **status threat, Latino threat narrative, racial threat theory, immigrant threat**

HART-CELLER ACT—*see* **Immigration and Naturalization Act of 1965**

H1B VISAS—temporary work permits for those workers with highly specialized expertise. *Chapter 3; see also* **temporary visas**

H2A VISAS—temporary work permits for seasonal agricultural workers. *Chapter 3; see also* **Bracero Program, farm labor, temporary visas**

H2B VISAS—temporary work permits for nonagricultural domestic workers. *Chapter 3; see also* **temporary visas**

IDENTITY PORTFOLIO—the multiple social categories that individuals ascribe to in creating a sense of self, including gender, education, ability/disability, income, ethnicity, race, national origin, language, religion, and occupation, among many others. Because identity is complex and multifaceted, multiple and overlapping identities mean that Latinos, for example, can identify with their national-origin group, or view themselves as belonging to a panethnic group, or identify as belonging to both simultaneously. *Chapter 16*

ILLEGAL IMMIGRATION RELIEF ACT (IIRA)—ordinance passed by the city of Hazleton, Pennsylvania, in 2006 to penalize landlords who rented to undocumented immigrants and businesses that hired them. *Chapter 15*

ILLOCUTIONARY FORCE—refers to the effect of a speech act; for example, the communication could be created with the intention of warning, promising, or advising. *Chapter 14*

IMMIGRANT CONTEXT—the concentration of the foreign-born population in a given geographic unit. *Chapter 17*

IMMIGRANT HEALTH ADVANTAGE—health-related advantage of Mexican immigrants (and, to a lesser extent, US-born Mexican Americans) relative to, for example, non-Hispanic whites, as seen in better Mexican immigrant chronic health for some types of cancers and especially many measures of cardiovascular function. *Chapter 5*

IMMIGRANT-LINKED FATE—internalized group discrimination that extends to a connection with Latino immigrants. Immigrant status has become one of the key factors in racializing immigrants. *Chapter 16; see also* **racialization**

IMMIGRANT THREAT—a widely held but largely inaccurate perception that immigrants represent a burden to the nation; often perpetuated in the media and by politicians. *Chapter 17*

IMMIGRATION AND NATURALIZATION ACT OF 1965—amendment to the Immigration and Nationality Act (also known as the Hart-Celler Act) that was signed into law by President Lyndon Johnson in October 1965. The federal law changed the criteria for legal immigration. It abolished the discriminatory national-origins quotas and prohibitions on the entry of certain nationalities (Eastern and Southern European, Asian, Middle Eastern, and African) in favor of a new system that gave each nation the same number of visas. The number of visas was allocated on the basis of family reunification criteria and US labor needs. The system was first applied to the eastern hemisphere in 1968 and to the western hemisphere in 1976. It put in place a ceiling for eastern Hemisphere immigration and for the first time put a ceiling on western hemisphere entrants. Before the Immigration and Naturalization Act of 1965, there had not been quotas on Mexican migration. *Chapter 2*

IMMIGRATION ENFORCEMENT—border and interior controls of unauthorized migration, including apprehensions and removals of migrants. Establishing the nature of the relationship between border enforcement and unauthorized migration has proved challenging. One hurdle is its endogeneity; that is, these two phenomena influence each other. *Chapter 4; see also* **border enforcement**

IMMIGRATION REFORM ACT OF 1965—*see* **Immigration and Naturalization Act of 1965**

IMMIGRATION REFORM ACT OF 1986 (IRCA)—*see* **Immigration Reform and Control Act**

IMMIGRATION REFORM AND CONTROL ACT (IRCA)—signed into law in 1986, IRCA legalized most unauthorized immigrants who arrived in the United States prior to January 1, 1982, and made it illegal to hire unauthorized immigrants. IRCA represented a change in the US migration policy. Its main elements were (1) sanctions on employers knowingly hiring undocumented migrants; (2) continuity and approval of temporary working programs (specifically, temporary agricultural workers); (3) an increase in resources for the Immigration and Naturalization Services (INS) and the Border Patrol for enforcing immigration law and for the surveillance of the US-Mexico border; and (4) an amnesty program and paths for regularizing the migratory situation of those who entered the United States before January 1, 1982, and had lived in the country ever since. *Chapter 3*

IMMIGRATION RESTRICTIONISTS—those who favor tighter limits on the number of people allowed to immigrate to the United States. *Chapter 8; see also* **restrictionist politics**

INDUSTRY 4.0—also known as the Fourth Industrial Revolution, based on the use of cyber-physical systems. It is preceded by three industrial revolutions: The first was based on the introduction of mechanical production equipment driven by water and steam power. The second was based on mass production achieved by the division of labor concept and the use of electrical energy. And the third was based on the use of electronics and information technology (IT) to further automate production (*Engineers Journal* 2014). There are fundamental trends associated with technological change: scientific and business models such as nanotechnology, biotechnology, the development of the Internet, clean technologies, robotics, and the so-called platform economy. While these changes are happening at different rates, they are technologically converging. In the wake of the digital transformation of the automotive industry, such technological changes, new business models, environmental regulations, smart cities, and consumer preferences will drive the trends in electrification, connectivity, autonomous management, and diverse mobility. *Chapter 11*

INFLOWS—*see* **annual inflow, in-migration**

IN-MIGRATION—the movement of people into a defined geographic region, such as a nation, state, or county. *Chapter 2; see also* **annual inflow, northbound flows**

IN-TRANSIT FLOWS—migratory movements across a country with the purpose of reaching another, third country and with no intention of settling down in the country of transit. *Chapter 3*

INTRAREGIONAL TRADE—export and import activity that occurs between regional neighbors, such as the countries of North America (trade outside the region is called interregional). *Chapter 11*

INVESTOR-STATE DISPUTE SETTLEMENT (ISDS)—a system created in NAFTA's chapter 11 that allows a foreign corporation to sue federal, state/provincial, or local governments before special panels of "experts" when the corporation claims that a government action or policy is taking away its property rights or reducing its potential profits. *Chapter 12*

KNOWLEDGE CAPITALS—large, wealthy metropolitan areas that serve as key nodes in the global flow of capital and are highly productive innovation centers with talented workforces and elite research universities. *Chapter 6*

LABOR-DRIVEN MIGRANTS—concentrated in working ages (15–64), population moving with the main purpose of finding a job and working in another country. *Chapter 3*

LABOR PRODUCTIVITY—the average amount of output per worker or per hour worked, where output is measured as the real (inflation-adjusted) value added in the sector or country. *Chapter 12*

LASANTI—the Los Angeles-San Diego-Tijuana region. This region was the eleventh largest economy in the world in 2016—larger than the economies of Spain and Russia—and is critically important for the economic well-being of the state of California, for the United States, and for Mexico. *Chapter 6*

LATINO THREAT NARRATIVE—the framing of immigration from Latin America as a grave threat to the United States, most commonly depicted metaphorically as a "flood" that would "drown" American culture and society or an "alien invasion" that would "conquer" and "occupy" the United States. *Chapter 2*

LEGAL PERMANENT RESIDENTS (LPRS)—noncitizens who are lawfully authorized to live permanently in the United States. *Chapter 3*

LESS-SKILLED WORKERS—workers with only a high school degree or less. *Chapter 8*

LUMP OF LABOR FALLACY—the idea that a relatively constant number of less-skilled jobs exists; this notion entails a zero-sum depiction of the labor market that ignores additional jobs that immigrants inevitably generate. *Chapter 8*

MANIFEST DESTINY—the nineteenth-century belief that the United States is an Anglo-Saxon Protestant country intended by God to occupy the North American continent all the way to the Pacific, which helped establish a dominant white national identity as justification for westward expansion and the conquest of people with different cultures and colored skin—red, black, brown, and yellow. *Chapter 13*

MAQUILADORAS—manufacturing assembly plants in Mexico that transform imported inputs into finished or semifinished goods for export (e.g., sewing imported textiles and fabrics into finished clothing). The maquiladora system predated NAFTA and was encouraged by policies whereby Mexico exempted the imported inputs from tariffs (provided that the assembled goods were exported) and the United States charged tariffs only on the value added in the goods imported from Mexico. Although this system is largely irrelevant now that NAFTA has reduced most tariffs to zero, the name is often applied to any kind of labor-intensive, export-oriented assembly operation that relies heavily on imported inputs. Originally, *maquiladora* meant "in-bond" production, because the Mexican tariffs on the inputs had to be paid into an escrow account until the producers could show proof that the assembled products had been exported. *Chapter 11*

MARKET ACCESS—openness of a country's markets to foreign goods and services. Market access reflects the government's economic policies regarding import substitution and free competition. *Chapter 10*

MARKETING SUPPORTS—a program that combined income and price subsidies for commercial farmers in specific regions of Mexico as well as for buyers, mainly multinational corporations, of agricultural imports from Mexico and domestically produced staples in Mexico. These supports encourage buyers to buy/produce commercial agricultural products from Mexico irrespective of price/income and are meant to reduce the effects on Mexican farmers of US government subsidies to American farmers. *Chapter 10; see also* **ASERCA; PROCAMPO**

MEXICAN AMERICAN HEALTH DISADVANTAGES—worse health in a variety of chronic health conditions when compared to non-Hispanic whites, such as diabetes, as well as higher rates of disability and underdiagnosis of mental health problems. *Chapter 5*

MEXICAN AUTOMOTIVE INDUSTRY (MAI)—refers to the production of vehicles (cars and light vehicles) in assembly plants and auto parts located in Mexico, whether they are foreign or Mexican capital. The automotive industry is considered the gasoline of the Mexican economy because of its enormous economic importance. *Chapter 11*

MEXICAN DIASPORA—the total population of Mexican origin outside of Mexico, born in Mexico or the United States; 36.3 million in 2017. *Chapter 9*

MEXICAN MIGRATION PROJECT (MMP)—a binational data gathering project currently based at Princeton University and the University of Guadalajara. Since 1987 the MMP has annually surveyed representative samples of households from communities throughout Mexico as well as out-migrant households from those communities located in the United States to gather detailed data on the US migratory experiences of household. *Chapter 2*

MEXICAN NATIONALISM—the narrative around national identity and the sense of belonging. The Mexican narrative invokes pride in such cultural features as the indigenous past and the cultural wealth of Mexico and has often been constructed around the conflictive relationship with other nations, particularly the United States. *Chapter 14*

MIGRANT CARAVANS—the flow of people moving from one country to another in large groups (groups of migrants often travel together for safety). *Chapter 3*

MIGRANT TRAIL—the dangerous route through the Mexican and US borderlands used for undocumented crossings. *Chapter 5*

MIGRANT WELL-BEING—the mental as well as physical health of migrants, especially as it is affected by the conditions under which they migrated and their **context of reception** upon arrival. *Chapter 5*

MIGRATION COLLAPSE SCENARIO—a computable general equilibrium (CGE) model constructed to include trade interactions on a worldwide scale that is used in this case to predict the impact of the elimination of all migration stocks and flows. *Chapter 9*

MIGRATION FLOWS—the number of people entering or leaving a given country with or without legal authorization. *Chapter 2; see also* **annual inflow, circular migration, in-migration, net migration, out-migration; return migration, northbound flows, outflows**

MIGRATION SYSTEM—geographic proximity, historical linkages, sustained social ties, and the building of large foreign-born communities among the six countries of North and Central America, especially those at the main destination countries, the United States and Canada. Within this system, Honduras, El Salvador, and Guatemala are mainly places of origin, whereas Mexico is a country of origin, transit, return, and, increasingly, destination. *Chapter 3*

MODES OF INCORPORATION—the wide range of ways immigrants adapt in a new country. *Chapter 5*

MOST FAVORED NATION (MFN) TARIFF—a somewhat misleading term, it means the lowest tariff that a country offers to any other member of the World Trade Organization (WTO) and is therefore, under WTO rules, obliged to give to imports from all other WTO members. However, this does not include the tariffs within a preferential trade agreement, which may be lower than MFN tariffs (the former are often but not always zero). *Chapter 12*

NAFTA PARADOX—the enrichment of work and concomitant impoverishment of employment. As Mexican workers become better trained and more qualified and their production increases in value, their incomes actually decrease. *Chapter 11*

NATIONAL-ORIGIN GROUP—the country or territory to which individuals can trace their ancestry. *Chapter 16*

NATIONALIST STEREOTYPES—characteristics assumed to be typical of a particular nationality. In nationalism discourses the set of features included are those related to the otherness of a nationality. *Chapter 14; see also* **stereotypes**

NATIVISM—a white nationalist movement based on anti-immigrant fear that immigrants will displace US-born (native) workers and bring social problems such as crime, revolution, violence, immorality, and disorder to the country. *Chapter 1*

NATIVIST NARRATIVE—*see* **nativism**

NEOLIBERALISM—policy model of social studies and economics that transfers control of economic factors to the private sector from the public sector. It draws on the basic principles of conventional neoclassical economics, suggesting that governments must limit subsidies, make reforms to tax laws in order to expand the tax base, reduce deficit spending, limit protectionism, and open up markets to trade. It also seeks to abolish fixed exchange rates, back deregulation, permit private property, and privatize businesses run by the state. *Chapter 10*

NET MIGRATION—the difference between the number of in-migrants and out-migrants, yielding a positive number when entries exceed exits and a negative number when exits exceed entries. *Chapter 2; see also* **annual inflow, in-migration, migration flows, out-migration, northbound flows, outflows**

NONCOMPETITIVE—applies when the cost of producing goods domestically is greater than the cost of producing them in another country. *Chapter 10*

NORTHBOUND FLOWS—Mexican-born individuals ages 15 or older who are not residents of Mexican border cities or the United States and who crossed into the United States from Mexico's northern border region. *Chapter 4; see also* **in-migration**

OFFSHORING—the relocation of some parts of a production process, often either parts or the assembly thereof, to another country. The term is often used interchangeably with "outsourcing," but strictly speaking outsourcing can be done domestically (by one firm buying inputs or contracting services from another firm) as well as internationally. Essentially, offshoring is outsourcing across international borders. *Chapter 12*

OPORTUNIDADES / OPPORTUNITIES—a social assistance program that provided cash for school attendance and nutrition, among other supports, and is credited for decreasing poverty, particularly in rural Mexico. *Chapter 9*

ORGANIZATION FOR ECONOMIC COOPERATION AND DEVELOPMENT (OECD)—Established in 1961, the OECD is a forum of industrialized countries that develops and promotes economic and social policies. Its mission is to "build strong economies in its member countries, improve efficiency, home market systems, expand free trade, and contribute to development in industrialized as well as developing countries. There were 30 member countries when the data set in this chapter was created. There are now 36 OECD member countries: Australia, Austria, Belgium, Canada, Chile, Czech Republic, Denmark, Estonia, Finland, France, Germany, Greece, Hungary, Iceland, Ireland, Israel, Italy, Japan, Korea, Latvia, Lithuania, Luxembourg, Mexico, the Netherlands, New Zealand, Norway, Poland, Portugal, Slovak Republic, Slovenia, Spain, Sweden, Switzerland, Turkey, the United Kingdom, and the United States. *Chapter 6*

OUTFLOWS—US residents who leave the United States. *Chapter 4; see also* **out-migration, return migration**

OUT-MIGRATION—the movement of people out of a defined geographic region, such as a nation, state, or county. *Chapter 2; see also* **return migration, outflows**

PANETHNIC IDENTITY—affiliation of individuals as members of a multiethnic group (e.g., Latino/Hispanic) despite diverse ethnic and national-origin backgrounds. For example, Latinos—the majority of whom are classified racially as white—comprise individuals who can trace their origin to over 22 distinct countries. However, due to a long history of racial inequality and discrimination, Latinos in the United States may view themselves as members of the same group. *Chapter 16*

POLITICAL MIGRANTS—people moving as a result of political turmoil or persecution in their countries of origin. *Chapter 3*

POST-NAFTA ERA—the period after the implementation of NAFTA in 1994. *Chapter 9*

PREFERENTIAL TRADE AGREEMENT—an agreement between two or more countries to reduce or eliminate tariffs and other barriers on trade between them while maintaining existing tariffs and barriers on trade with nations outside the agreement. Although often called *free trade agreements,* in reality they often involve considerable regulation of trade and do not necessarily imply the absence of any trade barriers. Preferential trade agreements may be regional, like NAFTA, but can also involve countries located in different global regions (such as KORUS, the South Korea–U.S. Free Trade Agreement). *Chapter 12*

PROCAMPO (*Programa de Apoyos Directos al Campo*/Program for Rural Funding)—The program Mexico created to support farmers with nonconditional payments decoupled from prices and agricultural production. *Chapter 9; see also* **decoupled payments**

PROPOSITION 187 (CALIFORNIA, 1994)—a ballot measure championed by Governor Pete Wilson to deny educational and health benefits to "illegal immigrants." *Chapter 13*

PROPOSITION 209 (CALIFORNIA, 1996)—a ballot measure championed by Governor Pete Wilson that banned affirmative action policies in government programs in California. *Chapter 13*

PROPOSITION 227 (CALIFORNIA, 1998)—a ballot measure championed by Governor Pete Wilson banning bilingual education in public schools. Proposition 227 had been the major plank of Wilson's high-profile gubernatorial campaign. *Chapter 13*

PURCHASING POWER PARITY (PPP)—a method of comparing income levels across countries that corrects for the fact that consumer goods and services are usually cheaper in a poorer, less developed country. *Chapter 12*

RACIALIZATION—ethnic groups that view themselves as members of a racial minority broadly categorized by skin color, language, and culture. *Chapter 16*

RACIALIZED PANETHNIC IDENTITY—the perception that various diverse groups from various national origins, such as Mexican American or Cuban American, are part of a larger racial minority based on skin color, language, culture, and immigrant status. *Chapter 16*

RACIAL THREAT THEORY—a theory that argues that larger concentrations of racial and ethnic minorities lead to greater feelings of threat and anxiety among the white population. *Chapter 17*

REACTIVE ETHNICITY—ethnic militancy in reaction to perceived discrimination by the mainstream. *Chapter 15*

REFUGEE SYSTEM—the provisions for protection of those fleeing threats from violent communities in a country other than the country of origin; the system can be open or it can incorporate restrictive measures inhibiting humanitarian protection such as those implemented by the Trump administration. *Chapter 3; see also* **asylum crisis**

REGRESSIONS—statistical models that allow us to estimate the effect of explanatory variables on the outcome of interest, migration in this case. *Chapter 7*

REMITTANCE FLOWS—*see* **remittances**

REMITTANCES—familial monetary transfers sent home by out-migrants. *Chapter 3*

RESTRICTIONIST POLITICS—programs and laws that restrict the number of immigrants allowed into the United States, such as banning Muslims, separating families at the border, and narrowing the grounds for asylum petitioners. *Chapter 13; see also* **immigration restrictionists**

RETURN MIGRATION—those leaving the United States to return to Mexico. *Chapter 3*

RULES OF ORIGIN—the regulations in any preferential trade agreement that determine how much of the value or content of a good has to be produced within the member countries in order to qualify for a tariff preference (usually a zero tariff). *Chapter 12*

RURAL HOUSEHOLDS—households related to farming or country life, characterized in less developed countries as units of production and consumption, that diversify their economic activities and income sources, including migration of family members. INEGI considers them as those in localities with less than 2,500 or 15,000 inhabitants. *Chapter 10*

RURAL MIGRATION—movement of people from the rural sector to the urban sector in the same country or to any of these sectors abroad, looking for better job opportunities. *Chapter 10*

SELECTIVITY—a phenomenon whereby those who choose to participate in a practice (such as immigration) are already better equipped (i.e., healthier) for what they have chosen to participate in than others who do not participate. *Chapter 5*

SOCIAL IDENTITY THEORY—social categorization whereby a person's sense of self is based on belonging to a particular group or groups. *Chapter 16*

SOCIAL POLICY—the political and social climate and legal practices that affect immigration and immigrant well-being, such as laws defining who can immigrate or apply for asylum as well as those aimed at defining who has access to public and subsidized (e.g., health care) programs. *Chapter 5*

SOUTHERN STRATEGY—a Republican political strategy to encourage racial polarization along party lines without appearing to be racist. Richard Nixon successfully used this strategy to win the previously Democratic South by capitalizing on white backlash to the civil rights legislation promoted under the Democratic leadership of Presidents John F. Kennedy and Lyndon Johnson. *Chapter 13; see also* **white backlash**

SPEECH ACTS (ALSO *DISCURSIVE ACTS*)—particular communicative interactions where the participants have the intention of changing the behavior of another. *Chapter 14*

SPEECH GENRES—categories of communicative interactions where language, written and oral, is used; these categories range from informal conversations, greetings and farewells, letters, speeches, and literary forms to such social media communications as Twitter. *Chapter 14; see also* **Twitter**

STATUS THREAT—anxiety about the devaluation of an individual's social status as part of an individual's identity as a member of a particular social group. *Chapter 1; see also* **group threat, white status, social identity theory, racial threat theory**

STEREOTYPES—a widely held but fixed and oversimplified image or idea of a particular type of person; often learned in childhood and deeply held. *Chapter 17;* see also **nationalist stereotypes**

SUBSISTENCE FARMERS—farmers producing food for family consumption, not for the market. *Chapter 10*

SUPPLY CHAINS—*see* **value chains**

SYMBOLIC POLITICS PERSPECTIVE—theory based on the insight that most political behavior is not rational but intuitive, driven by "symbolic predispositions" such as ideological beliefs, normative values, and prejudice. Political leaders lead by using rhetoric to appeal to their followers' symbolic predispositions and not their rational interests. *Chapter 15*

TEMPORARY FOREIGN WORKER PROGRAM—visas for employer-sponsored foreign workers laboring in seasonal industries. *Chapter 7; see also* **Bracero Program, temporary visas**

TEMPORARY VISAS—permits (visas) for noncitizen workers or students allowing residence for a fixed period of time in the United States. Most of these are *not* immigrants but rather students, tourists, businesspeople, exchange visitors, and temporary workers. *Chapter 3; see also* **Bracero Program, H1B visas, H2A visas, H2B visas, temporary foreign worker program**

TEMPORARY VISITORS—*see* **temporary visas**

TEMPORARY WORKER PROGRAM—*see* **temporary foreign worker program.**

TEMPORARY WORK VISAS—*see* **temporary visas.**

TRADABLE SECTORS—those industries that trade goods and services internationally; trade sectors include, for example, agricultural products; forest products; electronic products, chemical products; energy products; minerals and metals; textiles, apparel, and footwear; machinery; and transportation equipment. *Chapter 1*

TRADE AND PRODUCTION BLOC—a group of countries that has higher within-bloc trade shares of member countries than with countries outside the bloc. *Chapter 9*

TRADE BALANCE—difference between the value of a country's imports and exports for a given period. The balance of trade is the largest component of a country's balance of payments; the latter includes, among others, capital flows and remittances. *Chapter 10; see also* **trade flows, remittances, trade integration**

TRADE DIVERSION—in international trade, a business that is able to offer a lower-cost product for importation into a particular country tends to create a trade diversion away from another importer or local producers whose prices are higher for a similar product. *Chapter 10*

TRADE FLOWS—goods and services bought and sold between countries. *Chapter 1*

TRADE INTEGRATION—a measure of imports and exports between two or more countries. *Chapter 9*

TRADE LIBERALIZATION—the removal or reduction of restrictions or barriers on the free exchange of goods between nations. This includes the removal or reduction of tariff obstacles, such as duties and surcharges, and nontariff obstacles, such as licensing rules, quotas, and other requirements. Economists often view the easing or eradication of these restrictions as promoting free trade between nations. *Chapter 9*

TRADE WAR SCENARIO—a computable general equilibrium (CGE) model constructed to include trade interactions on a worldwide scale that is used here to predict the impact of nations retaliating against each other by raising tariffs. *Chapter 9*

TRUMP PARADOX—contradictions between the attitudinally perceived economic and social impacts of migration and trade compared to actual county economic and social exposure to Mexican trade and immigration. *Chapter 1*

TWITTER—a digital social network that has been in use in the past decade to communicate short messages directed at unspecified recipients about different kind of questions; this social network is particularly favored by President Trump. *Chapter 14*

UNAUTHORIZED IMMIGRANTS—*see* **undocumented migrants**

UNAUTHORIZED MIGRANTS—*see* **undocumented migrants**

UNDOCUMENTED IMMIGRANTS—*see* **undocumented migrants**

UNDOCUMENTED MIGRANTS—noncitizens who either overstay their visa or enter, live in, or work in the United States without satisfying the legal requirements for residence or employment. *Chapter 2*

UNDOCUMENTED MIGRATION—*see* **undocumented migrants**

UNIVERSITY OF CALIFORNIA–MEXICO INITIATIVE—the University of California's systemwide initiative to coordinate research and researchers in California and Mexico and to push for a broader policy agenda with Mexico. In addition to academic collaborations, the mission of the initiative is to "inform public policy [and] address issues of common interest." *Chapter 6*

VALUE ADDED—the increase in the value of a good or service based on the labor performed and capital invested in a given industry. By definition, it equals the gross (total) value of a product minus the cost of any inputs or raw materials purchased from another industry, country, or sector. *Chapter 12*

VALUE CHAINS—system of production in which the various stages of the production process (e.g., design, parts and components production, assembly, packaging, sales, distribution) are dispersed among different countries depending on where each stage can be performed at the lowest cost or under optimal conditions. *Chapter 9; see also* **automotive value chains, global value chains**

WHITE BACKLASH—reaction, in attitudes, voting, and mobilization, by whites to the perceived threat of growing diversity and globalization. *Chapter 1*

WHITE STATUS—traditionally, the highest position in the US racial hierarchy. *Chapter 1*

WORLD TRADE ORGANIZATION (WTO)—the successor to the General Agreement on Tariffs and Trade (GATT, 1947–94). The WTO was founded in

1995 to provide a multilateral forum for countries to reduce their trade barriers and to follow agreed-upon rules in imposing any tariffs or other barriers that they are allowed to adopt. The WTO agreement provides for dispute settlement panels in which member countries can file complaints against alleged violations of WTO rules by other members. As of 2018, the WTO had 164 members, including Canada, Mexico, and the United States. *Chapter 11*

ZERO TOLERANCE POLICIES—immigration policies that consist of criminally prosecuting all individuals caught trying to cross the border irregularly and that entail different types of detention, where migrants suffer poor living conditions and are often abused. Zero tolerance is likely to produce considerable, long-lasting trauma to detainees even though crossing the border irregularly per se (in particular, the first time) is not a crime. *Chapter 5*

References

INTRODUCTION

Badkern, M. 2012. Here's the real economic impact of Mexican immigrants on the US. *Business Insider,* July 29. Retrieved from www.businessinsider.com/mexican-immigration-us-economy-2012-7.

Huertas, G., and J. F. Kierkegards. 2019. Immigration: How the migrant Hispanic population's demographic characteristics contribute to US growth. Working Paper, PIIE, Peterson Institute for International Economics, February. Retrieved from https://www.piie.com/system/files/documents/wp19-3.pdf.

Huntington, S. P. 1996. *The Clash of Civilizations and the Remaking of the World Order.* New York: Simon and Schuster.

———. 2004. The Hispanic challenge. *Foreign Policy* 14 (March–April): 30–45. Retrieved from https://cla.umn.edu/sites/cla.umn.edu/files/the_hispanic_challenge-foreign_policy-2004_huntington.pdf.

Pastor, M. 2018. *State of Resistance: What California's Dizzying Descent and Remarkable Resurgence Mean for America's Future.* New York: New Press.

Schink, W., and D. Hayes-Bautista. 2017. Latino gross domestic product (GDP) report: Quantifying the impact of American Hispanic economic growth. *LDR Latino Donor Collaborator* (June). Retrieved from http://accf.org/wp-content/uploads/2017/08/Latino-GDP-Report-6.28.2017.pdf.

Spence, M. 2011. *The Next Convergence: The Future of Economic Growth in a Multispeed World.* New York: Farrar, Straus and Giroux.

CHAPTER 1

Altick, J. R., L. R. Atkeson, and W. L. Hansen. 2018. Economic voting and the 2016 election. Unpublished manuscript.

Autor, D., D. Dorn, and G. H. Hanson. 2016. The China shock: Learning from labor-market adjustment to large changes in trade. *Annual Review of Economics* 8: 205–40.

Autor, D., D. Dorn, G. H. Hanson, and K. Majlesi. 2016. *Importing Political Polarization? The Electoral Consequences of Rising Trade Exposure.* No. w22637. Cambridge, MA: National Bureau of Economic Research.

Blalock, H. M. 1967. *Toward a Theory of Minority-Group Relations.* New York: John Wiley & Sons.

Citrin, J., D. P. Green, C. Muste, and C. Wong. 1997. Public opinion toward immigration reform: The role of economic motivations. *Journal of Politics* 59(3): 858–81. Retrieved from www.journals.uchicago.edu/doi/abs/10.2307/2998640.

Colantone, I., and P. Stanig. 2018. The trade origins of economic nationalism: Import competition and voting behavior in Western Europe. *American Journal of Political Science* (April 18). DOI.org/10.1111/ajps.12358.

Davis, B., and J. Hilsenrath. 2016. How the China shock, deep and swift, spurred the rise of Trump. *Wall Street Journal*, August 11. Retrieved from www.wsj.com/articles/how-the-china-shock-deep-and-swift-spurred-the-rise-of-trump-1470929543.

Furman, J. 2018. How immigrants can make the economy, and the nation, stronger: Toxic nationalism will exacerbate the economic slowdown that fueled its emergence. *Market Watch* (July 18). Retrieved from www.marketwatch.com/story/how-immigrants-can-make-the-economy-and-the-nation-stronger-2018-07-18.

Green, J. 2017. *Devil's Bargain: Steve Bannon, Donald Trump, and the Storming of the Presidency.* New York: Penguin.

Green, J., and S. McElwee. 2018. The differential effects of economic conditions and racial attitudes in the election of Donald Trump. *Perspectives on Politics* 17(2): 1–22.

Greenstone, M., and A. Looney. 2010. Ten facts about immigration. Policy Memo. The Hamilton Project. Retrieved from www.brookings.edu/wp-content/uploads/2016/06/09_immigration.pdf.

Héricourt, J., and G. Spielvogel. 2014. Beliefs, media exposure and policy preferences on immigration: Evidence from Europe. *Applied Economics* 46(2): 225–39. DOI:10.1080/00036846.2013.844330.

Hood, M. V., III, and I. L. Morris. 1997 ¿Amigo o enemigo? Context, attitudes, and Anglo public opinion toward immigration. *Social Science Quarterly* 78(2): 309–23.

Hooghe, M., and R. Dassonneville. 2018. Explaining the Trump vote: The effect of racist resentment and anti-immigrant sentiments. *PS: Political Science & Politics* 51(3): 528–34. DOI: https://doi.org/10.1017/S1049096518000367.

Hopkins, D. J. 2010. Politicized places: Explaining where and when immigrants provoke local opposition. *American Political Science Review* 104(1): 40–60.

King, G. 2013. *A Solution to the Ecological Inference Problem: Reconstructing Individual Behavior from Aggregate Data.* Princeton, NJ: Princeton University Press.

Krogstad, J. M., and M. H. Lopez. 2015. Hispanic population reaches record 55 million, but growth has cooled. June 25. Pew Research Center, Washington, DC.

Margolis, M. F. 2018. How politics affects religion: Partisanship, socialization, and religiosity in America. *Journal of Politics* 80(1): 30–43.

McElvein, E. 2016. *Border Battle: New Survey Reveals Americans' Views on Immigration, Cultural Change.* Washington, DC: Brookings Institution Press.

Mendelberg, T. 2001. *The Race Card: Campaign Strategy, Implicit Messages, and the Norm of Equality.* Princeton, NJ: Princeton University Press.

Monnat, S. M. 2016. Deaths of despair and support for Trump in the 2016 presidential election. Research Brief 5. Department of Agricultural Economics, Pennsylvania State University, University Park.

Morgan, S. L. 2018. Status threat, material interests, and the 2016 presidential vote. *Socius* 4. DOI/10.1177/2378023118788217.

Mutz, D. 2018. Status threat, not economic hardship, explains the 2016 presidential vote. *Proceedings of the National Academy of Sciences* 115(19): E4330–E4339. DOI.org/10.1073/pnas.1718155115.

National Academy of Sciences, Engineering, and Medicine. 2017. *The Economic and Fiscal Consequences of Immigration.* Washington, DC: National Academies Press.

Quillian, L. 1995. Prejudice as a response to perceived group threat: Population composition and anti-immigrant and racial prejudice in Europe. *American Sociological Review* 60: 586–611.

Raudenbush, S. W., and A. S. Bryk. 2002. *Hierarchical Linear Models: Applications and Data Analysis Methods.* Vol. 1. Thousand Oaks, CA: Sage.

Rothwell, J. T., and P. Diego-Rosell. 2016. Explaining nationalist political views: The case of Donald Trump. November 2. Retrieved from https://papers.ssrn.com/sol3/papers.cfm?abstract_id=2822059.

Sears, D. O., and C. Funk. 1991. The role of self-interest in social and political attitudes. *Advances in Experimental Social Psychology* 24: 1–91.

Timberlake, J. M., J. Howell, A. B. Grau, and R. H. Williams. 2015. Who "*they*" are matters: Immigrant stereotypes and assessments of the impact of immigration. *Sociological Quarterly* 56(2): 267–99.

Valentino, N. A., V. L. Hutchings, and I. K. White. 2002. Cues that matter: How political ads prime racial attitudes during campaigns. *American Political Science Review* 96(1): 75–90.

CHAPTER 2

Capps, R., M. Fix, and J. Zong. 2016. *A Profile of Children with Unauthorized Immigrant Parents.* Washington, DC: Migration Policy Institute.

Chavez, L. R. 2001. *Covering Immigration: Population Images and the Politics of the Nation.* Berkeley: University of California Press.

———. 2008. *The Latino Threat: Constructing Immigrants, Citizens, and the Nation.* Stanford, CA: Stanford University Press.

Delva, J., P. Horner, R. Martinez, L. Sanders, W. D. Lopez, and J. Doering-White. 2013. Mental health problems of children of undocumented parents

in the United States: A hidden crisis. *Journal of Community Positive Practices* 13(3): 25–35.
Gelatt, J. 2016. Immigration status and the healthcare access and health of children of immigrants. *Social Science Quarterly* 97(3): 540–54.
Massey, D. S., R. Alarcón, J. Durand, and H. González. 1987. *Return to Aztlan: The Social Process of International Migration from Western Mexico.* Berkeley: University of California Press.
Massey, D. S., and C. Capoferro. 2008. The geographic diversification of U.S. immigration. In Douglas S. Massey, ed., *New Faces in New Places: The Changing Geography of American Immigration,* 25–50. New York: Russell Sage Foundation.
Massey, D. S., J. Durand, and N. Malone. 2002. *Beyond Smoke and Mirrors: Mexican Immigration in an Age of Economic Integration.* New York: Russell Sage Foundation.
Massey, D. S., J. Durand, and K. A. Pren. 2016. Why border enforcement backfired. *American Journal of Sociology* 121(5): 1557–1600.
Massey, D. S., and K. A. Pren. 2012a. Origins of the new Latino underclass. *Race and Social Problems* 4(1): 5–17.
———. 2012b. Unintended consequences of U.S. immigration policy: Explaining the post-1965 surge from Latin America. *Population and Development Review* 38: 1–29.
Massey, D. S., and A. Singer. 1995. New estimates of undocumented Mexican migration and the probability of apprehension. *Demography* 32: 203–13.
Migration Policy Institute. 2018. Profile of the unauthorized population: United States. Migration Policy Institute. Retrieved from www.migrationpolicy.org/data/unauthorized-immigrant-population/state/US#.
Passel, J. S., and D. Cohn. 2016. Overall number of U.S. unauthorized immigrants holds steady since 2009. Pew Research Center. Retrieved from www.pewhispanic.org/2016/09/20/overall-number-of-u-s-unauthorized-immigrants-holds-steady-since-2009/.
Urban Dictionary. 2018. Top definition for "train wreck." www.urbandictionary.com/define.php?term=train%20wreck.
US Embassy and Consulates in Mexico. 2018. Niños migrantes son prioridad para consulado. US Embassy and Consulates in Mexico. Retrieved from https://mx.usembassy.gov/es/ninos-migrantes-son-prioridad-para-consulado/.
Vargas, E. D., and V. D. Ybarra. 2017. U.S. citizen children of undocumented parents: The link between state immigration policy and the health of Latino children. *Journal of Immigrant Minority Health* 19(4): 913–20.
Wasem, R. E. 2011. *Unauthorized Aliens Residing in the United States: Estimates since 1986.* Washington, DC: Congressional Research Service.

CHAPTER 3

Bancomer Foundation, BBVA Research, and CONAPO (El Consejo Nacional de Población). 2018. *Yearbook of Migration and Remittances Mexico 2018.*

Retrieved from www.bbvaresearch.com/en/publicaciones/mexico-yearbook-of-migration-and-remittances-2018/.

Castillo, M.A., and M.L. Rojas. 2019. Un balance de la inmigración y de la migración de tránsito en México [A balance of immigration and migration in transit through Mexico]. In S. Giorguli and J. Sobrino, eds., *Dinámica demográfica del siglo XXI* [Dynamic demographics of the twenty-first century], vol. 2, 129–66. Mexico City: El Colegio de México, Center for Demographic, Urban, and Environmental Studies.

Chort, I., and M. de la Rupelle. 2016. Determinants of Mexico-U.S. outward and return migration flows: A state-level panel data analysis. *Demography* 53(5): 1453–76. DOI:10.1007/s13524-016-0503-9.

Consejo Nacional de Población (CONAPO). 2010. *Índices de intensidad migratoria México–Estados Unidos 2010* [Mexico–US migration intensity indexes 2010]. Mexico City: National Population Council.

Durand, J. 2016. *Historia mínima de la migración México Estados Unidos* [Brief history of Mexico-US migration]. Mexico City: El Colegio de México.

García-Guerrero, V.M., S. Giorguli, and C. Masferrer. 2018. Emerging demographic challenges and persistent trends in Mexico and the northern triangle of Central America. In G. Shultz, P. Cunningham, D. Fedor, and J. Timbie, eds., *Governance in an Emerging New World: Latin America in an Emerging World,* 6–15. Palo Alto, CA: Stanford University, Hoover Institution, EUA.

García-Guerro, V., C. Masferrer, and S.E. Giorguli. 2019. Future changes in age structure and different migration scenarios: The case of North and Central America. *Revista Latinoamericana de Población* 13(25): 36–53.

Garip, F. 2016. *On the Move: Changing Mechanisms of Mexico-U.S. Migration.* Princeton, NJ: Princeton University Press.

Gelatt, J., and J. Zong. 2018. Settling in: A profile of the unauthorized immigrant population in the United States. November Fact Sheets. Migration Policy Institute, Washington, DC. Retrieved from www.migrationpolicy.org/research/profile-unauthorized-immigrant-population-united-states.

Giorguli, S., and M.A. Angoa. 2019. ¿Una nueva era de la migración entre México y Estados Unidos? [A new era in migration between Mexico and the United States?]. In S. Giorguli and J. Sobrino, eds., *Dinámica demográfica del siglo XXI* [Dynamic demographics of the twenty-first century], vol. 2, 83–128. Mexico City: El Colegio de México, Center for Demographic, Urban, and Environmental Studies.

Giorguli, S., M.A. Angoa, and B. Jensen. 2018. Las experiencias migratorias de los padres: ¿Cómo influyen en el logro escolar de los hijos? [Migratory experiences of parents: How do they influence the educational achievement of their children?]. Paper presented at the 8th International Congress of the Latin American Population Association, Puebla, Mexico, October.

Giorguli, S.E., V.M. García-Guerrero, and C. Masferrer. 2016. A migration system in the making: Demographic dynamics and migration policies in North America and the Northern Triangle of Central America. Policy Paper.

El Colegio de México, Center for Demographic, Urban, and Environmental Studies. Retrieved from http://cedua.colmex.mx/images/_micrositios/amsitm/Giorguli_Garcia_Masferrer_2016.pdf.

Hanson, G., and C. McIntosh. 2016. Is the Mediterranean the new Rio Grande? U.S. and EU immigration pressures in the long run. *Journal of Economic Perspectives* 30(4): 57–82.

Instituto Nacional de Estadisticas y Geografía (INEGI). 2014. *Historical Statistics of Mexico, 2014–2015*, vol. 1, *Population*. Mexico City: National Institute of Statistics and Geography. Retrieved from http://internet.contenidos.inegi.org.mx/contenidos/productos/prod_serv/contenidos/espanol/bvinegi/productos/nueva_estruc/HyM2014/1.%20Poblacion.pdf.

———. 2015. *National Intercensal Survey 2015*. Mexico City: National Institute of Statistics and Geography.

Lida, C. 2006. Los españoles en el México independiente: 1821–1950. Un estado de la cuestión [The Spaniards in independent Mexico: 1821–1950. A state of affairs]. *Historia Mexicana* 56(2): 613–50.

Masferrer, C., V.M. García-Guerrero, and S. Giorguli. 2018. Connecting the dots: Emerging migration trends and policy questions in North and Central America. Migration Policy Institute, Washington, DC.

Masferrer, C., E.R. Hamilton, and N. Denier. 2019. Immigrants in their parental homeland: Half a million U.S.-born minors settle throughout Mexico. *Demography* 56(4): 1452–61.

Masferrer, C., and B.R. Roberts. 2012. Going back home? Changing demography and geography of Mexican return migration. *Population Research and Policy Review* 31(4): 465–96. DOI:10.1007/s11113-012-9243-8.

Massey, D.S., J. Durand, and K.A. Pren. 2015. Border enforcement and return migration by documented and undocumented Mexicans. *Journal of Ethnic and Migration Studies* 41(7): 1015–40.

Medina, D., and C. Menjívar. 2015. The context of return migration: Challenges of mixed-status families in Mexico's schools. *Ethnic and Racial Studies* 38(12): 2123–39.

Meissner, D., F. Hipsman, and T.A. Aleiikoff. 2018. The U.S. asylum system in crisis: Charting a way forward. September. Migration Policy Institute, Washington, DC. Retrieved from www.migrationpolicy.org/research/us-asylum-system-crisis-charting-way-forward.

Pew Research Center. 2018. U.S. unauthorized immigrant total dips to lowest level in a decade. Report, November 27. www.pewresearch.org/hispanic/wp-content/uploads/sites/5/2019/03/Pew-Research-Center_2018-11-27_U-S-Unauthorized-Immigrants-Total-Dips_Updated-2019-06-25.pdf.

Riosmena, F. 2004. Return versus settlement among undocumented Mexican migrants, 1980 to 1996. In J. Durand and D. Massey, eds., *Crossing the Border: Research from the Mexican Migration Project*, 265–80. New York: Russell Sage Foundation.

Riosmena, F., and D.S. Massey. 2012. Pathways to El Norte: Origins, destinations, and characteristics of Mexican migrants to the United States. *International Migration Review* 46(1): 3–36.

Selee, A. 2018. *Vanishing Frontiers: The Forces Driving Mexico and the United States Together.* New York: Public Affairs.

Statistics Canada. 2016. Census of Population, Statistics Canada Catalogue (no. 98–400-X2016184) [Table]. Retrieved from https://www12.statcan.gc.ca/census-recensement/index-eng.cfm.

United Nations, Department of Economic and Social Affairs, Population Division. 2017. World population prospects: The 2017 revision. Retrieved from https://population.un.org/wpp/Download/Standard/Population/.

Villarreal, A. 2014. Explaining the decline in Mexico-U.S. migration: The effect of the Great Recession. *Demography* 51(6): 2203–28.

Zúñiga, V., and S. Giorguli. 2019. Niñas y niños migrantes internacionales en México: La generación 0.5 [What children know about international migration: Generation 0.5]. Mexico City: El Colegio de México.

Zúñiga, V., and E. T. Hamann. 2015. Going to a home you have never been to: The return migration of Mexican and American-Mexican children. *Children's Geographies* 13(6): 643–55.

CHAPTER 4

Amuedo-Dorantes, C., and F. Lozano. 2015. On the effectiveness of SB1070 in Arizona. *Economic Inquiry* 53(1): 335–51.

Amuedo-Dorantes, C., and S. Pozo. 2014. On the intended and unintended consequences of enhanced U.S. border and interior immigration enforcement: Evidence from Mexican deportees. *Demography* 51: 2255–79.

Amuedo-Dorantes, C., T. Puttitanun, and A. P. Martinez-Donate. 2013. How do tougher immigration measures affect unauthorized immigrants? *Demography* 50(3): 1067–91.

Angelucci, M. 2012. U.S. border enforcement and the net flow of Mexican illegal migration. *Economic Development and Cultural Change* 60: 311–57.

Argueta, C. N. 2016. Border security: Immigration enforcement between ports of entry. Congressional Research Service. Report 7–5700. Congressional Research Service, Washington, DC. Retrieved from https://fas.org/sgp/crs/homesec/R42138.pdf.

Bohn, S., and T. Pugatch. 2015. U.S. border enforcement and Mexican immigrant location choice. *Demography* 52: 1543–70.

Cohn, D., J. S. Passel, and A. Gonzalez-Barrera. 2017. Rise in U.S. immigrants from El Salvador, Guatemala and Honduras outpaces growth from elsewhere. Pew Research Center. Retrieved from www.pewhispanic.org/2017/12/07/rise-in-u-s-immigrants-from-el-salvador-guatemala-and-honduras-outpaces-growth-from-elsewhere/.

Dávila, A., J. A. Pagan, and G. Soydemir. 2002. The short-term and long-term deterrence effects of INS border and interior enforcement on undocumented immigration. *Journal of Economic Behavior & Organization* 49: 459–72.

Encuesta sobre migración en la Frontera Norte de México (EMIF) / Border Survey of Mexican Migration. 1993–Present. Survey. Sponsored by El Colegio de la Frontera Norte (COLEF). Retrieved from www.colef.mx/emif/.

Espenshade, T. J. 1994. Does the threat of border apprehension deter undocumented U.S. immigration? *Population and Development Review* 20(4): 871–92.

Gathmann, C. 2008. Effects of enforcement on illegal markets: Evidence from migrant smuggling along the southwestern border. *Journal of Public Economics* 92(10): 1926–41.

Hanson, G., C. Liu, and C. McIntosh. 2017. Along the watchtower: The rise and fall of U.S. low-skilled immigration. Brookings Papers on Economic Activity. Retrieved from www.brookings.edu/bpea-articles/along-the-watchtower-the-rise-and-fall-of-u-s-low-skilled-immigration/.

Hanson, G. H., and C. McIntosh. 2009. The demography of Mexican migration to the U.S. *American Economic Review Papers and Proceedings* 99(2): 22–27.

———. 2010. The great Mexican emigration. *Review of Economics and Statistics* 92(4): 798–810.

Hanson, G. H., and A. Spilimbergo. 1999. Illegal immigration, border enforcement, and relative wages: Evidence from apprehensions at the U.S.-Mexico border. *American Economic Review* 89(5): 1337–57.

Massey, D., J. Durand, and K. A. Pren. 2014. Explaining undocumented migration to the U.S. *International Migration Review* 48(4): 1028–61.

———. 2016. Why border enforcement backfired. *American Journal of Sociology* 121(1): 1557–1600.

Passel, J., and D. Cohn. 2018. U.S. unauthorized immigrant total dips to lowest level in a decade. Pew Research Center. Retrieved from www.pewhispanic.org/2018/11/27/u-s-unauthorized-immigrant-total-dips-to-lowest-level-in-a-decade/.

Passel, J., D. Cohn, and A. Gonzalez-Barrera. 2012. Net migration falls to zero and perhaps less. Pew Research Center. Retrieved from http://assets.pewresearch.org/wp-content/uploads/sites/7/2012/04/PHC-Net-Migration-from-Mexico-Falls-to-Zero.pdf.

Pew Hispanic Center. 2007. Indicators of recent migration flows from Mexico. Retrieved from www.pewresearch.org/wp-content/uploads/sites/5/2011/09/33.pdf.

Pew Research Center. 2015. Modern immigration wave brings 59 million to U.S., driving population growth and change through 2065. Retrieved from www.pewhispanic.org/2015/09/28/modern-immigration-wave-brings-59-million-to-u-s-driving-population-growth-and-change-through-2065/.

US Census Bureau. 2015. Modern immigration wave brings 59 million to U.S., driving population growth and change through 2065. Pew Research Center, Hispanic Trends. Retrieved from www.pewhispanic.org/2015/09/28/modern-immigration-wave-brings-59-million-to-u-s-driving-population-growth-and-change-through-2065/.

US Department of Homeland Security. 2000–2018. Stats and Summaries. Customs and Border Protection. Retrieved from www.cbp.gov/newsroom/media-resources/stats.

Villarreal, A. 2014. Explaining the decline in Mexico-U.S. migration: The effect of the Great Recession. *Demography* 51: 2203–28.

Zenteno, R. 2012. Saldo migratorio nulo: El retorno y la política anti-inmigrante. *Coyuntura Demográfica* 2: 17–21.

CHAPTER 5

Afable-Munsuz, A., E.R. Mayeda, E.J. Pérez-Stable, and M.N. Haan. 2014. Immigrant generation and diabetes risk among Mexican Americans: The Sacramento area Latino study on aging. *American Journal of Public Health* 104(S2): S243–S250.

Arenas, E., N. Goldman, A.R. Pebley, and G. Teruel. 2015. Return migration to Mexico: Does health matter? *Demography* 52(6): 1853–68.

Arenas, E., S. Parker, L. Rubalcava, and G. Teruel. 2015. Evaluación del programa del Seguro popular del 2002 al 2005: Impacto en la utilización de servicios médicos, en el gasto en salud y en el mercado laboral. *El Trimestre Económico* 82(328): 807–45.

Beard, H.A., M. Al Ghatrif, R. Samper-Ternent, K. Gerst, and K.S. Markides. 2009. Trends in diabetes prevalence and diabetes-related complications in older Mexican Americans from 1993–1994 to 2004–2005. *Diabetes Care* 32(12): 2212–17.

Beltrán-Sánchez, H., and F. Riosmena. 2017. Socioeconomic inequalities in the risk of chronic disease between Mexicans residing in the U.S., their U.S. counterparts, and those in Mexico. In *Migration and Health: Reflections and Challenges about the Health of Migrants,* 53–68. Mexico City: National Population Council of Mexico (CONAPO). Retrieved from www.gob.mx/cms/uploads/attachment/file/390663/Migraci_n_y_salud_2017_web_final1.pdf.

Collins, S.R., M.Z. Gunja, M.M. Doty, and S. Beutel. 2016. Who are the remaining uninsured and why haven't they signed up for coverage? *Issue Brief (Commonwealth Fund)* 24: 1–20.

Cunningham, S.A., J.D. Ruben, and K.M.V. Narayan. 2008. Health of foreign-born people in the United States: A review. *Health & Place* 14(4): 623–35.

Diaz, C.J., L. Zeng, and A.P. Martinez-Donate. 2018. Investigating health selection within Mexico and across the U.S. border. *Population Research and Policy Review* 37(2): 181–204.

Eschbach, K., G.V. Ostir, K.V. Patel, K.S. Markides, and J.S. Goodwin. 2004. Neighborhood context and mortality among older Mexican Americans: Is there a barrio advantage? *American Journal of Public Health* 94(10): 1807–12.

Garcia, M.A., C. Garcia, C.-T. Chiu, M. Raji, and K.S. Markides. 2018. A comprehensive analysis of morbidity life expectancies among older Hispanic subgroups in the United States: Variation by nativity and country of origin. *Innovation in Aging* 2(2): 1–12. DOI:10.1093/geroni/igy014.

Garcia, M.A., J.L. Saenz, B. Downer, C.-T. Chiu, S. Rote, and R. Wong. 2017. Age of migration differentials in life expectancy with cognitive impairment: 20-year findings from the Hispanic-EPESE. *Gerontologist* 58(5): 894–903.

Gonzalez-Barrera, A., and J.M. Krogstad. 2017. What we know about illegal immigration from Mexico. Pew Research Center. Retrieved from www.pewresearch.org/fact-tank/2017/03/02/what-we-know-about-illegal-immigration-from-mexico/.

Hausmann, L.R., M.J. Hannon, D.M. Kresevic, B.H. Hanusa, C.K. Kwoh, and S.A. Ibrahim. 2011. Impact of perceived discrimination in health care on patient-provider communication. *Medical Care* 49(7): 626.

Holmes, S. 2013. *Fresh Fruit, Broken Bodies: Migrant Farmworkers in the United States*. Berkeley: University of California Press.

Horton, S. B. 2016. *They Leave Their Kidneys in the Fields: Illness, Injury, and Illegality among US Farmworkers*. Berkeley: University of California Press.

Hummer, R. A., and I. Gutin. 2018. Racial/ethnic and nativity disparities in the health of older U.S. men and women. Paper presented at Future Directions for the Demography of Aging: Proceedings of a Workshop.

Hummer, R. A., and M. D. Hayward. 2015. Hispanic older adult health and longevity in the United States: Current patterns and concerns for the future. *Daedalus* 144(2): 20–30.

Isacson, A., M. Meyer, and A. Hite. 2018. A national shame: The Trump administration's separation and detention of migrant families. Washington Office for Latin America, Washington, DC.

Jorgensen, C. 2017. Immigrant detention in the United States: Violations of international and human rights law. Human Rights Brief. Retrieved from http://hrbrief.org/hearings/immigrant-detention-united-states-violations-international-human-rights-law/.

Landale, N. S., J. H. Hardie, R. Oropesa, and M. M. Hillemeier. 2015. Behavioral functioning among Mexican-origin children: Does parental legal status matter? *Journal of Health and Social Behavior* 56(1): 2–18.

Lara, M., C. Gamboa, M. I. Kahramanian, L. S. Morales, and D. E. Hayes-Bautista. 2005. Acculturation and Latino health in the United States: A review of the literature and its sociopolitical context. *Annual Review of Public Health* 26: 367–97.

Martínez, Ó. 2013. *The Beast: Riding the Rails and Dodging Narcos on the Migrant Trail*. New York: Verso Books.

Masferrer, C., and B. Roberts. 2012. Going back home? Changing demography and geography of Mexican return migration. *Population Research and Policy Review* 31(4): 465–96.

Massey, D. S., J. Durand, and N. Malone. 2002. *Beyond Smoke and Mirrors: Mexican Immigration in an Era of Economic Integration*. New York: Russell Sage Foundation.

Massey, D. S., J. Durand, and K. A. Pren. 2015. Border enforcement and return migration by documented and undocumented Mexicans. *Journal of Ethnic and Migration Studies* 41(7): 1015–40.

Massey, D. S., and F. Riosmena. 2010. Undocumented migration from Latin America in an era of rising U.S. enforcement. *Annals of the American Academy of Political and Social Science* 630(1): 294–321.

McGuire, T. G., and J. Miranda. 2008. New evidence regarding racial and ethnic disparities in mental health: Policy implications. *Health Affairs* 27(2): 393–403.

Ortega, A. N., H. Fang, V. H. Perez, J. A. Rizzo, O. Carter-Pokras, S. P. Wallace, and L. Gelberg. 2007. Health care access, use of services, and experiences among undocumented Mexicans and other Latinos. *Archives of Internal Medicine* 167(21): 2354–60.

Ortega, B. 2018. Border patrol failed to count hundreds of migrant deaths on US soil. Retrieved from www.cnn.com/2018/05/14/us/border-patrol-migrant-death-count-invs/index.html.
Parrado, E. A., and E. Y. Gutierrez. 2016. The changing nature of return migration to Mexico, 1990–2010: Implications for labor market incorporation and development. *Sociology of Development* 2(2): 93–118.
Pedraza, F., and L. Zhu. 2015. The "chilling effect" of America's new immigration enforcement regime. *Pathways* (Spring): 13–17. Retrieved from https://inequality.stanford.edu/sites/default/files/Pathways_Spring_2015_Pedraza_Zhu.pdf.
Perreira, K. M., H. Yoshikawa, and J. Oberlander. 2018. A new threat to immigrants' health—The public-charge rule. *New England Journal of Medicine* 379(10): 901–3.
Riosmena, F., C. G. González, and R. Wong. 2012. El retorno reciente de Estados Unidos: Salud, bienestar y vulnerabilidad de los adultos mayores. *Coyuntura Demográfica* 2: 63–67.
Riosmena, F., R. Kuhn, and W. C. Jochem. 2017. Explaining the immigrant health advantage: Self-selection and protection in health-related factors among five major national-origin immigrant groups in the United States. *Demography* 54(1): 175–200.
Riosmena, F., A. M. Palloni, and R. Wong. 2013. Migration selection, protection, and acculturation in health: A bi-national perspective on older adults. *Demography* 50: 1039–64.
Ross, S. J., J. A. Pagán, and D. Polsky. 2006. Access to health care for migrants returning to Mexico. *Journal of Health Care for the Poor and Underserved* 17(2): 374–85.
Ryo, E. 2013. Deciding to cross: Norms and economics of unauthorized migration. *American Sociological Review* 78(4): 574–603.
Schafran, A., and P. Monkkonen. 2017. Beyond Chapala and Cancún: Grappling with the impact of American migration to Mexico. *Migraciones Internacionales* 6(21): 223–58.
Sullivan, M. M., and R. Rehm. 2005. Mental health of undocumented Mexican immigrants: A review of the literature. *Advances in Nursing Science* 28(3): 240–51.
Telles, E. E., and V. Ortiz. 2008. *Generations of Exclusion: Mexican Americans, Assimilation, and Race.* New York: Russell Sage Foundation.
Turra, C. M., and I. T. Elo. 2008. The impact of salmon bias on the Hispanic mortality advantage: New evidence from social security data. *Population Research and Policy Review* 27(5): 515–30.
Villarreal, A. 2014. Explaining the decline in Mexico-US migration: The effect of the Great Recession. *Demography* 51(6): 2203–28.
Wassink, J. T. 2016. Implications of Mexican health care reform on the health coverage of nonmigrants and returning migrants. *American Journal of Public Health* 106(5): 848–50.
Waters, M. C., and M. G. Pineau. 2016. *The Integration of Immigrants into American Society.* Washington, DC: National Academies Press.

CHAPTER 6

Barshay, J. 2018. Behind the Latino college degree gap: Latinos are the least likely to get a college education, new report says. *Hechinger Report*, June 16. Retrieved from hechingerreport.org/behind-the-latino-college-degree-gap/.

Bohn, S., and M. Cuellar Mejia. 2017. Higher education in California: Addressing California's skills gap. September. Public Policy Institute of California (PPIC), San Francisco.

California Department of Education. 2016. Statewide enrollment by ethnicity with county data. September 28. Sacramento.

———. 2017. California Assessment of Student Performance and Progress System (CAASPP). California Department of Education, Sacramento. Retrieved from www.cde.ca.gov/ta/tg/ca/.

Childtrends. 2014. Data Bank. Immigrant Children. Retrieved from www.childtrends.org/wp-content/uploads/2012/07/110_Immigrant_Children.pdf.

Guthrie, C., M. Fitzpatrick, C. Rebolledo-Gómez, and D. Toledo Figueroa. 2018. Raising the quality and equity of Mexico's education and skills system. In *Getting It Right: Strategic Priorities for Mexico*. Paris, France: OECD Publishing. DOI:https://doi.org/10.1787/9789264292062-en.

Harrup, A. 2018. Mexico to give minimum wage another boost. *Wall Street Journal*, December 17. Retrieved from www.wsj.com/articles/mexico-to-give-minimum-wage-another-boost-11545085238.

Instituto Nacional de Estadística y Geografía (INEGI) and Gobierno de Baja California. 2016. *Anuario estadístico y geográfico de Baja California, 2016* [Statistical and geographic yearbook of Baja California, 2016]. Retrieved from http://internet.contenidos.inegi.org.mx/contenidos/Productos/prod_serv/contenidos/espanol/bvinegi/productos/nueva_estruc/anuarios_2016/702825083663.pdf.

Jacobo, M., and B. Jensen. 2018. Schooling for U.S.-citizen students in Mexico. Civil Rights Project, University of California, Los Angeles. Retrieved from www.civilrightsproject.ucla.edu/research/k-12-education/immigration-immigrant-students/when-families-are-deported-schooling-for-us-citizen-students-in-mexico/Schooling-for-US-Citizens_Jacobo-and-Jensen_June19.pdf.

Johnson, H., and S. Sanchez. 2018. Just the facts: Immigrants in California. Public Policy Institute for California (PPIC), San Francisco.

Leal, J., and J. Parilla. 2016. Redefining global cities. Brookings Institution. Retrieved from www.brookings.edu/research/redefining-global-cities/.

Levy, S., and L.F. López-Calva. 2016. Figure on educational attainment by income, Mexico, 1996–2014. In *Labor Earnings, Misallocation, and the Returns to Education in Mexico*. IDB Working Paper Series No. IDB-WP-671, Inter-American Development Bank (IDB). Retrieved from https://publications.iadb.org/publications/english/document/Labor-Earnings-Misallocation-and-the-Returns-to-Education-in-Mexico.pdf.

Mission Statement. 2014. The U.S.-Mexico initiative: A strategic framework. Retrieved from https://ucmexicoinitiative.ucr.edu/docs/Strategic_framework_FINAL.pdf.

Mordechay, K. 2014. Vast changes and an uneasy future. Civil Rights Project, University of California, Los Angeles. Retrieved from www.civilrightsproject.ucla.edu/research/metro-and-regional-inequalities/lasanti-project-los-angeles-san-diego-tijuana/vast-changes-and-an-uneasy-future-racial-and-regional-inequality-in-southern-california/mordechayi-uneasy-future-lasantai-2014.pdf.

Reyes, K. 2017a. Más de 10 mil quedan sin lugar en la UABC [More than 10,000 are left without a place at the UABC]. *Frontera Info.*, August 11. Retrieved from www.frontera.info/EdicionEnlinea/Notas/Noticias/11082017/1245063-Mas-de-10-mil-quedan-sin-lugar-en-la-UABC.html.

———. 2017b. Quedan 12 mil fuera de "prepa" pública en BC [There are 12,000 out of public "prepa" in BC]. *Frontera Info.*, July 26. Retrieved from www.frontera.info/EdicionEnlinea/Notas/Noticias/26072017/1240285-Quedan-12-mil-fuera-de-prepa-publica-en-BC.html.

Shellenberger, M. 2018. *California in Danger.* Berkeley, CA: Environmental Progress.

Teruel, G., M. Reyes, and M. López. 2017. Mexico: Policy brief—análisis de coyuntura no. 1. In *Informe de coyuntura* (December): 15–22. Association of Universities Entrusted to the Society of Jesus in Latin America/AUSJAL, Lima, Peru. Retrieved from https://issuu.com/ausjal/docs/informe_coyuntura_diciembre.

Wong, T., G. Martinez Rosas, A. Luna, H. Manning, A. Reyna, P. O'Shea, T. Jawetz, and P. E. Wolgin. 2017. DACA recipients' economic and educational gains continue to grow. Center for American Progress, Washington, DC.

CHAPTER 7

Baker, B., and N. Rytina. 2013. Estimates of the unauthorized immigrant population residing in the United States: January 2012. Office of Immigration Statistics, US Department of Homeland Security. Retrieved from www.dhs.gov/sites/default/files/publications/ois_ill_pe_2012_2.pdf.

Bohn, S., M. Lofstrom, and S. Raphael. 2014. Did the 2007 legal Arizona workers act reduce the state's unauthorized immigrant population? *Review of Economics and Statistics* 96: 258–69.

Borjas, G. J. 2017. The labor supply of undocumented immigrants. *Labour Economics* 47: 1–13.

Borjas, G. J., R. B. Freeman, and L. K. Katz. 1997. How much do immigration and trade affect labor market outcomes? *Brookings Papers on Economic Activity* 1: 1–90. Retrieved from www.brookings.edu/bpea-articles/how-much-do-immigration-and-trade-affect-labor-market-outcomes/.

Chiquiar, D., and A. Salcedo. 2013. Mexican migration to the United States: Underlying economic factors and possible scenarios for future flows. Migration Policy Institute. Retrieved from www.migrationpolicy.org/research/mexican-migration-united-states-underlying-economic-factors-and-possible-scenarios-future.

Clemens, M., C. E. Montenegro, and L. Pritchett. 2008. The place premium: Wage differences for identical workers across the U.S. border. Center for Global Development. Retrieved from www.cgdev.org/sites/default/files/16352_file_CMP_place_premium_148.pdf.

Gandolfi, D., T. Halliday, and R. Robertson. 2015. Trade, migration, and the place premium: Mexico and the United States. Center for Global Development.

Retrieved from www.cgdev.org/sites/default/files/CGD-Working-Paper-396-Beyond-Fence-Gandolfi-Halliday-Robertson_0.pdf.

Genoni, M. E., G. Farfan, L. Rubalcava, G. Teruel, D. Thomas, and A. Velazquez. 2017. Mexicans in America. BREAD Working Paper. Retrieved from http://ibread.org/bread/working/511.

Gonzalez-Barrera, A. 2015. More Mexicans leaving than coming to the U.S. Pew Research Center. Retrieved from www.pewhispanic.org/files/2015/11/2015-11-19_mexican-immigration_FINAL.pdf.

Hanson, G. H. 2006. Illegal migration from Mexico to the United States. *Journal of Economic Literature* 44: 869–924.

Hanson, G. H., and C. McIntosh. 2009. The demography of Mexican migration to the United States. *American Economic Review Papers & Proceedings* 99: 22–27.

Hanson, G. H., and A. Spilimbergo. 1999. Illegal immigration, border enforcement, and relative wages: Evidence from apprehensions at the U.S.-Mexico border. *American Economic Review* 89: 1337–57.

King, M., S. Ruggles, J. T. Alexander, S. Flood, K. Genadek, M. B. Schroeder, B. Trampe, and R. Vick. 2010. Integrated public use microdata series, current population survey: Version 3.0 [machine-readable database]. Minnesota Population Center, Minneapolis.

Krogstad, J. M., J. S. Passel, and D. Cohn. 2017. 5 facts about illegal immigration in the U.S. Pew Research Center. Retrieved from www.pewresearch.org/fact-tank/2017/04/27/5-facts-about-illegal-immigration-in-the-u-s/.

Martin, P. 2018. Agriculture and international labor flows. Paper presented at the Kansas City Federal Reserve Bank Agricultural Symposium, July 18.

Massey, D. S., J. Durand, and K. A. Pren. 2014. Explaining undocumented migration to the U.S. *International Migration Review* 48: 1028–61.

National Research Council. 2013. *Options for Estimating Illegal Entries at the US-Mexico Border.* Washington, DC: National Academies Press. Retrieved from https://doi.org/10.17226/13498.

Orrenius, P. M. 2014. Enforcement and illegal migration. *IZA World of Labor* 81: 1–10.

Orrenius, P. M., and M. Zavodny. 2009. Tied to the business cycle: How immigrants fare in good and bad economic times. Migration Policy Institute. Retrieved from www.migrationpolicy.org/research/tied-business-cycle-how-immigrants-fare-good-and-bad-economic-times.

———. 2016. Unauthorized Mexican workers in the United States: Recent inflows and possible future scenarios. CGD Working Paper 436. Center for Global Development. Retrieved from www.cgdev.org/sites/default/files/unauthorized-mexican-workers-united-states-inflows.pdf.

Passel, J. S., and D. Cohn. 2015. Share of unauthorized immigrant workers in production, construction jobs falls since 2007. Pew Research Center. Retrieved from www.pewhispanic.org/files/2015/03/2015-03-26_unauthorized-immigrants-passel-testimony_REPORT.pdf.

Ruggles, S., K. Genadek, R. Goeken, J. Grover, and M. Sobek. 2015. Integrated public use microdata series: Version 6.0 [machine-readable database]. University of Minnesota, Minneapolis.

Warren, R. 2014. Democratizing data about unauthorized residents in the United States: Estimates and public-use data, 2010 to 2013. *Journal on Migration and Human Security* 2: 305–28.

Warren, R., and J. R. Warren. 2013. Unauthorized immigration to the United States: Annual estimates and components of change, by state, 1990 to 2010. *International Migration Review* 47: 296–329.

CHAPTER 8

Bean, F. D., S. K. Brown, and J. D. Bachmeier. 2015. *Parents without Papers: The Progress and Pitfalls of Mexican-American Integration*. New York: Russell Sage Foundation.

Bean, F. D., S. K. Brown, J. D. Bachmeier, Z. Gubernskaya, and C. D. Smith. 2012. Luxury, necessity and anachronistic workers: Does the United States need unskilled immigrant labor? *American Behavioral Scientist* 56(8): 1008–28.

Bean, F. D., S. K. Brown, and S. Pullés. 2018. Migration and the California dream: Past, present and future. Paper presented at the Immigrant California: Policies and Politics conference, University of California, San Diego, March 2.

Bean, F. D., B. L. Lowell, and L. Taylor. 1988. Undocumented Mexican immigrants and the earnings of other workers in the United States. *Demography* 25(1): 35–52.

Bean, F. D., and G. Stevens. 2003. *America's Newcomers and the Dynamics of Diversity*. New York: Russell Sage Foundation Press.

Cortes, P. 2008. The effects of low-skilled immigration on U.S. prices: Evidence from CPI data. *Journal of Political Economy* 116(3): 381–422.

Current Population Survey. 2010. Annual social and economic (ASEC) supplement [machine-readable data file]. Conducted by the Bureau of the Census for the Bureau of Labor Statistics, Washington, DC. US Census Bureau producer and distributor.

Fix, M., D. G. Papademetriou, and M. Sumption, eds. 2013. *Immigrants in a Changing Labor Market: Responding to Economic Needs*. Washington, DC: Migration Policy Institute.

Hall, M., and E. Greenman. 2015. The occupational risk of being illegal in the United States: Legal status, job hazard, and compensating differentials. *International Migration Review* 49: 406–42.

Hanson, G. H. 2013. The economics of illegal immigration in the United States: Policy implications. In M. Fix, D. G. Papademetriou, and M. Sumption, eds., *Immigrants in a Changing Labor Market: Responding to Economic Needs*, 53–68. Washington, DC: Migration Policy Institute.

Krugman, P. 2003. Lumps of labor. *New York Times,* October 7. Retrieved from www.nytimes.com/2003/10/07/opinion/lumps-of-labor.html.

Martin, P. 2009. *Importing Poverty? Immigration and the Changing Face of Rural America*. New Haven, CT: Yale University Press.

Minnesota Population Center. 2011. Integrated public use microdata series, International (Version 6.1) [machine-readable database]. University of Minnesota, Minneapolis.

National Academy of Sciences. 2015. *The Integration of Immigrants into American Society*. Washington, DC: National Academies Press. DOI:10.17226/21746.

———. 2016. *The Economic and Fiscal Consequences of Immigration*. Washington, DC: National Academies Press. DOI:10.17226/23550.

Passel, J.S., and D. Cohn. 2017. As Mexican share declined, U.S. unauthorized immigrant population fell in 2015 below recession level. Pew Research Center. Retrieved from www.pewresearch.org/fact-tank/2017/04/25/as-mexican-share-declined-u-s-unauthorized-immigrant-population-fell-in-2015-below-recession-level/.

Peri, G. 2013. The impact of immigrants in recession and economic expansion. In M. Fix, D.G. Papademetriou, and M. Sumption, eds., *Immigrants in a Changing Labor Market: Responding to Economic Needs*, 69–92. Washington, DC: Migration Policy Institute.

Telles, E., and V. Ortiz. 2008. *Generations of Exclusion: Mexican Americans, Assimilation, and Race*. New York: Russell Sage Foundation.

US Bureau of Labor Statistics. 2018. B-1. Employees on nonfarm payrolls by major industry sector, 1962 to date. Establishment data, historical employment. Retrieved from ftp://ftp.bls.gov/pub/suppl/empsit.ceseeb1.txt.

US Department of Health and Human Services. 2010. Vital stats. Centers for Disease Control and Prevention and National Center for Health Statistics. Retrieved from www.cdc.gov/nchs/vitalstats.htm and www.cdc.gov/nchs/data/statab/natfinal2003.annvoll_07.pdf.

Zolberg, A.R. 2006. *A Nation by Design: Immigration Policy in the Fashioning of America*. New York: Russell Sage Foundation.

CHAPTER 9

Bolt, J., R. Inklaar, H. de Jong, and J.L. van Zanden. 2018. Rebasing "Maddison": New income comparisons and the shape of long-run economic development. Maddison Project Database, version 2018. Maddison Project Working Paper 10. Retrieved from https://voxeu.org/article/rebasing-maddison.

Borjas, G.J. 2015. The wage impact of the Marielitos: A reappraisal. Retrieved from https://sites.hks.harvard.edu/fs/gborjas/publications/working%20papers/Mariel2015.pdf.

Brown, D., J. Hotchkiss, and M. Quispe-Agnoli. 2012. Does employing undocumented workers give firms a competitive advantage? FRB Atlanta Working Paper Series, 2012–02. http://dx.doi.org/10.2139/ssrn.2060242.

Burfisher, M., F. Lambert, and T. Matheson. 2019. NAFTA to USMCA: What is gained? *IMF Working Papers* 19(73): 1. DOI:10.5089/9781498303286.001.

Bustamante, J.A., C.W. Reynolds, and R. Hinojosa-Ojeda, eds. 1992. *U.S.-Mexico Relations: Labor Market Interdependence*. Palo Alto, CA: Stanford University Press.

Card, D. 1990. The impact of the Mariel boatlift on the Miami labor market. *ILR Review* 43(2): 245–57. Retrieved from journals.sagepub.com/doi/abs/10.1177/001979399004300205.

Congressional Budget Office. 2013. The economic impact of S. 744, the Border Security, Economic Opportunity, and Immigration Modernization Act. Retrieved from www.cbo.gov/sites/default/files/cbofiles/attachments/44346-Immigration.pdf.

Cuecuecha, A., and J. Scott. 2010. The effect of agricultural subsidies on migration and agricultural employment. Rural Development Research Report, No. 3, January. Woodrow Wilson Center, Mexico Institute. Retrieved from www.wilsoncenter.org/sites/default/files/Monograf%C3%ADa_Cuecuecha_Scott.pdf.

Fields, G. 2004. A guide to multisector labor market models. Cornell University, School of Industrial and Labor Relations. Retrieved from http://digitalcommons.ilr.cornell.edu/workingpapers/86/.

Gonzalez-Barrera, A. 2015. More Mexicans leaving than coming to the U.S. Trends. Pew Research Center. Retrieved from www.pewhispanic.org/wp-content/uploads/sites/5/2015/11/2015-11-19_mexican-immigration__FINAL.pdf.

Hanson, G., C. Liu, and C. McIntosh. 2017. Along the watchtower: The rise and fall of U.S. low-skilled immigration. Brookings Papers on Economic Activity. DOI:10.3386/w23753.

Hinojosa, R. 2013. The costs and benefits of immigration enforcement. Immigration reform: A system for the 21st century. Latin America Initiative. Rice University's Baker Institute for Public Policy. Retrieved from www.bakerinstitute.org/media/files/event/f46d9752/LAI-pub-HinojosaOjedaImmigrationEnforcement-040813.pdf.

———. 2019. North American Development Bank and Community Adjustment and Investment Program (CAIP): Historical trajectory and lessons learned. Mexico Center at the Baker Institute, Rice University, and Colegio de la Frontera Norte.

Hinojosa-Ojeda, R. 1994. The North American Development Bank forging in new directions in regional integration policy. *Journal of the American Planning Association* 60(3): 301–4.

———. 1999. North American integration and concepts of human rights: Reflections on 150 years of treaty making. *Southwestern Journal of Law and Trade in the Americas, Special Symposium Issue of the 150th Anniversary of the Treaty of Guadalupe Hidalgo* (March): 177–82.

———. 2002. Integration policy formation from the grassroots up: Transnational implications of Latino, labor, and environmental NGO strategies. In Jonathan Fox and David Brooks, eds., *Cross Border Dialogues: U.S. México Social Movement Networking*, 227–47. La Jolla: University of California, San Diego, Center for U.S.-Mexican Studies. Retrieved from www.naid.ucla.edu/uploads/4/2/1/9/4219226/_b13_2002.pdf.

———. 2010. Raising the floor for American workers: The economic benefits of comprehensive immigration reform. Center for American Progress and American Immigration Council. Retrieved from www.americanprogress.org/wp-content/uploads/2012/09/immigrationeconreport3.pdf.

———. 2011. The economic benefits of comprehensive immigration reform: General equilibrium approach. *Cato Journal: An Interdisciplinary Journal of Policy*

Analysis 32(1). Retrieved from www.naid.ucla.edu/uploads/4/2/1/9/4219226/a53_hinojosa_2012_cato_091511.pdf_published.pdf.

Hinojosa-Ojeda. R., J. Lewis, and S. Robinson. 1995. Regional integration options for Central America and the Caribbean after NAFTA. *Journal of North American Economics and Finance* 6(2): 121–48.

Hinojosa-Ojeda, R., and S. Robinson. 1991. Alternative scenarios of US-Mexico integration: A computable general equilibrium approach. CUDARE Working Papers 198585. University of California, Berkeley, Department of Agricultural and Resource Economics. DOI:10.22004/ag.econ.198585.

Ianchovichina, E., and T.L. Walmsley. 2012. *Dynamic Modeling and Applications for Global Economic Analysis.* Cambridge: Cambridge University Press.

Levy, S., and S. van Wijnbergen. 1992. Maize and the free trade agreement between Mexico and the United States. *World Bank Economic Review* 6(3): 481–502.

———. 1994. Labor markets, migration and welfare: Agriculture in the North American Free Trade Agreement. *Journal of Development Economics* 43(2): 263–78. Retrieved from www.researchgate.net/publication/4827653_Labor_markets_migration_and_welfare_Agriculture_in_the_North-American_Free_Trade_Agreement.

Lippolis, N. 2013. Our world in data. Retrieved from https://ourworldindata.org/grapher/employment-by-economic-sector?stackMode=relative&tab=data; http://www.public.asu.edu/~bherrend/Published%20Papers/Handbook%2013.pdf.

Massey, D.S., J. Durand, and N. Malone. 2002. *Beyond Smoke and Mirrors: Mexican Immigration in an Era of Economic Integration.* New York: Russell Sage Foundation. Retrieved from www.jstor.org/stable/10.7758/9781610443821.

McDonald, S., and K. Thierfelder. 2016. Globe v2: A SAM based global CGE model using GTAP data. Retrieved from www.cgemod.org.uk.

McDonald, S., K. Thierfelder, and S. Robinson. 2007. Globe: A SAM based global CGE model using GTAP data. USNA Working Paper No. 14.

Pastor, R. 2001. *Toward a North American Community: Lessons from the Old World for the New.* Washington, DC: Institute for International Economics.

Peri, G., and V. Yasenov. 2015. The labor market effects of a refugee wave: Applying the synthetic control method to the Mariel boatlift. Working Paper No. 21801. December. National Bureau of Economic Research. DOI:10.3386/w21801.

Pulaski, S., J. Capaldo, and K. Gallagher. 2019. Small gains and big risks: Evaluating the proposed United States-Mexico-Canada Agreement. GEGI Policy Brief 007. Retrieved from www.bu.edu/gdp/2019/06/07/small-gains-big-risks-evaluating-the-proposed-united-states-mexico-canada-agreement/.

Robert, E.S. 2011. Heading south: U.S.-Mexico trade and job displacement after NAFTA. May 3. Retrieved from https://secure.epi.org/files/page/-/BriefingPaper308.pdf.

Robinson, S., M.E. Burfisher, R. Hinojosa-Ojeda, and K.E. Thierfelder. 1991. Agricultural policies and migration in a US-Mexico free trade area: A computable general equilibrium analysis. Working Paper No. 617. December. Department of Agricultural and Resource Economics, University of California, Berkeley. Retrieved from https://tind-customer-agecon.s3.amazonaws.com/4b6d7869-24c6-4e65-8705-191126e2ac5c?response-content-disposition=inline%3B%20filename%2A%3DUTF-8%27%27agecon-cal-617.pdf&response-content-type=application%2Fpdf&AWSAccessKeyId=AKIAXL7W7Q3XHXDVDQYS&Expires=1560645897&Signature=8K3BsjfYYGZ4Wz8clDsL6VVxWPM%3D

———. 1993. Agricultural policies and migration in a U.S.-Mexico free trade area: A computable general equilibrium analysis. *Journal of Policy Modeling* 15(5–6): 673–701. DOI.org/10.1016/0161-8938(93)90009-F. An earlier version appeared in U.S. International Trade Commission, *Economy-Wide Modeling of the Economic Implications of an FTA with Mexico and a NAFTA with Canada and Mexico*. An Addendum to the Report on Investigation No. 332-317 under Section 332 of the Tariff Act of 1930. USITC Publication 2508, May 1992.

Robinson, S., and K.E. Thierfelder. 2018. NAFTA collapse, trade war and North American disengagement. *Journal of Policy Modeling* 40: 614–35.

Scott, J. 2010. Agricultural subsidies in Mexico: Who gets what? Centro de Investigación y Docencia Económicas. Retrieved from www.wilsoncenter.org/sites/default/files/Subsidizing_Inequality_Ch_3_Scott.pdf.

Taylor, J.E., D. Charlton, and A. Yúñez-Naude. 2012. The end of farm labor abundance. *Applied Economic Perspectives and Policy* 34(4): 587–98. DOI:10.1093/aepp/pps036.

Trade Adjustment Assistance Database. n.d. Retrieved from www.citizen.org/article/trade-adjustment-assistance-database/.

United States Census Bureau. U.S. international trade in goods and services. Historical series. Retrieved from www.census.gov/foreign-trade/statistics/historical/index.html.

United States Commission for the Study of International Migration and Cooperative Economic Development. 1990. *Unauthorized Migration: An Economic Development Response*. Washington, DC: US Government Printing Office.

United States Trade Representative (USTR). 2017. Summary of objectives for the NAFTA renegotiation. July 17. Retrieved from https://ustr.gov/about-us/policy-offices/press-office/press-releases/2017/july/ustr-releases-nafta-negotiating.

World Bank. Mexico trade statistics: Exports, imports, products, tariffs, GDP and related development indicator. WITS, World Integrated Trade Solution. Retrieved from https://wits.worldbank.org/CountryProfile/en/MEX.

World Trade Organization (WTO). Statistics: Databases, publications, and tools (including time series on international trade). Retrieved from www.wto.org/english/res_e/statis_e/data_pub_e.htm.

Yúñez-Naude, A., J. Villanueva, and V. Serrano. 2012. Spatial integration of Mexico and the United States in grain markets: The case of maize, wheat and sorghum. In *Subsidizing Inequality: Mexican Corn Policy since NAFTA*. Washington, DC: Mexico Institute, Woodrow Wilson International Center for Scholars. Retrieved from www.researchgate.net/publication/254387591_SPATIAL_INTEGRATION_OF_MEXICO_AND_UNITED_STATES_IN_GRAIN_MARKET_THE_CASE_OF_MAIZE_WHEAT_AND_SORGHUM.

CHAPTER 10

Banco de Información Económica (BIE). 2017. Agricultural GDP: Repository of economic information. Retrieved from Inegi.org.mx.

Bancomer Foundation, BBVA Research, and CONAPO (El Consejo Nacional de Población). 2017. Yearbook of migration and remittances Mexico 2017. Mexico. Retrieved from www.bbvaresearch.com/wp-content/uploads/2017/08/1707_AnuarioMigracionRemesas_2017.pdf.

Calderón, J. 2004. Diez años de TLCAN: Balance inicial. *Economía Informa* 327: 48–67. Retrieved from www.economia.unam.mx/publicaciones/reseconinforma/pdfs/327/06Calderon.pdf.

Charlton, D., and J. E. Taylor. 2016. A declining farm workforce: Analysis of panel data from rural Mexico. *American Journal of Agricultural Economics* 98(4): 1158–80. Retrieved from https://migrationcluster.ucdavis.edu/sites/g/files/dgvnsk821/files/2017-07/paper_charlton-declining-farm-workforce.pdf.

Comisión Federal de Competencia Económica (COFECE). 2015. Reporte sobre las condiciones de competencia en el sector agroalimentario. December 15. Mexico. Retrieved from www.cofece.mx/reporte-sobre-las-condiciones-de-competencia-en-el-sector-agroalimentario/.

Consejo Nacional de Población (CONAPO). 2017. Migratory geography. Retrieved from http://omi.gob.mx/es/OMI/Series_y_geografia_migratoria.

Dyer, G. 2007. Análisis cuantitativo de los efectos de transferencias al sector rural: Ingreso objetivo, PROCAMPO y Oportunidades [Quantitive analysis of the effects of transfers to the rural sector: Objective income, PROCAMPO, and Opportunities]. Final Report. July. Project Políticas y Gasto Público Federal en el Sector Rural en México [Federal public policies and expenditures in the rural sector in Mexico]. Inter-American Development Bank (IDB) and Mexico Ministry of Finance. Mimeo.

Dyer, G., A. Hernández-Solano, P. Meza-Pale, H. Robles-Berlanga, and A. Yúnez-Naude. 2018. Mexican agriculture and policy under NAFTA. Retrieved from https://cee.colmex.mx/2-principal/343-documentos-de-trabajo-2018.

Dyer, G. A., A. López-Feldman, A. Yúnez-Naude, and J. E. Taylor. 2014. Genetic erosion in maize's center of origin. *Proceedings of the National Academy of Sciences of the United States of America* (PNAS), September. Retrieved from www.pnas.org/search?fulltext=Genetic+erosion+in+maize%27s+center+of+origin&submit=yes&x=12&y=14.

Dyer, G., E. Taylor, and S. Boucher. 2006. Subsistence response to market shocks. *American Journal of Agricultural Economics* 88(2): 279–91. Retrieved from doi.org/10.1111/j.1467-8276.2006.00858.x.

Encuesta Nacional de Empleo (ENE). 2017. National survey of employment. Retrieved from Beta.inegi.org.mx.

Encuesta Nacional de Ocupación y Empleo (ENOE). 2017. National survey of occupation and employment. Retrieved from Beta.inegi.org.mx.

Fiess, N., and D. Lederman. 2004. Mexican corn: The effects of NAFTA. World Bank. Retrieved from http://documents.worldbank.org/curated/en/194601468300552482/Mexican-corn-the-effects-of-NAFTA.

Fitting, E. 2006. Importing corn, exporting labor: The neoliberal corn regime, GMOs, and the erosion of Mexican biodiversity. *Agriculture and Human Values* 23: 15–26.
Food and Agriculture Organization of the United Nations (FAOSTAT). 2017. Retrieved from www.fao.org/faostat/es/.
García Zamora, J., and S. Gaspar. 2017. TLCAN, crisis agrícola, empleo y migración internacional de México, 1980–2016 [Agricultural crisis: Employment and international migration in Mexico, 1980–2015]. Unidad Académica en Estudios del Desarrollo, México. Retrieved from http://recursoscomunesy migracion.org/Docs/publicaciones/CrisisagricolaempleoTLCymigracion1.pdf.
Indicadores estratégicos de ocupación y empleo. 2017. Retrieved from http://www.stps.gob.mx/gobmx/estadisticas/ehogares.htm.
Instituto Nacional de Estadísticas y Geografía (INEGI). 2017. Banco de información económica (BIE). Retrieved from http://www.inegi.org.mx/sistemas/bie.
Jaramillo, J. L., A. Yúnez-Naude, and V. Serrano. 2015. Spatial integration of Mexico-U.S. grain markets: The case of maize, wheat and sorghum. *EconoQuantum* 12(1): 57–70.
Lederman, D., W. F. Maloney, and L. Servén. 2004. Lessons from NAFTA for Latin America and the Caribbean: A Summary of Research Findings. Washington, DC: World Bank. Retrieved from http://siteresources.worldbank.org/DEC/Resources/BookNAFTAWorldBank.pdf.
Levy, S., and S. van Wijnbergen. 1994. Labor markets, migration and welfare: Agriculture in the North American Free Trade Agreement. *Journal of Development Economics* 43: 263–78.
Massey, D. 2012. America is losing as many illegal immigrants as it's gaining. Blog. April 12. Retrieved from http://blogs.reuters.com/great-debate/2012/04/12/america-is-losing-as-many-illegal-immigrants-as-its-gaining/.
Passel, J. S., D. Cohn, and A. Gonzalez-Barrera. 2012. *Net Migration from Mexico Falls to Zero—and Perhaps Less*. Washington, DC: Pew Hispanic Center.
Peri, G. 2016. Immigrants, productivity, and labor markets. *Journal of Economic Perspectives* 30(4): 3–30.
Robinson, S., M. E. Burfisher, R. Hinojosa-Ojeda, and K. E. Thierfelder. 1993. Agricultural policies and migration in a US-Mexico free trade area: A computable general equilibrium analysis. *Journal of Policy Modeling* 15(5–6): 673–701.
Secretaría de Comercio y Fomento Industrial (SECOFI). 1994. *Fracciones arancelarias y plazos de desgravación: Tratado de libre comercio de América del Norte: Estados Unidos*. Mexico City: Porrúa. Retrieved from https://catalog.hathitrust.org/Record/007202937.
Secretaría del Trabajo y Previsión Social (STPS). 2017. Workers in Mexico's primary sector: Occupation and employment series from Labor Ministry. Retrieved from Stps.org.mx.
Servicio de Información Agroalimentaria y Pesquera (SIAP). 2017a. Agricultural production. Retrieved from www.gob.mx/siap/acciones-y-programas/produccion-agricola-33119/.

———. 2017b. Foreign trade. Retrieved from https://w6.siap.gob.mx/comercio/.
Sistema de Información Agroalimentaria de Consulta (SIACON). 2017. Database. Retrieved from www.gob.mx/siap/prensa/sistema-de-informacion-agroalimentaria-de-consulta-siacon?idiom=es.
Sistema de Información Económica (SIE). 2017. Banco de México. Retrieved from www.banxico.org.mx/SieInternet.
Sumner, D. A., and J. V. Balagtas. 2007. Economic analysis of the Ingreso Objetivo Program in Mexico. Final Report. August. Project Políticas y Gasto Público Federal en el Sector Rural en México. Inter-American Development Bank (IDB) and Mexico Ministry of Finance. Mimeo.
Taylor, J. E., D. Charlton, and A. Yúnez-Naude 2012. The end of farm labor abundance. *Applied Economic Perspectives and Policy* 34(4): 587–98.
Taylor, J. E., G. Dyer, and A. Yúnez-Naude. 2005. Disaggregated rural economy-wide models for policy analysis. *World Development* 33(10): 1671–88.
Thomas, C. 2010. Globalization and the border: Trade, labor, migration, and agricultural production in Mexico. *McGeorge Law Review* 41: 867–89.
United States-Mexico-Canada Agreement (USMCA). 2018. Retrieved from https://ustr.gov/trade-agreements/free-trade-agreements/united-states-mexico-canada-agreement/united-states-mexico.
Yúnez-Naude, A. 2010. Las políticas públicas dirigidas al sector rural: El carácter de las reformas para el cambio estructural [Public policies aimed at the rural sector: The nature of reforms for structural change]. In A. Yúñez, ed., *Economía rural*, 23–62. Mexico City: El Colegio de México.
———. 2014. Old foods and new consumers in Mexico under economic reforms. *African Journal of Agricultural and Resource Economics* 9(1): 33–53. Retrieved from https://ageconsearch.umn.edu/bitstream/176464/2/3.%20Yunez%20Naude.pdf.
———. 2018. La agricultura y el sector rural [Agriculture and rural development]. In F. Hernández Trillo and R. Campos Vázquez, eds., *Buen diagnóstico, buena solución: Los retos de la economía mexicana* [Good diagnosis, good solution: Challenges of the Mexican economy]. Mexico City: Fondo de Cultura Económica.
Yúnez-Naude, A., G. Dyer, H. Cerón, M. Gurría, and P. Winters. 2007. Evaluación del impacto del PROCAMPO y propuesta de reformas a sistema de apoyos agropecuarios [Evaluation of the impact of PROCAMPO on the proposed reforms to the agricultural support system]. Final Report to the IDB and ASERCA-SAGARPA. May. Mimeo.
Yúnez-Naude, A., G. Dyer, and A. Hernández-Solano. 2020. El TLCAN y el sector agropecuario y rural mexicano: Mitos, realidades y perspectivas [NAFTA and the Mexican agricultural and rural sector: Myths, realities and perspectives]. In O. F. Contreras and G. Vega, eds., *La reestructuración de Norteamérica a través del libre comercio: Del TLCAN al TMEC* [The restructuring of North America through free trade: From NAFTA to TMEC (The new trade agreement)], 50–76. Mexico City: El Colegio de México and El Colegio de la Frontera Norte. Retrieved from https://libros.colmex.mx/ficha/?b=2949.

Yúnez-Naude, A., and A. Hernández-Solano. 2018. The Mexican agricultural sector two decades after NAFTA: Expectations, facts and policy challenges. In A. M. Buainain, M. Rocha de Sousa, and Z. Navarro, eds., *Globalization and Agriculture: Redefining Unequal Development,* 71–92. Lanham, MD: Lexington Books.

Yúnez-Naude, A., A. Martínez, and M. Orrantia. 2007. *Elementos técnico económicos para evaluar los fundamentos que tendría una controversia comercial contra el maíz originario de los Estados Unidos de América* [Technical economic elements for evaluating the fundamentals that have created a commercial controversy over corn from the United States]. Colección Estudios e Investigaciones, Centro de Estudios para el Desarrollo Rural Sustentable y Soberanía Alimentara (CEDRSSA). Mexico City: Cámara de Diputados.

CHAPTER 11

Albin, Ó. 2017. Perspectivas del sector automotriz [Automotive industry outlook]. Presentation to INA, Industria Nacionales de Autopartes, A.C., August 22, Querétaro, Mexico.

Asociación Mexicana de la Industria Automotriz (AMIA). 2017. Exportación por región de destino. *Boletín de información estadística para diciembre de 2017.* [Export by region of destination. Statistical information bulletin for December 2017.] Retrieved from www.amia.com.mx/expregion.html.

Autor, D. 2015. Why are there still so many jobs? The history and future of workplace automation. *Journal of Economic Perspectives* 29(1): 3–30.

Baumol, W. 1967. Macroeconomics of unbalanced growth: The anatomy of urban crisis. *American Economic Review* 57(3): 415–26.

Bensusán, G., J. Carrillo, and I. Ahumada. 2011. ¿Es el sistema nacional de relaciones laborales mexicano un obstáculo o una ventaja para la competitividad de las CMNs? [Is the Mexican national labor relations system an obstacle or an advantage for the competitiveness of the MNCs?]. *Revista Latinoamericana de Estudios del Trabajo* 16(25): 121–54.

Boyer, R., and M. Freyssenet. 2002. *The Productive Models.* London: Palgrave Macmillan/Gerpisa.

Carrillo, J. 1993. La Ford en México: Restructuración industrial y cambio en las relaciones sociales [Ford in Mexico: Industrial restructuring and change in social relations]. PhD diss., El Colegio de México.

Centro de Estudios de las Finanzas Públicas (CEFP). 2017. *La industria automotriz en México y el tratado de libre comercio en América del Norte (TLCAN)* [The automotive industry in Mexico and the free trade agreement in North America (NAFTA)]. Boletín, Sector Industrial, Cámara de Diputados LXIII Legislativa. Retrieved from www.cefp.gob.mx/publicaciones/boleco/2017/becefp0072017.pdf.

Comisión Económica para América Latina y el Caribe (CEPAL). 2017. *La inversión extranjera directa en América Latina y el Caribe* [Foreign direct investment in Latin America and the Caribbean]. Santiago de Chile: Organización de las Naciones Unidas.

Coriat, B. 1992. *Pensar al revés: Trabajo y organización en la empresa japonesa* [Thinking backwards: Work and organization in the Japanese company]. Mexico City: Siglo XXI.

Gortari, Alonso, 2018, How much of your car is made in Mexico, EconoFact Network, Edward R. Murrow Center for a Digital World, Tufts University June 20.

Covarrubias, A. 2014. *Explosión de la industria automotiz en México: De sus encadenamientos actuales a su potencial trasformador* [Explosion of the automotive industry in Mexico: From its current chains to its transformed potential]. Analysis No. 1/2014. Mexico City: Friedrich Ebert Stiftung.

García, H., and J. Carrillo. 2017. Determinación de un salario digno para el sector automotriz en México: Metodología y resultados de investigación [Determination of the minimum wage in the automotive sector in Mexico: Methodology and research results]. Paper presented at the X AMET Congress "Del TLCAN al ATCE: Las instituciones, las promesas y los resultados" [From NAFTA to ATCE: Institutions, promises, and results]. Hermosillo, Mexico, October.

Heim, S. 2016. The development of the Mexican automotive industry and the strategy of the Japanese car makers and suppliers: Production/product policies, competitiveness, labor cost, and division of labor. Paper presented at the First Seminar of the Asian Research Center on the Intimate and Public Spheres, Kyoto University, June.

INA, 2017, Perspectiva del Sector Automotriz, Industria Nacional de Autopartes, A.C., Mexico, PPT presentation, 87 pages

Instituto Nacional de Estadísticas y Geografía (INEGI) and Asociación Mexicana de la Industria Automotriz (AMIA). 2016. Estadísticas a propósito de la industria automotriz [Statistics on the automotive industry]. Retrieved from http://internet.contenidos.inegi.org.mx/contenidos/Productos/prod_serv/contenidos/espanol/bvinegi/productos/nueva_estruc/automotriz/702825079963.pdf.

McKinsey Global Institute. 2017. *A Future That Works: Automation, Employment and Productivity.* New York: McKinsey Global Institute/McKinsey & Company.

Moreno-Brid, J., and E. Garry. 2015. El salario mínimo en México: En falta con la Constitución mexicana y una aberración en América Latina [The minimum wage in Mexico: Missing the Mexican constitution and an abberation in Latin America]. In M. Á. Mancera, ed., *Del salario mínimo al salario digno* [From the mínimum wage to the living wage], 105–21. Mexico City: Consejo Económico y Social de la Ciudad de México.

Organización Internacional de Fabricantes de Automóviles (OICA). 2018. Production and sales statistics. Organización Internacional de Fabricantes de Automóviles. Retrieved from www.oica.net/category/sales-statistics.

Secretaría de Economía. 2018. Inversión extranjera directa: Conjunto de datos. Flujos totales de IED hacía México por país de origen, según tipo de inversión, sector económico o entidad federativa [Foreign direct investment: Data set. Total FDI flows to Mexico by country of origin, according to type of investment, economic sector, or state]. Retrieved from http://catalogo.datos.gob.mx/dataset/inversion-extranjera-directa.

Secretaria de Economia, 2018, Registro Nacional de Inversiones Extranjeras (RNIE), Secretaría de Economía, Mexico.

Shaiken, H. 2016. The NAFTA paradox. *Berkeley Review of Latin American Studies.* Retrieved from http://clas.berkeley.edu/sites/default/files/shared/docs/tertiary/BRLASSpring2014-Shaiken.pdf.

CHAPTER 12

Autor, D. H., D. Dorn, and G. H. Hanson. 2016. The China shock: Learning from labor-market adjustment to large changes in trade. *Annual Review of Economics* 8: 205–40.

Autor, D. H., D. Dorn, L. F. Katz, C. Patterson, and J. Van Reenen. 2020. The fall of the labor share and the rise of superstar firms. *Quarterly Journal of Economics* 135(2): 645–709.

Bernstein, J. 2018. Trump's preliminary deal with Mexico is better for workers on both sides of the border than prior trade deals. *Washington Post,* August 28. Retrieved from www.washingtonpost.com/news/posteverything/wp/2018/08/28/trumps-preliminary-deal-with-mexico-is-better-for-workers-on-both-sides-of-the-border-than-prior-trade-deals/.

Bivens, J. 2017a. *Adding Insult to Injury: How Bad Policy Decisions Have Amplified Globalization's Costs for American Workers.* Washington, DC: Economic Policy Institute.

———. 2017b. *Inequality Is Slowing US Economic Growth: Faster Wage Growth for Low- and Middle-Wage Workers Is the Solution.* Washington, DC: Economic Policy Institute.

Blecker, R. A. 2014. The Mexican and U.S. economies after twenty years of NAFTA. *International Journal of Political Economy* 43(2): 5–26.

———. 2016. Integration, productivity, and inclusion in Mexico: A macro perspective. In A. Foxley and B. Stallings, eds., *Innovation and Inclusion in Latin America: Strategies to Avoid the Middle Income Trap,* 175–204. New York: Palgrave Macmillan.

———. 2019. NAFTA. In R. E. Looney, ed., *Handbook of International Trade Agreements: Country, Regional and Global Approaches,* 147–65. Abingdon: Routledge.

Blecker, R. A., and G. Esquivel. 2013. Trade and the development gap. In A. Selee and P. Smith, eds., *Mexico and the United States: The Politics of Partnership,* 83–110. Boulder, CO: Lynne Rienner.

Bolio, E., J. Remes, T. Lajous, J. Manyika, E. Ramirez, and M. Rossé. 2014. *A Tale of Two Mexicos: Growth and Prosperity in a Two-Speed Economy.* San Francisco, CA: McKinsey Global Institute.

Caliendo, L., and F. Parro. 2015. Estimates of the trade and welfare effects of NAFTA. *Review of Economic Studies* 82(1): 1–44.

Campbell, P. 2018. What does the revamped NAFTA deal mean for carmakers? *Financial Times,* August 28. Retrieved from www.ft.com/content/bbd27960-aac1-11e8-94bd-cba20d67390c.

Cordera, R., and E. Provencio, eds. 2020. *Cambiar el Rumbo: El Desarrollo Tras la Pandemia* [Changing course: Post-pandemic development]. Mexico

City: Grupo Nuevo Curso de Desarrollo/Universidad Nacional Autónoma de México. Retrieved from www.nuevocursodedesarrollo.unam.mx/docs/GNCD_CambiaIerumbo.pdf.

De Loecker, J., J. Eeckhout, and G. Unger. 2020. The rise of market power and the macroeconomic implications. *Quarterly Journal of Economics* 135(2): 561–644.

Dussel Peters, E., and K. P. Gallagher. 2013. NAFTA's uninvited guest: China and the disintegration of North American trade. *CEPAL Review* 110: 83–108.

Esquivel, G. 2015. *Extreme Inequality in Mexico*. Mexico City: OXFAM.

Fickling, D., and A. Trivedi. 2018. Trump's Mexico trade deal looks like a lemon. *Bloomberg*, August 28. Retrieved from www.bloomberg.com/view/articles/2018-08-28/trump-s-mexico-trade-deal-looks-like-a-lemon.

Gallagher, K. P., J. C. Moreno-Brid, and R. Porzecanski. 2008. The dynamism of Mexican exports: Lost in (Chinese) translation? *World Development* 36(8): 1365–80.

Grupo Nuevo Curso de Desarrollo. 2017. *En defensa del interés nacional ante la coyuntura crítica, ¿Qué hacer?* Mexico City: Universidad Nacional Autónoma de México. Retrieved from www.nuevocursodedesarrollo.unam.mx/docs/GNCDEnDefensaIntNal.050217.pdf.

Hakobyan, S., and J. McLaren. 2016. Looking for local labor market effects of NAFTA. *Review of Economics and Statistics* 98(4): 728–41.

Harrup, A., R. Whelan, and P. Vieira. 2018. Trump's goal for NAFTA rewrite looks unattainable in 2018: Mexican economy minister Ildefonso Guajardo says he expects negotiations to go beyond May 18. *Wall Street Journal*, May 16. Retrieved from www.wsj.com/articles/mexico-doesnt-see-nafta-talks-wrapping-up-before-deadline-1526389121.

Ibarra, C. A., and J. Ros. 2019. The decline of the labor income share in Mexico, 1990–2015. *World Development* 122: 570–84.

Miller, S. 2018. Investor-state dispute settlement faces hurdles on the road ahead. *CSIS Trade Vistas*, May 10. Retrieved from https://tradevistas.csis.org/investor-state-dispute-settlement-faces-hurdles-road-ahead/.

Moreno-Brid, J. C. 2013. Industrial policy: A missing link in Mexico's quest for export-led growth. *Latin American Policy* 4(2): 216–37.

Moreno-Brid, J. C., R. A. Blecker, I. Salat, and J. Sanchez. 2018. Modernización del TLCAN y sus implicaciones para el desarrollo de la economía mexicana [Modernization of NAFTA and its implications for the development of the Mexican economy]. *Revista de Economía Mexicana = UNAM Yearbook*, Year 3, no. 3: 249–98.

Moreno-Brid, J. C., and J. Ros. 2009. *Development and Growth in the Mexican Economy: A Historical Perspective*. New York: Oxford University Press.

Moreno-Brid, J. C., J. Santamaría, and J. C. R. Valdivia. 2005. Industrialization and economic growth in Mexico after NAFTA: The road travelled. *Development and Change* 36(6): 1095–1119.

Piketty, T. 2014. *Capital in the Twenty-First Century*. Cambridge, MA: Harvard University Press.

Public Citizen. 2018. Investor-state dispute settlement (ISDS): Extraordinary corporate powers in "trade" deals. Retrieved from www.citizen.org/our-work/globalization-and-trade/investor-state-system.

Rodrik, D. 2014. Mexico's growth problem. *Project Syndicate* (online), November 13. Retrieved from www.project-syndicate.org/commentary/mexico-growth-problem-by-dani-rodrik-2014-11.

Romalis, J. 2007. NAFTA's and CUSFTA's impact on international trade. *Review of Economics and Statistics* 89(3): 416–35.

United States Trade Representative (USTR). 2017. Summary of objectives for the NAFTA renegotiation. Updated, November. USTR, Washington, DC.

Whalen, J. 2018. Trump's USMCA delivers big wins to drugmakers, oil companies and tech firms. *Washington Post*, October 2. Retrieved from www.washingtonpost.com/business/economy/trumps-usmca-delivers-big-wins-to-drugmakers-oil-companies-and-tech-firms/2018/10/02/2d68ad10-c66f-11e8-b1ed-1d2d65b86doc_story.html.

Zepeda, E., T. A. Wise, and K. P. Gallagher. 2009. *Rethinking Trade Policy for Development: Lessons from Mexico under NAFTA.* Carnegie Policy Outlook, December. Washington, DC: Carnegie Endowment for International Peace.

Zumbrun, J. 2018a. Trump's NAFTA rewrite holds promise for labor unions. *Wall Street Journal*, August 30. Retrieved from www.wsj.com/articles/trumps-nafta-rewrite-holds-promise-for-labor-unions-1535653247.

———. 2018b. What the U.S.-Mexico trade pact says. *Wall Street Journal*, August 27. Retrieved from www.wsj.com/articles/what-the-u-s-mexico-trade-pact-says-1535403635.

Zumbrun, J., and R. Whelan. 2018. U.S., Mexico could resolve issues holding up NAFTA talks as early as Monday. *Wall Street Journal*, August 26. Retrieved from www.wsj.com/articles/u-s-mexico-could-resolve-issues-holding-up-nafta-talks-as-early-as-monday-1535307970.

CHAPTER 13

Almaguer, T. 1994. *Racial Fault Lines: The Historical Origins of White Supremacy in California.* Berkeley: University of California Press.

America's changing colors: What will the U.S. be like when whites are no longer the majority? 1990. *Time*, April 9.

Babbit, B. 1983. Quoted in G. A. Geyer, States conduct own foreign policy. *Houston Post*, November 10. Retrieved from www.csmonitor.com/1985/0919/erace.html.

Buchanan, P. J. 2007. *State of Emergency: The Third World Invasion and Conquest of America.* New York: St. Martin's Press.

Chapman, L. 1992. Quoted in William Langewiesche, The border (part two): A vast and silent invasion. *Atlantic Monthly* 269(5): 53–92. Retrieved from https://www.theatlantic.com/past/docs/issues/92may/border2.htm.

Dunn, T. J. 1996. *The Militarization of the U.S.-Mexico Border, 1978–1990: Low Intensity Conflict Doctrine Comes Home.* Austin: University of Texas Press, 1996.

Ganz, J. 2018. Trump's new target in the politics of fear: Citizenship. *New York Times,* July 23. Retrieved from www.nytimes.com/2018/07/23/opinion/trump-birthright-citizenship-mccarthy.html.

Geyer, G. A. 1983. States conduct own foreign policy. *Houston Post,* November 10, 13.

Gomez, L. 2007. *Manifest Destinies: The Making of the Mexican-American Race.* New York: New York University Press.

Hayes-Bautista, D. E., W. Schink, and J. Chapa. 1988. *The Burden of Support: Young Latinos in an Aging Society.* Stanford, CA: Stanford University Press.

Hernández, K. L. 2010. *Migra! A History of the Border Patrol.* Berkeley: University of California Press.

Huntington, S. 1996. *The Clash of Civilizations and the Remaking of the World Order.* New York: Simon & Schuster.

———. 2004a. The Hispanic challenge. *Foreign Policy* 14 (March–April): 30–45.

———. 2004b. *Who Are We? The Challenges to America's National Identity.* New York: Simon & Schuster.

Kennedy, P. 1987. *The Rise and Fall of Great Powers: Economic Change and Military Conflict from 1500–2000.* New York: Random House.

———. 1993. *Preparing for the 21st Century.* New York: Random House.

Klein, E. 2018. White threat in a browning America: How demographic change is fracturing our politics. *Vox,* July 30. Retrieved from https://www.vox.com/policy-and-politics/2018/7/30/17505406/trump-obama-race-politics-immigration.

Lamm, R. D. 1985. The melting pot: Half empty? *Christian Science Monitor,* September 19. Retrieved from www.csmonitor.com/1985/0919/erace.html.

Langewiesche, W. 1992. The border (part two): A vast and silent invasion. *Atlantic Monthly* 269(5): 53–92. Retrieved from www.theatlantic.com/past/docs/issues/92may/border2.htm.

Miller, H. 2018. Arizona lawmaker: Immigration a "threat" because "there aren't enough white kids." *Huffington Post,* June 14.

Montejano, D. 1987. *Anglos and Mexicans in the Making of Texas.* Austin: University of Texas Press.

———. 1999. On the future of Anglo-Mexican relations in the United States. In D. Montejano, ed., *Chicano Politics and Society in the Late Twentieth Century,* 234–57. Austin: University of Texas Press.

Operation blockade. 1993. *El Paso Times,* September 29, 1.

Phillips, K. 1969. *The Emerging Republican Majority.* New Rochelle, NY: Arlington House.

Saenz, R. 2018. Declining white population is spawning fear, bias. *San Antonio Express-News,* July 21. Retrieved from https://www.mysanantonio.com/opinion/commentary/article/Declining-white-population-is-spawning-fears-bias-13092533.php.

Sheer, R. 1978. Colby calls Mexico bigger threat than Russia. *Los Angeles Times,* June 6, 11.

Tavernise, S. 2018. Fewer births than deaths among whites in majority of U.S. states. *New York Times,* June 20. Retrieved from www.nytimes.com/2018/06/20/us/white-minority-population.html.

Weinberger, C., and P. Schweizer. 1996. *The Next War.* Washington, DC: Gateway Books.

CHAPTER 14

Bakhtin, M. [1979] 2008. *Estética de la creación verbal* [Aesthetics of verbal art]. Mexico City: Siglo XXI.
Bhabha, H. K., ed. 1990. *Nation and Narration.* Abingdon: Routledge.
Brading, D. 1995. Patriotismo y nacionalismo en la historia de México [Patriotism and nationalism in the history of Mexico]. *AHí Actas* 12: 1–18. Retrieved from https://cvc.cervantes.es/literatura/aih/pdf/12/aih_12_6_005.pdf.
Duranti, A. 1997. *Linguistic Anthropology.* Cambridge: Cambridge University Press.
EFE Agencia. 2019. Acusan a AMLO de mentir a sus seguidores sobre respuesta a los ataques de Trump contra México [They accuse AMLO of lying to his followers about the response to Trump's attacks against Mexico]. *El Diario,* April 31. Retrieved from www.msn.com/es-us/noticias/mexico/acusan-a-amlo-de-mentir-a-sus-seguidores-sobre-respuesta-a-los-ataques-de-trump-contra-m%C3%A9xico/ar-BBVsjws?li=BBqdmGW&ocid=iehp&%252525 25200cid=slider#page=2.
Guillen López, T. 2018. Quoted in L. Santiago and C. E. Shoichet, Trump says caravan migrants are turning back. Mexico says most are still at the border. CNN World, December 12. Retrieved from https://edition.cnn.com/2018/12/11/americas/mexico-caravan-trump/index.html.
Lomnitz, C. 2010. Por mi raza hablará el nacionalismo revolucionario (arqueología de la unidad nacional) [For my race will speak revolutionary nationalism (archaeology of national unity)]. *Nexos,* February 1. Retrieved from www.nexos.com.mx/?p=13506.
———. 2016. *La nación desdibujada: México en trece ensayos* [The nation blurred: Mexico in thirteen trials]. Mexico City: Malpaso.
López Obrador, A. M. 2019. Quoted in R. Jardínez Hernández, A mano alzada pide AMLO decider sobre respuesta a Trump [A show of hands asks AMLO to decide on a response to Trump]. W Radio, April 29. Retrieved from http://wradio.com.mx/radio/2019/03/30/nacional/1553908336_432908.html.
Meyer, L. 2006. Estados Unidos y la evolución del nacionalismo defensivo mexicano [The United States and the evolution of Mexican defensive nationalism]. *Foro Internacional* 46(3): 421–64. Retrieved from www.redalyc.org/articulo.oa?id=59918501.
Morelos, J. M. 1813. *Sentimientos de la nación* [Feelings of the nation]. Retrieved from www.ordenjuridico.gob.mx/Constitucion/1813.pdf.

CHAPTER 15

Alvarez, R. M., and T. L. Butterfield. 2000. The resurgence of nativism in California? The case of proposition 187 and illegal immigration. *Social Science Quarterly* 81(1): 167–79. DOI:10.2307/42864374.

Associated Press. 1993. Board in Miami repeals an English-only law. *New York Times*, May 19. Retrieved from www.nytimes.com/1993/05/19/us/board-in-miami-repeals-an-english-only-law.html.

———. 2017. Miami-Dade officials approve decision against "sanctuary city" designation. Fox News, February 18. Retrieved from www.foxnews.com/us/2017/02/18/miami-dade-officials-approve-decision-against-sanctuary-city-designation.html.

Barry, E. 2006. City's immigration law turns back clock: Latinos leave Hazleton, Pa., in droves in the old coal town's crackdown. *Los Angeles Times*, November 9, A10. Retrieved from www.latimes.com/archives/la-xpm-2006-nov-09-na-hazleton9-story.html.

Beckett, K. 1997. *Making Crime Pay: Law and Order in Contemporary American Politics*. New York: Oxford University Press.

Birkbeck, M. 2007. Crowd shows Hazleton mayor the love: Several hundred people mass in support of Barletta and his illegal immigrant crackdown. *Morning Call* (Allentown, PA), June 4.

Bonilla-Silva, E. 2003. "New racism," color-blind racism, and the future of whiteness in America. In E. Bonilla-Silva and A. W. Doane, eds., *White Out: The Continuing Significance of Racism*, 271–84. New York: Routledge.

Brubaker, R. 2002. Ethnicity without groups. *European Journal of Sociology/Archives européennes de sociologie* 43(2): 163–89.

Burke, M. 2016. Activity among white supremacists continues to surge. *USA Today*, June 16. Retrieved from www.usatoday.com/story/news/nation/2016/06/16/activity-among-white-supremacists-continues-surge/85931440/.

Calavita, K. 1996. The new politics of immigration: Balanced-budget conservatism and the symbolism of Proposition 187. *Social Problems* 43: 284–305.

Carroll, R. 2016. "You were born in a Taco Bell": Trump's rhetoric fuels school bullies across US. *The Guardian*, June 9. Retrieved from www.theguardian.com/us-news/2016/jun/09/california-primary-trump-rhetoric-school-bully.

Chavez, L. R. 2001. *Covering Immigration: Popular Images and the Politics of the Nation*. Berkeley: University of California Press.

———. 2008. *The Latino Threat: Constructing Immigrants, Citizens, and the Nation*. Palo Alto, CA: Stanford University Press.

Cooney, L. 2010. Local author bases stories on growing up in Hazleton. *Standard-Speaker*, January 11.

Coser, L. A., ed. [1956] 1998. *The Functions of Social Conflict*. International Library of Sociology, vol. 9. New York: Routledge.

Easton, D., and J. Dennis. 1969. *Children in the Political System*. New York: McGraw-Hill.

Edelman, M. 1977. *Political Language: Words That Succeed and Policies That Fail*. New York: Academic Press.

Engstrom, D. W. 1997. *Presidential Decision Making Adrift: The Carter Administration and the Mariel Boatlift*. Lanham, MD: Rowman & Littlefield.

Fennick, R. 2007. Fox's visit offers best incentive to hit the polls. *Times Leader*, November 4. Retrieved from www.timesleader.com/?s=Fox+visit+best+incentive+to+hit+the+polls.

Flores, R. D. 2014. In the eye of the storm: How did Hazleton's restrictive immigration ordinance affect local interethnic relations?" *American Behavioral Scientist* 58(13): 1743–63.

———. 2018. Can elites shape public attitudes toward immigrants? Evidence from the 2016 U.S. presidential election. *Social Forces* 96(4). DOI.org/10.1093/sf/soy001.

Fox, L. 2015. South Boston brothers held on high bail in alleged hate crime. *Boston Globe*, November 26. Retrieved from www.bostonglobe.com/metro/2015/11/25/south-boston-brothers-held-high-bail-hate-crime/ExrzAn4GAI94aqVVXBB6UM/story.html.

Haberman, M. 2016. Donald Trump's immigration message may resound in New Hampshire. *New York Times*, February 5. Retrieved from www.nytimes.com/2016/02/06/us/politics/donald-trumps-immigration-message-may-resound-in-new-hampshire.html.

Haller, W., A. Portes, and S. M. Lynch. 2011. Dreams fulfilled, dreams shattered: Determinants of segmented assimilation in the second generation. *Social Forces* 89(3): 733–62.

Hart, A. 2018. "She represents California, not Arkansas": Feinstein's rival presses her on immigration. *Sacramento Bee*, January 17. Retrieved from www.sacbee.com/news/politics-government/capitol-alert/article195004389.html.

Hyman, H. H. 1959. *Political Socialization*. New York: Free Press.

Jordan, M. 2006. States and towns attempt to draw the line on illegal immigration. *Wall Street Journal*, July 12. Retrieved from www.wsj.com/articles/SB115266944904204220.

Longazel, J. 2013. Moral panic as racial degradation ceremony: Racial stratification and the local-level backlash against Latino/a immigrants. *Punishment and Society* 15: 96.

Lopez, I. H. 1997. *White by Law: The Legal Construction of Race*. New York: New York University Press.

Maghbouleh, N. 2017. *The Limits of Whiteness: Iranian Americans and the Everyday Politics of Race*. Palo Alto, CA: Stanford University Press.

Marrow, H. B. 2011. *New Destination Dreaming: Immigration, Race, and Legal Status in the Rural American South*. Palo Alto, CA: Stanford University Press.

Mendelberg, T. 2001. *The Race Card: Campaign Strategy, Implicit Messages, and the Norm of Equality*. Princeton, NJ: Princeton University Press.

Portes, A., and R. G. Rumbaut. 2001. *Legacies: The Story of the Immigrant Second Generation*. Berkeley: University of California Press.

Portes, A., and A. Stepick. 1993. *City on the Edge: The Transformation of Miami*. Berkeley: University of California Press.

Powell, M., and M. García. 2006. Pa. city puts illegal immigrants on notice. *Washington Post*, August 22.

Republican National Committee. 2013. Growth and opportunity project. July 16. Retrieved from https://gop.com/growth-and-opportunity-project.

Romero, M. 2016. How Latino voters and legislators are changing California politics. *Los Angeles Times*, September 27. Retrieved from www.latimes.com/opinion/op-ed/la-oe-romero-latino-impact-on-california-democrats-20160927-snap-story.html.

Rove, K. 2013. More white votes alone won't save the GOP. To win the presidency in 2016, the party needs to do better with Hispanics. *Wall Street Journal,* June 26. Retrieved from www.wsj.com/articles/SB10001424127887323 8739045785694806967466 50.

Santa Ana, O. 2002. *Brown Tide Rising: Metaphoric Representations of Latinos in Contemporary American Public Discourse.* Austin: University of Texas Press.

Sears, D. O. 1993. Symbolic Politics: A Socio-Psychological Theory. In S. Iyengar and W. J. McGuire, eds., *Explorations in Political Psychology,* 113–49. Durham, NC: Duke University Press.

Segarra, L. M. 2017. Donald Trump: Puerto Rico wants "everything to be done for them." *Time,* September 30. Retrieved from http://time.com/4963903 /donald-trump-puerto-rican-leaders-want-everything-to-be-done-for-them/.

Tarone, L. A. 2006. Groundbreaking: After passionate debate, Hazleton passes illegal immigration law. *Standard-Speaker,* July 14. Retrieved from http:// forum.skyscraperpage.com/showpost.php?p=2181238&postcount=35.

Trump, D. 2015. Presidential announcement speech. June 16. Retrieved from http://time.com/3923128/donald-trump-announcement-speech/.

———. 2018. Remarks by President Trump after review of border wall prototypes. White House Portal. Retrieved from www.whitehouse.gov/briefings-statements/remarks-president-trump-review-border-wall-prototypes-san-diego-ca/.

Waters, M. C., and P. Kasinitz. 2015. The war on crime and the war on immigrants: Racial and legal exclusion in 21st century United States. In N. Foner and P. Simon, eds., *Fear, Anxiety, and National Identity: Immigration and Belonging in North America and Europe,* 115–43. New York: Russell Sage Foundation.

CHAPTER 16

Arington, M. 1990. English-only laws and direct legislation: The battle in the states over language minority rights. *Journal of Law & Politics* 7: 325.

Barreto, M. A., S. Manzano, R. Ramirez, and K. Rim. 2009. Mobilization, participation, and solidaridad: Latino participation in the 2006 immigration protest rallies. *Urban Affairs Review* 44(5): 736–64.

Barreto, M. A., and G. M. Segura. 2014. *Latino America: How America's Most Dynamic Population Is Poised to Transform the Politics of the Nation.* New York: Public Affairs.

Beltrán, C. 2010. *The Trouble with Unity: Latino Politics and the Creation of Identity.* New York: Oxford University Press.

Citrin, J., and D. O. Sears. 2014. *American Identity and the Politics of Multiculturalism.* New York: Cambridge University Press.

Cobas, J. A., J. Duany, and J. R. Feagin. 2016. *How the United States Racializes Latinos: White Hegemony and Its Consequences.* New York: Routledge.

Garcia-Rios, S., F. Pedraza, and B. Wilcox-Archuleta. 2018. Direct and indirect xenophobic attacks: Unpacking portfolios of identity. *Political Behavior* 41(3): 1–24.

Hajnal, Z., and M. Baldassare. 2001. *Finding Common Ground: Racial and Ethnic Attitudes in California.* San Francisco: Public Policy Institute of California.

HoSang, D. 2010. *Racial Propositions: Ballot Initiatives and the Making of Postwar California.* Berkeley: University of California Press.

Huddy, L., S. Feldman, and F. Cassese. 2007. On the distinct political effects of anxiety and anger. In G. E. Marcus, W. R. Neuman, M. MacKuen, and A. N. Crigler, eds., *The Affect Effect: Dynamics of Emotion in Political Thinking and Behavior,* 202–30. Chicago: University of Chicago Press.

Lavariega Monforti, J., and G. R. Sanchez. 2010. The politics of perception: An investigation of the presence and sources of perceptions of internal discrimination among Latinos. *Social Science Quarterly* 91(1): 245–65.

Marcus, G. E., W. R. Neuman, and M. MacKuen. 2000. *Affective Intelligence and Political Judgment.* Chicago: University of Chicago Press.

Masuoka, N., and J. Junn. 2013. *The Politics of Belonging: Race, Public Opinion, and Immigration.* Chicago: University of Chicago Press.

Mora, G. C. 2014. *Making Hispanics: How Activists, Bureaucrats, and Media Constructed a New American.* Chicago: University of Chicago Press.

Neuman, W. R., G. E. Marcus, A. Crigler, and M. MacKuen. 2007. Theorizing affect's effects. In W. R. Neuman, G. E. Marcus, A. Crigler, and M. MacKuen, eds., *The Affect Effect: Dynamics of Emotion in Political Thinking and Behavior,* 1–20. Chicago: University of Chicago Press.

Ortiz, V., and E. Telles. 2012. Racial identity and racial treatment of Mexican Americans. *Race and Social Problems* 4(1): 41–56.

Padilla, F. M. 1985. *Latino Ethnic Consciousness: The Case of Mexican Americans and Puerto Ricans in Chicago.* Notre Dame, IN: University of Notre Dame Press.

Pedraza, F. I., and M. A. Osorio. 2017. Courted and deported: The salience of immigration issues and avoidance of police, health care, and education services among Latinos. *Aztlan: A Journal of Chicano Studies* 42(2). Retrieved from www.franciscoipedraza.com/wp-content/uploads/PedrazaOsorio_Aztlan Acceptance2017.pdf.

Perlmann, J. 2005. *Italians Then, Mexicans Now: Immigrant Origins and the Second-Generation Progress, 1890–2000.* New York: Russell Sage Foundation.

Portes, A., and R. L. Bach. 1985. *Latin Journey: Cuban and Mexican Immigrants in the United States.* Berkeley: University of California Press.

Ramirez, R. 2013. *Mobilizing Opportunities: The Evolving Latino Electorate and the Future of American Politics.* Charlottesville: University of Virginia Press.

Rumbaut, R. G. 2009. Pigments of our imagination: On the racialization and racial identities of "Hispanics" and "Latinos." In J. Cobas, J. A. Duany, and J. Feagin, eds., *How the United States Racializes Latinos: White Hegemony and Its Consequences,* 15–36. New York: Routledge.

Sanchez, G. R. 2006. The role of group consciousness in Latino public opinion. *Political Research Quarterly* 59(3): 435–46.

Sanchez, J. R. 2007. *Boricua Power: A Political History of Puerto Ricans in the United States.* New York: New York University Press.

Santa Ana, O. 2017. The rhetoric of our celebrity demagogue. *Aztlan: A Journal of Chicano Studies* 42(2): 267–83.
Tajfel, H., and J.C. Turner. 1979. An integrative theory of intergroup conflict. *Social Psychology of Intergroup Relations* 33(47): 74.
Telles, E.M., and V. Ortiz. 2008. *Generations of Exclusion: Mexican-Americans.* New York: Russell Sage Foundation.
Valdez, Z. 2016. Agency and structure in panethnic identity formation: The case of Latino/a entrepreneurs. In J. Cobas, J.A. Duany, and J. Feagin, eds., *How the United States Racializes Latinos: White Hegemony and Its Consequences,* 200–213. New York: Routledge.
Valentino, N.A., T. Brader, E.W. Groenendyk, K. Gregorowicz, and V.L. Hutchings. 2011. Election night's alright for fighting: The role of emotions in political participation. *Journal of Politics* 73(1): 156–70.
Valentino, N.A., V.L. Hutchings, A.J. Banks, and A.K. Davis. 2008. Is a worried citizen a good citizen? Emotions, political information seeking, and learning via the internet. *Political Psychology* 29(2): 247–73.
Zepeda-Milan, C. 2017. *Latino Mass Mobilization: Immigration, Racialization, and Activism.* New York: Cambridge University Press.

CHAPTER 17

Abrajano, M.A., and M. Alvarez. 2010. *New Faces, New Voices: The Hispanic Electorate in America.* Princeton, NJ: Princeton University Press.
Abrajano, M., and Z. Hajnal. 2015. *White Backlash: Race, Immigration, and Party Politics.* Princeton, NJ: Princeton University Press.
Bobo, L., and D. Johnson. 2000. Racial attitudes in a prismatic metropolis: Mapping identity, stereotypes, competition, and views on affirmative action. In L. Bobo et al., eds., *Prismatic Metropolis: Inequality in Los Angeles,* 81–163. New York: Russell Sage Foundation.
California Department of Finance. 2019. Enacted Budget. Retrieved from www.ebudget.ca.gov/.
Fellowes, M.C., and G. Rowe. 2004. Politics and the new American welfare state. *American Journal of Political Science* 48: 362–73.
Fraga, L., J. Garcia, R. Hero, M. Jones-Correa, V. Martinez-Ebers, and G. Segura. 2012. *Latinos in the New Millennium: An Almanac of Opinion, Behavior, and Policy Preferences.* New York: Cambridge University Press.
Hajnal, Z., and M.R. Rivera. 2014. Immigration, Latinos, and white partisan politics: The new democratic defection. *American Journal of Political Science* 58(4): 773–89.
Hero, R.E., and R.R. Preuhs. 2006. From civil rights to multiculturalism and welfare for immigrants: An egalitarian tradition across American states? *Du Bois Review* 3(2): 317–40.
Hopkins, D.J. 2010. Politicized places: Explaining where and when immigrants provoke local opposition. *American Political Science Review* 104(1): 40–60.
Lee, T. 2000. Racial attitudes and the color line(s) at the close of the twentieth century. In P. Ong, ed., *The State of Asian Pacific Americans: Race Relations,* 103–8. Los Angeles: LEAP.

Monogan, J. E. 2013. The politics of immigrant policy in the 50 U.S. states, 2005–2011. *Journal of Public Policy* 33(1): 35–64.

National Conference of State Legislators (NCSL). 2012–18. State laws related to immigration and immigrants. Retrieved from www.ncsl.org/research/immigration/state-laws-related-to-immigration-and-immigrants.aspx.

Rivera, M. 2015. Immigration, public opinion, and state policy responsiveness. PhD diss.

Soss, J., R. C. Fording, and S. F. Schram. 2008. The color of devolution: Race, federalism, and the politics of social control. *American Journal of Political Science* 52(3): 536–53.

Contributors

James D. Bachmeier, Temple University
Matt Barreto, University of California, Los Angeles
Frank D. Bean, University of California, Irvine
Hiram Beltrán-Sánchez, University of California, Los Angeles
Robert A. Blecker, American University
Susan K. Brown, University of California, Irvine
Jorge Carrillo, El Colegio de la Frontera Norte
René D. Flores, University of Chicago
Patricia Gándara, University of California, Los Angeles
Victor M. García-Guerrero, El Colegio de México
Silvia E. Giorguli, El Colegio de México
Yatziry Govea-Vargas, El Colegio de México
Angela E. Gutierrez, University of California, Los Angeles
Zoltan L. Hajnal, University of California, San Diego
Raúl Hinojosa-Ojeda, University of California, Los Angeles
Rafael Elías López Arellano, CIESAS
Regina Martínez Casas, Center for Research and Advanced Studies in Social Anthropology
Claudia Masferrer, El Colegio de México
Douglas S. Massey, Princeton University
David Montejano, University of California, Berkeley

Jorge Mora-Rivera, Instituto Tecnológico de Monterrey
Juan Carlos Moreno-Brid, Universidad Nacional Autónoma de México
Gary Orfield, University of California, Los Angeles
Pia M. Orrenius, Federal Reserve Bank of Dallas
Megan Reynolds, University of Utah
Fernando Riosmena, University of Colorado, Boulder
Sherman Robinson, Peterson Institute for International Economics
Isabel Salat, Barcelona Graduate School of Economics
Gary Segura, University of California, Los Angeles
Roberto Suro, University of Southern California
Edward Telles, University of California, Irvine
Karen Thierfelder, US Naval Academy
Justin Vinneau, University of California, Berkeley
Antonio Yúnez-Naude, El Colegio de México
Madeline Zavodny, University of North Florida
René Zenteno, University of Texas, San Antonio

Index

ability/disability, 275
ACA (Affordable Care Act), 83
acculturation, 82
ACLU (American Civil Liberties Union), 216
ACS (American Community Survey), 19, 20, 103, 261n3(ch7), 262nn6,15
affirmative action, Proposition 209 (California, 1996), 268n1(ch16), 281
Affordable Care Act (ACA), 83
Africa: African national-origin quotas, 120, 276; Immigration and Nationality Act of 1956 (INA), 33
Agency for Support and Services to Agricultural Marketing/Agencia de Servicios a la Commercialización y Desarrollo de Mercados Agropecuarios (ASERCA). *See* ASERCA (Agencia de Servicios a la Comercialización y Desarrollo de Mercados Agropecuarios/ Support and Services to Agricultural Marketing)
age structure, demographic transition and, 273
agglomeration models, 265n3(ch11)
aggregates by scenario, GDP and, 143 table9.2
AGR (average growth rate), 122 table8.1, 150, 264n7
agricultural commodities in Mexico, 150 table10.1

agricultural imports from Mexico, 278. *See also* marketing supports
agricultural output, 151, 259n2(ch1), 271
agricultural producers, 273, 283. *See also* commercial farmers; subsistence farmers
agricultural production: NAFTA and, 131; US-Mexico migration and trade in, 149–51. *See also* trade in agriculture and US-Mexico migration
agricultural sector jobs, 262n15
agricultural trade liberalization, 141
agricultural workers, Mexican, crossing into US, 156 fig.10.4
Agriculture and Fisheries Information System/Servicio de Información Agroalimentaria y Pesquera (SIAP), 264n7
Agrifood Information Consulting System/ Sistema de Información Agroalimentaria de Consulta (SIACON), 153, 156
agroecological conditions, 273
alternative energies, 161 table11.1, 162fig.11.1
alternative immigration, NAFTA and, 142–46
Alvarez, Ramon, 265n4(ch11)
American Civil Liberties Union (ACLU), 216
American Community Survey (ACS), 19, 20, 103, 261n3(ch7), 262nn6,15

325

326 | Index

AMIA (Asociación Mexicana de la Industria Automotriz/Mexican Association of the Automotive Industry), 162 fig.11.1, 167 fig.11.3, 169
amnesty program, 276. *See also* DACA (Deferred Action for Childhood Arrivals); DAPA (Deferred Action for Parents of Americans)
Amuedo-Dorantes, Catalina, 71
anger, 231–32, 234 table16.2, 237–40, 239 fig.16.3
Anglo-Saxon Protestants, 3–4, 192, 278
annexation of northern Mexico, 10, 193, 271
annual inflow, 33, 271, 277, 279, 280. *See also* in-migration
"Antibilingual" referendum (Miami, Dade County), 222
anti-immigrant backlash, 244–54; California and, 252–53; conclusion, 253–54; defined, 271; evidence of broader policy backlash, 247–50; immigrants' role in backlash equation, 250–51; measuring immigrant context, 247; overview, 11, 244; possibilities of broader backlash, 245–47; test of racial threat story, 250. *See also* white backlash
anti-immigrant politics. *See* immigrant scapegoating by political elites; Latino responses to anti-immigrant politics; nativist appeal, historical/political contexts of Trump's
anxiety, 18, 195, 220, 223, 254, 275, 281, 283. *See also* threats
apprehensions of migrants: border militarization and, 38, 40, 41; Border Patrol and, 34, 73 fig.4.3, 105 fig.7.2, 272; Bracero Program and, 35; from Central America, 56; cost of living, 139; data on, 262n9; decline in, 141; feedback loop between border enforcement and, 36–37, 37 fig.2.2; immigration enforcement and, 72, 81, 276; intent to return after repatriation, 74; NAFTA and, 135 fig.9.2; new unauthorized Mexican immigrant workers and, 105 fig.7.2, 136 table9.1; Operation Wetback and, 34; peak year for, 136 table9.1; repatriation after, 66; risk perception, 70; Trump on Mexico's, 211; US/Mexico GDP per, 135 fig.9.2
Arizona, 193, 195, 197, 234 table16.2, 237, 238 fig.16.2, 271

Arrellano, Rafael Elías López, 10, 204–13
ASERCA (Agencia de Servicios a la Comercialización y Desarrollo de Mercados Agropecuarios/Support and Services to Agricultural Marketing), 154–55, 271. *See also* marketing supports; neoliberalism; trade liberalization
Asia: Asian national-origin quotas, 120, 276; Asians, 95, 273; Immigration and Nationality Act of 1956 (INA), 33. *See also specific countries*
Asociación Mexicana de la Industria Automotriz/Mexican Association of the Automotive Industry (AMIA), 162 fig.11.1, 167 fig.11.3, 169
assembly operations: automation, 171–72; CKD and, 160; FDI and, 163, 265n3(ch11); Fordism, 171; maquiladora system and, 278; value chains and, 272, 284. *See also* maquiladoras
asylum crisis, 57, 209, 271, 282
Audi AG, 167 fig.11.3
Australia, 260n6, 280
Austria, 280
Automex, 160
automotive industry: competitiveness, 160; digital transformation of, 277; NAFTA and, 160; steel production and, 265n2(ch11). *See also* CKD (Completely Knocked Down); Mexican automotive industry (MAI); *specific automotive manufacturers*
automotive sector, US-Mexico, 159–73; automotive sales in Mexico, 162 fig.11.1; conclusion, 172; exponential new technologies, 170–72; FDI by country of origin, 163 fig.11.2; importance of, 159–64; integration of automotive chains, 164–65, 166 table11.2; NAFTA paradox, 169–70; overview, 159; rules of origin, 178, 180, 181, 282; Technological Development in, 160; technology level and productivity, 166–69
automotive value chains, 164, 272, 275. *See also* global value chains; value chains
autonomous management trends, 277
auto parts, 165, 265n3(ch11), 272. *See also* OEM (original equipment manufacturer)
Autor, David, 19, 20
average annual employment, 262n10, 266n6(ch12)
average growth rate (AGR), 122 table8.1, 150, 264n7

Babbit, Bruce, 194
baby boom cohort, 95, 114, 121–23, 134, 272
Bachmeier, James D., 7, 113–25
backward linkages, 178, 272
Baja California, 7, 89–90, 92, 99, 100
Bajío (west central) mega region, 167, 167 fig.11.3, 168 fig.11.4
balance of payments, 283
ballot initiatives, 10, 268n1(ch16), 281. *See also* Proposition 187 (California, 1994); Proposition 209 (California, 1996); Proposition 227 (California, 1998)
Banco de Información Económica/Repository of Economic Information (BIE), 156 fig.10.4
bank deregulation, 280
Bank of Mexico (Banxico), 153 fig.10.2, 177 fig.12.2, 264n3
Banxico (Bank of Mexico). *See* Bank of Mexico (Banxico)
Barletta, Lou, 216, 219–20
Barreto, Matt, 11, 227–43
barriers on trade, 281, 284
Bean, Frank D., 7, 113–25
Belgium, 280
Belize, 266n14(ch14)
Beltrán-Sánchez, Hiram, 7, 78–87
berry production, 264n2
Bhabha, H.K., 205
BIE (Banco de Información Económica/Repository of Economic Information), 156 fig.10.4
bilingual education, 268n1(ch16), 281. *See also* Proposition 227 (California, 1998)
biliteracy, seal of, 99
biodiversity, 273
biotechnology, 161 table11.1, 276
BIP (Border Industrialization Program of 1965), 136 table9.1, 137, 138, 272
birthrate: in Central America, 111; demographic transition and, 273; family migrations and, 263n5; in Mexico, 104, 262n14
blacks, 194, 195, 197, 216, 273
Blecker, Robert A., 9, 174–88
BLS (US Bureau of Labor Statistics), 262n10, 265n5(ch12)
BMW, 167, 167 fig.11.3
Bolshevik Revolution, 193
border controls of unauthorized migration: IRCA and, 276; Light Up the Border campaign, 198–99; national security narrative, 194–96; political campaigns and, 202; rural migration and, 156–57. *See also* apprehensions of migrants; removals of migrants
border crossings: costs of, 156; coyote services, 39–40; death rates from, 40; decrease in, 136 table9.1; tracking of, 272; zero tolerance policies and, 285. *See also* Border Survey of Mexican Migration/Encuesta Sobre Migración en la Frontera Norte de México (EMIF)
border enforcement: call for National Guard troops for, 199; causal effect on first undocumented trips, 42, 42 fig.2.4; defined, 272; ending of Mexican unauthorized migration and, 70–71; feedback loop between apprehensions and, 37 fig.2.2; post-9/11 legislation and, 263n1; unauthorized migration and, 276. *See also* immigration enforcement
Border Industrialization Program of 1965 (BIP), 136 table9.1, 137, 138, 272
border militarization, consequences of, 32–46; border enforcement and, 272; context for migrant decision making, 41–44; Latino threat narrative, 35–38, 195; militarization consequences, 38–41; overview, 32–33; train wreck metaphor, 44–46; watershed of 1965, 33–35. *See also* border enforcement; Border Patrol
Border Patrol: apprehension and, 34, 105 fig.7.2; apprehensions of migrants, 66, 74; budget of, 32, 37, 38 fig.2.3, 39, 40, 42, 73 fig.4.3; investment in, 72; IRCA and, 276; Latino threat narrative and, 36, 37; Operation Blockade, 195; staffing, 32, 106, 107, 108, 262n14; staff of, 73 fig.4.3; Trump on, 209, 210
Border Survey of Mexican Migrants/Encuesta Sobre Migración en la Frontera Norte de México (EMIF), 63–64, 66, 68 fig.4.2, 69, 72, 76, 272
border wall: Mexican nationalism and, 207–9; support for, 21, 28 table1.3; Trump administration and, 142; Trump and, 5, 46, 113
Borjas, George, 104
Bosch, 167
bottom ninety-nine percenters, 273
Boxer, Barbara, 199
Bracero Agreement, 33

Bracero Program: annual emigration from Mexico during, 64; concerns over, 110; creation of, 6, 137, 194; defined, 33, 272; end of, 33, 34, 37, 111, 120–21, 137; expansion of, 35; GDP and, 135 fig.9.2; Mexican-born population in U.S. during, 51 fig.3.1; timeline, 136 table9.1. *See also* farm labor; H2A visas; temporary foreign worker program
Brazil, 266–67n14(ch14)
Brookings Institution, 89
Brown, Susan K., 7, 113–25
"browning of America" ideology, 200–201, 202
Brunei, 260n6
Buchanan, Pat, 198
Buick, 160
Bush, George H. W., 197
Bush, George W., 136 table9.1, 198
Bush, Jeb, 214
Bustamante, Cruz, 224
buyers: marketing supports for, 155, 278; multinational corporations as, 155, 278

CAIP (Community Adjustment and Investment Program), 263n11
CAIP DEA (Community Adjustment and Investment Program Designated Eligible Areas), 140
Caliendo, L., 265n2(ch12)
California: annexation of northern Mexico and, 193, 271; anti-immigrant backlash in, 11, 252–53; anti-immigrant initiatives, 12; anti-Mexican sentiment in, 198–200, 202; ballot initiatives, 268n1(ch16), 281; Department of Education, 90; family ratio of income by education level, 94 fig.6.3; GDP's annual percentage change in, 115 fig.8.1; immigrant scapegoating in, 10, 223–24; Latino politicians, 223–24; nativist appeal, contexts for Trump's, 198–200; Operation Gatekeeper, 195; Proposition 30, 252–53; as traditional destination, 39, 41; Trump favorability, 237; University of California-Mexico Initiative, 284. *See also* Proposition 187 (California, 1994) and; Proposition 209 (California, 1996); Proposition 227 (California, 1998); Wilson, Pete
Canada: auto part exports, 165; Mexican exports to, 262n12; Mexico's relations with, 6; migration flows and, 50; migration stocks from, 55, 55 table3.2; NAFTA and, 164; as OECD member, 280; refugees in, 56–57; total and foreign-born population of, 54, 54 table3.1; TPP and, 260n6; in trade and production bloc, 132; USMCA and, 181; as WTO member, 285
CAND (Cuban American National Foundation), 222
capital flows, 277, 283. *See also* knowledge capitals
Carrillo, Jorge, 9, 159–73
Carter, Jimmy, 221
Casas, Regina Martínez, 10, 204–13
Catch & Release, 209
CCES (Cooperative Congressional Election Survey), 21, 26
Census Bureau. *See* US Census Bureau
Center for Research and Teaching in Economics/Centro de Investigación y Docencia Económicas (CIDE), 96
Center for US-Mexican Studies (USMEX), 99, 100
Central America: 2016 election anger relationship, 238 fig.16.2; annual growth rates, 60 fig.3.2(B); birthrates, 111; fertility rates, 60 fig.3.2(A); immigrants from, 54; instability in, 111; out-migration from, 140–41, 263n4; response to racism scale in, 233 table16.1, 234 table16.2; total and foreign-born population in, 54 table3.1; Trump favorability, 233; working age population in, 61 fig.3.2(C); xenophobic comments against, 212
Central American flows: across Mexico to US, 6, 49; aging population and, 59; future profile of, 50; migrant caravans, 53, 209; new immigration surpassing Mexico, 272; political turmoil and natural disasters, 56
Centro de Estudios Superiores en Antropología Social (CIESAS), 96
Centro de Investigación y Docencia Económicas/Center for Research and Teaching in Economics (CIDE), 96
Centro mega region, 167, 167 fig.11.3, 168 fig.11.4
CEPAL (Comisión Económica para América Latina y el Caribe/Economic Commission for Latin America and the Caribbean), 170
CGE (computable general equilibrium) model, 130, 142, 263n3, 275, 279, 284
Chapa, Jorge, 202

Chapman, Leonard, 194
Chapultepec Conference of 1946, 136 table9.1
Chavez, L. R., 35
chemical products, 259n2(ch1), 283
Chicago Board of Trade, 149
Child Health Care Program, 246
children of migration, future of, 88–101; conclusion, 100; creation of, 88–89; data collection, 97–98; demonstration projects, 98–100; educational challenges in California, 93–95; educational challenges in Mexico, 91–93; inequality in Mexico and US, 89–91; overview, 88; relationship establishment between US-Mexico institutions, 96–97; University of California-Mexico Initiative, 95–96
Chile: income inequality in, 90, 90 fig.6.1; as OECD member, 280; TPP and, 260n6
China: Chinese imports, 17, 19, 259n1(ch1); export-promotion policies, 186; high-skilled temporary technical workers from, 119; LPRs from, 117, 118 fig.8.2; migration stocks from, 54; nonimmigrant admissions from, 118 fig.8.3; retaliation tariffs on US exports, 184; supply chain comparison to, 168
Chiquiar, D., 262n7
CIDE (Centro de Investigación y Docencia Económicas/Center for Research and Teaching in Economics), 96
CIESAS (Centro de Estudios Superiores en Antropología Social), 96
CIR (comprehensive immigration reform), 136, 142, 143, 143 table9.2
circular migration, 33, 131, 134, 136 table9.1, 272–73, 279
citizenship, 193, 199, 202
civil rights: civil rights legislation, 282; civil rights movement, 33, 197; Civil Rights Project at UCLA, 96; lack of, 45, 225. See also white backlash
CKD (Completely Knocked Down), 159–60
The Clash of Civilizations and the Remaking of the World Order (Huntington), 3, 200–201
clean technologies, 276
Clemens, Michael, 102, 261n1(ch7)
Clinton, Bill, 138
CMPS (Collaborative Multi-Racial Post-Election Survey), 227, 229, 232, 268n2(ch16), 273

cohorts: baby boom cohort, 121, 123, 272; birth cohort size, 104, 107–8; Mexican labor supply cohorts, 70; unauthorized worker migration and, 107 table7.1; of young Central Americans, 59; of young Mexicans, 111; of young working age adults, 59
Colby, William, 194
COLEF (El Colegio de la Frontera Norte), 66, 96
Collaborative Multi-Racial Post-Election Survey (CMPS), 227, 229, 232, 268n2(ch16), 273
Colombia, 266–67n14(ch14)
Colorado, 193, 271
Comisión Económica para América Latina y el Caribe/Economic Commission for Latin America and the Caribbean (CEPAL), 170
commercial farmers, 149, 273, 278. See also marketing supports
communication interactions, 265n3(ch11), 282. See also social media communications; speech acts; speech genres
Community Adjustment and Investment Program Designated Eligible Areas (CAIP DEA), 140
competitiveness: automotive industry and, 160; free competition, 278; less-skilled workers and, 115–17
complementarity in US-Mexico automotive sector, 159–73
Completely Knocked Down (CKD), 159–60
comprehensive immigration reform (CIR), 136, 142, 143, 143 table9.2
computable general equilibrium (CGE) model, 130, 142, 263n3, 275, 279, 284
concomitant impoverishment of employment, 279. See also NAFTA paradox
conditional cash transfer programs, 263n12
Congressional Research Service, 43
connectivity trends, 171, 277
construction industry, US. See US construction industry
consumption: corn and, 151, 273; increased aggregate demand and, 115; intrabranch consumption, 271; patterns of, 170; rural households as unit of, 282; shifts in, 132; in subsistence farming, 283
context of reception, 80, 273, 279
Continental, 167
conventional neoclassical economics, 280
Cooperative Congressional Election Survey (CCES), 21, 26

corn production: corn biodiversity, 157, 273; corn tariffs, 138–39; cropland in, 264n7; imports and exports, 264n8; in Mexico, 131, 148; migration of Mexican farmworkers and, 153 fig.10.2; trade liberalization under NAFTA and, 131, 151–53; volume of imports under/over tariff rate quota, 152 fig.10.1
corrections spending, 251 fig.17.1
cost of living, 261n1(ch7)
COVID-19 pandemic, 157–58, 174, 184
coyote services, 39–40
CPI-W use, 262n10
CPS (Current Population Survey), 103, 261n2(ch6), 261n3(ch7), 262n6, 262n14
crime: criminal justice spending, 248–49; immigrant incarceration rates, 136 table9.1; immigrants and, 266–67n14(ch14), 268nn1–2; newspaper coverage and rates of in Hazleton, PA, 217, 218 fig.15.1, 219; as social problem, 279; zero tolerance policies, 285
Cross-Border Business Pathway, 99–100
Cruz, Ted, 222
Cuba, 220–21
Cuban American National Foundation (CAND), 222
Cuban Americans, 221–22, 224, 233, 234 table16.2, 238 fig.16.2
culture categorization, 281. *See also* racialization; racialized panethnic identity
Curiel, Gonzalo, 193
Current Population Survey (CPS), 103, 261n2(ch6), 261n3(ch7), 262nn6,14
cyber-physical systems, 276
Czech Republic, 280

DACA (Deferred Action for Childhood Arrivals), 100, 136 table9.1, 209
DAPA (Deferred Action for Parents of Americans), 136 table9.1
Dassonevilee, Ruth, 18
Davis, Bob, 259n1(ch1)
DEA (Designated Eligible Areas), 140
declinism, 200
decoupled payments, 154, 273, 281. *See also* PROCAMPO (Programa de Apoyos Directos al Campo/Program for Rural Funding)
Deferred Action for Childhood Arrivals (DACA), 100, 136 table9.1, 209
Deferred Action for Parents of Americans (DAPA), 136 table9.1

deficit spending reduction, 280
deflation, 262n10
De León, Kevin, 223, 224
Delphi, 167
Democratic Party, 202, 209, 226. *See also* Clinton, Bill; Johnson, Lyndon B.; Obama, Barack
demographic factors: baby boom cohort, 272; demographic hump, 131; demographic projections, 50; demographic transition, 69–70, 273; dynamics of, 58, 273; Mexican migration increases and, 121–23. *See also* age structure; baby boom cohort; educational upgrading; fertility decline; fertility transition; sex distribution; territorial location of population
Denmark, 280
Department of Homeland Security (DHS). *See* US Department of Homeland Security (DHS)
dependency ratios, 58, 273
deportations: change in county output under, 144 fig.9.4; children and, 45–46; Operation Wetback, 194; post-9/11 legislation and, 263n1; postwar US-Mexico trade and migration policy initiatives and, 136 table9.1; rural migration and, 156–57; Trump administration and, 142; US/Mexico GDP per, 135 fig.9.2
deregulation, bank, 185, 280
Designated Eligible Areas (DEA), 140
destination countries, 279
developed countries, economic convergence and, 273
developing countries: corn biodiversity and, 273; economic convergence and, 273; OECD and, 280; rural households in, 282. *See also* OECD (Organization for Economic Cooperation and Development); purchasing power parity (PPP); *specific countries*
development policies, 149, 273
DHS (US Department of Homeland Security), 36, 72, 103, 137
Diaz de la Portilla, Miguel, 222
disability/ability, 275, 278
discrimination: CMPS and, 268n2(ch16); internalized group discrimination, 275; national-origins quotas/prohibitions, 276; perceived, 228, 268n3, 281. *See also* reactive ethnicity
discursive acts, defined, 282

dispute settlement panels, WTO and, 285
diversification, 52, 282
diversity: diverse ethnic backgrounds, 280–81; diverse mobility trends, 171, 277; diverse national-origin backgrounds, 280–81; perceived threat of, 284
division of labor concept, 276
domestic produced goods, 278, 280. *See also* marketing supports
Dominican Republic, 216, 218, 224, 234 table16.2, 239, 241
Dorn, D., 20
driver's licenses, 224
drug trade: in hypothetical Mexican crisis scenario, 196; immigrant health and, 82; Trump on, 208–9, 209, 214, 215
dual citizens, defined, 273
Durand, Jorge, 38, 42, 44, 50
duties, trade liberalization and, 284

Eastern European national-origin quotas, 120, 193, 276
Eastern Hemisphere immigration, 276
ecological inference, 260n5(ch2)
econometric estimates, 265n2(ch12)
economic activities diversification, of rural households, 282
Economic Census, 19
Economic Commission for Latin America and the Caribbean. *See* CEPAL (Comisión Económica para América Latina y el Caribe/Economic Commission for Latin America and the Caribbean)
economic conditions, 106, 262n13
economic convergence, 175; defined, 273
economic declines, Great Recession of 2008, 275
economic development and integration, NAFTA and, 132–35
economic downturn, ending of Mexican unauthorized migration and, 69
economic factors, 280
economic growth, Lewis model of, 132–33
economic impacts of migration and trade, Trump Paradox and, 284
economic inequality, 89–90, 273. *See also* income inequality; wage inequality
economic issues, 278; anti-Mexican sentiment and, 199. *See also* Mexican economy
economic policies: market access and, 278; US-Mexico trade deal policies and, 184–87. *See also* OECD (Organization for Economic Cooperation and Development)
Economic Policy Institute (EPI), 139
economic sector, Mexican and US employment by, 133 fig.9.1
economics models, 280. *See also* neoliberalism
education, 235 table16.2; California Department of Education, 90; children of migration and, 91–93, 93–95; degrees of, 273; demographic transition and, 273; educational attainment, 92 fig.6.2, 274; educational benefits of Proposition 187, 268n1(ch16), 281; educational upgrading, 274; high school completion movement, 274; income gap and levels of, 94 fig.6.3; LASANTI and, 88–101; as social category, 275. *See also* higher education
educational upgrading, 121, 274
efficiency, 280. *See also* OECD (Organization for Economic Cooperation and Development)
El Colegio de la Frontera Norte (COLEF), 66, 96
elections: 2016 election, 25 table1.1, 27 table1.2; 2018 House election, 28 table1.3
electoral politics, immigrant scapegoating in, 197
electrical energy, 276
electrification trends, 171, 277
electronic products, 259n2(ch1), 283
electronics, 276
El Salvador: Mexico's relations with, 6; migration flows and, 50; migration stocks from, 55, 55 table3.2; in migration system, 279; as place of origin, 53; political turmoil and natural disasters, 56; population growth rates, 58; total and foreign-born population of, 54, 54 table3.1
The Emerging Republican Majority (Phillips), 197
EMIF (Encuesta sobre Migración en la Frontera Norte de México /Border Survey of Mexican Migrants), 63–64, 66, 68 fig.4.2, 69, 72, 76, 272
empirical framework for US-Mexico migration policies, NAFTA and, 130–32
employment: types of, 274. *See also* farm labor; Mexican total employment

employment, Mexican, by economic sector, 133 fig.9.1
employment, US, by economic sector, 133 fig.9.1
employment-based visa programs, 110, 274
employment in Mexico, Mexican farmworkers crossing into US and, 154 fig.10.3
Encuesta Mensual de la Industria Manufacturera, 265n5(ch12)
Encuesta sobre Migración en la Frontera Norte de México /Border Survey of Mexican Migrants (EMIF), 63–64, 66, 68 fig.4.2, 69, 72, 76, 272
energy products, 259n2(ch1), 283
environmental regulations, 161 table11.1, 185, 277
EPI (Economic Policy Institute), 139
equity, 273
Espenshade, T.J., 260n5(ch4)
Estonia, 280
ethnicity: ethnic composition of Hazleton, PA, 217 table15.1; ethnic militancy, 281; ethnic minorities, 281; reactive ethnicity, 220, 223, 226, 281. *See also* panethnic identity; racialization; racial threat theory
European Union (EU), 184
Evangelicals, 235 table16.2, 238 fig.16.2
E-Verify, 110
exchange rates, fixed, neoliberalism and, 280
EXP (Exportations), 161 table11.1
exponential new technologies, 161 table11.1, 170–72
Exportations (EXP), 161 table11.1
exports: exported outputs, 278; Industrialization for Export, 160; maquiladora system and, 178; Mexican exports, 262n12; Mexican exports effects on migration, 106; Mexico-US exports, 264n6; NAFTA and, 151; noncompetitive crops, 151; principal exports of Mexico, 166 table11.2; ratio to output, 264n4; trade balance and, 283; trade integration, 284. *See also* intraregional trade
expropriation clause, 182
ex situ/in situ conservation, 273

FACE (Facts about Cuban Exiles), 222
Facts about Cuban Exiles (FACE), 222
family: family consumption, 283; family migrations, 263n5; family ratio of income by education level, 94 fig.6.3; family reunification criteria, 276. *See also* subsistence farmers
farmers: PROCAMPO and Mexican, 281; US government subsidies to American, 278. *See also* subsistence farmers
farming: rural households, 282. *See also* rural households
farm labor: defined, 274; demand for, 157; migration flow of, 157. *See also* Bracero Program; H2A visas
farmworkers, Mexican: corn production and migration of, 153 fig.10.2; crossing into US, 154 fig.10.3
FDI (foreign direct investment): in automotive industry by mega region, 168 fig.11.4; automotive industry in Mexico and, 109; by country of origin in automotive sector, 163 fig.11.2; defined, 274; MAI and, 162, 163fig.11.2; models of agglomeration and, 265n3(ch11); NAFTA and, 175; overestimation of, 264n1(ch11)
federal laws, Immigration and Naturalization Act of 1965, 276
feedback loop, between apprehensions and border enforcement, 37 fig.2.2
fertility issues: fertility decline, 6, 273, 274; fertility rate, 260n4(ch4), 274; fertility rates, 60 fig.3.2, 122; fertility transition, 57, 273, 274; fertility trends, 273
Fiat Chrysler, 167 fig.11.3
field crop production in Mexico, 264n8
Finland, 280
First Industrial Revolution, 276
fiscal reforms, 185, 265n2(ch11)
Fitting, Elizabeth, 151
5G technology, 171
fixed exchange rates, 280
Flores, René D., 10, 214–26
Florida, 10, 234 table16.2, 238 fig.16.2, 239
food staples, 273. *See also* corn biodiversity
Fordism, 171
Ford Motor Company, 164, 167, 167 fig.11.3
foreign-born community building, 279
foreign capital, 278
foreign corporations. *See* ISDS (investor-state dispute settlement)
foreign direct investment (FDI). *See* FDI (foreign direct investment)
foreign goods/services, 278. *See also* market access

foreign workers: employment-based visa programs, 274; temporary foreign worker program, 283
forest products, 259n2(ch1), 283
Formadores Project, 99
formal sectors, average annual employment, 262n10
Fourth Industrial Revolution, 276. See also Industry 4.0
France, as OECD member, 280
free competition, 278
free exchange of goods, 284
free trade agreement (FTA), 264n6, 281
free trade expansion, 280. See also OECD (Organization for Economic Cooperation and Development)
FTA (free trade agreement), 264n6, 281
full-time employment, 262n10, 274

Gándara, Patricia, 88–101
Garcetti, Eric, 224
García-Guerrero, Victor M., 6, 49–62
Garcia-Rios, Sergio, 229
García Zamora, J., 151
Gaspar, S., 151
GDP (gross domestic product): aggregates by scenario, 143 table9.2; annual percentage change in for US and California, 115 fig.8.1; FDI as share of, 140 fig.9.3, 175–76, 176 fig.12.1; of field crops in Mexico, 156 fig.10.4, 157; impacts of trade and migration on, 130, 134, 139; labor productivity and, 176 fig.12.1; MAI and, 161–62; NAFTA and, 175–76; per US apprehensions and deportations, 135 fig.9.2; raising of, 132; trade policy scenarios, 142–46. See also GLOBE model
gender, as social category, 275
General Agreement on Tariffs and Trade, 284–85
General Social Survey, 36
genetically modified seeds (GMS), 157, 274
geographic proximity, 279
Germany, 280
GI Bill, 274
Giorguli, Silvia E., 6, 49–62
global chains. See global value chains
global flow of capital, 277. See also knowledge capitals
globalization, perceived threat of, 284
global production chains, 160. See also global value chains

global supply chains, 161. See also global value chains
global value chains, 160–61, 174, 272, 274. See also automotive value chains; value chains
GLOBE model, 130, 142, 275. See also CGE (computable general equilibrium) model
GM (General Motors), 160, 161, 167, 167 fig.11.3
GMS (genetically modified seeds), 157, 274
Gobierno de Baja California, 91
Goldwater, Barry, 197
goods: rules of origin and, 282; value added, 284
Govea-Vargar, Yatziry, 8, 148–58
government interventions, 273. See also development policies
Great Depression, 194, 275
Great Recession of 2008, 6, 49, 52, 57, 63, 64, 65, 67, 69, 70, 71, 72, 76, 77, 104, 111, 114, 115, 121, 156, 160, 262n7, 275
Greece, 280
gross domestic product (GDP). See GDP (gross domestic product)
group anger: changes in probability of, 238 fig.16.2; Latinos responses to anti-immigrant politics and, 230–32; overview, 11; predicted probability of, 239 fig.16.3
group position theory, 18
group threat, 11, 18, 227, 283
group threat theory, 275. See also immigrant threat; Latino threat narrative; racial threat theory; status threat
GTAP data set, 263n3
Guadalajara, University of, 278
Guatemala, 223; Mexico's relations with, 6; migration flows and, 50; migration stocks from, 55, 55 table3.2; in migration system, 279; as place of origin, 53; political turmoil and natural disasters, 56; total and foreign-born population of, 54, 54 table3.1; total fertility rate (TFR), 58
Gulf War I, 200
Gutierrez, Angela E., 11, 227–43

H1B visas, 53, 275
H2A visas, 53, 109, 111, 119, 274, 275. See also Bracero Program; farm labor; temporary visas

H2B visas, 53, 111, 119, 275. See also temporary visas
Hajnal, Zoltan L., 11, 244–54
Hanson, Gordon, 20, 70, 108
Hart-Celler Act. See Immigration and Naturalization Act of 1965
harvested output, 271
Hayes-Bautista, David, 202
Hazleton, PA: crime and, 268n2(ch15); demographics, 216; ethnic and racial composition of, 217 table15.1; IIRA of 2006, 216, 275; immigrant scapegoating in, 10; newspaper coverage and crime rates in, 218 fig.15.1
health benefits, Proposition 187 (California, 1994) and, 268n1(ch16), 281
health care services, 224
health issues of Mexican-origin population, 6–7, 78–87, 278; Child Health Care Program, 246; contemporary mobility trends, 78–79; health of Mexican migrant returnees, 84–85; health of Mexican-origin population in US, 79–84; Medicaid program, 246; overview, 78; policy recommendations, 86
health of Mexican migrant returnees, health issues of Mexican-origin population and, 84–85
health of Mexican-origin population in US, health issues of Mexican-origin population and, 79–84
heterogeneous flows management, Mexico-US migration system and, 59–62
high-identifying/low-identifying Mexican Americans, 229
high-skilled temporary technical workers, 119
Hilsenrath, Jon, 259 n1(ch1)
Hinojosa-Ojeda, Raúl, 8, 15–31, 129–47
Hispanic Challenge narrative, 3
historical contexts for Trump's nativist appeal. See nativist appeal, historical/political contexts of Trump's
historical linkages, 279
home market systems, 280. See also OECD (Organization for Economic Cooperation and Development)
Honda, 167 fig.11.3
Honduras: homicide rates, 266n14(ch14); Mexico's relations with, 6; migration flows and, 50; migration stocks from, 55, 55 table3.2; in migration system, 279; as place of origin, 53; total and foreign-born population of, 54, 54 table3.1; working age group in, 58–59
Hooghe, Marc, 18
Hopkins, D.J., 268n1(ch17)
Horton, Willie, 197, 199
households: MMP survey of, 278. See also rural households
Hungary, 280
Huntington, Samuel P., 3, 200–201

ICE (Immigration and Customs Enforcement), 135 fig.9.2, 210
Iceland, 280
ICT (information and communication technology), 171
IDB (Inter-American Development Bank), 91
identity portfolio, 229; defined, 275
ideological beliefs, symbolic politics perspective theory and, 283
IIRA (Illegal Immigration Relief Act) (Pennsylvania, 2006), 216, 275
IIRIRA (Illegal Immigration Reform and Immigrant Responsibility Act of 1996), 38
illegal alien discourse, 35, 194
illegal immigrants, Proposition 187 (California, 1994) and, 268n1(ch16), 281
Illegal Immigration Reform and Immigrant Responsibility Act of 1996 (IIRIRA), 38
Illegal Immigration Relief Act (Pennsylvania, 2006) (IIRA), 216, 275
illocutionary force, 205, 275
ILO (International Labor Organization), 183
ILO Department of Statistics (ILOSTAT), 133 fig.9.1
ILOSTAT (ILO Department of Statistics), 133 fig.9.1
IMF (International Monetary Fund), 262n12, 265n4(ch12)
IMMEX (Manufacturing, Maquiladora, and Export Services), 160, 161 table11.1
immigrant context, 247, 275
immigrant health advantage, 79, 275
immigrant-linked fate, 230, 232, 234 table16.2, 275
immigrant-linked threat, racism scale and, 234 table16.2
immigrants: crime and, 136 table9.1, 266–67n14(ch14), 268nn1–2(ch15); panethnic identities and, 228–29; perceptions of, 273. See also context of reception

immigrant scapegoating by political elites, social consequences of, 214–26; anti-immigrant rhetoric of Trump, 224–26; backlash in California and, 223–24; overview, 10, 214–15; political rhetoric, 201, 215; reactive ethnicity in Florida and, 220–22; social effects of in Pennsylvania, 215–20
immigrant status categorization, 275, 281. *See also* racialization; racialized panethnic identity
immigrant threat, 247, 275
immigrant workers, Mexican: data adjustments, 262n6; estimated number of unauthorized, 105 fig.7.1
immigration: NAFTA and, 139–41; social policy and, 282
immigration, Eastern Hemisphere, Immigration and Naturalization Act of 1965 and, 276
immigration, Western Hemisphere, Immigration and Naturalization Act of 1965 and, 276
Immigration and Customs Enforcement (ICE), 135 fig.9.2, 210
Immigration and Nationality Act of 1956 (INA), 33
Immigration and Naturalization Act of 1965, 6, 33, 37, 64, 120, 136 table9.1, 137, 275, 276
Immigration and Naturalization Services (INS), 194; IRCA and, 276
immigration enforcement, 70, 212, 272; defined, 276; impacts of, 72–76. *See also* border enforcement
immigration flows, 102–12, 272. *See also* Central American flows
immigration law enforcement, 276; zero tolerance policies, 285
immigration reform, effects of Mexican migration on US labor market and, 120–21
Immigration Reform Act of 1965. *See* Immigration and Naturalization Act of 1965
Immigration Reform Act of 1986. *See* Immigration Reform Act of 1986 (IRCA)
Immigration Reform and Control Act of 1986 (IRCA), 43, 51, 64, 134, 136 table9.1, 137, 263n1, 276. *See also* IRCA (Immigration Reform and Control Act of 1986)
immigration restrictionists, 120; defined, 276

immigration restrictions, 282. *See also* restrictionist politics; restrictive measures
immorality, as social problem, 279
imports: of corn from Mexico, 157; importation/exportation of automotive parts, components, and systems, 272; imported inputs, 278; import substitution, 278; Mexico-US imports, 264n6; MFN and, 279; NAFTA and, 150; noncompetitive crops, 150; principal imports of Mexico, 166 table11.2; ratio to output, 264n5; trade balance and, 283; trade integration, 284; by US counties per capita, 22 fig.1.1
in-bond production, 278. *See also* maquiladoras
incarceration: rates for immigrants, 136 table9.1; Trump administration and, 142
income, 235 table16.2, 238 fig.16.2, 275; annual wages, 262n10; demographic transition and, 273; educational attainment and, 92 fig.6.2; family ratio of income by education level in Southern California, 94 fig.6.3; income gap by education levels, 94 fig.6.3; income inequality, 90 fig.6.1, 273–74; income level comparisons, 281. *See also* purchasing power parity (PPP)income per capita, 273; income subsidies, 278. *See also* marketing supports; NAFTA paradox and, 279
India, 54, 117, 118 fig.8.2, 119
India, 168
individual behavior, 260n5(ch2). *See also* micro level analysis
Industrialization by Import Substitution (ISI), 160, 161 table11.1
Industrialization for Export, 160, 161 table11.1
industrialized countries. *See* OECD (Organization for Economic Cooperation and Development)
industrial modernization, 160
industrial production, Border Industrialization Program of 1965 (BIP), 136 table9.1, 137, 138, 272
industrial revolutions, 276
Industry 4.0, 9, 161 table11.1, 170–71, 172; defined, 276. *See also* Fourth Industrial Revolution
INEGI (Instituto Nacional de Estadisticas y Geografía/National Institute of Statistics, Geography, and Informatics), 91, 169, 264n2, 282

INEGI (Instituto Nacional de Estadística y Geografía/National Institute of Statistics, Geography, and Informatics), 163
inequality in Mexico and US: children of migration and, 89–91; of income in OECD countries, 90 fig.6.1; increases in, 179; social inequalities, 172. *See also* racial inequality
inflows, 277. *See also* annual inflow; in-migration; net migration inflows
informal conversation, 282
informal sectors, 262n10, 263n9
information and communication technology (ICT), 171
information technology (IT), 265n2(ch11), 276
infotainment innovations, 171
in-migrants, net migration and, 280
in-migration, 42, 133 fig.9.1, 271, 279, 280; defined, 277; net migration and. *See* net migration. *See also* annual inflow; northbound flows
innovation centers, 277. *See also* knowledge capitals
inputs, value added goods/services and, 284
INS (Immigration and Naturalization Services), 194
INSABI (Instituto de Salud para el Bienestar/Institute of Health for Wellness)), 85
Instituto de Mexicanos en el Extranjero (IME), 97
Instituto de Salud para el Bienestar/Institute of Health for Wellness (INSABI), 85
Instituto Nacional de Estadísticas y Geografía/National Institute of Statistics, Geography, and Informatics (INEGI), 91, 163, 169, 264n2
integration of automotive chains, in automotive sector, US-Mexico, 164–65, 166 table11.2
Inter-American Development Bank (IDB), 91
internal migration trends, 273
International Labor Organization (ILO), 183
international migration trends, 273
International Monetary Fund (IMF), 262n12, 265n4(ch12)
International Organization for Automobile Manufacturers. *See* OICA (Organización Internacional de Fabricantes de Automóviles/International Organization for Automobile Manufacturers)
international trade. *See* trade diversion
Internet, development of, 276
intrabranch consumption, 271
intrafirm/interfirm trade, 272
in-transit flows, 53; defined, 277
intraregional trade, 172, 277
investments in Mexico, 265n2(ch11)
Investor-State Dispute Settlement (ISDS), 182
IRCA (Immigration Reform and Control Act of 1986), 43, 51, 64, 134, 137, 263n1, 276; NAFTA and, 137–39
Ireland, as OECD member, 280
irrigated areas, corn cropland in, 264n7
ISDS (Investor-State Dispute Settlement), defined, 277
Israel, 280
Italy, 280

Jalisco, Mexico, 264n2
Japan: auto part exports, 165; dominance in auto industry, 169; nonimmigrant admissions from, 118 fig.8.3; as OECD member, 280; TPP and, 260n6
job growth/population growth comparison, effects of Mexican migration on US labor market and, 114, 115 fig8.1
job opportunities, rural migration and, 282
Johnson, Lyndon B., 197, 276, 282

Kennedy, John F., 282
Kennedy, Paul, 200
KIA, 167 fig.11.3
knowledge capitals, 89; defined, 277
Korea, 280
KORUS (South Korea-US Free Trade Agreement), 281
Ku Klux Klan, 193

labor adjustment issues, NADBank and, 263n11
labor competition: effects of Mexican migration on US labor market and, 115–17; less-skilled workers and, 115–17
labor-driven migrants, 56; defined, 277
labor-intensive parts components, 177–78
labor market: immigrant/native workers as complementary, 263n10; visa allocations and, 276. *See also* lump of labor fallacy
labor productivity, 176; defined, 277; economic convergence and, 273; GDP and, 176 fig.12.1

labor segmentation, 169
labor shortages, 120, 194, 272. *See also* Bracero Program
Lamm, Richard, 195
language, 275, 282. *See also* communication interactions; speech acts; speech genres
language categorization, 281. *See also* racialization; racialized panethnic identity
LASANTI (Los Angeles-San Diego-Tijuana) region, 7, 88–101; defined, 277
Latino context on corrections spending, 251 fig.17.1
Latino/Hispanic categorization, 227–28
Latino identity racialization, 11
Latino immigrants, immigrant-linked fate, 275
Latino responses to anti-immigrant politics, 227–43; conclusion, 241–42; group anger, 230–32; overview, 11, 227; political participation, 238–41; racialized panethnic identity, 227–30; racism and immigrant-linked fate, 232; Trump favorability, 232–38
Latinos: anti-immigrant politics, Latinos responses to, 227–43; CMPS and, 268n2(ch16), 268n3, 273; identification as, 269n3; identifying as, 275; panethnic identity and, 281; population size, 269n6; racism toward, perceived, 268n3; regressive government policy in heavily Latino states, 248 table17.1
Latino threat narrative, 35, 275; border militarization and, 35–38; defined, 277
Latvia, 280
legal migration: legal authorization, 279; legal immigration criteria, 276; legal immigration quotas, 137. *See also* legislation; restrictive measures
legal permanent residents (LPRs): from countries of next largest migration, 118 fig.8.2; defined, 56, 277; flow trends and, 117, 118 fig.8.2; migration from Mexico, 118 fig.8.2
legal status groups, 34 fig.2.1
legislation: ballot initiatives, 268n1(ch16); border control legislation, 209; IIRIRA of 1996, 263n1; IRCA of 1986, 263n1; IRCA of 1990, 263n1; post-9/11 legislation, 263n1
less-skilled workers, 277; effects of Mexican migration on US labor market and, 115–17; labor competition and, 115–17; native working-age population and, 122

letters, 283
Levy, Santiago, 91
Levy and Sweder von Wijnbergen, 263n6
Lewis, W. Arthur, 263n8
Lewis model of economic growth, 132–33
licensing rules, 284
Lighthizer, Robert, 180, 182–83, 183
Light Up the Border campaign, 198–99
Lithuania, 280
local employment, 274
local immigrant populations, 268n1(ch17)
local tax rates, 268n1(ch17)
López-Calva, Luis Feipe, 91
López Obrador, Andrés Manuel, 91, 149, 183, 186, 187, 206, 210–12
Los Angeles-San Diego-Tijuana region (LASANTI), 7. *See also* LASANTI (Los Angeles-San Diego-Tijuana region)
low-cost products, trade diversion and, 283
low-skilled immigrants: demand for, 108–9; earning in US, 261n1(ch7); numbers of, 65; temporary worker program for, 103, 110–11. *See also* less-skilled workers
low-skilled workers, 65, 103, 108–11, 110, 261n1(ch7)
low-wage immigrant labor market, 263n10
LPRs(legal permanent residents). *See* legal permanent residents (LPRs)
lump of labor fallacy, 9, 115; defined, 277
Luxembourg, 280
luxury services, 115–16

machinery, 259n2(ch1), 283
macro level analysis, 260n5(ch2)
MAGA (Make America Great Again) campaign slogan. *See* Make America Great Again (MAGA) campaign slogan
MAI (Mexican automotive industry). *See* Mexican Automotive Industry (MAI)
main destination countries, 279. *See also* Canada; United States
Make America Great Again (MAGA) campaign, 10, 16, 191, 200–201, 201
Malaysia, 260n6
Manifest Destiny, 10, 192; defined, 278. *See also* dominant white national identity
Manufacturing, Maquiladora, and Export Services (IMMEX), 160, 161 table11.1
manufacturing assembly plants, 278. *See also* maquiladoras
manufacturing jobs in United States, 275
Maquiladora Program, 136 table9.1, 161 table11.1. *See also* Border Industrialization Program of 1965 (BIP)

maquiladoras, 265n3(ch11); defined, 278. *See also* NAFTA (North American Free Trade Agreement)
maquiladora system, 178, 278
Mariel boatlift, 220-21
market access, 157; defined, 278
marketing supports, 155, 271, 278. *See also* ASERCA (agencia de servicios a la comercialización y desarrollo de mercados agropecuarios / support and services to agricultural marketing); PROCAMPO
Marsicano, Mike, 217
Masferrer, Claudia, 6, 49-62
Massey, Douglas S., 5, 32-46, 36, 38, 42, 44
Mazda, 167 fig.11.3
McIntosh, Craig, 70
measuring immigrant context, anti-immigrant backlash and, 247
media: inaccurate perceptions of, 275; right-wing media, 199, 214
Medicaid program, 246, 248
Menendez, Bob, 222
mental health issues: migrant well-being, 279; underdiagnosis of, 278
Mexican American health disadvantages, 79-80, 278
Mexican Americans: racialization of Latino identity, 228; rhetoric against, 224; xenophobic comments against, 229
Mexican Americans, US-born, immigrant health advantage of, 275
Mexican American War, 3, 193, 271
Mexican Association of the Automotive Industry/Asociación Mexicana de la Industria Automotriz (AMIA), 162 fig.11.1, 167 fig.11.3, 169
Mexican Automotive Industry (MAI), 265n2(ch11); beginnings of, 159; defined, 278; main automotive clusters in Mexico, 167 fig.11.3; milestones in, 161 table11.1; NAFTA and, 265n5(ch11); wages and employment, 265n5(ch11)
Mexican automotive industry (MAI): defined, 278; Mexican economy and, 278
Mexican Automotive Vehicles/Vehículos Automotrices Mexicanos (VAM), 160. *See also* VAM (Vehículos Automotrices Mexicanos/Mexican Automotive Vehicles)
Mexican-born population in U.S., 51 fig.3.1, 155, 262n7

Mexican CAIP, 263n11
Mexican capital, 278
Mexican Censos Económicos, 265n5(ch12)
Mexican Census, 58
Mexican Consumer Price Index (CPI), 262n10
Mexican diaspora, 139; defined, 278
Mexican economy, MAI and, 278
Mexican emigration's rise and fall, ending of Mexican unauthorized migration and, 64-66
Mexican farm laborers (braceros), 194, 272; decrease in, 157. *See also* Bracero Program
Mexican immigrants, 23 fig.1.1B; chronic health issues, 275; data adjustments, 262n6; immigrant health advantage of, 275; percent by US counties, 22 fig.1.1; in US and annual rate of change, 65 table4.1
Mexican immigration, nativism and, 193-94
Mexicanization, 206
Mexican migration: effects on US labor market of, 113-25; in legal status groups, 34 fig.2.1
Mexican Migration Project (MMP), 36-37, 38, 44, 278
Mexican migration quotas, 276
Mexican nationalism, 205; defined, 279
Mexican nationalism, Mexico-US relations and, 204-13; border wall, 207-9; conflicts, 205-7; considerations, 212; migration and otherness, 209-11; overview, 10, 204-5; social power, 205; speech genres, 205
Mexican-origin population: health of, 78-87; as percentage of unauthorized migrants in US, 119 fig.8.4
Mexican peso crisis of 1994, 64
Mexican real wage, 262n10
Mexican Revolution, 206
Mexican side of border, Border Industrialization Program of 1965 (BIP), 136 table9.1, 137, 138, 272
Mexican total employment, 262n10
Mexican unauthorized migration, ending of, 63-77; border enforcement and, 70-71; conclusion, 76-77; demographic transition and, 69-70; economic downturn and, 69; EMIF and, 66; immigration enforcement impacts, 72-76; Mexican emigration's rise and fall, 64-66; overview, 63-64; undocumented border crossing and, 67-69

Mexican-US migration. *See* children of migration, future of; educational imperative; LASANTI; Mexican migration, effects on US labor market; Mexican-origin population, health of; Mexican unauthorized migration; recession; removals; US attitudes; US labor market, effects of Mexican migration on; US policies

Mexico: annexation of northern Mexico, 10, 193; auto part exports, 165; China's export policies and, 186; corn production in, 264n7; cropland in corn in northern, 264n7; demographics of, 58–59; economic development of, 186–87; FDI in automotive industry by mega region, 168 fig.11.4; fertility transition, 274; homicide rates, 266–67n14(ch14); hypothetical Mexican crisis scenario, 196–97; LPRs from, 117, 118 fig.8.2; manufacturing employment under NAFTA, 266n6(ch12); Mexican independence, 204; migration stocks from, 55, 55 table3.2; minimum wage, 91, 180, 181, 185–87, 186, 274; monetary policy of, 185–86, 187; net migration from, 263n4; net migration inflows from, 262n7; nonimmigrant admissions from, 118 fig.8.3; as OECD member, 280; out-migration from, 263n4; as place of origin, transit, return and destination, 53; principal exports and imports, 166 table11.2; total and foreign-born population of, 54, 54 table3.1; TPP and, 260n6; in trade and production bloc, 132; US Embassy and Consulates in, 46; USMCA and, 181; as WTO member, 285. *See also* Mexican Automotive Industry (MAI); Mexican nationalism, Mexico-US relations and

Mexico migration, FDI and, 140 fig.9.3

Mexico question? nativist appeal, contexts for Trump's, 196–97

Mexico-US migration system, current, 49–62; heterogeneous flows management, 59–62; North America-Central America migration system, 53–59; overview, 49–50; strong linkages construction, 50–57

MFN (most favored nation) tariff, 181, 279

Michoacán, Mexico, 264n2

micro level analysis, 260n5(ch2)

Middle Eastern national-origin quotas, 33, 120, 276

migrant caravans, 53, 209–11; defined, 279

migrant flow, data adjustments, 261n4(ch7)

migrant trail, 81; defined, 279

migrant well-being, 79; defined, 279

migration collapse scenario, 143; defined, 279

migration flows, 39, 263n1, 280; defined, 279; effects of, 206; migration of family members, 282; net migration and. *See* net migration. *See also* annual inflow; circular migration; in-migration; net migration; northbound flows; outflows; out-migration; return migration; unauthorized migration; undocumented immigrants

migration patterns, 272–73. *See also* circular migration

migration policies, changing, NAFTA and, 129–47

migration policy initiatives, US-Mexico trade and migration policy initiatives, 136 table9.1

Migration Policy Institute, 45

migration stocks and flows: in migration collapse scenario, 279; in North America, 55 table3.2

migration system, 53; defined, 279

migratory employment, 274

migratory movements, 277. *See also* in-migration; in-transit flows; northbound flows

minerals and metals, 259n2(ch1), 283

minimum wage, 91, 180, 181, 185–87, 265n5, 274

Ministry of Labor and Social Welfare, Government of Mexico. *See* STPS (Secretaría del Trabajo y Previsión Social—Gobierno de México/Ministry of Labor and Social Welfare, Government of Mexico)

MMP (Mexican Migration Project), 36–37, 37 fig.2.2, 38, 44, 278

mobilization. *See* white backlash

modes of incorporation, 82, 279

Montejano, David, 10, 191–203

Montenegro, L., 261n1(ch7)

Monterrey Technology Center (MTC), 167

Mora-Rivera, Jorge, 8, 148–58

Morelos y Pavón, José María, 204

Moreno-Brid, Juan Carlos, 9, 174–88

mortality trends, 273

most-favored nation (MFN) tariff, 181, 279

340 | Index

MS-13, 198
MTC (Monterrey Technology Center), 167
multiethnic groups. *See* panethnic identity
multinational corporations, 278. *See also* marketing supports
Muslims, 200–201, 225, 282
Mutz, Diana, 17

NADB (North American Development Bank), 263n11
NADBank (North American Development Bank), 131, 138, 263n11
NADBank Community Adjustment and Investment Program (NADN CAIP), 140
NADB CAIP (North American Development Bank Community Adjustment and Investment Program), 140
NAFTA (North American Free Trade Agreement), 278, 281; alternative immigration and, 142–46; ASERCA and, 271; automotive industry and, 160; conclusion, 146; corn imports and, 264n8; economic development and integration? 132–35; effects of, 206; empirical framework for US-Mexico migration policies, 130–32; expropriation clause, 182; immigration and, 139–41; IRCA and, 136 table9.1, 137–39; MAI and, 159, 265n5(ch11); migration policies, changing, 129–47; outputs in nonservice sectors under trade war of, 144 fig.9.4; overview, 8, 9, 15, 129–30; postwar US migration, 135–37; status of goals, 175–77; tariff reductions, 265n2(ch12); trade and labor migration, 132–35; trade policies, changing, 129–47; trade policies and, 142–46; trade policy initiatives, 135–37; Trump era, 141–42; USMCA and, 165, 166, 174, 183; US-Mexico trade deal policies and, 175–77. *See also* ISDS (investor-state dispute settlement); NAFTA paradox; post-NAFTA era
NAFTA new trade agreement outcomes, US-Mexico trade deal policies and, 182–84
NAFTA paradox: automotive sector, US-Mexico and, 169–70; defined, 279. *See also* NAFTA (North American Free Trade Agreement)
nanotechnology, 161 table11.1, 276
Napolitano, Janey, 95
NAS (National Academy of Sciences), 17

National Academy of Sciences (NAS), 17
National Auto Parts Industry/Industria Nacional de Autopartes (INA), 265n4(ch11)
National Commission of Minimum Wages. *See* CONASAMI (Comisión Nacional de Salarios Mínimos/National Commission of Minimum Wages)
National Immigration Institute, 210
National Institute of Statistics, Geography, and Informatics, 169. *See also* INEGI (Instituto Nacional de Estadísticas y Geografía/National Institute of Statistics, Geography, and Informatics)
nationalism discourses, 279. *See also* Mexican nationalism, Mexico-US relations and; nationalist stereotypes
nationalist stereotypes, 206, 283; defined, 279. *See also* stereotypes
national-origin group, 228, 268n5, 275, 276; defined, 279; political participation models by, 240 fig.16.4; racialized panethnic identity and, 281; racism scale items by, 233 table16.1
National Population Council. *See* CONAPO (Consejo Nacional de Población/ National Population Council)
National Science Foundation, General Social Survey, 36
National Security Council, 200–201
national security narrative, 181; hypothetical Mexican crisis scenario, 196–97; nativist appeal, contexts for Trump's, 194–96; perceived foreign threats, 200–201
National Survey of Employment. *See* ENE (Encuesta Nacional de Empleo/National Survey of Employment)
National Survey of Occupation and Employment. *See* ENOE (Encuesta Nacional de Ocupación y Empleo/ National Survey of Occupation and Employment)
National Survey of Urban Employment. *See* ENEU (Encuesta Nacional de Ocupación y Empleo Urbano/National Survey of Urban Employment)
native-born Americans, 271. *See also* anti-immigrant backlash; white backlash
nativism: defined, 279; in Hazleton, PA, 217–19
nativist appeal, historical/political contexts of Trump's, 191–203; California 1994, 198–200; conclusion, 201–2; Make

America Great Again (MAGA) campaign, 200–201; Mexican immigration and nativism, 193–94; Mexico question, 196–97; national building and national identity, 192–93; national security narrative, 194–96; overview, 10, 191; scapegoating in electoral politics, 197–98; white backlash, 200–201
Near-Peer Mentoring Project, 99
neoliberalism, 151, 271; defined, 280
Netherlands, 280
net migration, 43, 133 fig.9.1, 279; defined, 280; inflows, 262n7; from Mexico, 263n4. *See also* annual inflow; in-migration; migration flows; northbound flows; outflows; out-migration
Nevada, 193, 271
New Jersey, 233, 234 table16.2, 237, 238 fig.16.2
new materials, 161 table11.1
New Mexico, 193, 271
New York, 233, 234 table16.2, 236 fig.16.1, 237, 238 fig.16.2
New Zealand, 260n6, 280
The Next War (Weinberger and Schweizer), 196–97
9/11 terrorist attacks, 199, 200–201
Nissan, 161, 167 fig.11.3
Nixon, Richard M., 197, 282
nonagricultural domestic workers, 119. *See also* H2B visas
noncitizens, 53, 56, 268n1(ch16), 277, 283, 284. *See also* legal permanent residents (LPRs); temporary visas; undocumented migrants
noncommercial interactions, 265n3(ch11)
noncompetitive crops, 150, 154; defined, 280
non-Hispanic whites, 202, 275, 278
nonimmigrants, 118, 118 fig.8.3. *See also* temporary visitors; unauthorized migrants
nonservice sectors, outputs under NAFTA trade war in, 144 fig.9.4
nontariff obstacles: trade liberalization and, 284. *See also* licensing rules; quotas/prohibitions
non-US citizens. *See* noncitizens
normative values, symbolic politics perspective theory and, 283
Norte (northeast) mega region, 167, 167 fig.11.3, 168 fig.11.4

North America: migration flows and, 50; migration stocks and flows in, 55 table3.2; North America-Central America migration system, 53–59; total and foreign-born population in, 54 table3.1; working age population in, 60 fig.3.2
North American Development Bank (NADBank), 131, 138, 263n11
North American Development Bank Community Adjustment and Investment Program (NADB CAIP), 140
North American Free Trade Agreement (NAFTA). *See* NAFTA (North American Free Trade Agreement)
northbound border crossers, 272
northbound flows, 49, 64, 68 fig.4.1, 277, 279, 280; defined, 260n3(ch4), 280; net migration and. *See* net migration. *See also* in-migration
Norway, 280

Obama, Barack, 136 table9.1, 191, 198, 214
OECD (Organization for Economic Cooperation and Development), 90, 90 fig.6.1, 262n10, 274; defined, 280. *See also specific member countries*
OEM (original equipment manufacturer), 160, 164, 166, 168, 169, 170, 264n1(ch11), 265n3(ch11), 265n5(ch11)
offshoring, 179; defined, 280. *See also* outsourcing
Operation Blockade, 37, 40, 195
Operation Gatekeeper, 37, 40, 195
Operation Hold the Line, 195. *See also* Operation Blockade
Operation Safeguard, 195
Operation Wetback, 136 table9.1, 194
Oportunidades (Opportunities), 139, 141; defined, 280
Orange county, CA, 261n2(ch6)
Orfield, Gary, 88–101
Organization for Economic Cooperation and Development (OECD), 90, 90 fig.6.1, 262n10; defined, 280
original equipment manufacturer (OEM), 161, 164, 167, 168, 264n1(ch11), 265n3(ch11); wage scale and, 169, 170
origin countries: in migration system, 279; political migrants and, 281
Orrenius, Pia M., 7, 102–12
otherness, 279. *See also* nationalist stereotypes

outflows, 66, 279, 280; defined, 280; net migration and. *See* net migration. *See also* out-migration; return migration
out-migrant households, MMP survey of, 278
out-migrants: net migration and, 280; remittances and, 282
out-migration, 42, 133 fig.9.1, 279, 280; defined, 280; net migration and; root causes of, 263n12; from southeastern Mexico and Central America, 263n4. *See also* net migration; outflows; return migration
output/input, 144 fig.9.4, 271. *See also* labor productivity
outsourcing, 180, 280. *See also* offshoring
overstay, data adjustments, 261n4(ch7)

packaging, value chains and, 284
panethnic identity, 228, 280. *See also* racialized panethnic identity
Parro, F., 265n2(ch12)
parts and components production, 284
part suppliers, 272
part-time employment, 262n15, 274
Pastor, Robert, 138
payroll employment survey, BLS (US Bureau of Labor Statistics), 262n10
Pedraza, Francisco, 229
Peña Nieto, Enrique, 206, 207–8, 209
People Without Borders, 209
permits. *See* temporary visas; visas
Peru, 260n6
Pew Research Center, 65, 103, 260n1(ch4)
Philippines, 54, 117, 118 fig.8.2
Phillips, Kevin, 197, 200
physical health issues, 279
platform economy, 276–77
Poland, 280
policy recommendations, 86, 102–12
political behavior, 283
political climate, 282. *See also* social policy
political contexts for Trump's nativist appeal. *See* nativist appeal, historical/political contexts of Trump's
political elites, social consequences of immigrant scapegoating by, 214–26
political engagement, 11, 268n5
political migrants, 55; defined, 281
political participation models, 238–41, 240 fig.16.4
politics. *See* political contexts for Trump's nativist appeal; racialized politics; Southern strategy

Polk, James K., 3
population composition, 273. *See also* demographic dynamics
population growth: family migrations and, 263n5; rates of, 60 fig.3.2
population nonreplacement, 122
Portugal, 280
post-9/11 legislation, Secure Fence Act of 2006, 263n1
postwar US migration, 136 table9.1; NAFTA and, 135–37
poverty, Great Recession of 2008, 275
PPP (purchasing power parity), 281
preferential trade agreements, 175, 281; defined, 282; MFN and, 279. *See also* KORUS (South Korea-US Free Trade Agreement); NAFTA (North American Free Trade Agreement); rules of origin
prejudice, symbolic politics perspective theory and, 283
Pren, K. A., 36, 38, 42, 44
Preparing for the 21st Century (Kennedy), 200
price evolution, 264n8
price/income, 278. *See also* marketing supports
price subsidies, 278. *See also* marketing supports
pride: in cultural features of indigenous past, 279; in cultural wealth of Mexico, 279. *See also* Mexican nationalism
Princeton University, MMP at, 278
Pritchett, L., 261n1(ch7)
private property ownership, 280
private sector, 280
PROCAMPO (Programa de Apoyos Directos al Campo/Program for Rural Funding), 139, 141, 154, 278, 281. *See also* marketing supports
production, 274; evolution of, 162 fig.11.1; production levels, 274
production process: global value chains, 274; offshoring, 280; value chains, 284. *See also* offshoring; outsourcing
production workers, Mexican, hourly compensation of, 177 fig.12.2
Programa de Apoyos Directos al Campo/Program for Rural Funding (PROCAMPO). *See* PROCAMPO (Programa de Apoyos Directos al Campo/Program for Rural Funding)
Program for Direct Support to Rural Areas/Programa de Apoyos Directos al Campo (PROCAMPO). *See* PROCAMPO

(Programa de Apoyos Directos al Campo/Program for Rural Funding)
Project SOL (Secondary Online Learning), 98–99
Proposition 30 (California), 252–53
Proposition 187 (California, 1994), 12, 199, 223–24, 231, 252, 268n1(ch16); defined, 281
Proposition 209 (California, 1996), 199, 231, 268n1(ch16); defined, 281
Proposition 227 (California, 1998), 199, 231, 268n1(ch16); defined, 281
protectionism, 141, 184, 280
Public Citizen, 139
public sector, 280
Puerto Rico, 193, 234 table16.2, 238 fig.16.2
purchasing power parity (PPP), 176; defined, 281

quotas/prohibitions, 276, 284

race: panethnic identity and racial discrimination, 281; race baiting in electoral politics, 197; racial composition of Hazleton, PA, 217 table15.1; racial diversity, 269n1; racial inequality, 228, 281; US racial hierarchy, 284
racialization, 11, 228; defined, 281
racialized panethnic identity, 227–30, 230; defined, 281
racialized politics, 4–5, 9–10, 189–90, 191, 204–5, 214–15, 227, 244. See also anti-immigrant backlash; anti-immigrant politics; immigration scapegoating; Latino response; Mexican nationalism; Mexico-US relations; political elites; Trump, nativist appeal of; US politics
racial minorities, 281. See also racialization; racial threat theory
racial polarization, 197, 198, 282. See also Southern strategy
racial threat theory, 248, 275, 283; defined, 281
racism: CMPS and, 268n3; economic duress and, 201; as important issue, 238 fig.16.2; Latinos responses to anti-immigrant politics and, 232; perceived, 268n3
racism scale: immigrant-linked threat and, 234 table16.2; by national origin group, 233 table16.1
raw materials, 272; Tier Three suppliers, 161; value added goods/services and, 284

reactive ethnicity, 220, 220–22, 223, 226; defined, 281
Reagan, Ronald, 137, 196
REAL ID Act, 246
recession, 63–77
refugee systems, 56; defined, 281–82; Mariel refugees, 220–21. See also asylum crisis
regional neighbors. See intraregional trade; NAFTA (North American Free Trade Agreement); preferential trade agreements
regressions, 106, 107–9, 282
regressive government policy, 248 table17.1
regressive taxes, 249
regular employment, 274
regulation of trade, 281. See also preferential trade agreements
regulations. See rules of origin
relative income gaps, 273
religion, 275
remittances, 52, 106, 110; defined, 282; FDI and, 140 fig.9.3; immigration reform and, 131; remittance flows, 282, 283
removals of migrants, 63–77, 276
Rendón, Anthony, 224
repatriated Mexicans, 73 fig.4.4, 73 table4.2, 74, 75 table4.2, 194. See also deportations
Repository of Economic Information. See BIE (Banco de Información Económica/Repository of Economic Information)
Republican Party: anti-Latino rhetoric and, 226; Buchanan's 1992 campaign, 198; Bush's 1988 campaign, 197; in California, 224; Cubans and, 222; Goldwater's 1964 campaign, 197; Latinos and, 197–98, 202; Nixon's 1968 campaign, 197; Reagan's 1980/1984 campaigns, 197; Romney's 2012 campaign, 214; Trump's 2016 campaign, 198; Wilson's 1994 gubernatorial campaign, 199. See also specific politicians
Republican vote share, 20, 24, 25 table1.1, 29
research methodology: data adjustments, 261n4(ch7); data and methods for Trump support, trade, and immigration, 19–21; ordinary least squared (OLS) regression data analysis models, 259–60n3. See also surveys

research programs, 272; Border Survey of Mexican Migrants/Encuesta Sobre Migración en la Frontera Norte de México (EMIF), 66; CPS (Current Population Survey); ENEU (Encuesta Nacional de Ocupación y Empleo Urbano/National Survey of Urban Employment); IPUMS (Integrated Public Use Microdata Series); regressions, 282; SIPP (Survey of Income and Program Participation); University of California-Mexico Initiative, 284. *See also* CMPS (collaborative multi-racial post-election survey); MMP (Mexican Migration Project)
restrictionist politics, 192, 223, 282. *See also* immigration restrictions; restrictive measures; "Save Our State" Initiative, Proposition 187 (California, 1994) (SOS)
restrictive measures, 263n1; refugee system and, 281–82; trade liberalization and, 284; of Trump administration, 136 table9.1; USMCA and, 157–58. *See also* immigration restrictions; legislation; restrictive politics
return countries, in migration system, 279
returnees, Seal of Biliteracy, 99
return migration, 51, 279, 282; defined, 282; to Guatemala, 56; rising, 262n7
reverse Trump favorability, 234 table16.2, 238 fig.16.2
Reynolds, Megan, 7, 78–87
right-wing media, 199, 214
Riosmena, Fernando, 7, 78–87
The Rise and Fall of Great Powers (Kennedy), 200
Riverside county, CA, 261n2(ch6)
Robinson, Sherman, 8, 129–47, 263n6
robotics, 161 table11.1, 172, 276
Rodrik, Dani, 177
Romalis, J., 265n2(ch12)
Romney, Mitt, 20, 21, 22 fig.1.1, 22 fig.1.1A, 23, 26, 198, 214
Roper poll of 1992, 199
Rubio, Mario, 222
rules of origin, 178, 180, 181; defined, 282. *See also* preferential trade agreements
Rural Development Advance (RDA), 140
rural households, 149, 156; defined, 282
rural migration, 149; defined, 282
rural sector, 282. *See also* ENOE (Encuesta Nacional de Ocupación y Empleo/ National Survey of Occupation and Employment)

Salat, Isabel, 9, 174–88
Salcedo, A., 262n7
San Bernardino county, CA, 261n2(ch6)
sanctuary states, 224
San Diego county, CA, 261n2(ch6)
satellites companies, 265n3(ch11)
"Save Our State" Initiative, Proposition 187 (California, 1994) (SOS), 223, 252, 268n1(ch16). *See also* Proposition 187 (California, 1994)
SBA (Small Business Association), 140
SBO (Survey of Business Owners and Self-Employed), 20
scapegoating. *See* immigrant scapegoating
Schink, Werner, 202
Schwarzenegger, Arnold, 224
Seal of Biliteracy, 99
seasonal employment, 119, 262n15, 272, 274, 283. *See also* Bracero Program; H2A visas; seasonal agricultural workers; temporary foreign worker program
Second Industrial Revolution, 276
Secretaría de Educación Pública (SEP), 97
Secretaría de Relaciones Exteriores (SRE), 97
Secure Fence Act of 2006, 263n1
seed management of corn, 273
Segura, Gary, 11, 227–43
Seguro Popular program, 85. *See also* Instituto de Salud para el Bienestar (INSABI)
selectivity, defined, 282
sending countries, 117, 118 fig.8.2. *See also* China; India; Philippines
Sensenbrenner Bill (HR 4437), 231, 241
Sentimientos de la Nación (Feelings of a nation) (Morelos y Pavón), 204
separation of families, 282
service-oriented economy, 132–33
services, value added, 284
short-term work visas, 272. *See also* Bracero Program
SIACON (Sistema de Información Agroalimentaria de Consulta/Agrifood Information Consulting System), 153, 156
SIAP (Servicio de Información Agroalimentaria y Pesquera/Agriculture and Fisheries Information System), 264n7
Singapore, 260n6
SIPP (Survey of Income and Program Participation), 103, 262n6

Sistema de Información Agroalimentaria de Consulta/Agrifood Information Consulting System (SIACON), 153, 156
skin color categorization, 281. *See also* racialization; racialized panethnic identity
Slovak Republic, 280
Slovenia, 280
Small Business Association (SBA), 140
smart cities, 277
social categorization, 275, 282. *See also* identity portfolio; social identity theory; *specific categories*
social climate, 282. *See also* social policy
social consequences of immigrant scapegoating by political elites, 214–26
social dumping, 169
social groups, status threat and, 283
social identity theory, 229, 283; defined, 282
social impacts of migration and trade, 284
social media communications, 205, 283. *See also specific platforms*
social policies, 86; defined, 282. *See also* OECD (Organization for Economic Cooperation and Development)
social power: discourse as resource of, 273; Mexican nationalism and, 205
social problems, 279. *See also specific social problems*
social status, devaluation of, 283
socioeconomic factors: demographic transition and, 273. *See also* age structure; birthrate; education; income
SOS ("Save Our State" Initiative, Proposition 187) (California, 1994), 223, 252, 268n1(ch16). *See also* Proposition 187 (California, 1994)
South American, 268n4
Southern European national-origin quotas, 120, 193, 276
Southern Strategy, 197
Southern strategy, defined, 282
South Korea, 118 fig.8.3
South Korea-US Free Trade Agreement (KORUS), 281
Spain, 280
speech acts, 205; defined, 282
speeches, 283
speech genres, 205; defined, 282. *See also* greetings and farewells; informal conversation; letters; speeches
spending analysis, 269n5
Spilimbergo, Antonio, 108

state privatization of businesses, neoliberalism and, 280
statistical models: predicting Republic vote share, 25 table1.1; predicting Trump vote in 2016, 27 table1.2; predicting voting in 2018 House election, 28 table1.3
status threat, 275; defined, 283
steam power, 276
steel and aluminum imports, 180, 181, 209, 265n2(ch11)
STEM education, 100
stereotypes, 226, 247, 279; defined, 283. *See also* nationalist stereotypes
strong linkages construction, Mexico-US migration system and, 50–57
students, noncitizen, 283. *See also* temporary visas
subsidized programs: neoliberalism and, 280; social policy and, 282
subsistence farmers, 155, 273; defined, 283
supply chains, 132, 174, 265n3(ch11), 274. *See also* value chains
surcharges, trade liberalization and, 284
Suro, Roberto, 6, 63–77
surplus labor, 263n9
Survey of Business Owners and Self-Employed (SBO), 20
Survey of Income and Program Participation (SIPP), 103, 262n6
surveys: ACS (American Community Survey), 261n3(ch7); BLS (payroll employment survey), 262n10; CPS (Current Population Survey), 261n2(ch6), 261n3(ch7); respondents, 260n3(ch4). *See also* research programs
sustainability, 273, 279
Sweden, 280
Switzerland, 280
symbolic politics perspective theory, 215; defined, 283. *See also* ideological beliefs; normative values; prejudice

tariffs: elimination of, 281; on imported steel and aluminum, 265n2(ch11); NAFTA and, 131; reduction of, 265n2(ch12), 278, 281; tariff exemptions, 278; tariff payments, 272; tariff preference, 282; tariff rate quotas, 152 fig.10.1; trade liberalization and, 284; WTO and, 284–85. *See also* MFN (most favored nation) tariff; preferential trade agreements; rules of origin
tax reform laws, 280

346 | Index

tax revenues, 269n4
Technological Convergence, 161 table11.1, 171
Technological Development, in automotive sector, US-Mexico, 160, 166–69
Telles, Edward, 15–31
temporary agricultural workers, IRCA and, 276
temporary foreign worker program, 110, 283. *See also* Bracero Program; temporary visas
temporary guest workers, 194
temporary legal Mexican workers, 119
temporary visas, 33, 56, 124, 275. *See also* Bracero Program; H1B visas; H2A visas; H2B visas; temporary foreign worker program
temporary visitors, 117, 118 fig.8.3, 283
temporary worker agreements, 272. *See also* Bracero Program
temporary worker program. *See* temporary foreign worker program
temporary working programs, 110–11, 276, 283
temporary work visas, 52–53. *See also* H1B visas; H2B visas; temporary visas
test of racial threat story, 250
Texas, 234 table16.2, 238 fig.16.2, 271; annexation of northern Mexico and, 193; Latinos in, 202; as traditional destination, 39, 41
textiles, apparel, and footwear, 259n2(ch1), 283
theories: social identity theory, 282; symbolic politics perspective theory, 283
Thierfelder, Karen, 8, 129–47
Third Industrial Revolution, 276
Thomas, Chantal, 151
threats: anti-immigrant threat, 279; Latino threat narrative, 277; perceived foreign threats, 199–201; perceived threat of diversity, 284; perceived threat of globalization, 284; Trump administrations protectionism as, 141. *See also* group threat; Latino threat narrative; nativism; racial threat theory; refugee system; status threat; white backlash
Tier Four companies, 161, 168
Tier One companies, 161, 167, 168, 169, 265n1(ch11)
Tier Three companies, 161, 168
Tier Two companies, 161, 167, 168
Tijuana, 89, 99
top one-percenters, 273

tourists, 283
Toyota, 164, 167 fig.11.3
TPP (Trans-Pacific Partnership Act), 21, 260n6
tracking data of US-Mexico border crossings, 272. *See also* Border Survey of Mexican Migration/ Encuesta Sobre Migración en la Frontera Norte de México (EMIF)
tradable sectors, defined, 18
trade, regulation of, 281. *See also* barriers on trade; intraregional trade; preferential trade agreements
trade agreements, 281; TPP and, 260n6. *See also* free trade agreements; preferential trade agreements
trade and labor migration, NAFTA and, 132–35
trade and production bloc, defined, 132, 283
trade balance: defined, 283. *See also* remittances; trade flows; trade integration
trade balances, 149
trade barriers, 281; WTO and, 284–85. *See also* preferential trade agreements
trade bloc, defined, 263n7
trade contributions, FDI and, 140 fig.9.3
trade diversion, 151, 264n6; defined, 283
Trade Expansion Act of 1962, 181
trade exposure, Chinese imports and, 259n1(ch1)
trade flows, 18; defined, 283; FTA and, 264n6
trade in agriculture and US-Mexico migration, 148–58; agricultural production, trade, and rural migration trends, 149–51; changes in, 155–57; conclusion, 157–58; corn and trade liberalization under NAFTA, 151–53; overview, 148; trends in, 153–55
trade integration, 127–28, 130; defined, 284; high trade deficits, 164. *See also* agriculture, trade in; complementarity; NAFTA (North American Free Trade Agreement); sustainable complementarity; US-Mexico automotive sector; US-Mexico trade deal; US policies
trade interactions: globe model, 275; in migration collapse scenario, 279; trade war scenario and, 284
trade liberalization, 130, 151, 271; defined, 284; focus on, 134; NAFTA and, 138, 141. *See also* NAFTA (North American

Free Trade Agreement); USMCA (United States-Mexico-Canada Agreement)
trade policies: NAFTA and, 129–47, 135–37, 142–46; repercussions for immigration, 109–10; trade policy scenarios, 142–46
trade sectors, 259n2(ch1), 283; defined, 283. *See also* agricultural products; chemical products; electronic products; energy products; forest products; machinery; minerals and metals; textiles, apparel, and footwear; transportation equipment
trade shares of GDP, 135 fig.9.2
trade war scenario, 143; defined, 284; trade interactions and, 284
train wreck metaphor, border militarization and, 44–46
transit countries, in migration system, 279
Trans-Pacific Partnership Act (TPP), 21; question on, 260n6
transportation equipment, 259n2(ch1), 283
Treaty of Guadalupe Hidalgo, 193, 271
trends, 273; effects of Mexican migration on US labor market and, 117–20; in trade in agriculture and US-Mexico migration, 153–55; of traditional location crossings, 39; unauthorized immigration from Mexico decline and, 104–5
Trump, Donald J., 9; 2016 election, 238 fig.16.2, 239 fig.16.3; 2016 election campaign, 200–201, 206, 214, 241–42; 2016 election of, 191; anti-immigration policies of, 136 table9.1; anti-Latino rhetoric of, 11, 191, 212; on border wall, 207, 208; favorability, 232–38; NAFTA and, 136 table9.1, 174, 180; Nafta and, 209; percent voting for in 2016, 22 fig.1.1; rules of origin of auto parts and, 265n2(ch11); Twitter, 10; Twitter use, 207, 209–10, 284; use of perceived foreign threats, 199–200; white nationalists and, 46; white nativism and, 202. *See also* Make America Great Again (MAGA) campaign slogan; nativist appeal, contexts for Trump's
Trump administration: anti-immigrant policies, 253; anti-immigration policies of, 130; domestic policies, 185; NAFTA and, 141, 141–42, 164; protectionism of, 184; protectionist rhetoric/threats of, 141; protectionist threats of, 141; restrictive measures, 282; restrictive measures of, 136 table9.1, 142; tariffs imposed by, 181; USMCA and, 141, 183, 184
Trump favorability, 236 fig.16.1; Latinos responses to anti-immigrant politics and, 232–38
Trump favorability interaction models, 234 table16.2, 236 fig.16.1
Trump Paradox: anti-trade and anti-immigrant attitudes account for Trump support, no actual immigration or trade, 26–29; conclusion, 29–31; data and methods for Trump support, trade, and immigration, 19–21; defined, 13–15, 16, 284; economic self-interest, anti-immigrant attitudes and racial resentments, 18–19; exposing of, 12; false US-Mexico narrative, 16–19; overview, 15–16; research showing, 16, 18, 30; Trump support greater where there are fewer Mexican immigrants and less trade, 22–26. *See also* border militarization, consequences of; US-Mexico False Narrative, use of
Turkey, 280
Twitter, 10, 205, 209–10, 283, 284. *See also* social media communications

UCLA NAID (University of California, Los Angeles, North American Integration and Development Center), 139–40
UCSD (US-Mexican Studies Center at UC, San Diego), 96, 100, 261n4
unauthorized flows: annual percentage change in, 68 fig.4.2; of northbound Mexicans, 68 fig.4.1
unauthorized immigrants, 276. *See also* undocumented migrants
unauthorized immigration from Mexico, policy implication of decline in, 102–12; conclusion, 111–12; determinant of unauthorized worker inflows from Mexico, 106–7; estimating number of unauthorized immigrant workers, 103–4; overview, 102–3; policy considerations, 109–10; regression results, 107–9; temporary worker programs, 110–11; trends in, 104–5
unauthorized labor: as crop workers, 262n15; dependency on, 262n15
unauthorized Mexican immigrant workers, estimated number of, 105 fig.7.1
unauthorized Mexican immigrant workers, new, 105 fig.7.2

unauthorized Mexican migrants, 271
unauthorized migrants in US: percentage of Mexican-origin, 119 fig.8.4. *See also* undocumented migrants
unauthorized migration, 35, 279; border enforcement and, 276. *See also* Mexican unauthorized migration, ending of
unauthorized workers, data adjustments, 261n4(ch7)
undocumented crossings, 136 table9.1, 279; ending of Mexican unauthorized migration and, 67–69. *See also* migrant trail
undocumented immigrants: IIRA of 2006 and, 275; IRCA and, 276. *See also* undocumented migrants
undocumented labor, exploitation of, 134–35
undocumented migrants: border enforcement and, 42 fig.2.4; Bracero Agreement and, 33; defined, 284; estimated size of US population of, 43 fig.2.5; reporting of, 268n1(ch16); sanctuary states, 224
undocumented migration, 35, 279; 1994 California elections and, 199. *See also* undocumented migrants
unemployment, Great Recession of 2008, 275
United Kingdom: migration stocks from, 54; nonimmigrant admissions from, 118 fig.8.3; as OECD member, 280
United States: GDP's annual percentage change in, 115 fig.8.1; Mexican exports to, 262n12; migration stocks from, 55, 55 table3.2; as OECD member, 280; outflows, 280; total and foreign-born population of, 54, 54 table3.1; TPP and, 260n6; in trade and production bloc, 132; as WTO member, 285. *See also* out-migration; return migration
United States-Mexico-Canada Agreement (USMCA). *See* USMCA (United States-Mexico-Canada Agreement)
units of consumption, rural households and, 282
units of production, rural households and, 282
Universidad Autónoma de Baja California (UABC), 96
Universidad Nacional Autónoma de México (UNAM), 96–97
University of California, Los Angeles, North American Integration and Development Center (UCLA NAID), 139–40

University of California Curriculum Integration (UCCI), 100
University of California-Mexico Initiative, 95; children of migration and, 95–96; defined, 284
UN projections, 58–59
unskilled workers, 169
urban sector, 263n9; Border Patrol strategies in, 195; MAI and, 161 table11.1; migration to, 282. *See also* ENEU (Encuesta Nacional de Ocupación y Empleo Urbano/National Survey of Urban Employment)
urban sectors, migration flows and, 132–33
US-born (native) high school dropouts, 262n14
US-born (native) workers, 279. *See also* nativism
US-born children of illegal immigrants, 199
US-born Mexican Americans, immigrant health advantage of, 275
US Bureau of Labor Statistics, 265n5(ch12)
US Bureau of Labor Statistics (BLS) payroll employment survey, 262n10
US CAIP, 263n11
US Census, 19, 58
US Census Bureau, 20, 103, 260n1(ch4)
US Commission for the Study of International Migration and Cooperative Economic Development, 138
US construction industry: construction permits, 106, 107 table7.1, 262nn10–11; Great Recession and, 76, 104, 121; home construction bubble, 67, 70; slowdown in, 65; unauthorized migrants and, 109, 121, 124
US Department of Homeland Security (DHS), 36, 72, 103, 137
US government subsidies to American farmers, 278. *See also* marketing supports
US labor market, effects of Mexican migration on, 113–25; demographic factors in increased Mexican migration, 121–23; future growth and integration, 123–24; immigration reform, 120–21; job growth/population growth comparison, 114, 115 fig8.1; labor competition, 115–17; less-skilled workers, 115–17; overview, 113–14; trends in Mexican migration, 117–20
USMCA (United States-Mexico-Canada Agreement): alternative trade policy scenarios and, 129–30, 142, 143 table9.2,

144, 146; binational market access of agricultural products, 157; COVID-19 pandemic and, 157–58, 174, 184; future renegotiation mandate, 9; ISDS under, 182; key changes in automotive sector, 180–81; labor organizing rights of Mexican workers, 9, 186; minimum wage requirement, 9, 91, 186; NAFTA and, 130, 136, 136 table9.1, 149, 165, 166, 174, 183; overview, 8, 9; restrictive measures and, 157–58; review of, 182–84; trade liberalization in, 134; Trump administration and, 141, 183, 184, 186; wage disparity and, 169, 175
USMEX (Center for US-Mexican Studies), 99, 100
US-Mexican Studies Center at UC, San Diego (UCSD), 96, 100, 261n4
US-Mexico automotive sector. *See* automotive sector, US-Mexico
US-Mexico border: {{lt}}Edit Me{{gt}}, 276; borderlands, 279. *See also* border enforcement; border militarization, consequences of; Border Patrol
US-Mexico-California Collaborative, 11
US-Mexico migration. *See* trade in agriculture and US-Mexico migration
US-Mexico trade and migration policy initiatives, 135–37, 136 table9.1
US-Mexico trade deal policies, 174–88; economic policies, 184–87; industries, jobs, and inequality, 177–80; NAFTA and, 175–77; NAFTA new trade agreement outcomes, 182–84; overview, 174–75; USMCA deal on automobiles, 180–81
US residents: on Cuban Americans, 221; as outflows, 280; out of status Latinos, 45. *See also* out-migration; return migration
US trade: adjustment policies, 140; with China, 20; deficit, 1, 164, 179, 200, 207–9, 275; with Mexico, 20; national security provision, 181; negative impacts from, 17; policy initiatives, 135–37; in total trade of agricultural commodities in Mexico, 150 table10.1. *See also* NAFTA (North American Free Trade Agreement); USMCA (United States-Mexico-Canada Agreement); US-Mexico trade deal policies
Utah, 193, 271

Valentino, Nicholas, 231
value added, 178, 284

value chains, 132, 272, 275, 284. *See also* automotive value chains; global value chains
VAM (Vehículos Automotrices Mexicanos/ Mexican Automotive Vehicles), 160
Venezuela, 266n14(ch14)
Videgaray Caso, Luis, 208
Villaraigoza, Antonio, 224
Villarreal, Andrés, 69
Vinneau, Justin, 7, 78–87
violence: as social problem, 279; Trump's anti-immigrant rhetoric and, 225; violence-related flows, 57, 193
visas: employment-based visa programs, 110, 274; Immigration and Naturalization Act of 1965 and, 276; visa violations, 261n4(ch7). *See also* H1B visas; H2A visas; H2B visas; temporary visas
Volkswagen AG, 164, 167 fig.11.3
voting, 202; 2016 election, 17; Latino vote, 202; statistical analysis of, 20–29; white American vote, 246; white backlash and, 284. *See also* white backlash

wages and employment: minimum wage, 91, 180, 181, 185–87, 265n5, 274; US wage defined, 262n10; wage inequality, 273–74. *See also* CONASAMI (Comisión Nacional de Salarios Mínimos/National Commission of Minimum Wages); ENEU (Encuesta Nacional de Ocupación y Empleo Urbano/National Survey of Urban Employment); ENOE (Encuesta Nacional de Ocupación y Empleo/ National Survey of Occupation and Employment)
"war on terror," 199–200
Wasem, Ruth Ellen, 43
Weinberger, Casper, 196–97
welfare system, 215, 223, 245–46, 247, 249, 250, 269n1
Western Hemisphere immigration, 276
westward expansion, 278. *See also* Manifest Destiny
white backlash: defined, 284; Huntington and, 201; Nixon and, 282; Republican Party and, 197; Trump and, 16, 200–201. *See also* anti-immigrant backlash
white national identity, 278. *See also* Manifest Destiny
white nationalist movements, 46, 193, 279. *See also* nativism

whites: white nativist movement, 193–94; white status, 18, 283, 284; white supremacists, 225. *See also* white backlash
Who Are We? (Huntington), 201
Wilcox, Bryan, 229
Wilcox, Kim, 95
Wilson, Pete, 199, 202, 268n1(ch16), 281
WISER (World Institute for Strategic Economic Research), 20, 260n4(ch2)
workers, less-skilled: defined, 277; demographic changes and, 122–24, 123; Great Recession of 2008 and, 121; labor competition and, 113, 115–17; Mexican seasonal agriculture workers, 119; unauthorized, 111. *See also* low-skilled immigrants
workers, noncitizen, 53, 56, 283, 284. *See also* temporary visas
working-age population: annual growth rates, 58, 61 fig.3.2, 121, 122 table8.1; decline in less-skilled, 117, 123; decline in native-born, 121, 123; demographic change in, 132, 266n6; dependency ratios and, 273; labor-driven migrants and, 277; Mexicans in US as percentage of, 51
work permits: employment-based visa programs, 110, 274; temporary permits, 275. *See also* H1B visas; H2A visas; H2B visas; temporary visas
World Bank: adjustment programs, 139; fertility rate data from, 260n4(ch4); imports and exports of goods/services, 135 fig.9.2; remittance and trade share of GDP, 140 fig.9.3; World Development Indicators, 176 fig.12.1, 265n3(ch12)
World Development Indicators, 176 fig.12.1, 262n14, 265n3(ch12)
World Institute for Strategic Economic Research (WISER), 20, 260n4(ch2)
World Trade Organization (WTO), 135 fig.9.2, 165, 181, 186, 279, 284–85
World War II: bracero recruitment after, 6; economic and job growth after, 7, 113; GDP during, 135 fig.9.2; GI Bill, 121, 274; labor shortages, 120, 194, 272. *See also* Bracero Program
Wyoming, 193, 271

Yúnez-Naude, Antonio, 8, 148–58

Zavodny, Madeline, 7, 102–12
Zenteno, René, 6, 63–77
zero-sum depiction of labor market, 9, 115, 159, 277. *See also* lump of labor fallacy
zero tolerance policies, 81, 285

Founded in 1893,
UNIVERSITY OF CALIFORNIA PRESS
publishes bold, progressive books and journals
on topics in the arts, humanities, social sciences,
and natural sciences—with a focus on social
justice issues—that inspire thought and action
among readers worldwide.

The UC PRESS FOUNDATION
raises funds to uphold the press's vital role
as an independent, nonprofit publisher, and
receives philanthropic support from a wide
range of individuals and institutions—and from
committed readers like you. To learn more, visit
ucpress.edu/supportus.

www.ingramcontent.com/pod-product-compliance
Lightning Source LLC
Chambersburg PA
CBHW030518230426
43665CB00010B/669